T0339486

Workers' Voice, HRM Practice, and Leadership in the Public Sector

Much is talked and written about well-being in the workplace, but many wonder whether 'putting people first' is just a facade and that were it not for employment legislation, union representation and the high profile of human rights issues, employers would regard employees as a necessary burdensome financial evil, as in days gone by. Some scholarly research has focused on the reactions of employees to the quality of working life and well-being at work and much of this suggests high levels of dissatisfaction, disaffection and disengagement. In *Workers' Voice, HRM Practice, and Leadership in the Public Sector: Multidimensional Well-Being at Work*, Nicole Cvenkel avers that whilst it is known that public sector employees are even less satisfied than those in the private sector, there has been very little research into the effects of working life experiences on employee well-being in public sector organisations. There is even some doubt about whether a well-being philosophy that can be applied in the private sector can readily be extended to the public sector. The push towards New Public Management (NPM) means organisations continue to undergo significant reform processes around efficiency, costs and public service delivery. All these changes place additional demands on public sector employees who are at times also subject to intensive scrutiny by stakeholder groups, who may regard the recourse to well-being initiatives as a poor use of public funds. The author has researched in the UK local government sector and that is the setting for the debate in this book, about whether and how an employee well-being ideology can be successfully promoted and maintained in an NPM environment, given continuous reform and expenditure reduction. In a local government case organisation that the author researched, limited resources, reduction in budgets, redundancies, increased workloads, lack of trust and the existence of a 'controlled' working environment were all found to be central to a climate of bullying and unfairness. Although the organisation was committed to the adoption of HRM 'best practice' and initiatives geared towards promoting employees well-being, employees still believed they were being bullied and treated unfairly. It was found that different perspectives on the psychological contract, fairness and bullying at work were highlighted by managerial and non-managerial employees. The author's conclusions contribute to a clearer understanding than hitherto of workers' voice in relation to work, leader-member exchanges and well-being in the public sector, and she offers a model depicting employees' understanding of what their quality of working life, line manager's leadership and well-being should be that might be used by organisational leaders, researchers, policy makers, human resources managers and other practitioners and consultants to move towards a more holistic, multidimensional well-being at work paradigm.

Dr. Nicole Cvenkel (nee Baptiste) obtained her PhD in Human Resource Management and Organisational Behaviour at Roehampton University Business School. Her research focused on employees' perspectives and reactions to HRM practices, the quality of working life, line management leadership and well-being at work.

Workers' Voice, HRM Practice, and Leadership in the Public Sector

Multidimensional Well-Being at Work

Nicole Cvenkel

Routledge
Taylor & Francis Group

LONDON AND NEW YORK

First published 2020
by Routledge
2 Park Square, Milton Park, Abingdon, Oxon, OX14 4RN

and by Routledge
605 Third Avenue, New York, NY 10017

First issued in paperback 2021

Routledge is an imprint of the Taylor & Francis Group, an informa business

© 2020 Taylor & Francis

The right of Nicole Cvenkel to be identified as author of this work
has been asserted by her in accordance with sections 77 and 78 of the
Copyright, Designs and Patents Act 1988.

Publisher's Note
The publisher has gone to great lengths to ensure the quality of this reprint but
points out that some imperfections in the original copies may be apparent.

Library of Congress Cataloging-in-Publication Data
A catalog record for this book has been requested

ISBN 13: 978-1-03-208212-7 (pbk)
ISBN 13: 978-1-4094-5325-3 (hbk)

Typeset in Sabon
by Apex CoVantage, LLC

Contents

Figures

Tables

Preface

Much is talked and written about well-being in the workplace, but many wonder whether 'putting people first' is just a facade and that were it not for employment legislation, union representation and the high profile of human rights issues, employers would regard employees as a necessary burdensome financial evil, as in days gone by. Some scholarly research has focused on the reactions of employees to the quality of working life and well-being at work and much of this suggests high levels of dissatisfaction, disaffection and disengagement.

In *Workers' Voice, HRM Practices, and Leadership in the Public Sector: Multidimensional Well-Being at Work*, Dr. Nicole Cvenkel avers that whilst it is known that public sector employees are even less satisfied than those in the private sector, there has been very little research into the effects of working life experiences on employee well-being in public sector organisations. There is even some doubt about whether a well-being philosophy that can be applied in the private sector can readily be extended to the public sector.

The push towards New Public Management (NPM) means organisations continue to undergo significant reform processes around efficiency, costs and public service delivery. All these changes place additional demands on public sector employees who are at times also subject to intensive scrutiny by stakeholder groups, who may regard recourse to well-being initiatives as a poor use of public funds. The author has researched in the UK local government sector and that is the setting for the debate in this book, about whether and how an employee well-being ideology can be successfully promoted and maintained in an NPM environment, given continuous reform and expenditure reduction. In a local government organisation that the author has researched, limited resources, reduction in budgets, redundancies, increased workloads, lack of trust and the existence of a 'controlled' working environment were all found to be central to a climate of bullying and perceived unfairness.

Although the organisation was committed to the adoption of HRM 'best practice' and initiatives geared towards promoting employees wellbeing, employees still believed they were being bullied. It was found that different perspectives on the psychological contract, fairness, ineffective leadership and bullying at work were highlighted by managerial and non-managerial employees. The author's conclusions contribute to a clearer understanding than hitherto known of workers' voice in relation to work and well-being in the public sector, and Dr. Cvenkel offers a model depicting employees' understanding of what their quality of working life and well-being should be that might be used by researchers, policy makers, human resources managers and other practitioners and consultants to move towards a more holistic, multidimensional well-being at work paradigm.

Introduction
An agenda for research

Well-being in the workplace is one of the essential domains for contemporary organisations. Several reasons can be advanced for the importance of studying employee well-being at work. Historically, in the late nineteenth century, employers paid little attention to employee well-being, though there were some exceptions in employers like Quaker Cadbury family and Lever Brothers who generally cared about employees' well-being and introduced practices that assisted employees in the workplace and in life outside work. However, most employers at that time held a different view and generally regarded employees as a necessary but burdensome financial evil. Social and economic history shows that it took centuries to develop the employment relationship where well-being is recognised as an organisational responsibility. However, one often wonders, under the organisational facade of 'putting people first', whether this attitude is still uppermost in contemporary employers thinking but is being stopped by the now pressing 'best practice' and employment legislation standards, unions and human rights corporatives.

The nature of global, technological, economic, demographic and social changes in the twenty-first century have affected, and will continue to affect work, workers and management in the coming decades as emphasis is placed on revolutions in business concepts and incremental progress, a little cheaper, better and faster. These changes have transformed the way people live and work, revolutionising the rules of the game, creating a 24/7 service work culture, resulting in individuals working longer hours and experiencing job insecurity. All of these have implications for increased work-related stress and negative well-being. Work-related stress and mental health are another salient principles of growing importance for policy makers and organisations as the growing intensity and pressures of work are major problems facing British workers, and workers globally. The CIPD, 2019 Health and Well-Being at Work research states that stress is one of the main causes of short- and long-term absence, particularly in the public sector, and that organisations are considerably more likely to report that stress-related absence has increased rather than decreased over the last year, which is also associated with increased presenteeism (CIPD, 2019). The CIPD research also found that heavy workloads remain the common cause of stress, and, newly, an increase proportion blame management style, relationships at work and non-work factors (relationships/family) as some main causes of stress at work. The research further reveals that common mental health conditions (i.e. anxiety and depression) have increased in nearly three-fifths of organisations, with an increasing proportion of organisations have included mental ill-health among their main causes of short- and long-term stress-related absence (CIPD, 2019). Moreover, the research states that public sector organisations are more likely to report an increase in common mental health conditions compared with the private or non-profit sectors (CIPD, 2019; Gov.UK, 2018).

Stress and mental ill-health have contributed to an increase in presenteeism and leaveism. Hesketh and Cooper (2014) defines 'presenteeism' as people coming into work when they are sick and 'leaveism' relates to people using allocated time off such as annual leave to work, or if they are unwell, or working outside contracted hours. Hesketh and Cooper further avers that presenteeism and leaveism have been observed in nearly two-thirds of organisations in the UK over the last year, and that the average absence levels are just one indicator of the health and well-being of employees within an organisation. Hesketh and Cooper claim that presenteeism and leaveism can also indicate organisational issues, such as long-hours culture or excessive workloads. These behaviours can adversely affect employees' health and well-being: working when ill or not taking opportunities to relax outside work may have far greater impact on employees' long-term physical and mental health, as well as organisational productivity, than their absence (CIPD, 2019; Gov.UK., 2018; Hesketh and Cooper, 2014). Organisations with a well-being strategy are now more likely to take steps to discourage presenteeism and leaveism but those with senior leaders and line managers that have embraced the importance of an employee well-being agenda have a significant role to play in creating a culture where people do not work when ill and are encouraged to go home if they are unwell, as well as to discourage employees taking work home that cannot be completed in normal working hours or employees working while on leave or holiday to catch up (CIPD, 2019; Hesketh and Cooper, 2014).

Rising workloads is a major reason why some employees feel they cannot complete their work in the time available and need to work outside the normal working hours (Hesketh and Cooper, 2014). Increasing organisational workloads have been placing an ever-increasing burden on those of working age in the delivery of products and services, which in turn has implications for sickness absence rates and patterns, and is a driver of employee behaviour and health and well-being. The negative effects of the levels of stress, pressure and mental ill-health experienced by individuals have health implications such as depression and anxiety and other psychological and physical well-being factors, resulting in high cost to business and the public purse (Black, 2008; Harrington, 2013). Ill-health relating to stress at work and mental ill-health have doubled between 1990 and 2007 and continues to increase in most industry sectors in 2019 (CIPD, 2019). In the twenty-first-century workplace, stress and mental ill-health are now the major causes of employee absence followed by certain diseases and musculoskeletal conditions (Harrington, 2013; Spurgeon et al., 2009). This is also echoed by the World Health Organisation that also predicted soaring levels of stress and other mental health problems in the next few years (WHO, 1992).

According to Harrington (2013), stress is not just limited to emotional experiences but also encompasses the physiological, behavioural and cognitive. He further points out that the precise definition of stress is generally elusive but it is commonplace to regard stress as undesirable and harmful to one's health and well-being. The cost of workers' ill-health to organisations and the UK economy is astronomical, resulting in 35 million working days lost in the United Kingdom yearly to occupational ill-health and injury, with absence due to sickness costs of around 12 billion each year (CIPD, 2007; Silcox, 2007). Beven and Hayday (2001) argue that sickness absence is an issue of growing concern among employers in the UK owing to changing legislation, increased competitive pressures and the greater awareness of the costs incurred as a result of absence. According to Personnel Today (2017), recent research shows that workplace absence and presenteeism are costing the UK economy GBP18 billion yearly in lost productivity. Research also found that there has been an increasing trend of workplace absence year-on-year since 2011 predicting the cost of absence to increase to £21 billion in 2020, and increase to £26 billion in 2030 (www.personneltoday.com). In the public sector British employees' average absence levels are 8.4 days per employee compared to 4.4 days for the private sector, costing around £4 billion a year to the taxpayer (HSE, 2009). The Department of Works and Pension 2016 research reveals that ill-health among working age people costs the UK economy £100 billion and sickness absence costs employers £9 billion a year (DWP, 2017).

The CIPD, 2019, Health and Well-Being at Work research found that on average public sector employees had 8.4 days of absence over the last year, compared with 4.4 days in private sector services, 5.6 days in manufacturing and production and 6.3 in the non-profit sector. While absence levels in the private services and non-profit sectors have shown a steady decline over the last decade, the CIPD 2019 research found that there has been little change in public sector absence over the last few years, and at the beginning of the decade (i.e. 2010), the public sector absence levels were 9.3 days (CIPD, 2019; Gov.UK., 2018). The Office of National Statistics 2017 research found that despite the economic downturn, sickness absence fell to a low of 131.7 million days in 2013 but there were increases in 2014 and 2015 (Comer, 2017). Although there was some reduction in absences throughout the UK labour market, there was an increase in presenteeism, as people coming into work when they are ill has more than tripled since 2010 and is at a record high in UK organisations as stress, mental ill-health (e.g. anxiety and depression) at work rises (CIPD, 2019; DWP, 2017). The CIPD, 2019 research reveals that causes of long-term absence are mental ill-health (59%), stress (54%), musculoskeletal injuries (54%), acute medical conditions (45%) and work/non-work-related injuries/accidents (19%) (CIPD, 2019).

The challenges and tensions of work, work-related stress and employee absence have implications for worker satisfaction and well-being. Brown et al. (2006) state that the majority of British workers (i.e. 15 million or more) are in fact dissatisfied with their jobs. In support, Gallup survey points out that more than 80% of Britain's workers lack any real commitment to their jobs and a quarter of those are 'actively disengaged' or truly disaffected with their workplaces, lacking inspiration and engagement with their work, and the problem hasn't gotten any better (Flade, 2003). Therefore, research evidence suggests that workers in larger organisations report higher levels of more stress, work intensity, a lack of influence and more dissatisfaction than those in smaller and medium-sized organisations (CIPD, 2019). As such, CIPD's (2010) research found that public sector employees are less satisfied than their private sector counterparts. What is of particular interest to the discussion presented here is whether well-being philosophy can be extended to the public sector? The UK public sector, as with many public sectors worldwide, continues to undergo significant reform processes around efficiency and costs. The push towards New Public Management (NPM) has led to considerable changes within funding models, governance structures and joint public service delivery. All these changes place additional demands on public sector employees, leading to an increase in the stresses they face relative to their normal work (Morphet, 2008). Additionally, public sector employees are at times subject to intensive scrutiny by stakeholder groups, who may regard recourse to well-being initiatives a poor use of the public purse (Baptiste, 2009).

In this context, it is not at all clear whether a 'well-being' philosophy or culture can thrive or deliver all that is espoused, and the well-being at work literature has made little comment on its applicability to differing contexts and employee groups not least in the public sector. To this end, the business case evidence for promoting employee well-being seems clear and this influences the implementation that people management practices can have on employees. Likewise, the evidence of increasing work-related stress and mental ill-health occurring in the public sector over the last decade all have implications for employee well-being. Based on this discussion, employees' well-being at work in the public sector is shown to be a fascinating and essential area of investigation to explore employees' perceptions of work, line management leadership and well-being given the public sector approach to manage employee well-being in a New Public Management (NPM) environment that also focuses on reformation and expenditure reduction.

Based on the preceding, this book will prove to be a valuable publication, as there is a need to go beyond the current conceptualisation of employee well-being in the literature towards a more holistic multidimensional well-being at work paradigm that can be used for policy and practice in organisations, scholarly research, government institutions, professionals and consultants to better understand employees' evaluation of high commitment HRM practices, the meaning employees give to the quality of working life, line management leadership and well-being at work.

References

Baptiste, N.R. (2009) 'Fun and Well-Being: Insights from Senior Managers in a Local Authority', *Employee Relations*, Vol. 31(6): 600–612.

Beven, S., and Hayday, S. (2001) *Costing Sickness Absence in the UK*, The Institute of Employment Studies, IES Report 382, Brighton, UK: A Report prepared for UNUM and published by IES.

Black, D.C. (2008) *Working for a Healthier Tomorrow*, London: TSO.

Brown, A., Charlwood, A., Forde, C., and Spencer, D. (2006) *Changing Job Quality in Britain 1998–2004*, DTI Employment Relations Research Series, No. 70, London: DTI.

Chartered Institute of Personnel and Development (CIPD, 2007) *New Directions in Managing Employee Absence: An Evidence-Based Approach*, Research in Practice, London: Chartered Institute of Personnel and Development.

Chartered Institute of Personnel and Development (CIPD, 2010) *Employee Outlook Recovery Yet to Reach the Workplace*, Quarterly Survey Report, Spring 2010, London: Chartered Institute of Personnel Development.

Chartered Institute of Personnel and Development (CIPD, 2019) *Health and Well-Being at Work*, Public Sector April 2019, In Partnership with Simply health, Reference 7837, London.

Comer, M. (2017) *Office for National Statistics*, www.ons.gov.uk/employmentand labourmarket/peopleinwork/labourproductivity/articles/sicknessabsencein thelabourmarket/2016 (accessed 3rd June, 2019).

Department of Works & Pensions (2017) 'Improving Lives, the Work, Health and Disability Green Chapter', Presented to Parliament by the Secretary of State for Work and Pensions and the Secretary of State for Health by Command of Her Majesty, October 2016, London.

Flade, P. (2003) 'Great Britain's Workforce Lacks Inspiration', *Gallup Management Journal*, The Gallup Organisation's Employee Engagement Index Survey, http://gmj.gallup.com/content/9847/great-britains-workforce-lacks-inspiration.aspx (accessed 12th July, 2010).

GOV.UK (2018) 'Local Government, NHS 10-Year Plan and a Prevention Opportunity', *Press Release*, www.gov.uk/government/news/local-government-nhs-10-year-plan-and-a-prevention-opportunity

Harrington, R. (2013) *Stress, Health and Well-Being: Thriving in the 21st Century*, Belmont, CA, USA: Wadsworth Cengage Learning.

Health and Safety Executive (2009) *Health and Safety Statistics 2008/2009*, London: HSE.

Hesketh, I., and Cooper, C.L. (2014) 'Leaveism at Work', *Occupational Medicine*, Vol 64(3): 146–147, https://academic.oup.com/occmed/article/64/3/146/1439077

Morphet, J. (2008) *Modern Local Government*, London: Sage Publications.

Personnel Today (2017) 'Cost of Absence to UK Economy Rises to 18 Billon', www.personneltoday.com/pr/2017/03/cost-of-absence-to-uk-economy-rises-to-18-billion/ (accessed 1st June, 2019).

Silcox, S. (2007) 'Health Work and Well-Being: Rising to the Public Sector Attendance Management Challenge', *ACAS Policy Discussion Chapter*, (6), May.

Spurgeon, P., Mazelan, P., Barwell, F., and Flanagan, H. (2009) *New Directions in Managing Employee Absence: An Evidence-Based Approach*, London: CIPD.

World, Health Organisation (WHO) (1992) *Basic Document*, 39th Edition, Geneva: WHO.

Part I

Theoretical developments in HRM, New Public Management and well-being research agendas

1 Building a foundation for workplace health and well-being in the public sector

Introduction

The rising dependencies on the global market and continued increased workloads have, and continues to, place an ever-increasing burden on those of working age in the delivery of products and services. In turn, increased workloads, line management relationship, and work-life conflicts and relationships are among the highest causes of stress-related absence at work, presenteeism and leaveism that have a negative effect on the health and well-being of workers, resulting in high cost to business and the public purse (CIPD, 2019; Hesketh and Cooper, 2014; MacDonald, 2005). For example, public sector absence levels (and associated costs) are now estimated to be nearly nine days per employee every year; with stress and other mental health conditions now being the main causes of employee absence. Moreover, the concentration on problems such as absenteeism, presenteeism, leaveism and accidental injury is giving way to a broader vision of what a healthier and happier and more productive workforce can achieve in terms of higher performance and productivity. Therefore, the fundamental principle outlined by policy makers are that all working age people have the opportunity to make the optimum contribution to their organisations while enjoying a safer, more satisfying and healthier working life (Black, 2008). This vision has been embraced by cutting edge companies that have invested deeply in the well-being of their workforce and are now reaping the benefits, as it appears that well-being at work is increasingly being recognised as an important factor in determining organisational success (CIPD, 2019).

This book draws from research that explored employees' perspectives and reactions to HRM practices, line management leadership, the quality of working life and how such experiences have contributed to employees' well-being at work in the local government context in North West England. This chapter establishes the research territory and identifies the research aims, objectives, justification and conceptual framework for the research. The structure of the book is outlined and the chapter concludes with a summary of the key issues discussed.

Establishing the research territory

Well-being in the workplace is one of the essential domains for contemporary organisations. Several reasons can be advanced for the importance of studying employee well-being at work. Historically, in the late nineteenth century, employers paid little attention to employee well-being, though there were some exceptions in employers (Quaker Cadbury family and Lever Brothers) who generally cared about employees' well-being and introduced practices that assisted employees in the workplace and in life outside work (Cooper and Robertson, 2001; Newall, 2002). However, most employers at that time held a different view and generally regarded employees as a necessity but burdensome financial evil was a far more frequent phenomenon (Currie, 2001). Social and economic history shows that it took centuries to develop the employment relationship where well-being is recognised as an organisational responsibility (Cooper and Robertson, 2001). However, one often wonders if, under the organisational façade of 'putting people first', whether this attitude is still uppermost in contemporary employers thinking but is being stopped by the now pressing 'best practice' and employment legislation standards, unions and human rights corporative.

The nature of global, technological, economic, demographic and social changes in the twenty-first century have affected, and will continue to affect work, workers and management in the coming decades as emphasis is placed on revolutions in business concepts and incremental progress, a little cheaper, better and faster (Armstrong and Brown, 2001; Berman et al., 2010; CIPD, 2008; Cascio, 2010; MacDonald, 2005). These changes have transformed the way people live and work, revolutionising the rules of the game, creating a 24/7 service work culture, resulting in individuals working longer hours and experiencing job insecurity. All of these have implications for increased work-related stress, mental ill-health and negative well-being (ESRC, 2006; Green and Whitfield, 2009). ESRC (2010) further argues that the risk of losing jobs is greater in large organisations and has shifted from blue to white collar workers with professionals experiencing much of the job losses.

Work-related stress and mental ill-health are other salient principles of growing importance for policy makers and organisations as the growing intensity and pressures of work are major problems facing British workers (DWP, 2005; HSE, 2004, 2007, 2009). The cost of workers' ill-health to organisations and the economy is astronomical, with the average cost of sickness absence in the United Kingdom (UK) being £600 per employee per year, resulting in 35 million working days lost yearly to occupational ill-health and injury with absence due to sickness costs of around £12 billion in 2007 and is now predicted to be GBP21 billion in 2020 and GBP26 billion in 2030 (CIPD, 2007, 2019; HSE, 2004, 2009; Silcox, 2007). In the public sector, the CIPD, 2019 Health and Well-Being at Work research points out an increased focus on mental health, which remains the most common cause of long-term absence in the public sector and other organisations. Public sector British employees' average absence levels are 8.4 days per employee over the last year compared to 4.4 days for the private sector services, 5.6 days in manufacturing and production and 6.3 in the non-profit sector (DWP, 2005, 2017). While absence levels in the private services and non-profit sectors have shown a steady decline over the last decade, there has been little change in public sector absence over the last few years (CIPD, 2019). Public sector absence is costing around £4 to £9 billion a year to the taxpayer and approximately £100 billion to the British economy (DWP, 2005, 2017; HSE, 2000, 2009; Silcox, 2007). Therefore, promoting and maintaining employee well-being in the public sector in particular is essential given the high absence levels and cost to individuals, organisations and the economy as a whole.

The challenges and tensions of work, work-related stress, mental ill-health and employee absence have implications for worker satisfaction and positive well-being. Guest and Conway (1999) and Brown et al. (2006) argue that the level of worker satisfaction and worker well-being in Britain is considerably lower than suggested by Workplace Employment Relations Survey (WERS) 2004 survey (Kersley et al., 2006). Brown et al. state that a majority of British workers (15 million or more) are in fact dissatisfied with their jobs and recommend an urgent policy towards worker well-being and its likely incremental impact (Brown et al., 2006; Fisher et al., 2004). In support, the Gallup survey points out that more than 80% of Britain's workers lack any real commitment to their jobs and a quarter of those are 'actively disengaged' or truly disaffected with their workplaces, lacking inspiration and engagement with their work, and the problem hasn't gotten any better (Flade, 2003; MacLeod and Clarke, 2009). Echoing this view, Green and Whitfield (2009) claim that workers in larger organisations report higher levels of more stress, work intensity, a lack of influence and more dissatisfaction than those in smaller and medium-sized organisations (CIPD, 2019). In support, CIPD's (2010) research found that public sector employees are less satisfied than their private sector counterparts.

The UK public sector, as with many public sectors worldwide, continues to undergo significant reform processes around efficiency and costs (Morphet, 2008; Noblet et al., 2006). These have been associated with a number of pressures that have been a catalyst for public sector reform (Bach et al., 2005). In particular, local government reforms tend to focus on improved management of resources and redefinition of roles and responsibilities (Noblet et al., 2006). All these changes place additional demands on public sector employees, leading to an increase in the stresses they face relative to their normal work (Morphet, 2008). Additionally, public sector employees are at times subject to intensive scrutiny by

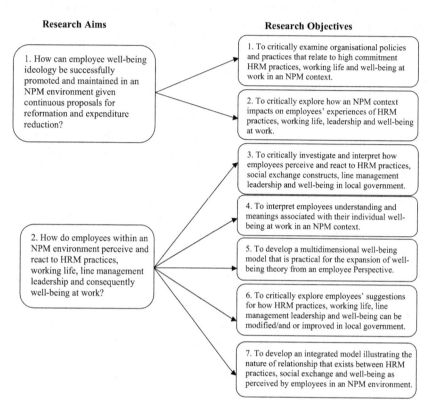

Research Aims

1. How can employee well-being ideology be successfully promoted and maintained in an NPM environment given continuous proposals for reformation and expenditure reduction?

2. How do employees within an NPM environment perceive and react to HRM practices, working life, line management leadership and consequently well-being at work?

Research Objectives

1. To critically examine organisational policies and practices that relate to high commitment HRM practices, working life and well-being at work in an NPM context.

2. To critically explore how an NPM context impacts on employees' experiences of HRM practices, working life, leadership and well-being at work.

3. To critically investigate and interpret how employees perceive and react to HRM practices, social exchange constructs, line management leadership and well-being in local government.

4. To interpret employees understanding and meanings associated with their individual well-being at work in an NPM context.

5. To develop a multidimensional well-being model that is practical for the expansion of well-being theory from an employee Perspective.

6. To critically explore employees' suggestions for how HRM practices, working life, line management leadership and well-being can be modified/and or improved in local government.

7. To develop an integrated model illustrating the nature of relationship that exists between HRM practices, social exchange and well-being as perceived by employees in an NPM environment.

Figure 1.1 Relationship between the research aims and objectives

stakeholder groups, who may regard recourse to 'well-being initiatives' a poor use of the public purse (Baptiste, 2009).

To this end, Black (2008) suggests that the business case evidence for promoting employee well-being is far from proven (ESRC, 2006, 2010). Echoing this view, Guest (2002) points out the impact that management implementation of people management practices can have on employees (Pfeffer, 2005; Purcell and Hutchinson, 2003); and the evidence of increasing work-related stress, mental ill-health, presenteeism and leaveism occurring in the public sector over the last decade (Hesketh and Cooper, 2014; Silcox, 2007) all have implications for employee well-being. Thus, this is a fascinating and essential area of investigation. Whilst the issue of employee well-being at work has reached a new level of importance in the minds of policy makers and managers, there is still little evidence that attention has been paid to the 'workers' voice' in their evaluation of HRM practices, the quality of working life and well-being at work in the public sector. Research within this area remains relatively untapped. Furthermore, understanding employees' expectations of the psycho-social factors affecting behaviour, the meaning of work experiences and well-being, and employees' perceptions of how their well-being can be improved are all lacking in the evidence base (ESRC, 2010; HSE, 2007; Mowbray, 2009). Based on the preceding discussions, this book takes local government as its setting and seeks to contribute towards the debates in these areas. This book explores how public sector employees perceives HRM practices, line management leadership, their quality of working life and consequently their well-being at work in a New Public Management (NPM) environment given continuous proposals for reformation and expenditure reduction.

The relationships between the research aims and objectives of the research illustrated in this book are summarised in Figure 1.1.

Research rationale

The health and well-being of people of working age is of fundamental importance to Britain's future (Black, 2008). Growing evidence suggests that work can help improve physical and mental health, reduce health inequalities and offer improved opportunities in life (DWP, 2005, 2017; HSE, 2009). The debate about the impact of working life on employee well-being has been intensified with the publication of Dame Carol Black's (2008) review *Working for a Healthier Tomorrow*; the CIPD's research on the *Health and Well-Being of Work Survey* (CIPD, 2019); the Kersely et al. (2006) research on *Inside the Workplace: Findings from the 2004 Workplace Employment Relations Survey*; the Department of Health research on *Commissioning Framework for Health and Well-Being* (DOH, 2007); and the Department of Works and Pensions research, *Health, Work and Well-Being: Caring for Our Future – A Strategy for the Health and Well-Being of Working Age People* (DWP, 2005). The central messages in these reviews are that promoting the health and well-being of employees is not only a good thing in itself, but it also promotes the well-being of the organisations for which they work, including so-called bottom-line performance indicators such as profits and targets (Black, 2008; CIPD, 2019; DOH, 2007; DWP, 2005; ESRC, 2006; HSE, 2009). Black (2008) further states that the failure of many organisations to grasp this is as a result of a lack of information. Black avers that the key importance in the promotion of employee well-being is job design, management organisation and minimisation of work-related stress.

This policy position is based on evidence from the review by PricewaterhouseCoopers (PwC) research (PwC, 2008) that considered the wider business case for workplace wellness programmes and the economic business case for UK employers. The evidence indicates that the costs of well-being programmes can in many circumstances be translated into benefits in the form of *cost savings* rather than increased income or revenue flows, which can all impact positively upon intermediate measures that can be followed through to financial benefits (HSE, 2009; PwC, 2008).

Furthermore, Williams and Cooper (1999) emphasise that when people come to work the whole person comes to work not just the part that does the job. Central to this view, Thompson and Bates (2009) indicate that it is important for organisations to understand that when they employ individuals it is essential to recognise that they have employed a 'human being' to perform a particular task and presumably add value to the organisation. Echoing this view Bolton and Houlihan (2007) maintain that organisations need to recognise that their human resources are precisely that: *human*; they are not simply a resource and they will be a far from optimal resource if their humanity is not recognised, respected and supported. In essence, the journey to workplace health and well-being can start with a 'leap of faith' as it is most needed for the challenges organisations and individuals face in the twenty-first century.

Central to this view, Bates and Thompson (2007) argue that the idea that an organisation's most valuable resource is its human resource – its people – is an idea that has been around for a long time now and sadly it often remains at a rhetorical level and does not rise above the status of an empty slogan. What is of particular importance to this argument here is that, in order to view employees as the most valuable asset it may require 'going back to the basics' of the notion that people are more valuable than 'carbon chapter' or placed 'ninth' in the list of organisational priorities (Figure 1.2).

It is important for organisations to have the understanding that people can work more effectively, may be more creative, productive, stimulated and fulfilled when their well-being is promoted (Baptiste, 2008, 2009). Echoing this view, Cartwright and Cooper (2009) state that organisations that take care of their employees, such care is reciprocated (Rousseau, 1995; George, 2009) and can have positive effects on the bottom line (Black, 2008), citizenship behaviour (Coyle-Shapiro and Conway, 2005), enhance service delivery (Noblet et al., 2006), reduction in absenteeism (CIPD, 2019; Hesketh and Cooper, 2014; Silcox, 2007), improved performance (Mowbray, 2009) and personal fulfilment (CIPD, 2007; Grant et al., 2007; MacDonald, 2005). Therefore, it is essential to better understand the needs of the employees that can promote and maintain employee well-being that contributes to an organisation's overall strategic objectives and performance. This can only be done by getting 'below the surface' of people issues, understanding what really matters to employees, and to explore employees' reactions to work, the quality of working life, line management leadership and their perceptions regarding how their well-being is defined, promoted and can be improved.

In general, employers know relatively little about their employees apart from basic personal details required at the commencement of

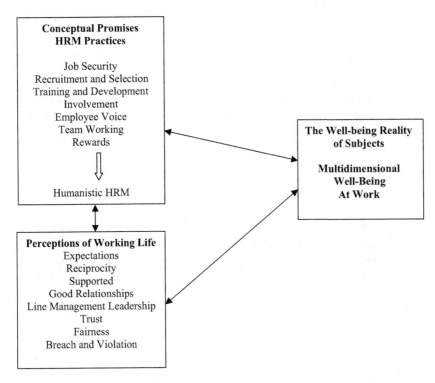

Figure 1.2 Conceptual framework

employment (Williams and Cooper, 1999). Therefore, understanding employees' perspectives and the meaning they give to their lived working life experiences and well-being within organisations have been overlooked. This is demonstrated by scanning through HRM journals where a substantial amount of research focuses on quantitative measures of employees' experiences of the employment relationship, neglecting to consider that individuals' lived experiences cannot be measured but require instead, an in-depth understanding of what 'lies beneath the melting ice' of employees' working life realities and experiences and well-being within organisations.

Conceptual framework of the research

The conceptual framework for this research outlined in Figure 1.2, shows the framework of analysis: conceptual promises, perceptions of working life and the well-being reality of subjects.

This book utilises a conceptual framework that identifies and differentiates between three kinds of entities: conceptual promises (i.e. HRM ideas); perceptions of working life (social exchange constructs) – that is, the psychological contract (PC), perceived organisational support (POS), leader-member exchange (LMX) and organisational justice (OJ); and well-being reality of subjects (i.e. multidimensional well-being conceptualisation as a relevant concept of the reality of subjects). The conceptual framework is based on the premise of the existence of different employee groups within organisations, and a high commitment HRM approach to the employment relationship. The identification and analysis of the three conceptual entities stems from human resource management, social exchange and employee well-being literatures. These literatures can generate a range of new insights and debates about understanding employees' perspectives and reactions to HRM, quality of working life and consequently well-being at work.

The *conceptual promises* relate to structures and practices that underline HRM policy formulation as well as the high commitment HRM practices that were adopted by Pfeffer (2005) and later amended by Marchington and Wilkinson (2005) for the UK context. It is viewed as the employer's obligation to the psychological contract to provide 'best-practice' high commitment HRM practices as part of its people management strategy espoused to enhance commitment, fairness at work and performance. Supporting this view, Wood and Menezes (1998) and Grant and Shields (2002) assert that discursive practices can contribute to the construction of social reality, and more specifically to shaping the identity, attitudes and behaviour of organisational stakeholders. Proponents of HRM practices or 'conceptual promises' will believe that it is correct and valid, and will seek to use it to change social structures and relationships (Grant and Shield, 2002; Guest and Conway, 2004; Marchington and Wilkinson, 2005; Pfeffer, 2005). Conceptual promises exist in organisations in an expressive order; they exist in the realm of ideas (i.e. Humanistic HRM or Cost Minimisation HRM) that are later developed as HRM policies to be implemented in the management of human capital.

Perceptions of working life is explored through the lens of widely used social exchange constructs (mentioned previously) (Coyle-Shapiro and Conway, 2005; Eisenberger et al., 1986; Graen et al., 1982; Guest and Conway, 2004; Rousseau, 1995). These social exchange theories have been used to explain the employment relationship and are considered relevant and appropriate in this research. It bridges the thinking between HRM practices and well-being at work and will explain how employees relate to the adopted HRM practices and consequently well-being.

The *well-being reality of subjects* – well-being has been widely researched in literature and human well-being has been the focus of substantial and ongoing research (Cooper et al., 2001; CIPD, 2019; Guest and Conway, 2004; Guest, 2002; ESRC, 2006, 2010; Linley et al., 2010; Whitfield, 2009). Major lines of research that characterise the quality of life and performance originate from stress and health literatures. These research argue that worker performance and quality of life are hindered by strain or boredom affecting performance as well as their well-being (Cooper et al., 2001; Seligman, 2000). Although well-being is very much talked about it is not effectively defined (Renwick, 2003). The literature focuses on psychological, physical and social well-being dimensions (Baptiste, 2009; Currie, 2001; Grant et al., 2007; Kersley et al., 2006; Warr, 2002). From a broader perspective, well-being also generally relates to work-life balance, wellness management programmes, health promotions, employee support (e.g. access to counselling service, employee assistance programme (EAP), financial education and stop smoking support), job satisfaction, insurance/protection initiatives, job-related well-being and contentment (CIPD, 2019; Guest, 2002; Kersley et al., 2006; PwC, 2008; Warr, 2002; Wood and de Menezes, 1998). This book argues that there is a need to go beyond the current conceptualisation of well-being in the literature towards a more holistic multidimensional well-being paradigm that can be used for policy and practice in organisations to better understand the meaning employees give to well-being at work from an HRM perspective.

Structure of the book

This book is divided into three parts with a total of 14 chapters. Part I explores the *Theoretical developments in HRM, New Public Management and Well-Being Research Agendas*; Part II explores the *Methodological and Ethical Considerations for employee well-being research*; and Part III explores the *Workers' Voice: HRM Practices, Line Management Leadership and Well-Being at Work*. This book starts with an Introduction to an agenda for research into workplace well-being. Chapter 1 builds a foundation for workplace health and well-being in the public sector and introduces the research context, rationale and theoretical framework of the study. Chapter 2 reviews literature around the dynamics and key principles of an NPM environment and its political context. The local government case organisation is reviewed. The effects of NPM changes on employee well-being and the employment relationship are also presented in this chapter. Chapter 3 introduces the theoretical debases in 'high commitment' human resources management, social exchanges and high performing organisations literatures. The relationships that exists between HRM, social exchanges and well-being at work is established. Chapter 4 reviews the historical and current literature that relates to well-being at work and presents a holistic multidimensional well-being model that looks at the individual, groups, and the organisational dimensions that should be considered to promote diverse employee well-being domains at work. Chapter 5 provides an in-depth methodological approach to workplace well-being research and is written in the first person to allow readers a closer look into the research and respondents' reality during the time of data collection. Chapter 6 explores research that looked at employees' quality of working life through the lens of the observations and documentary analysis. This chapter provides readers with a closer view of the work environment and working life realities of the public sector employees.

Chapter 7 presents research that explore well-being at work in the public sector during tough times with restricted resources. It raises the question whether well-being at work can be promoted in the public sector with limited budgets and increasing targets? Implications for policy makers and manager are discussed. Chapter 8 explores line management leadership and implications for job satisfaction, service delivery and performance. Chapter 9 explores public sector senior managers' perspectives that relates to workplace well-being and fun initiatives. The chapter outlines what senior managers require to promote and maintain their well-being in the public sector. Chapter 10 evaluates the quality of working life and the meaning of the job of public sector workers and the implications of these experiences on their mental health, well-being and performance. Chapter 11 explores employees' reactions and evaluation of HRM practices, definition of well-being and improvements of well-being at work in the public sector. Chapter 12 explores the concepts of well-being as it relates to managers and employees' perspectives of their understanding and meaning ascribed to well-being at work. Insights of the importance of well-being and recommendations for how well-being can be improved is explored. Chapter 13 investigates managers and employees accounts of the responsiveness of their line managers to the promotion of their well-being. Reactions to HRM, working life realities and improvements in line management leadership to promote well-being are discussed. The chapter also illustrates the multidimensional well-being model as well as the integrated model depicting employees' interpretation of what their quality of working life and well-being at work should be. Chapter 14 reviews the main research discussed throughout the book through the exploration of the key findings that arose from managers and employees' perspective and reactions to HRM, the quality of working life, social exchanges, line management leadership and well-being at work. Implications for local government, public sector employees, policy makers, organisational leaders, HR practitioners, managers and researchers are discussed.

Research limitations and future research are also discussed, focusing on what happens next for well-being at work in the public sector in the North West England given the new coalition government's proposal for additional expenditure reduction, and now with the 'Brexit', which relates to the UK's decision in a June 23, 2016, referendum to leave the European Union (EU) and the European Single Market. This decision has macro implications for uncertainty with trade agreements and global markets and has caused the British pound to fall to its lowest level against the American dollar in 30 years (Kenton, 2019). The Brexit vote also has political upheaval that resulted in the resignation of Prime Minister David Cameron and most recently Prime Minister Theresa May, which created a platform for a leadership contest to choose May's successor from the Tory party. The nature of Brexit has to be decided by the new leader. There have been numerous debates regarding Brexit, but there are still a lot of grey areas regarding the best way forward. Given this challenging and precarious situation, one can only imagine the micro implications of Brexit on the health and well-being of public sector employees as well as the working aged population in the UK as a whole. The author postulates that the findings and recommendations from this research can be used as a road map to contribute to the dialogue and debates in this area.

Conclusion

This chapter established the motivation for this study and the research questions, which explored employees' perspectives and reactions to HRM practices and working life and how such experiences have contributed to their well-being at work in the context of local government in the North West of England. The aims of this research are to investigate how employee well-being ideology can be successfully promoted and maintained in an NPM environment given continuous proposal for reformation and expenditure reduction; and to explore how employees within an NPM environment perceive and react to HRM practices, working life and consequently well-being at work.

This chapter reviewed the research territory, which identified challenges and pressures of the changing nature of work. These have implications relating to long working hours, increased workloads, job insecurity and increasing work-related stress that have implications for mental and physical ill-health. This in turn can lead to rising sickness absence, which has a high cost to businesses and the public purse. It is noted that sickness absence, presenteeism and leaveism are higher in the public sector than in the private sector and non-profit organisations with British workers rated as being dissatisfied with their jobs. Now, the recent Brexit challenges have added another layer to the potential challenges that public sector organisations and other organisations will face, which will have far-reaching implications for employees' health and well-being at work. These changes create a platform for the importance of research into well-being at work, with particular reference to public sector employees. Well-being ideology has been embraced by the UK government which commissioned well-being research and supported the notion that well-being is essential for people of working age and can help improve the physical and mental health of employees. Moreover, as more organisational leaders prioritise employee well-being as an important strategy, senior and line managers should better understand and value their most important resource, *people*, as through human capital, services can be delivered effectively, performance can be enhanced, savings can be made and organisations can be more effective and efficient. The theoretical framework used in the study draws from HRM, Social Exchange and Well-being literatures using social exchange as a lens to explain the relationship between HRM practices, line management leadership and well-being at work. The structure of the book is outlined using a graphical road map illustration. The next chapter reviews the New Public Management environment that establishes the context of the research.

References

Armstrong, M., and Brown, D. (2001) *New Dimensions in Pay Management, (Developing Practice)*, London, UK: Chartered Institute of Personnel and Development.

Bach, S., Kessler, I., and White, G. (2005) 'Employment Relations and Public Services "Modernisation" under Labour', *Personnel Review*, Vol. 34(6): 626–633.

Baptiste, N.R. (2008) 'Tightening the Link between Employee Well-Being at Work and Performance: A New Dimension for HRM', *Management Decisions*, Vol. 46(2): 284–309.

Baptiste, N.R. (2009) 'Fun and Well-Being: Insights from Senior Managers in a Local Authority', *Employee Relations*, Vol. 31(6): 600–612.

Bates, J., and Thompson, N. (2007) 'Workplace Well-Being: An Occupational Social Work Approach', *Illness, Crisis and Loss*, Vol. 15(3): 273–284.

Berman, E.M., Bowman, J.S., West, J.P., and Van Wart, M.R. (2010) *Human Resource Employment Relations in the Public Services*, London: Routledge.

Black, D.C. (2008) *Working for a Healthier Tomorrow*, London: TSO.

Bolton, S., and Houlihan, M. (2007) 'Beginning the Search for the H in HRM', in S. Bolton and M. Houlihan (Eds.) *Searching for the H in Human Resource Management: Theory, Practice and Workplace Context*, Basingstoke: Palgrave Macmillan.

Brown, A., Charlwood, A., Forde, C., and Spencer, D. (2006) *Changing Job Quality in Britain 1998–2004*, DTI Employment Relations Research Series, No. 70, London: DTI.

Cartwright, S., and Cooper, C.L. (2009) *The Oxford Handbook of Organisational Well-Being*, Oxford: Oxford University Press.

Cascio, W.F. (2010) 'The Changing World of Work', in P.A. Linley, S. Harrington, and N. Garcea (Eds.) *Oxford Handbook of Positive Psychology and Work*, pp. 13–23, Oxford: Oxford University Press.

Chartered Institute of Personnel and Development (CIPD, 2007) *New Directions in Managing Employee Absence: An Evidence-Based Approach*, Research in Practice, London: Chartered Institute of Personnel and Development.

Chartered Institute of Personnel and Development (CIPD, 2008) *Bully at Work and the 2007 Code of Practice*, London: Chartered Institute of Personnel Development.

Chartered Institute of Personnel and Development (CIPD, 2010) *Employee Outlook Recovery Yet to Reach the Workplace*, Quarterly Survey Report, Spring 2010, London: Chartered Institute of Personnel Development.

Chartered Institute of Personnel and Development (CIPD, 2019) *Health and Well-Being at Work*, Public Sector April 2019, In Partnership with Simply-health, Reference 7837, London.

Cooper, C.L., Dewe, P.J., and O'Driscoll, M.P. (2001) *Organisational Stress: A Review and Critique of Theory, Research and Application*, Newbury Park, CA: Sage Publications.

Cooper, C.L., and Robertson, I. (2001) *Well-Being in Organisations: A Reader for Students and Practitioners*, Chichester: John Wiley and Sons Limited.

Coyle-Shapiro, J.A.-M., and Conway, N. (2005) 'Exchange Relationships: An examination of Psychological Contracts and Perceived Organisational Support', *Journal of Applied Psychology*, Vol. 90: 774–781.

Currie, D. (2001) *Managing Employee Well-Being*, Oxford: Chandos Publishing Oxford Limited.

Department of Works and Pensions (2005) *Health, Work and Well-Being: Caring for Our Future: A Strategy for the Health and Well-Being of Working Age People*, Research Report with Department of Health and Health and Safety Executive, HWW1, October.

Department of Works and Pensions (2017) 'Improving Lives, the Work, Health and Disability Green Chapter', Presented to Parliament by the Secretary of State for Work and Pensions and the Secretary of State for Health by Command of Her Majesty, October 2016, London.

Department of Health (DOH, 2007) *Departmental Report: The Health and Personal Social Services Programmes,* London: The Stationery Office.

Economic and Social Research Council (ESRC) (2006) *Health Well-Being of Working Age People: The Employee's Perspectives*, London: ESRC.

Economic and Social Research Council (ESRC) (2010) *Well-Being and Working Life: Towards an Evidence-Based Policy Agenda*, London: HSE/ESRC.

Eisenberger, R., Huntington, R., Hutchison, S., and Sowa, D. (1986) 'Perceived Organisational Support', *Journal of Applied Psychology*, Vol. 71(3): 500–507.

Fisher, D., Harris, L., Kirk, S., Leopold, J., and Leverment, Y. (2004) 'The Dynamics of Modernization and Job Satisfaction in the British National Health Service', *Review of Public Personnel Administration*, Vol. 24(4): 283–290.

Flade, P. (2003) 'Great Britain's Workforce Lacks Inspiration', *Gallup Management Journal*, The Gallup Organisation's Employee Engagement Index Survey, http://gmj.gallup.com/content/9847/great-britains-workforce-lacks-inspiration.aspx (accessed 12th July, 2010).

George, C. (2009) *The Psychological Contract: Managing and Developing Professional Groups*, Work and Organisational Psychology, Berkshire: Open University Press.

Graen, G.B., Novak, M.A., and Sommerkamp, P. (1982) 'The Effects of Leader-Member Exchange and Job Design on Productivity and Satisfaction: Testing a Dual Attachment Model', *Organisational Behaviour and Human Performance*, Vol. 30: 109–131.

Grant, A., Christianson, M., and Price, R. (2007) 'Happiness, Health or Relationships? Managerial Practices and Employee Well-Being Tradeoffs', *The Academy of Management*, Vol. 21(3): 51–63.

Grant, D., and Shields, J. (2002) 'In Search of the Subject: Researching Employee Reactions to Human Resource Management', *Journal of Industrial Relations*, Vol. 44(3): 313–334.

Green, F., and Whitfield, K. (2009) 'Employees Experiences at Work', in W. Brown, A. Bryson, J. Forth, and K. Whitfield (Eds.) *The Evolution of the Modern Workplace*, Cambridge: Cambridge University Press.

Guest, D. (2002) 'Human Resource Management, Corporate Performance and Employee Well-Being: Building the Worker into HRM', *Journal of Industrial Relations*, Vol. 44(3): 335–358.

Guest, D., and Conway, N. (1999) *How Dissatisfied Are British Workers? A Survey of Surveys*, London: IPD.

Guest, D., and Conway, N. (2004) *Employee Well-Being and the Psychological Contract*, London: CIPD.

Health and Safety Executive (2000) *Securing Health Together*, London: HSE.

Health and Safety Executive (2004) *Management Standards for Work-Related Stress*, 3rd November, London: HSE.

Health and Safety Executive (2007) *Workplace Health, Safety and Welfare: A Short Guide for Management*, London: Health and Safety Executive.

Health and Safety Executive (2009) *Health and Safety Statistics 2008/2009*, London: HSE.

Hesketh, I., and Cooper, C.L. (2014) 'Leaveism at Work', *Occupational Medicine*, Vol. 64(3): 146–147, https://academic.oup.com/occmed/article/64/3/146/1439077

Kenton, W. (2019) *Brexit*, Investopedia Markets, https://investopedia.com/terms/b/brexit.asp (accessed 1st June, 2019).

Kersley, B., Alphin, C., Forth, J., Bryson, A., Bewley, H., Dix, G., and Oxenbridge, S. (2006) *Inside the Workplace: Findings from the 2004 Workplace Employment Relations Survey*, London: Routledge.

Linley, P.A., Harrington, S., and Garcea, N. (Eds.) (2010) *Oxford Handbook of Positive Psychology at Work*, Oxford: Oxford University Press.

MacDonald, L.A.C. (2005) *Wellness at Work: Protecting and Promoting Employee Well-Being*, London: Chartered Institute of Personnel and Development.

MacLeod, D., and Clarke, N. (2009) *Engaging for Success: Enhancing performance through employee engagement*. A report to government, Great Britain. Department for Business, Innovation and Skills (BIS), http://hdl.voced.edu.au/10707/149387.

Marchington, M., and Wilkinson, A. (2005) *Human Resource Management at Work: People Management and Development*, London: CIPD.

Morphet, J. (2008) *Modern Local Government*, London: Sage Publications.

Mowbray, D. (2009) *The Well-Being and Performance Agenda*, www.the-stress-clinic.net (accessed 15th May, 2010).

Newall, S. (2002) *Creating the Healthy Organisation: Well-Being Diversity and Ethics at Work*, London: Thomson Learning.

Noblet, A., Rodwell, J., and McWilliams, J. (2006) 'Organisational Change in the Public Sector: Augmenting the Demand Control Model to Predict Employee Outcomes under New Public Management', *Work and Stress*, Vol. 20(4): 335–352.

Pfeffer, J. (2005) 'Producing Sustainable Competitive Advantage through Effective Management of People', *Academy of Management Executive*, Vol. 19(4): 95–108.

PricewaterhouseCoopers (2008) *Building the Case for Wellness*, www.working-forhealth.gov.uk (accessed 20th July, 2010).

Purcell, J., and Hutchinson, S. (2003) *Bringing Policies to Life: The Vital Role of Front Line Managers in People Management*, London: CIPD.

Renwick, D. (2003) 'HR Managers, Guardians of Employee Well-Being?', *Personnel Review*, Vol. 32(3): 341–359.

Rousseau, D.M. (1995) *Psychological Contracts in Organisations: Understanding Written and Unwritten Agreements*, Thousand Oaks, London: Sage Publications.

Seligman, M.E.P. (2000) 'Positive Psychology', in J. Gillham (Ed.) *The Science of Optimism and Hope, Research Essays in Honour of Martin E.P. Seligman*, New York: Templeton Foundation Press.

Silcox, S. (2007) 'Health Work and Well-Being: Rising to the Public Sector Attendance Management Challenge', *ACAS Policy Discussion Chapter*, (6), May.

Thompson, N., and Bates, J. (Eds.) (2009) *Promoting Workplace Well-Being*, London: Palgrave Macmillan.

Warr, P. (2002) *Psychology at Work*, Suffolk: Penguin Group Books.

Whitfield, K. (Ed.) (2009) 'Employee Well-Being and Working Life: Towards an Evidence-Based Policy Agenda, an ESRC/HSE Public Policy Project', Report on a public policy seminar held at HSE, February, London.

Williams, S., and Cooper, L. (1999) *Dangerous Waters: Strategies for Improving Well-Being at Work*, Chichester: John Wiley and Sons.

Wood, S., and de Menezes, L. (1998) 'High Commitment Management in the UK: Evidence from the Workplace Industrial Relations Survey and Employers WERS' Manpower and Skills Practices Survey', *Human Relations*, Vol. 51: 485–515.

2   New Public Management environment

Introduction

The British economy is facing one of its greatest challenges in recent history. In 2008, the global economy plunge into turmoil and the recession is notable as it is born out of a financial crisis after a long period of growth and prosperity. This resulted in a fall in output and employment had returned to pre-recessionary levels, and labour productivity has declined (van Wanrooy et al., 2011). Van Wanrooy et al. (2011) further assert that employment in the private sectors have behaved very differently. Private sector employment fell substantially during 2008 and 2009 as the recession hit. In contrast, public sector employment rose during this period. Since 2010, the picture has been reversed, with private sector employment rising while public sector employment has fallen (CIPD, 2019). There has also been a pattern of unstable growth, and uncertainty. Public sector organisations are stretched further to 'weather the storms' of challenging financial crisis which places a tighter and perhaps unforgiving squeeze on there already limited resources within a New Public Management (NPM) environment. Has public sector employees' working life experiences and well-being suffered during the economic upheaval and NPM?

An exploration of organisational phenomenon such as employees' perspectives and reactions to HRM practices, working life and well-being would be impossible without the understanding of the surrounding environment in which organisations and people function. The assumption is that exploring employees' work experiences and well-being in a New Public Management environment requires a contextual background of this working environment which can affect individuals' experiences, ideologies, values, attitudes and behaviours. The environment focus of this research is a United Kingdom (UK) context in a local government organisation in North West (NW) England over the period 2005 to 2007 under the New Labour government. This chapter reviews the key principles and political context that underpin the NPM environment, followed by the characteristics of the local government case organisation, and the consequences of NPM on employee well-being and the employment relationship. The chapter concludes with a summary and conclusion of the key issues discussed.

Dynamics of an New Public Management environment

New Public Management (NPM) theory has been applied in the public sector because of funding limitations and the growing expenditure due to technological progress and an aging population (Simonet, 2013). The UK public sector in Northern England has been selected for the analysis in this book because it is the forefront of NPM for political and historical reasons. Simonet (2013) states that historically, the UK has had continuing fiscal crisis that led to an International Monetary Fund (IMF) intervention as early as the 1970s, with much of the blame placed on the civil service. NPM theory reforms can be traced to the ascendancy of neo-liberal ideas of the early 1980s, economic shocks (e.g. the oil crisis in the 1970s and the recession of the early 1980s), the desire to balance government budgets in the late 1990s, and a revival of neoconservatism among the governing elite (Cribb, 2008). In emerging and transition economies, NPM was advocated by most international finance institutions (e.g. The World Bank and the IMF) as a means to emphasise good governance (OECD, 1995; Simonet, 2013). The NPM ideology and key trends that provide the context in which decisions are made in the public sector environment have implications for human resource management, working life and well-being at work for public sector employees (Boyne, 2002; Livesey et al., 2006). These include diminishing confidence in government, declining budgets, increasing demands for service and productivity and human resource activities.

Diminishing confidence in government has resulted in a steady erosion of trust in government which can erode the morale and well-being of employees in the public service and impede performance (Anderson and Bateman, 1997; Lyons, 2007). Berman et al. (2010) assert that rebuilding trust is an important challenge facing the public sector at all levels. Central to this view, Pate et al.'s (2007) research revealed a relative distrust of senior management in the public sector. The CIPD, 2019 Health and Well-Being at Work survey findings echoes this view as employees noted that relationships with management was the second major cause for work-related stress, and mental ill-health, which in turn have negative implication for negative well-being, absenteeism, presenteeism and leaveism behaviours in the public sector (CIPD, 2019). Albrecht and Travaglione's (2003) study also support this view suggesting that effective organisational communication, procedural justice, organisational support and satisfaction with job security predicts trust in public sector senior management (Boyne, 2002; Reichers et al., 1997). They further argue that trust in senior management influences affective and continuance commitment, cynicism towards change and turnover intention (Helliwell and Wang, 2010; Zeffane and Connell, 2003).

Moreover, declining budgets due to the reduction in funding from central government and political pressures to curb future expenditure have implications for the challenges and tensions faced by public sector workers that can influence their well-being (Dibben and James, 2007; Massey and Pyper, 2005). Budget limitations have also set the platform for alternative work arrangements to help keep costs down due to changes in work contracts and working time scheduling have radically transformed the nature of work in public sector organisations (Beaumont et al., 2007; Jackson and Lapsley, 2003; Sparks et al., 2001). These approaches have reformed and re-engineered initiatives, resulting in new approaches to the delivery of goods and services with greater efficiency (Beaumont et al., 2007; Drewry, 2005). Central to declining budgets is restructuring, through downsizing and upsizing, which paves the way for workforce reductions linked to privitisation, deregulation, budget or service cuts and programme terminations (Berman et al., 2010; Cunha and Cooper, 2002; Simonet, 2013). Changing organisational structures resulted in the breaking down of monolithic public service organisations into separate units, with more devolved management practice paving the way for more direct budget responsibilities (Bach, 1999; Jackson and Lapsley, 2003). Another key principle is the demand for productivity where all levels in the public sector are under pressure to improve performance without rising costs (Dibben and James, 2007). Modell (2001) states that legitimacy-seeking and efficiency enhancing rationales form part of senior management's rhetoric for performance management in the public sector. Modell further argues that the differing nature of the interrelationships between stakeholders will influence the extent of performance management in service provided organisations.

Moreover, decentralisation of human resource activities and responsibilities to line managers facilitates greater flexibility and discretion in the implementation of human resource management practices (Berman et al., 2010; Gould-Williams, 2007). This allows managers to play an active role in terms of having greater scope to alter job roles and develop other forms of flexibility (Gould-Williams, 2007). It is important to mention here, that line managers were given the responsibility for people management, but with limited funding and budgets, it is likely that they were not effectively trained to provide the required support to employees to effectively promote their health, mental health and well-being at work as well as deliver HRM functions. This point is validated by the CIPD, 2019 Health and Well-Being Survey that claims levels of absenteeism, presenteeism, leaveism and mental health challenges remain growing issues in the public sector and many organisations are also failing to provide line managers with the skills and support they require in these areas (CIPD, 2019). Line managers play a key role in managing employee absence and promoting well-being, but the CIPD research states that half of respondents agree that their line managers have bought in to the importance of well-being and a minority believe their managers have the confidence and competence to support mental health (CIPD, 2019). Changes within the organisation were also accompanied by competition between service units that produced an organisational dynamics different from that underpinning the traditional bureaucracy (Stewart, 2003). Central to this view, Harris (2007) points out that public sector reform will influence changes in HR's role and services which will impact on the function's ability to act as an 'employee champion' due to reduced employee contact and more fragmented HR roles. However, it has increased managerial flexibility and discretion over hiring, discipline and other employment relations practices (Dibben and James, 2007).

NPM ideology rejects traditional models of HRM for a more assertive managerialism with tighter control of resources (Dibben and James, 2007; Green, 2009), changes in organisational structures (Bach, 1999) and enhanced efficiency which are all associated with more intensive working practices (Cribb, 2008; Dibben, 2007). It also entails downsizing (Cunha and Cooper, 2002), pay determination (Kirkpatrick et al., 2005), areas of management, resource utilisation, tighter control of performance (Bach and Kessler, 2008) and a dilution of union influence (Dibben and James, 2007). In the area of HRM, reform strategies are context specific and shaped by the cultural and institutional details of each organisation. This approach is associated with institutional theory (Scott, 2004) which relates to processes by which structures, rules, norms and routines become established as authoritative guidelines for social behaviour (Harrow, 2002).

The development of HRM practice in the public sector appears to be shrouded by the lack of autonomy for creativity and innovation (Bach, 1999). Central to this view, Kessler and Coyle-Shapiro (2000) argue that the development of local HR practices in the public services were quite limited, with practices sharing similar features, suggesting mimicking or copying. Bach and Kessler (2008) maintain that the reluctance of service units to use their HR discretion was ascribed to the limited and inadequate HR capacity/specialists and trade unionists, and managers unwillingness to exercise their HR discretion, fearing variation in style and resulting in more problems (Dibben and James, 2007; Morphet, 2008). Bach and Kessler, also point out that these values constrain the risks executives and managers are prepared to take, remaining aware that their employment policies may become subject to closer public scrutiny than would likely be applied to a private sector organisation. Therefore, managers promote vigilance not to expose ministers or other public officials to risk through unacceptable or controversial practices (Livesey et al., 2006; Massey and Pyper, 2005).

The HR literature focuses on management styles for the efficient use of human resources being linked to high-commitment (Guest, 2002; Gould-Williams, 2007). Moreover, Purcell (2006) claim that management styles in the public sector are more in common with cost minimisation than a high-commitment approach to HRM. Kessler and Coyle-Shapiro (2000) support this view and claim that devising new HR practices to meet 'business' needs was to ensure that labour costs were reduced by tackling sickness absence and altering the composition of the workforce. Central to management style was the introduction of professional managers in the public sector to curb the entrenched power of professionals, as tensions existed between managers and professionals who had differing goals and orientations (Bach and Kessler, 2008). Nevertheless, Kirkpatrick et al. (2005) point out that senior managers have become increasingly reliant on professionals to deliver on central government targets, thus strengthening professional control of services. Central to this view, Bach (2004: 192) advocates that the emphasis placed on strengthening managerial prerogatives have implications for employee voice with the potential to erode trade union influence.

Furthermore, partnership working signified attempts to move away from adversarial relations towards mutuality (Masters and Albright, 2003). This approach reflected government attempts to improve flexible working practices, setting an example as a model employer of 'best practice' ideology towards improving the quality of working life for staff (DOH, 2007). Partnership working was used to influence a change in relationships with trade unions in an effort to remove tensions through union involvement at the workplace level (Bach, 2004). Supporting these views, Kickert (2003) argues that the provision of services through inter-organisational working, places greater emphasis on integrated working shifting to a more pragmatic mixed approach where 'what works best is used'.

The political context

Local government has an important contribution to make as part of a single system of government geared towards meeting the needs of the locality leading to the well-being of citizens (Lyons, 2007). Politics is an important context of the public sector (Berman et al., 2010). This research was conducted during the time New Labour was in government (i.e. 1997 to 2010). However, there was a change in government on 10 May 2010, from New Labour to Conservatives/Liberal Democrats. The central objective for New Labour was making life better for people by ensuring that policy making was more 'joined up' and strategic (Green, 2009; Morphet, 2008). New Labour professed to focus on public service users by delivering high quality and efficient public services, union recognition, partnership working, individual employment rights, and the improvement of public service performance with the creation of greater 'fairness' at work (Dibben and James, 2007; Massey and Pyper, 2005). Essential to New Labour's policies was the espousal of wellness initiatives and health and safety 'best practice' standards for the promotion of the health and well-being of the working age population (Black, 2008; HWWE, 2010), equal opportunities, the promotion of a trust culture, diversity and working time arrangements (Lewis and Campbell, 2007). Central to New Labour's professed ideology of promoting and maintaining employee health and well-being of the working aged population, the UK's public sector engaged in activities to improve employee well-being by introducing and promoting well-being strategies and programmes. However, the CIPD, 2019 research on Health and Well-being in the UK's public sector states that public sector organisations remain divided in how strategic and proactive employee well-being programmes should be with two-fifths having a standalone well-being strategy, while a similar proportion are much more reactive than proactive (CIPD, 2019). Furthermore, the CIPD, health and well-being research point out that an average level of employee absenteeism this year was 5.9 days per employee per year, which was the lowest rate ever recorded by this survey. The research also states that presenteeism and leaveism remain common, as well as an increased focus on mental health, which remains the most common cause of long-term absence and is a growing issue for nearly three-fifths of organisations (CIPD, 2019). Despite public sector organisations espousal of reducing employee absence and increasing employee well-being activities, there remain clear divisions in the value organisations place on employee well-being and how strategic, targeted and comprehensive they are in their approach to achieve positive organisational outcomes (CIPD, 2019). According to the CIPD research, financial well-being is a more neglected aspect of health and well-being activity and a minority of public sector organisations (13%) have a financial well-being strategy that takes into account the needs of different employee groups. CIPD findings show that over a quarter of respondents in the public sector (28% compared with 22% in the private sector) believe that poor financial well-being is a significant cause of employee stress in their organisations, and just 21% agree that their employees demonstrate the knowledge and skills to make the right reward and benefit choices to meet their financial needs (CIPD, 2019). However, budgetary constraints tend to have greater influence on the purchase of well-being benefits in the public sector than managing identified health issues in the organisation, but this is also true in the private and non-profit sectors (Hesketh and Cooper, 2014).

The local government case organisation

The research was carried out in a local authority in the North West of England situated in Greater Manchester (GM) that comprises ten metropolitan borough towns. Cushman and Wakefield (2015) state that Manchester is the fastest growing city region outside London and is rated as Britain's most creative city essential for good business. The local government case organisation is located south of Manchester bordering on

Cheshire with a population of 285 thousand and is the seventh most socially polarised nationally (Livesey et al., 2006). It is highly affluent with areas of deprivation, and has a vibrant economy with the highest level of activity in GM (Audit Commission, 2008; ONS, 2007). The local authority is responsible for the provision of a wide range of public services including ensuring the mental health and well-being of the community. The local authority was formed in 1974 and under the New Labour government had elected councillors resulting in no political majority, which affected decision making and consequently impinged on a lack of clear direction. The organisation is rated as a four-star performing council (Audit Commission, 2008), it employs 11,000 full-time and part-time staff making it the largest employer in the borough, with a revenue budget in the financial year 2004/2005 of £269 million. The local authority has a management structure of five operating directorates/departments[1] and an overall vision for a 'cleaner, greener, safer, stronger future for the council through seven strategic priorities'[2] (Arms Length Management Report (ALMO), 2006; Audit Commission, 2008).

Following a period of political and financial stability and indeed economic well-being throughout the 1990s the authority was subject to a range of pressures and difficulties in the succeeding decade. The Comprehensive Performance Assessment (Livesey et al., 2006) highlighted overall improvements in performance throughout all directorates which include: financial strategies and budget monitoring; meeting residents' expectations and support provisions; improvements in service capacity; value for money; information communication technology development; use of resources with the focus on internal control; and improvements in approach to customer care by addressing stakeholder satisfaction in services provided and inequalities in residents' health and well-being (Audit Commission, 2008). These improvements resulted in financial uncertainty for the council with a then economic crisis, a looming financial deficit and a pressing need to respond to performance measures outlined by the Audit Commission imposed by Central Government (Audit Commission, 2008; Noblet et al., 2006).

The ALMO's (2006) report revealed that the local authority's response to these combined pressures involved fairly radical changes in the general structure and operations of the council as well as the more specific management of the employment relationship. For example, directorates/departments were merged for greater efficiency and effectiveness. The council resorted to capital asset reduction which resulted in the abolition of traditional work offices for managers and professionals. These were replaced with a 'new way of working' strategy which involved 'hot-desking', mobile and home working. Moreover, flexible working initiatives were also offered throughout the local government organisation.

Demographic characteristics of the case borough as highlighted by the Office for National Statistics (2007) showed that the Metropolitan borough's population was 12% of GM and 4% of the NW region. For the purpose of confidentiality, the case borough will be referred to XYZ borough. Overall, the same percentage proportion was reflected in the gender division and age ranges, with females outnumbering males by 7% in XYZ borough, 5% in GM and 6% in the NW (Forth and Stokes, 2006). Weekly earnings are higher in XYZ borough as compared to GM and the NW region. This also applied to education as a larger percentage; (i.e. 19% more) individuals were qualified with skills as compared to GM and the NW region (Forth and Stokes, 2006; DOH, 2007; ONS, 2007). The XYZ borough had more individuals in managerial professional occupations than GM and NW and less in non-managerial occupations as compared to the other two areas.

The consequences of New Public Management on employee well-being

The public sector has been the centre for continuous politically sensitive reform that has been underpinned by the NPM approach that focuses on the move from hierarchical formalised approach, with an emphasis on avoiding mistakes and application of rules (Butterfield et al., 2005). It also involves the existence of bureaucracy and red tape (Bozeman, 1993, 2000) to espousal of decentralisation, values of innovation, enterprise and management problem solving (Clarke et al., 2000; McLaughlin et al., 2008). Other features involve a shift towards value for money, supported by techniques of performance management, budgeting, costing, balance scorecard and key performance indicators (Jackson and Lapsley, 2003). The modernisation of the public sector consequently affected, and still affects, public sector workers in the areas of declining public service ethos (Needham, 2007), increasing criticism of the quality of public services and failure to meet citizens expectations (Dibben and James, 2007), work intensification and delivery of public services (Noblet et al., 2006), pay and rewards (Folger, 1977), fairness and equity (Harrow, 2002; Dibben et al., 2007; Marsden, 2007), employment security (Dibben, 2007), increased absenteeism, mental health challenges, financial well-being, presenteeism, and leaveism (CIPD, 2019; Hesketh and Cooper, 2014), and even less discussed employee well-being (Baptiste, 2007, 2009; Emmott, 2006).

A key notion of well-being is reflected in the rewards strategies adopted in the public sector as well as fairness and equity. There are ongoing debates in terms of levels of rewards in the public sector compared with private sector employment, especially at the highest and least skilled ends where there is perception of unfairness existing between public service pay and private sector payments practices (e.g. merit pay, performance-related pay) (Folger, 1977; Cropanzano and Folger, 1991). The development of pay determination has implications for the career systems of management and staff (Kirkpatrick et al., 2005). Supporting this view, Ferlie and Steane (2002) argues that this trend signalled a shift away from a predominantly career-based model of employment in which public servants remained in the public sector for their whole working life. Ferlie further states that instead, a position-based system emerged in which the best-suited candidate was selected for each individual position from internal or external sources (Ferlie and Steane, 2002; Morphet, 2008). Essential to career advancement is employees' skills and development (Redman and Wilkinson, 2009). Marchington and Wilkinson (2005) assert that commitment to employee development is associated with the high-commitment HRM agenda which contrast sharply with the cost minimisation approach of the NPM area (Bach and Kessler, 2008). Moreover, this approach is based on employees' willingness to develop their careers as their working life experiences are filled with the tensions and pressures of performance targets. This in turn generates cumbersome procedures and 'mountains' of paper work, which taps into their already limited time to discharge their duties, thus undermining morale and well-being (Massey and Pyper, 2005). This notion of fairness or justice has been defined by Cropanzano and Folger (1991) as the fairness of procedures for allocating rewards, and is often contrasted with distributive justice which relates to the fairness of the allocated rewards themselves (Harrow, 2002). It can be noted that in cases of perceived injustice, employees will withdraw goodwill and then when they believe that procedures are fairly implemented, they will tolerate temporary departure from distributive justice in rewards (Emmott, 2006; Folger and Cropanzano, 1998).

Furthermore, Kirkpatrick et al. (2005: 176) maintain that the pressures faced by the public sector workforce have been intensified by performance and audit regimes, short-term approach to people management, and the target culture, which has affected staff morale and well-being. Public service performance has remained central to the reform agenda (OECD, 1996) and relates to efficient and effective use of resources, reflected in higher quality public services (Guest and Conway, 2002, 2004). Therefore, greater emphasis has been placed on performance targets allied to recognition that improved organisational performance in a service context is dependent on improved employee performance (Lyons, 2007). Stewart (2003) critiques this approach and argues that a service culture like the public sector driven by performance measurements produces difficulties to elicit the type of employee performance needed to produce better-quality services. Schlesinger and Heskett (1992) further declare that the quality of service customers want requires an 'empowerment' approach (Purcell and Hutchinson, 2003). They also contended that in treating workers more humanely, hiring customer-focussed individuals, treating employees fairly, and de-industrialisation of the service sector can allow workers to give enhanced quality service to customers. Schneider and Bowen (1995) critique this view and argue that the contemporary nature of service work is increasingly harmful to workers. Central to this view, Ritzer (1999: 116) refers to this as the McDonaldization of society portraying customer service work as variously, fake, invasive, emotionally draining, demeaning, highly routinised and alienating. In essence, the nature of service work in the public sector has implications for employee well-being.

Findings from WERS's 1998 and 2004 surveys (Cully et al., 1999; Kersley et al., 2006) shows that public sector workers were more likely than employees in the private sector to experience stress and absence from work through illness. Central to this view, Guest and Conway (2002) reported that levels of satisfaction, trust and commitment are all lower in the public sector. This is also significant and has detrimental consequences for recruitment and retention, particularly for professional groups (Green and Whitfield, 2009; George, 2009). Moreover, Organisation for Economic Co-operation and Development (OECD) (1996) and Harrow (2002) maintain that public sector values of merit, equity, fairness and ethical behaviour continue to influence human resource policies and practices. The public sector ideologies of fairness and ethical behaviour are likely to pave the way for the doctrine of employee well-being being viewed as a '*good thing to do*' under the banner of 'corporate social responsibility', where MP's, senior executives and managers can all pat themselves on the back for a day, for an espoused '*good deed*' done before they return to their 'bottom line' focus.

Another key consequence of modernisation that can affect public service employees' well-being is employment insecurity (Gaunt and Benjamin, 2007). Dibben (2007) avers that employment security is a key issue for public service workers in Britain. Boyne et al. (2002) also state that the erosion of employment security has affected the professional autonomy of the public servant, which has been undermined with the pledge of job cuts as a result of NPM philosophies for efficiency and enhanced service delivery and performance. Public sector job insecurity has in essence negatively affected different groups of workers in different ways (Gould-Williams, 2007). Thus resulting in challenges confronted by government of 'squaring the circle' of higher demands in the context of fiscal constraints (Foster and Plowden, 1996). These are likely to affect HRM activities, the quality of working life and employee well-being in the public sector.

To this end, based on the aforementioned challenges and tensions experienced by public sector employees in an NPM environment, it is important to question whether employee well-being ideology can be viewed strategically by senior managers and successfully promoted and implemented in a NPM environment given continuous proposals for modernisation, reformation, expenditure reduction and improved service delivery and performance without rising costs. It is likely that these challenges and continuous changes in an NPM environment, coupled with political and global market pressures will negatively affect public sector employees' reactions to HRM practice, quality of work life and well-being at work.

This book seeks to address these research questions and to contribute towards the debates in these areas.

Conclusion

This chapter provided the contextual background of the NPM environment in which the study was conducted. The complexities of an NPM environment include challenges and tensions of diminishing confidence in government resulting in mistrust, declining budgets, increasing demands for productivity and service delivery which have implications for HR practice in the public sector. The political context of the work environment and its functioning was explored, noting that data was collected when New Labour was in government and has implications for the study. The local government case organisation is one of the ten Metropolitan Borough councils in Greater Manchester and the council attained a four-star accreditation for its performance. The Audit Commission review of the local authority suggested improvements in efficiency savings and procedural changes in keeping with the modernisation agenda. This resulted in tightening of resources by the council, capital asset reduction, restructuring, changes in working times arrangements and merging of directorates for greater effectiveness and efficiency.

These challenges faced in the local government case organisation have implications for work intensification in the delivery of public services, criticism of the quality of services delivered, increasing work-related stress and pressures, pay and rewards, fairness and equity, employment insecurity and consequently well-being. These challenges give rise to the question whether or not the 'well-being ideology' can be successfully promoted and maintained in an NPM environment given continuous proposals for reformation and expenditure reduction. This study seeks to contribute towards the debates in these areas.

Notes

1 Chief executives, environment and economy, adults and communities, children and young people, and business services (AC, 2008).
2 Children and young people; sustainable environment; physical and economic environment; safer, stronger communities; older people; excellent services and a well run council.

References

Albrecht, S., and Travaglione, A. (2003) 'Trust in Public-Sector Senior Management', *International Journal of Human Resource Management*, Vol. 14(1): 76–92.

Anderson, L.M., and Bateman, T.S. (1997) 'Cynicism in the Workplace: Some Causes and Effects', *Journal of Organisational Behaviour*, Vol. 18: 449–469.

Arms Length Management Organisations (ALMO) (2006) *Guidance and Arms Length Management of Local Authority Housing, (2004 Housing) and the supplement, to the Guidance on Arms Length Management,* June 2006, Wetherby, West Yorkshire.

Audit Commission (2008) *Better Outcomes, Annual Reports and Accounts 2007/2008, HC824,* London: The Stationary Office.

Bach, S. (1999) 'Personnel Managers: Managing to Change?', in S. Corby and G. White (Eds.) *Employment Relations in the Public Services,* London: Routledge.

Bach, S. (2004) *Employment Relations in the Health Service: The Management of Reforms,* London: Routledge Publisher.

Bach, S., and Kessler, I. (2008) 'HRM and the New Public Management', in P. Boxall, J. Purcell, and P. Wright (Eds.) *The Oxford Handbook of Human Resource Management,* pp. 469–488, Oxford: Oxford University Press.

Baptiste, N.R. (2007) 'Line Management Leadership: Implications for Employee Well-Being', in G.P. Clarkson (Ed.) *Developing Leadership Research, Chapters from the Northern Leadership Academy Fellow 2007 Conference,* pp. 229–238, Leeds: Leeds University Business School, Leeds University Press Financial Services.

Baptiste, N.R. (2009) 'Fun and Well-Being: Insights from Senior Managers in a Local Authority', *Employee Relations,* Vol. 31(6): 600–612.

Beaumont, P., Pate, J., and Fischbacher, M. (2007) 'Public Sector Employment: Issues of Size and Composition in the UK', in P. Dibben, P. James, I. Roper, and G. Wood (Eds.) *Modernising Work in Public Services: Redefining Roles and Relationships in Britain's Changing Workplace,* Basingstoke: Palgrave Macmillan.

Berman, E.M., Bowman, J.S., West, J.P., and Van Wart, M.R. (2010) *Human Resource Employment Relations in the Public Services,* London: Routledge.

Black, D.C. (2008) *Working for a Healthier Tomorrow,* London: TSO.

Boyne, G.A. (2002) 'Public and Private Management: What's the Difference', *Journal of Management Studies,* Vol. 39(1): 97–122.

Boyne, G.A., Poole, M., and Jenkins, G. (2002) 'Human Resources Management in the Public and Private Sectors: An Empirical Comparison', *Public Administration,* Vol. 77(2): 407–420.

Bozeman, B. (1993) 'A Theory of Government "Red Tape"', *Journal of Public Administration Research and Policy,* Vol. 3: 273–303.

Bozeman, B. (2000) *Bureaucracy and Red Tape,* Upper Saddle River, NJ: Prentice Hall.

Butterfield, R., Edwards, C., and Woodall, J. (2005) 'The New Public Management and Managerial Roles: The Case of the Police Sergeant', *British Journal of Management,* Vol. 16: 329–341.

Clarke, J., Gewirtz, S., and McLaughlin, E. (Eds.) (2000) *New Managerialism, New Welfare?* London: Sage Publications.

Chartered Institute of Personnel and Development (CIPD, 2019) *Health and Well-Being at Work,* Public Sector April 2019, In Partnership with Simplyhealth, Reference 7837, London.

Cribb, A. (2008) 'Organisational Reform and Health-Care Good', *Journal of Medicine and Philosophy,* Vol. 33: 221–240.

Cropanzano, R., and Folger, R. (1991) 'Procedural Justice and Worker Motivation', in R.M. Steers and L.W. Porter (Eds.) *Motivation and Worker Behaviour,* pp. 131–143, 5th Edition, New York: McGraw Hill.

Cully, M., O'Reilly, A., Millward, J., Forth, S., Woodland, W., Dix, G. and Bryson, A. (1999) *British at Work: As Depicted by the 1998 Workplace Employee Relations Survey*, London: Routledge Publishers.

Cunha, R.C., and Cooper, C.L. (2002) 'Does Privatization Affect Corporate Culture and Employee Well-Being?', *Journal of Managerial Psychology*, Vol. 17(1): 21–49.

Cushmon and Wakefield (2015) *Winning in Growth Cities 2015/2016, A Cushman and Wakefield Capital Markets Research Publication*, www.cushmonwakefield.com.

Department of Health (2007) *Commissioning Framework for Health and Well-Being*, London: DOH, 7th March, www.dh.gov.uk/publications.

Dibben, P. (2007) 'Employment Security and Job Insecurity in Public Services: Tow Sides of the Same Coin?', in P. Dibben, P. James, I. Roper, and G. Wood (Eds.) *Modernising Work in Public Services: Redefining Roles and Relationships in Britain's Changing Workplace*, Basingstoke: Palgrave Macmillan.

Dibben, P., and James, P. (2007) 'Introduction: Is "Modern" Necessarily Better?', in P. Dibbens, P. James, I. Roper, and G. Wood (Ed.), *Modernising Work in Public Services: Redefining Roles and Relationships in Britain's Changing Workplace*, pp. 1–2, Basingstoke: Palgrave MacMillan.

Dibben, P., James, P., Roper, I., and Wood, G. (2007) *Modernising Work in Public Services: Redefining Roles and Relationships in Britain's Changing Workplace*, Basingstoke: Palgrave MacMillan.

Drewry, G. (2005) 'Citizen's Charters: Service Quality Chameleons', *Public Management Review*, Vol. 7(3): 321–340.

Emmott, M. (2006) 'Employee Attitudes in the Public Sector', in *Reflections on Employee Well-Being and the Psychological Contract*, London: Chartered Institute of Personnel and Development.

Ferlie, E., and Steane, P. (2002) 'Changing Developments in New Public Management', *International Journal of Public Administration*, Vol. 25(12): 1459–1469.

Folger, R. (1977) 'Distributive and Procedural Justice: Combined Impact of Voice and Improvement of Experienced Inequity', *Journal of Personality and Social Psychology*, Vol. 35(2): 108–119.

Folger, R., and Cropanzano, R. (1998) *Organisational Justice and Human Resource Management*, London: Sage Publications.

Forth, J., and Stokes, L. (2006) A Regional Perspective on Employment Relations: Tabulations from the 2004 Workplace Employment Relations Survey, *Report to the Advisory, Conciliation and Arbitration Services (ACAS)*, Final Report 8th September 2006.

Foster, C., and Plowden, F. (1996) *The State under Stress*, Buckingham: Open University Press.

Gaunt, R., and Benjamin, O. (2007) 'Job Insecurity, Stress and Gender', *Community Work and Family*, Vol. 10(3): 341–355.

George, C. (2009) *The Psychological Contract: Managing and Developing Professional Groups*, Work and Organisational Psychology, Berkshire: Open University Press.

Gould-Williams, J. (2007) 'HR Practices, Organisational Climate and Employee Outcomes: Evaluating Social Exchange in Local Government', *International Journal of Human Resource Management*, Vol. 18(9): 1627–1647.

Green, I. (2009) *Public Management: A Critical Text*, Basingstoke: Palgrave Macmillan.

Green, F., and Whitfield, K. (2009) 'Employees Experiences at Work', in W. Brown, A. Bryson, J. Forth, and K. Whitfield (Eds.) *The Evolution of the Modern Workplace*, Cambridge: Cambridge University Press.

Guest, D. (2002) 'Human Resource Management, Corporate Performance and Employee Well-Being: Building the Worker into HRM', *Journal of Industrial Relations*, Vol. 44(3): 335–358.

Guest, D., and Conway, N. (2002) *Pressure at Work and the Psychological Contract*, Research Report, London: CIPD.

Guest, D., and Conway, N. (2004) *Employee Well-Being and the Psychological Contract*, London: CIPD.

Harris, L. (2007) 'The Changing Nature of the HR Function in UK Local Government and Its Role as "Employee Champion"', *Employee Relations*, Vol. 30(1): 34–47.

Harrow, J. (2002) 'New Public Management and Social Justice: Just Efficiency or Equity as Well?', in K. McLaughlin, S.P. Osborne, and E. Ferlie (Eds.) *New Public Management: Current Trends and Future Prospects*, pp. 141–159, London: Routledge, Taylor and Francis Group.

Health Work and Well-Being Executive (HWWE) (2010), www.workingforhealth. gov.uk/ (accessed 10th April, 2010) working in partnership with DOH, DWP, HSE, Welsh Assembly Government, and The Scottish Government.

Helliwell, J.F., and Wang, S. (2010) 'Trust and Well-Being', NBER Working Chapter Series 15911, National Bureau of Economic Research, MA, Cambridge.

Hesketh, I., and Cooper, C.L. (2014) 'Leaveism at Work', *Occupational Medicine*, Vol. 64(3): 146–147, https://academic.oup.com/occmed/article/64/3/146/ 1439077

Jackson, A., and Lapsley, I. (2003) 'The Diffusion of Accounting Practices in the New Managerial Public Sector', *International Journal of Public Sector Management*, Vol. 16(5): 359–372.

Kersley, B., Alphin, C., Forth, J., Bryson, A., Bewley, H., Dix, G., and Oxenbridge, S. (2006) *Inside the Workplace: Findings from the 2004 Workplace Employment Relations Survey*, London: Routledge.

Kessler, I., and Coyle-Shapiro, J. (2000) 'New Forms of Employment Relations in the Public Services', *Industrial Relations Journal*, Vol. 31(1): 17–34.

Kickert, W.J.M. (2003) 'Beneath Consensual Corporatism: Traditions of Governance in the Netherlands', *Public Administration*, Vol. 81(1): 119–140.

Kirkpatrick, I., Ackroyd, S., and Walker, R. (2005) *The New Managerialism and Public Service Professions*, Basingstoke: Palgrave.

Lewis, J., and Campbell, M. (2007) 'Work/Family Balance Policies in the UK since 1997: A New Departure?', *Cambridge University Press*, Vol. 36(3): 365–381.

Livesey, D., Machin, A., Millard, B., and Walling, A. (2006) 'Public Sector Employment 2006: Seasonally Adjusted Series and Recent Trends', Office for National Statistics, Labour Market Trends, December.

Lyons, M. (2007) *Lyons Inquiry into Local Government, Place-Shaping: A Shared Ambition for the Future of Local Government*, London: The Stationery Office.

Marchington, M., and Wilkinson, A. (2005) *Human Resource Management at Work: People Management and Development*, London: CIPD.

Marsden, D. (2007) 'Pay and Rewards in Public Services: Fairness and Equity', in P. Dibben, P. James, I. Roper, and G. Wood (Eds.) *Modernising Work in Public Services: Redefining Roles and Relationships in Britain's Changing Workplace*, Basingstoke: Palgrave Macmillan.

Massey, A., and Pyper, R. (2005) *Public Management and Modernisation in British*, Basingstoke: Palgrave Macmillan.

Masters, M., and Albright, R. (2003) 'Federal Labour-Management Partnerships: Perspectives, Performance and Possibilities', in J. Brock and D. Lipsky (Eds.) *Going Public: The Role of Labor Management Relations in Delivering Quality Government Services*, IRRA Series, Urbana: University of Illinois.

McLaughlin, K., Osborne, S.P., and Ferlie, E. (2008) *New Public Management: Current Trends and Future Prospects*, London: Taylor and Francis Group.

Modell, S. (2001) 'Performance Measurement and Institutional Processes: A Study of Managerial Responses to Public Sector Reform', *Management Accounting Research*, Vol. 12: 437–464.

Morphet, J. (2008) *Modern Local Government*, London: Sage Publications.

Needham, C. (2007) 'A Declining Public Sector Ethos?', in P. Dibben, P. James, I, Roper, and G. Wood (Eds.) *Modernising Work in Public Services: Redefining Roles and Relationships in Britain's Changing Workplace*, Basingstoke: Palgrave Macmillan.

Noblet, A., Rodwell, J., and McWilliams, J. (2006) 'Organisational Change in the Public Sector: Augmenting the Demand Control Model to Predict Employee Outcomes under New Public Management', *Work and Stress*, Vol. 20(4): 335–352.

Office for National Statistics (2007) *UK Standard Industrial Classification of Economic Activities 2007 (SIC 2007)*, Structure and Explanatory Notes, Editor, Lindsay Prosser, Office of National Statistics, Palgrave McMillan, Cardiff Road, Newport, South Wales.

Organisation for Economic Co-Operation and Development (1995) *Governance in Transition: Public Management Reform in OECD Countries*, Paris, France: OECD.

Organisation for Economic Co-Operation and Development (OECD) (1996) *Integrating People Management into Public Service Reform*, Paris: OECD.

Pate, J., Beaumont, P., and Stewart, S. (2007) 'Trust in Senior Management in the Public Sector', *Employee Relations*, Vol. 29(5): 458–468.

Purcell, J. (2006) 'Best Practice and Best Fit: Chimera or cul-de-sac?' *Human Resources Management Journal*, Vol. 9(3): 26–41.

Purcell, J., and Hutchinson, S. (2003) *Bringing Policies to Life: The Vital Role of Front Line Managers in People Management*, London: CIPD.

Redman, T., and Wilkinson, A. (2009) *Contemporary Human Resource Management, Text and Cases*, London: Pearson Education.

Reichers, A.E., Wanous, J.P., and Austin, J.T. (1997) 'Understanding and Managing Cynicism about Organisational Change', *Academy of Management Executive*, Vol. 11(1): 48–59.

Ritzer, G. (1999) *Enchanting a Disenchanted World*, Thousand Oaks, London: Pine Forge Press.

Schlesinger, L.A., and Heskett, J. (1992) 'De-Industrialising the Service Sector', in T. Swartz, D. Brown, and S. Brown (Eds.) *Advances in Services Marketing and Management: Research and Practice*, pp. 159–176, Greenwich, CT: JAI Press.

Schneider, B., and Bowen, D. (1995) *Winning the Service Game*, Boston, MA: Harvard Business School Press.

Scott, W.R. (2004) 'Institutional Theory', in G. Ritzer (Ed.) *Encyclopaedia of Social Theory*, Thousand Oaks, CA: Sage Publications.

Simonet, D. (2013) 'The New Public Management Theory in the British Health Care System: A Critical Review', *Administration and Society*, Vol. 47(7): 1–25.

Sparks, K., Faragher, B., and Cooper, C.L. (2001) 'Well-Being and Occupational Health in the 21st Century Workplace', *Journal of Occupational and Organisational Psychology*, Vol. 74: 489–509.

Stewart, J. (2003) *Modernising British Local Government: An Assessment of Labour's Reform Programme*, Basingstoke: Palgrave Macmillan.

Van Wanrooy, B., Bewley, H., Bryson, A., Forth, J., Freeth, S., Stokes, L., and Wood, S. (2011) 'The 2011 Workplace Employment Relations Study (WERS)', First Findings, commissioned by BIS, ESRC, ACAS, UKCES, and NIESR, London, Department for Business, Innovation and Skills.

Zeffane, R., and Connell, J. (2003) 'Trust and HRM in the New Millennium', *International Journal of Human Resource Management*, Vol. 14(1): 3–11.

3 Theoretical debates in HRM, social exchange and high performing organisations

Introduction

This chapter reviews the literature that is considered appropriate and links directly with the key themes of the research in this book. This chapter is divided into three main sections. The first section discusses the three streams of human resource management (HRM) literature. This is followed by a theoretical debate in Employee Relations and high commitment HRM practices in British workplaces. The third section discusses social exchange theories (i.e. the psychological contract, perceived organisational support, leader-member exchange and organisational justice) that are widely used in literature to explain the relationship between social actors in organisations and the employment relationship. Social exchange theories are considered relevant in this study as it is the bridge to assist with understanding employees' reactions to HRM practices, quality of working life and well-being at work in the public sector.

Three streams of HRM literature

The HRM literature is divided into three key streams: the prescriptive, the critical and the small but growing body of employee-focused literature (Gibb, 2001; Grant and Shields, 2002; Guest, 2002). The dominant prescriptive stream of research within the field of HRM has explored the link between HRM and organisational performance (Bach and Kessler, 2009; Gould-Williams, 2003; Guest, 1997, 1999; Huselid et al., 1997) and is an essential determinant of the organisational success which distinguishes high-performing organisations (Boxall et al., 2008; Price, 2007).

Over the past decade, there has been much interest in the notion of 'best practice' HRM sometimes referred to as 'high performance work systems' (Appelbaum et al., 2000; Appelbaum et al., 2000; Keenoy, 1990), 'high commitment' (Boxall et al., 2009; Guest, 2001) or 'high involvement' (Belt and Giles, 2009; Wood, 2008). Research on HRM focuses on a particular set of high commitment HRM practices that are suggested to be able to improve employee and organisational performance and the bottom line for all organisations (Huselid, 1995; Legge, 2005; Marchington and Wilkinson, 2005; Purcell, 2006; Wood, 2008). There is no agreed assumption as to which HRM practices actually constitute 'best practice' and the debate is ongoing with researchers using ranges between 7 and 28 practices (Gould-Williams, 2003, 2004; Huselid, 1995; Wood, 2008). HRM practices associated with high worker satisfaction include trust, team working, involvement/participation, employee voice, fair rewards, job security, job design, equal opportunities, family-friendly and anti-harassment practices (Gould-Williams and Davies, 2005; Guest, 2002; White et al., 2003).

By contrast, Grant and Shields (2002) argue that HRM is disdained as a blunt instrument to bully workers' and is associated with increased job intensity, reduced security and high levels of worker anxiety (Grant and Shields, 2002; Guest, 2002; Monks, 1998). In an effort to demonstrate value in organisations, human resource professionals (HRPs) should adopt seemingly contrasting roles of both the strategic partner and employee champion (CIPD, 2005; Storey, 2007; Ulrich, 1997). There are many debates around such conceptualisations and typologies and the particular challenge of HRM positioning itself as a business part-ner (Storey, 1992; Ulrich, 1997). Likewise, there are conflicting debates about HRM role of an employee advocate which places HRPs in an impossible situation of attempting to simultaneously champion employ-ees while being part of the management team (Harrington and Rayner, 2010). Such a conflict has resulted in the criticism of the philosophy and components of HRM for creating an environment in which bullying can remain unchallenged, be allowed to thrive, or actually be encouraged in an indirect way, thus becoming a source of bullying itself (Lewis and Rayner, 2003). Proponents of the critical stream claim that HRM views the worker purely as a resource or commodity to be exploited for the benefit of the organisation (Keenoy, 1990; Legge, 2005; Willmott, 1993). HRM is also viewed as another management initiative to secure greater control and reinforcement of management prerogatives, raising the spec-tre of inhuman resource management (Grant and Shields, 2002; Town-ley, 1994). Yet other researchers claim that HRM looms as a 'wolf in sheep's clothing', that in practice HRM has not worked, performance has not been significantly enhanced, and workers and management remain locked into their conflicting positions (Keenoy, 1990; Legge, 2005).

The third stream of HRM literature is employee-focused literature which is one of the central focuses of the research presented in this book. Proponents of this stream of literature argue that there is neglect of work-ers' reactions to HRM and attempts to re-centre the employee as the primary subject of HRM (Gibb, 2001; Grant and Shields, 2002; Guest, 1997, 2002; Guest and Peccei, 1994; Legge, 2005; Wilkinson et al., 2004). The reactions of employees' to HRM practices have attracted little schol-arly attention and even less research have been conducted into the effects of those practices on employee well-being (Baptiste, 2008, 2009; Deery, 2002; Gibb, 2001; Grant and Shields, 2002; Guest, 2002). Researchers further argue that studies linking HRM and performance never go beyond considering workers' as subjects of HRM, instead employees are left disenfranchised – their verdict on HRM being seriously ignored (Gallie et al., 2001; Guest, 1997, 2002). Yet other researchers' point out that the growing body of employee-focused literature fails to provide an adequate basis for understanding the association between HRM and the employee. It also ignores inputs from employees and believes that the dearth of research into employee reactions leaves us unable to evaluate HRM (Clark et al., 1998; Gibb, 2001). Furthermore, there is a lack of clarity as to whether or not employees are as enthusiastic about the model as their employers, since their views are not accorded the same space (Gibb, 2001; Grant and Shields, 2002). However, Grant and Shields (2002) and Gibb (2001) also point out that attempts to assess employee reactions are affected by conceptual and methodological limitations. Where large-scale surveys of HRM do exist they generally fail to appraise employees' reactions to HRM, and employee presence is mostly incidental rather than fundamental, leaving us unable to evaluate HRM. This led to a strong call for the 'employee voice' to be heard in HRM research (Guest, 2002).

Research findings reveal a mixed but overall positive picture of the state of HRM highlighting positive results, suggesting employees 'like' for HRM which contradicts the views that HRM is 'talked up' by management and is ineffectual (Guest, 1997). Guest also suggests that the greater number of HR practices used are more likely to enhance a more positive psychological contract, greater satisfaction, fairness of treatment, trust in management and lower levels of work pressure (Guest and Conway, 2002; Guest, 1990). Gibb's study found that employees report areas of strengths and weaknesses of HRM and highlighted strengths to include the provision of training and development, rewards and levels of personal motivation (Baptiste, 2009; Gibb, 2001). By contrast, weaknesses of HRM in employees' estimation existed in the management of staffing levels, aspects of recruitment and retention, levels of morale, and a reduction in the worker's voice (Gibb, 2001). It also included a more responsive management, insufficient line management commitment (Baptiste, 2008, 2009; Browning and Edgar, 2004), unfairness, inconsistency in the application of HRM policies (Bryson et al., 2006), and poor communication (Baird, 2002). According to O'Donnell and Shields (2002) HRM practices are likely to meet with negative employee reactions where they are incompatible with employees' prior experience and expectations, and where they conflict with the underlying, as opposed to espoused, organisational values. Therefore, O'Donnell and Shields (2002) suggest that, however configured, 'best-practice' HRM is likely to fall short of its own criteria for success, unless it is attuned to existing employees' perceptions of the employment relationship.

Employment relations and high commitment HRM practices in British workplaces

The UK government has commissioned Workplace Employment Relations Surveys (WERS) since 1980 to explore and understand the operation of workplaces in a time of substantial economic and social uncertainty. The WERS series have mapped employment relations extensively over three decades and provides insight into the state of the employment relations and working life inside British workplaces (van Wanrooy et al., 2011). WERS's research also provide understanding of complex and diverse employment relationships by taking a step inside the workplace and collecting a wide range of information from managers, employees and their representatives. Kersley et al. (2006) survey is the sixth in the series of study conducted by the Department for Business, Innovation and Skills (BIS), The Economic and Social Research Council (ESRC), the Advisory, Conciliation and Arbitration Service (Acas), The UK Commission for Employment and Skills (UKCES) and the National Institute of Economic and Social Research (NIESR), and is considered one of the most authoritative sources of information on employment relations in Great Britain (van Wanrooy et al., 2011).

British workplaces have had to respond to the economic downturn, and recent recession that impacted structures and practices of employment relations and the experiences, health and well-being of workers, particularly workers in the public sector that also have to function within a NPM environment. Van Wanrooy et al. (2011) assert that job security, rewards and satisfaction are all central to understanding how employees relate to their work, and the importance of these has been heightened in the current economic climate. These challenges are likely to result in breakdown and conflict in the employment relationship resulting in poor relationships between management and employees as well as collective disputes. Van Wanrooy et al. (2011) state that employees' experiences at work are not only shaped by the type of work they do, but also how they are managed. If employees are not committed to their workplace, and are dissatisfied with their pay, these will affect their approach to their work (Guest, 2002; van Wanrooy et al., 2011). HRM literature suggests that employees will have a positive result with the use of high-commitment HRM practices that are geared towards increasing satisfaction, commitment and performance.

The 'bundles' of high commitment HRM practices adopted in this research and throughout the book were drawn from Pfeffer (2005) and are now widely recognised and universally accepted, and have been modified by Marchington and Wilkinson (2005) for the UK context (Kinnie et al., 2005; Wood and de Menezes, 1998). These include (1) employment security and internal labour markets, (2) selective hiring and sophisticated selection, (3) extensive training, learning and development, (4) employee involvement, information sharing and worker voice, (5) self-managed teams/team working, (6) high compensation contingent on performance, and (7) reduction of status differentials/harmonisation. These practices are discussed in greater depth here:

1   *Employment Security and Internal Labour Markets* – Employment security is a key theme that affects an individual's well-being and underpins the other six HR practices as it is unrealistic to ask for employees' loyalty, intellectual competences and commitment without reciprocating an expectation of employment security and future careers (Guest and Conway, 2002; Pfeffer, 2005). The changing nature of the workplace hinders employers' ability to offer job security but instead employers offer the possibility of internal transfers, flexibility in employment, challenging jobs, a competitive package and a promise of opportunities to learn valuable skills (Marchington and Grugulis, 2000). Workplace Employment Relations Survey (WERS)'s 2004 survey reveals that internal recruitment offers advantages of cost savings, guaranteeing tacit knowledge from recruits who have an understanding of the internal workings of the workplace (Kersley et al., 2006). This approach facilitates flexibility and enables organisations to promote employment security as it allows organisations to react quickly and cheaply to environmental changes (Atkinson, 1984; Redman and Wilkinson, 2009). In contrast, the 2011 WERSs report reveal that employees that had experienced changes as a result of the recession were less likely to agree that their job was secure as the more changes they had experience, the less likely they were to feel secure in their job (van Wanrooy et al., 2011). However, Legge (2005) points out that while in some circumstances employees will have flexibility, the interest of employee and employer will not always coincide. Legge further declares that flexibility cannot unequivocally be seen as a good thing and can have negative implications for increasing work-related stress and pressure, workloads, extending working hours, and blurring the distinction between work and home which can all affect employees' health and well-being at work (Baptiste, 2008, 2009).

2   *Selective hiring and sophisticated selection* – Recruitment is the most critical human resource function for organisational survival or success (Saks, 2005). It is one of the most common job responsibilities of employment relations managers demonstrating key decisions for efficiency and the quality of diversity of applicants from their recruitment strategies (Redman and Wilkinson, 2009). WERS's 2004 survey confirms that diverse recruitment channels are used by managers in British workplaces in recruitment of new employees (Kersley et al., 2006). WERS's 2011 survey highlighted that employers used a diverse range of recruitment options (e.g. shift-working, annual

hours' contracts, zero hours' contracts, fixed-term and temporary contracts, use of agency workers, temporary staff, and contracting in and out) to staff the workplace in response to the recession (van Wanrooy et al., 2011). From a broader perspective, a competitive strategy used by organisations is 'employer branding' to attract a high quality pool of job applicants (McCormack and Scholarios, 2009; Saks, 2005). Moreover, systematic selection is now regarded as a critical function of HRM and is an essential part of an organisation's strategic capability for adapting to competition (Marchington and Wilkinson, 2005). This facilitates the achievement of key organisational outcomes (Storey, 2007), and can bring about increased commitment and motivation from employees that may result in positive work attitudes and behaviour that may lead to higher performance (Marchington and Wilkinson, 2005). In essence, this also has implications for employee well-being at work.

3   *Extensive training, learning and development* – Training and development is used in organisations to increase competitiveness through raising skill levels, greater effectiveness, insulate organisations from skills shortages, safeguard productivity and 'value-added' (Price, 2007; Redman and Wilkinson, 2009). It is also an essential practice that can promote employee well-being at work (Baptiste, 2009). At the level of the individual, training can increase knowledge and opportunities, prepare employees for future jobs, give access to more highly rewarded work and career progression (Redman and Wilkinson, 2009). From an organisational perspective, training and development is likely to bring about increased commitment and motivation amongst employees that can ultimately enhance employee well-being at work (Kersley et al., 2006). From a national perspective, Lord Leitch's (2006) report suggests that skills development and training unlocks potential talent that can lead to high productivity, creation of wealth and social justice in Britain. Extending this view, WERS's 2004 survey reveals that more than four-fifths of workplaces provided training that included Investors in People (IiP) accreditation (Kersley et al., 2006). From a regional perspective, WERS's 2004 survey indicates that three-fifths of employees in the North West (NW) of England received training and just over half of the region's employees were satisfied with training received with one-fifth expressing dissatisfaction (Forth and Stokes, 2006).

4   *Employee involvement, information sharing and worker voice* – Employee involvement/participation (EIP) is an essential component of the high commitment paradigm (Marchington and Wilkinson, 2005; Wood, 2008). EIP is a process by which individual employees are given greater freedom to make decisions autonomously (Cox et al., 2006), and includes inter-relations between supervisors and subordinates towards an end result (Strauss, 2006). According to Handel and

Levine (2004) EIP can improve organisational outcomes and should be embedded and integrated within organisational practice which has implications for organisational citizenship behaviour, free speech and dignity (Bolton and Houlihan, 2007). Moreover, Marchington and Wilkinson (2005) differentiate EIP into direct communication, upward problem solving or representative participation. Communication is a key theme in EIP that can affect an individual's well-being as it ensures that employees are informed about organisational issues as well as guaranteeing successful team working, where employee suggestions can contribute to organisational performance (Pilbeam and Corbridge, 2006). Critiquing this view, Dundon and Wilkinson (2009) suggest that information communicated may be political, power-centred and that messages may be used to reinforce managerial prerogatives. Other critics advocate upward problem solving as being inherently unitarist in nature and that feedback given to workers in an attitude survey is based on a managerial agenda, as information asked for tends to be set by employers (Bolton and Houlihan, 2007). The WERS's 2011 survey reveals that managers are using a variety of methods that can enhance levels of employee engagement through communication, involving staff in workplace meetings, the use of team briefings, the use of problem solving groups, and provision of information. Moreover, the survey also found that a majority of employees feel that manage are good at seeking their views, fewer employees feel that they influence decision-making, most employees suggested that they would like to have influence over final decisions (van Wanrooy et al., 2011). As a consequence, less than half of the employee are satisfied with their level of involvement in workplace decisions (van Wanrooy, 2011).

Moreover, emails have also been shown to have a negative effect on workplace stress and employee well-being (Taylor et al., 2008). WERS's 2004 survey highlights that EIP was similar throughout the UK with a greater disposition of EIP in the NW of England than elsewhere (Kersley et al., 2006). From a practice perspective, NW managers agreed that employees were involved and consulted in decision making but employees' view tended to be more negative as a little more than one-third disagreed and considered managers' poor in this area (Mathieson and Lucas, 2007). Twenty-seven per cent of employees rated managers' poor in responding to suggestions from employees (Forth and Stokes, 2006).

Employee voice is also viewed as an essential component of the high commitment paradigm (Huselid, 1995; Dundon and Wilkinson, 2009; Pfeffer, 2005). According to Kersley et al., (2006) employees experience greater satisfaction when they are invited by management to voice their opinions in decision making events that can bring about increased commitment, motivation and can lead to higher performance (Gould-Williams, 2004; Guest and Conway, 2002; Mowbray, 2009). Tapping into employees' ideas and drawing on their tacit knowledge may be embraced as a solution to the problems of managing in an increasingly competitive marketplace (Marchington and Wilkinson, 2005). WERS's 2004 survey reveals that in the NW employee voice was demonstrated through direct consultation with staff through unions (as nationally) (Kersley et al., 2006). WERS also indicate that in the NW employee voice was demonstrated predominantly through consultative committee and various communication strategies (Forth and Stokes, 2006).

5 *Self-managed teams/team working* – Self-managed teams are seen as an integral part of high performance work systems and provide workers with greater autonomy, influence and responsibility over task completion and inter-dependent skills (Appelbaum et al., 2000). Echoing this view, Barker (1999) claims that self-managed teams are viewed as an evolutionary development in the management of work from a traditional bureaucratic structure to a more decentralised, participative and democratic form of controlling work activity. According to Pfeffer, 2005) organisations benefit from self-managed teams by eliminating supervision that is not needed, from greater employee motivation, productivity and commitment and from enhancing the capacity to promote a varied and satisfying work experience. WERS's 2004 survey reveals that four fifths of all workplaces had core employees working in formally designed teams and the majority of workplaces encouraged collaborative working amongst core employees in the absence of formal teams (Kersley et al., 2006).

Team working is integral to achieving more creative solutions and better organisational performance through people (Pfeffer, 2005). Tapping into the power of teams' organisations can experience excellent results and better decision making (Marchington and Wilkinson, 2005). It also facilitates a way of pooling ideas (Pilbeam and Corbridge, 2006), improvement in work processes and report higher levels of employee satisfaction (Barker, 1999). Organisations function better when employees are encouraged to work together rather than on their own as team working has a positive effect on performance and social interaction (Gould-Williams, 2004). However, a more subversive side of team working is that it can be introduced in the context of cost cutting and can result in forms of peer surveillance and control, work intensification, and limited autonomy (Barker, 1999). WERS's 2004 survey reveals that team working was present among core employees in almost three quarters of all workplaces with the incident of team working varying substantially according to work being done by employees (Kersley et al., 2006). From a NW perspective, it was reported that team working skills were higher than the national average (Forth and Stokes, 2006). In essence, both self-managed teams and team working have implications for employee well-being at work.

6   *High compensation contingent on performance* – It is important that organisations remunerate employees adequately. This is associated with procedural justice (Folger and Cropanzano, 1998) that may affect their psychological contract (Coyle-Shapiro, 2001; George, 2009) and material well-being (Currie, 2001). Supporting this view, Gould-Williams (2003) suggests that workers should be adequately rewarded for their effort and points out that when employees perceive that the management team, shareholders or other parties are benefiting from their diligent efforts they become discouraged. This negative perception may be perceived as a psychological contract breach (Rousseau, 2001), and unfair treatment (Folger and Cropanzano, 1998), affecting the quality of workplace relationships, productivity and well-being at work (Baptiste, 2008, 2009). According to Pfeffer (2005) higher than average compensation and performance-related rewards both send a signal to employees that they deserve to be rewarded for superior contributions. However, Marchington and Wilkinson (2005) highlight that in order for high compensation to be effective it needs to be at a level in excess of that for comparable workers in other organisations so as to attract and retain high-quality labour. WERS's 2004 survey reveals that rewards were used in organisations to extract greater effort from employees and to increase employees' motivation and commitment to the goals of the organisation (Kersley et al., 2006). WERS's 2011 study found that during the recession, 48% of public sector employees reported increased workloads and less pay, wage cuts or freezes, access to training restricted, contracted working hours reduced, and job insecurity compared with 27% in the private sector (van Wanrooy et al., 2011). These changes, especially pay is likely to be one of the key factors affecting how employees feel about their jobs and well-being. From a North West (NW) perspective, employees were least satisfied with the amount of pay they received with only one-third expressing satisfaction and 43% expressing dissatisfaction (Forth and Stokes, 2006; Kersley et al., 2006; Mathieson and Lucas, 2007).

7   *Reduction of status differentials/harmonisation* – The reduction of status differentials encourages employees to offer ideas within an 'open' management culture towards promoting a single status and harmonisation (Pilbeam and Corbridge, 2006). This aims to break down artificial barriers among different groups of staff, thus encouraging team working and flexibility (Redman and Wilkinson, 2009). Marchington and Wilkinson (2005) advocate that symbolic manifestation of egalitarianism promotes a message to manual workers and lower grade staff that they are valuable assets who deserve to be treated in a similar way to their more senior colleagues (Gould-Williams,

2004). In essence, this practice may have implications for interactional justice (Bies, 1987), social justice equity (Harrow, 2002), the psychological contract (George, 2009; Guest and Conway, 2002; Rousseau, 2001), and employee well-being at work (Baptiste, 2008). From a NW perspective, WERS's 2004 survey highlights that two-thirds of workplaces in the region and nationally had a formal written equal opportunity policy (Kersley et al., 2006; Mathieson and Lucas, 2007). The WERS's 2011 survey state that Britain's workforce is increasingly diverse and legislation has sought to help achieve equal opportunity at work. While workplace policies have changed to reflect this situation, practice on the ground has changed little since 2004 (van Wanrooy et al., 2011).

The preceding review discusses the varied streams of HRM literature and the high commitment HRM practices as outlined by Pfeffer and Marchington and Wilkinson as well as the WERS 2004 and 2011 surveys. Relevant gaps identified include: the under-researched area in the employee-focused HRM literature as it relates to employees' perspectives and reactions to HRM practices and well-being at work; and the methodological weakness of HRM literature that is fundamentally underpinned in a realist tradition. This research proposes to contribute towards the debate in the employee-focus HRM literature by emphasising the worker's voice in the evaluation of HRM and well-being at work. Likewise, this book advocates an alternative methodological conceptualisation to investigate the worker's voice and reactions to HRM, quality of working life and well-being at work, through the use of a mixed method approach as opposed to the traditional quantitative approach used by other researchers. The next section reviews literature on social exchange theories as it relate to understanding employees' perspectives and reactions to the employment relationship.

Social exchange and the employment relationship

Social exchange behaviour originated from Gouldner (1960), and Blau (1964) as a dominant theoretical framework that is used in literature to interpret behaviour and to examine the employment relationship as exemplified by research on the psychological contract (George, 2009; Guest and Conway, 2002; Rousseau, 2001), perceived organisational support (Coyle-Shapiro and Conway, 2005), leader member exchange (Graen et al., 1982), and organisational justice and its consequences on employee attitudes and behaviours.

Social exchange theories are used in this research study as a lens to explain employees' perspectives and reactions to HRM practices, their quality of working life and well-being at work in the public sector. The employment relationship when viewed from a social exchange perspective can be categorised as consisting of social and/or economic exchanges (Aryee et al., 2002). The situation and conditions that are likely to lead to adverse employee responses, such as workplace stressors, mental ill-health and negative well-being, are those that are likely to evoke strong feelings of inequality and unfairness (Cropanzano and Folger, 1991). By contrast, positive employee attitudes depend on employees' perceptions of how much the employing organisation cares about their well-being and values their contribution (Wayne et al., 1997). Proponents of social exchange suggest that organisations treatment of its employees is with the expectation that such treatment will be reciprocated in kind (Blau, 1964; Gouldner, 1960). Trust is regarded as a critical factor underpinning social exchanges in an act of initiating social exchange relationships (Cropanzano and Folger, 1991). Central to this view, WERS's 2004 survey reveals that British employees are becoming less trusting of their managers and employers (Kersley et al., 2006).

The psychological contract

The use of the term 'the psychological contract' (PC) first emerged in the 1960s by Argyris (1960) and Schein (1965) that used it to explain the relationship between workers and their organisations. Schein (1965) argues that a key to satisfaction and performance at work was a shared understanding between the worker and employer of what each expected from the other. The more contemporary view of the PC draws from the work of Rousseau (2001) that offered suggestions on how the PC can be defined and argues that the PC was best viewed only from the perspective of employees on the grounds that an organisation cannot 'perceive', should not be anthropomorphised and therefore cannot have a PC. However, critics argue that the PC should not only be viewed from the employee but should also involve the employer as it fails to recognise the role of managers as 'agents' of the organisation as well as evidence that workers readily anthropomorphise their organisations (Guest, 2002). Rousseau claims that promises are based on behaviour rather than expectations that can arise from a variety of sources. Rousseau (2001:9) defines the PC as 'individual beliefs, shaped by the organisation, regarding terms of an exchange agreement between the individual and their organisation'. Echoing this view, George (2009) suggest that the PC is promissory, implicit, reciprocal, perceptual and based on expectations. Schein (1965) views the PC as unwritten, a powerful determiner of behaviour in organisations influencing organisational goals, power relationships, motivation, employee commitment, loyalty and enthusiasm for the organisation.

From an HRM perspective, Guest (1997) conceptualises the PC by turning the focus on the state of the PC consisting of three components – trust, fairness and delivery of the deal (Guest, 2002; Guest and Conway,

2002). Guest also suggests that several HRM policies and practices might affect the PC, and through these, work-related health and well-being (Guest, 2002). For the purpose of the research discussed in this book, the high-commitment HRM practices that are discussed are likely to promote fulfilment and more particularly prevent violation of the PC (Coyle-Shapiro and Kessler, 2000). The presence of such HRM practices create some obligation on the part of the employer to keep their side of the exchange (Guest and Conway, 2002). Guest further highlights that a friendly work climate with strong organisational support, the scope for direct EIP in the work itself, and communication are consistently associated with a more fulfilled and less violated PC (Guest and Conway, 2002). Therefore, work climate can be created at senior levels but it is the local organisational 'agents' and the way they act to implement HRM practices that are important. The making and delivery of promises have the major bearing on a positive PC and, through this, on employee well-being (Baptiste, 2009; Guest, 1990). Central to this view, Baptiste (2008) states that employees usually perceive the organisation based on the relationship they have with their line managers.

The PC is likely to be useful in considering well-being at work as it represents a potentially important mediator between managerial policy and practice and employee outcomes (Guest, 1997, 2002). The PC addresses the subjective perceptions of employees. It recognises that it is not enough to link policy and practice to outcomes but that it is necessary to explore how they are perceived by employees as a first step in understanding their impact (Coyle-Shapiro and Kessler, 2000). Central to this view, Guest and Conway (2002) argue that what is critical is how management behaviour stands up against the promises made, the obligations these entail and the expectation of what constitutes appropriate behaviour. Robinson and Morrison (1995) suggest that diverse groups of workers within an organisation may view the PC differently and can have varied emphasis on fulfilment of the PC. Rousseau (2001) advocate that the PC is a dynamic construct which is likely to change during the employee's organisational life and throughout the employer-employee relationship (Coyle-Shapiro and Kessler, 2000). George's (2009) review of the PC of professional workers suggests that the profession forms an important part of this dynamic relationship of mutual obligation and exchange relationship. George further points out that the PC may be more complex for professional workers as there may be a choice as to whether this relationship should be with the organisation or the profession as 'perceived promises' may come from a variety of sources. To prevent violation, Coyle-Shapiro (2001) and George (2009) point out that the PC of professional and managerial workers requires career progression, compensation, management of change, and responsibility to name a few (Baptiste, 2009).

The realities of managerial work show the challenges that managers can face. Managers have certain distinct functions as compared to owners of the organisations or its employees. In the contemporary business environment, managers increasingly need to focus on cost management and competitive strategies (Baptiste, 2009). Clark and Salaman (1998) observe that the key characteristics of management work emerging from studies over the last 40 years include brevity, spontaneity, fragmentation and discontinuity, adaptation to circumstances, unreflectivity, a focus on immediacy, doing, and on tangible, concrete activities. Moreover, senior managers' daily realities are inundated with social and moral problems in corporate life (Jackall, 1988), often further challenging espoused rationality, efficiency, the PC and well-being at work.

The PC construct is usually described as being either transactional, which focuses on the concrete content of the employment contract and relational, which emphasises the degree of social exchange and interdependence between workers and their employers (Rousseau, 2001; Robinson and Morrison, 1995). Blancero et al. (1996) state that contract violation can have implications for changes in the nature of the PC from relational to transactional. In support, George (2009) argues that professional workers may have transactional contracts as many take a series of short-term jobs as a stepping stone to further their career aspirations and tend to have low levels of affective commitment (Meyer and Allen, 1997).

Workers physical and psychological health are major problems facing contemporary organisations that are likely to have implications for the PC violation. Rousseau (2001) argues that the PC breach or violation is a subjective experience based on a person's perception that another has failed to fulfil adequately the promised obligations of the PC (Robinson and Rousseau, 2001; Coyle-Shapiro and Kessler, 2000; Guest and Conway, 2002). George (2009) point out that contract violation influences behaviour and becomes salient when broken or violated. This view is substantiated by Robinson and Morrison (1995) who characterise contract violation as inherently perceptual as experienced by the employee, is cognitive and reflects a mental calculation of what one has received relative to what one was promised. Coyle-Shapiro and Kessler (2000) advocate that contract breach has implications for emotional and effective state accompanied by feelings of bitterness, indignation, perception of betrayal, psychological distress, a careerist orientation to work, employee voicing displeasure to management, a sense of injustice, reduction in trust and increased cynicism and mistreating (George, 2009; Rousseau, 2001). Most commonly cited causes of PC breach and violation include organisational downsizing and restructuring (Robinson and Morrison, 1995), loss of job and redundancy (Rousseau, 2001), and organisational change.

According to Coyle-Shapiro and Kessler (2000) employees redress the balance in the relationship through reducing their commitment and their willingness to engage in organisational citizenship behaviour when they perceive their employer as not having fulfilled its part in the exchange process. Blancero et al. (1996) indicate that the interconnection of social exchange and psychological contract processes suggest that PC breach mediates the effects of POS and LMX and intention to quit and that violation fully mediates the effects of breach on commitment and trust and partially mediates the effect of breach on turnover intentions.

Social exchange constructs underpinning the psychological contract

Social Exchange constructs that are widely used in literature to underpin the PC include perceived organisational support (POS), leader-member exchange (LMX) and organisational justice (OJ) which are mutually dependent elements. Organisation support theory supposes that to determine the organisation's readiness to reward increased work effort and to meet socio-emotional need, employees develop global beliefs concerning the extent to which the organisation values their contribution and cares about their well-being (Eisenberger et al., 1990). POS is valued as assurance that aid will be available from the organisation when it is needed to carry out one's job effectively and to deal with stressful situations (Dulac et al., 2008). Echoing this view, Coyle-Shapiro and Kessler (2000) advocate that POS has important consequences for employee performance and well-being and involve favourable treatment from the organisation in terms of fairness, supervisory support, recognition, rewards, distributive justice, autonomy and job conditions (Eisenberger et al., 1990; Wayne et al., 1997).

However, Eisenberger et al. (1990) point out that individuals feel less valued in large organisations where highly formalised policies and procedures may reduce flexibility in dealing with employees' individual needs. Thus, Wayne et al., (1997) argue that employers value employees dedication and loyalty, whereas employees who are emotionally committed to the organisation show heightened performance, job involvement, reduction in psychological and psychosomatic strains, citizenship behaviour, reduced absenteeism, and a lessened likelihood of quitting their job (Eisenberger et al., 1990; Meyer and Allen, 1997; Wayne et al., 1997).

Another relevant theory that underpins the PC is Leader-Member Exchange (LMX). This is derived from social exchange theory and developed by Graen and colleagues and is based on the notion that leaders develop unique types of relationships with individual subordinates (Eisenberger et al., 1990; Graen et al., 1982; Linden and Maslyn, 1998). Employees and leader attitudes and behaviours are influenced by the quality of these relationships (Linden and Maslyn, 1998). These relationships range from low-quality, in which the relationship is based strictly on the transactional PC to high-quality based on the relational PC which involves mutual liking, trust, commitment, respect and influence (Graen et al., 1982; Wayne et al., 1997). Linden and Maslyn (1998) argue that the reciprocal relationship in high-quality LMX fosters employee attitudes and behaviours and are beneficial to managers and organisations. Proponents of LMX view this relationship as a 'vertical dyad linkage' where leaders can distribute rewards based on their position in the organisation and exchange results in both economic and social outcomes and rewards (Cooper et al., 2001).

LMX theory proposes that leaders employ a different style of leadership depending on the relationship they have with their subordinates (Pinnington and Edwards, 2000). Martin et al. (2005) advocate that people with an internal locus of control develop better quality relations with their manager and this in turn results in more favourable work-related reactions (Peters and Waterman, 1982). Research by Offerman and Hellman (1996) highlight that leader behaviours did relate to stress experienced by staff and leaders' view of what relates to subordinate stress did not always coincide with the factors that subordinates themselves associated with stress. The relationship of leader delegation and subordinate participation to lower subordinate reports of stress were particularly underestimated by leaders (Bernerth et al., 2007). Echoing this view, Lepak and Snell (2005) suggest that supervisor behaviour can affect employee well-being and suggests that those seeking to create healthier workplaces should not neglect supervisor behaviour as potentially influential (Baptiste, 2009, 2008). Central to this view, Baptiste (2009) also states that line management leadership practices can promote well-being at work which in turn can enhance the effectiveness of service delivery and performance within local government organisations. In support, Detert and Burris (2007) argue that leadership behaviour has the strongest impact on the voice behaviour, engagement and well-being of the best-performing employees (Bhal and Ansari, 2007; Baptiste, 2008, 2009).

The CIPD, 2019 health and well-being research state that the role of leadership is integral in ensuring that employee well-being is taken seriously at an operational level and integrated into line manager training and guidance and should be on senior leaders agenda. Likewise, the CIPD research also reveals that one-third of senior leaders encourage a focus on mental well-being through their actions and behaviour, and an increased proportion of managers' attribute management style as a cause of stress (43% this year compared with 32% in 2018) (CIPD, 2019). Moreover, leaders and managers are important role models in fostering healthy behaviour at work, and the CIPD, 2019 findings underline how harmful the impact can be if managers are not equipped with the competence and confidence to go about their people management role in the right way. According to Cropanzano and Folger (1991), there is strong empirical evidence supporting the relationship between POS and LMX, job enrichment, job satisfaction, employee engagement, commitment, work-related well-being, organisational citizenship behaviour (OCB) and employee experience (Eid and Larson, 2008; Graen et al., 1982).

Another relevant theory that underpins the PC is organisational justice (OJ) theory which is a construct defining the quality of social interaction at work. It focuses on perceptions of fairness in organisations that can affect individuals' psychological, physical and social well-being (Cropanzano, 1993). The term OJ seeks to categorise and to explain the views and feelings of organisational participants about their own treatment and that of others (Folger and Cropanzano, 1998; DOH, 2004). OJ is known to play an important role in the health and well-being of employees and how perceived justice relates to factors that influence susceptibility to illness and negative feelings, increasing risk of mental distress, sickness absence and self-rated health status (Beardwell and Claydon, 2007; Cropanzano, 1993). Employees' experiences of OJ are important to their perception of fairness. Brewester et al. (2004) and Cooper et al. (2001) propose that fairness matters to people because it helps them to deal with uncertainty, and suggest that people especially need fairness judgements when they are concerned about potential problems associated with social interdependence and concerns with whether or not one can trust others (Black, 2008; Atkinson, 2007: Cooper et al., 2001).

The CIPD, 2019 health and well-being research reveal that a supportive, and inclusive culture and committed leadership, will make a real impact towards employees' perceptions of fairness and well-being. In support of this view, Meechan (2018) avers that organisations need leaders who are not afraid to show compassion and lead by example. Senior and line managers that demonstrate compassionate leadership means that they will have empathy for someone else's circumstances, alive to the suffering of others, non-judgemental, tolerant of personal distress and approachable but going further by feeling compelled to take action and make a difference (Meechan, 2018). Worline and Dutton (2017) argue that compassion fuels competitive advantage through collaboration by building trust and respect, service delivery by motivating a philanthropic approach to emotions, and building customer loyalty. Compassion fuels innovation by motivating creative ideas, fuels employee and customer engagement, and adaptability by alleviating the pain caused by change processes and sparking passion that motivates resourceful change (Poorkavoos, 2016; Worline and Dutton, 2017). Barriers to compassion in the workplace include: HR Policy that is too restrictive and not being able to adapt to individual circumstances, cultural norms of what is, or is not acceptable in the workplace, pressure from senior management too focused on outputs, managers not feeling empowered to make decisions themselves that enable them to be compassionate, too busy to stop and show care, low emotional intelligence, managers who genuinely don't care about their teams and focus only on getting the job done whatever the costs (Poorkavoos, 2016).

Moreover, OJ is a multidimensional construct with three distinct but overlapping dimensions: distributive justice, procedural justice, and interactional justice (Bies, 1987). *Distributive justice* refers to fairness of outcomes, that is, pay, reward equity, outcomes of decisions taken in an organisation, and employees' response to these, forms the basis for distributive justice (Cooper et al., 2001; Cully et al., 1999). *Procedural justice* relates to the extent to which employees perceive they have opportunities to make their views heard – known as 'voice' (Folger and Cropanzano, 1998). Supporting this view, Moorman (1991) suggests that procedures seem most fair when they take into account the opinions and voices of all organisational stakeholders. It also relates to procedures that are applied consistently across people and over time, are free from bias such as vested interest, and reflect ethical standards of propriety (Baptiste, 2008; Beardwell and Claydon, 2007; Folger and Cropanzano, 1998). *Interactional justice theory* is a term introduced by Bies (1987) and underpins an 'interpersonal' subcomponent that pertains to treating employees with dignity and respect (Bolton and Houlihan, 2007) and relate to communication qualities such as adequate and honest explanations (Beis, 1987).

To this end, despite the field of social exchange and reciprocity being well-researched areas, Coyle-Shapiro and Conway (2005) note that there is a dearth of empirical studies, which have considered social exchange processes in the manager-employee relationship as it relates to: the use of a variety of research methods (i.e. mixed methods using qualitative and quantitative approaches) to better address the employer-employee relationship; and greater focus on employee implications on ways to improving employees' attitude and behaviour that relates to employee health and well-being, as most of the literature is managerialist in focus. Likewise, there is the need for research that seeks to improve the lives of individual employees through focusing on health and well-being enhancement, stress reduction and employee fulfilment. Even further, there is limited empirical research that reviews different employee groups' perceptions of fairness, leader-member-exchange, perceived support and well-being at work. Based on these gaps, this study seeks to contribute towards the debate in these areas.

References

Appelbaum, E., Bailey, T., Berg, P., and Kalleberg, A. (2000) *A Manufacturing Competitive Advantage: The Effects of High-Performance Work Systems on Plant Performance and Company Outcomes*, New York: Cornell University Press.

Argyris, C. (1960) *Understanding Organisational Behaviour*, Homewood, IL: Dorsey.

Arms Length Management (AMLO) (2006), *Stockport AMLO, Stockport*, Department of Communities and Local Government, York: National Federation of ALMOs.

Aryee, S., Budhwar, P.S., and Chen, Z.X. (2002) 'Trust as a Mediator of the Relationship Between Organisational Justice and Work Outcomes: Test of a Social Exchange Model', *Journal of Organisational Behaviour*, Vol. 23(3): 267–285.

Atkinson, C. (2007) 'Trust and the Psychological Contract', *Employee Relations*, Vol. 29(3): 227–246.

Atkinson, J. (1984) 'Manpower Strategies for Flexible Organisations', *Personnel Management*, August: 28–31.

Bach, S., and Kessler, I. (2009) 'HRM and the New Public Management', in P. Boxall, J. Purcell, and P. Wright (Eds.) *The Oxford Handbook of Human Resource Management*, pp. 469–488, Oxford: Oxford University Press.

Baird, M. (2002) 'Changes, Dangers, Choice and Voice: Understanding What High Commitment Means for Employees and Unions', *The Journal of Industrial Relations*, Vol. 44(3): 359–375.

Baptiste, N.R. (2008) 'Tightening the Link between Employee Well-Being at Work and Performance: A New Dimension for HRM', *Management Decisions*, Vol. 46(2): 284–309.

Baptiste, N.R. (2009) 'Fun and Well-Being: Insights from Senior Managers in a Local Authority', *Employee Relations*, Vol. 31(6): 600–612.

Barker, J.R. (1999) *The Discipline of Teamwork*, California: Sage Publications.

Beardwell, J., and Claydon, T. (2007) *Human Resources Management: A Contemporary Approach*, 5th Edition, Financial Times, Prentice Hall, London: Pearson Publishers.

Belt, V., and Giles, L. (2009) 'High Performance Working: A Synbook of Key Literature', UK Commission for Employment and Skills, Evidence Report 4, August.

Bernerth, J.B., Armenakis, A.A., Feild, H.S., and Walker, H.J. (2007), Justice, Cynicism, and Commitment: A Study of Important Organizational Change Variables, *Journal of Applied Behavioral Science*, Vol. 43(3): 303–326, September 2007.

Bhal, K.T., and Ansari, M.A., (2007), Leader-member exchange-subordinate outcomes relationship: role of voice and justice, *Leadership and Organization Development Journal*, Vol. 28(1): 20–35.

Bies, R.J. (1987) 'The Predicament and Injustice: The Management of Moral Outrage', in L.L. Cummings and B.M. Staw Greenwich (Eds.) *Research in Organisational Behaviour*, pp. 289–319, CT: JAI.

Black, D.C. (2008) *Working for a Healthier Tomorrow*, London: TSO.

Blancero, D., Johnson, S.A., and Lakshman, C. (1996) 'Psychological Contracts and Fairness: The Effect of Violations on Customer Service Behaviour', *Journal of Market-Focused Management*, Vol. 1: 49–63.

Blau, P.M. (1964) *Exchange and Power in Social Life*, New York: Wiley Publishers.

Bolton, S., and Houlihan, M. (2007) 'Beginning the Search for the H in HRM', in S. Bolton and M. Houlihan (Eds.) *Searching for the H in Human Resource Management: Theory, Practice and Workplace Context*, Basingstoke: Palgrave Macmillan.

Boxall, P., Purcell, J., and Wright, P.M. (Eds.) (2008) *The Oxford Handbook of Human Resources Management*, Oxford: Oxford University Press.

Brewster, C., Mayrhofer, W., and Morley, M. (2004) *Human Resource Management in Europe: Evidence of Convergence?*, London: Elsevier Butterworth Heinemann.

Browning, V. and Edgar, F. (2004) 'Reactions to HRM: An Employee Perspective from South Africa and New Zealand', *Journal of the Australian and New Zealand Academy of Management*, Vol. 10(1): 1–13.

Bryson, A., Charlwood, A., and Forth, J. (2006) 'Worker Voice, Managerial Response and Labour Productivity: An Empirical Investigation', *Industrial Relations Journal*, Vol. 37(5): 438–455.

Chartered Institute of Personnel Development (CIPD, 2005) *Annual Survey Report*, 2005: Training and Development, London, England: CIPD, 2005.

Chartered Institute of Personnel and Development (CIPD, 2019) *Health and Well-Being at Work*, Public Sector April 2019, In Partnership with Simplyhealth, Reference 7837, London: Chartered Institute of Personnel and Development.

Clark, T., Mabey, C., and Skinner, D. (1998) 'Experiencing HRM: The Important of the Inside Story', in C. Mabey, D. Skinner, and T. Clark, (Eds.) *Experiencing Human Resource Management*, pp 4–16, London: Sage Publishers.

Clark, J., and Salaman, G. (1998) 'Telling Tales: Management Gurus' Narratives and the Construction of Managerial Identity', *Journal of Management Studies*, Vol. 35(2): 137–161.

Cooper, C.L., Dewe, P.J., and O'Driscoll, M.P. (2001) *Organisational Stress: A Review and Critique of Theory, Research and Application*, Newbury Park, CA: Sage Publications.

Cox, A., Zagelmeyer, S., and Marchington, M. (2006) 'Embedding Employee Involvement and Participation at Work', *Human Resource Management Journal*, Vol. 16(3): 250–267.

Coyle-Shapiro, J.A.-M., and Conway, N. (2005) 'Exchange Relationships: An Examination of Psychological Contracts and Perceived Organisational Support', *Journal of Applied Psychology*, Vol. 90: 774–781.

Coyle-Shapiro, J.A., and Kessler, I. (2000) 'Consequences of the Psychological Contract for the Employment Relationship: A Large Scale Survey', *Journal of Management Studies*, Vol. 37(7): 903–930.

Coyle-Shapiro, J.A. (2001) 'Managers: Caught in the Middle of a Psychological Contract Muddle', Annual meeting of the Academy of Management, August, Washington, DC, Annual meeting of the Academy of Management.

Cropanzano, R. (Ed.) (1993) *Justice in the Workplace: Approaching Fairness in Human Resource Management*, New York: Lawrence Erlbaum.

Cropanzano, R., and Folger, R. (1991) 'Procedural Justice and Worker Motivation', in R.M. Steers, and L.W. Porter (Eds.) *Motivation and Worker Behaviour*, pp. 131–143, 5th edition, New York: McGraw Hill.

Cully, M., O'Reilly, A., Millward, J., Forth, S., Woodland, G., Dix, G., and Bryson, A. (1999) *British at Work: As Depicted by the 1998 Workplace Employee Relations Survey*, London: Routledge Publishers.

Currie, D. (2001) *Managing Employee Well-Being*, Oxford: Chandos Publishing and Oxford: Oxford Limited.

Deery, S. (2002) 'Employee Reactions to Human Resource Management: A Review and Assessment', *The Journal of Industrial Relations*, Vol. 44(3): 458–466.

Department of Health (2004) *Choosing Health: Making Healthier Choices Easier*, London: Public Health White Chapter, DH.

Detert, J.R., and Burris, E.R. (2007), Leadership Behavior and Employee Voice: Is the Door Really Open?, *Academy of Management Journal*, Vol. 50(4): 869–884.

Diener, E. (1996) 'Traits Can Be Powerful, But Are Not Enough: Lessons from Subjective Well-Being', *Journal of Research in Personality*, Vol. 30: 389–399.

Diener, E., Oishi, S., and Lucas, R.E. (2003) 'Personality, Culture, and Subjective Well-Being: Emotional and Cognitive Evaluations of Life', *Annual Review Psychology*, Vol. 54: 403–425.

Dulac, T., Coyle-Shapiro, J., and Henderson, D. (2008), 'Not All Responses to Breach Are the Same the Interconnection of Social Exchange and Psychological Contract Processes in Organisations', *Academy of Management Journal*, Vol. 51(6): 1079–1098.

Dundon, T., and Wilkinson, A. (2009) 'Employee Participation', in T. Redman and A. Wilkinson (Eds.) *Contemporary Human Resource Management: Text and Cases*, pp. 405–416, 3rd Edition, London: Pearson Education.

Eisenberger, R., Fasolo, P., and Davis-LaMastro, V. (1990) 'Perceived Organisational Support and Employee Diligence, Commitment, and Innovation', *Journal of Applied Psychology*, Vol. 75(1): 51–59.

Folger, R., and Cropanzano, R. (1998) *Organisational Justice and Human Resource Management*, London: Sage Publications.

Forth, J., and Stokes, L. (2006) 'A Regional Perspective on Employment Relations: Tabulations from the 2004 Workplace Employment Relations Survey', Report to the Advisory, Conciliation and Arbitration Services (ACAS), Final Report 8th September.

Gallie, D., Felstead, A., and Green, F., (2001) 'Employer Policies and Organisational Commitment in Britain 1992–1997', *Journal of Management Studies*, Vol. 38(8): 1081–1101.

George, C. (2009) *The Psychological Contract: Managing and Developing Professional Groups*, Work and Organisational Psychology, Berkshire: Open University Press.

Gibb, S. (2001) 'The State of Human Resource Management: Evidence from Employees' Views of HRM Systems and Staff', *Employee Relations*, Vol. 23(4): 318–336.

Gouldner, A.W. (1960) 'The Norm of Reciprocity: A Preliminary Statement', *American*.

Gould-Williams, J. (2003) 'The Importance of HR Practices and Workplace Trust in Achieving Superior Performance: A Study of Public-Sector Organisations', *International Journal of Human Resource Management*, Vol. 14(1): 28–54.

Gould-Williams, J. (2004) 'The Effects of High Commitment HRM Practices on Employee Attitude: The Views of Public Sector Workers', *Public Administration*, Vol. 82(1): 63–81.

Gould-Williams, J., and Davies, F. (2005) 'Using Social Exchange Theory to Predict the Effects of HRM Practice on Employee Outcomes: An Analysis of Public Sector Workers', *Public Management Review*, Vol. 7(1): 25–47.

Grant, D., and Shields, J. (2002) 'In Search of the Subject: Researching Employee Reactions to Human Resource Management', *Journal of Industrial Relations*, Vol. 44(3): 313–334.

Graen, G.B., Novak, M.A., and Sommerkamp, P. (1982) 'The Effects of Leader-Member Exchange and Job Design on Productivity and Satisfaction: Testing a Dual Attachment Model', *Organisational Behaviour and Human Performance*, Vol. 30: 109–131.

Guest, D. (1990) 'Human Resource Management and the American Dream', *Journal of Management Studies*, Vol. 27(4): 377–397.

Guest, D. (1997) 'Human Resource Management and Performance: A Review and Research Agenda', *International Journal of Human Resource Management*, Vol. 8(3): 263–276.

Guest, D.E. (1999) 'Human Resource Management – The workers' verdict', *Human Resource Management Journal*, Vol. 9(3): 5–25.

Guest, D. (2001) 'Human Resource Management: When Research Confronts Theory', *International Journal of Human Resource Management*, Vol. 12(7): 1092–1106.

Guest, D. (2002) 'Human Resource Management, Corporate Performance and Employee Well-Being: Building the Worker into HRM', *Journal of Industrial Relations*, Vol. 44(3): 335–358.

Guest, D.E., and Peccei, R. (1994) 'The Nature and Causes of Effective Human Resource Management', *British Journal of Industrial Relations*, Vol. 39(2): 207–236.

Guest, D., and Conway, N. (2002) *Pressure at Work and the Psychological Contract*, Research Report, London: CIPD.

Handel, M.J., and Levine, D.I. (2004) 'Editors' Introduction: The Effects of New Work Practices on Workers', *Industrial Relations*, Vol. 43: 1–43.

Harrington, S., and Rayner, C. (2010) 'Look Before You Leap or Drive Right In? The Use of Moral Courage in Response to Workplace Bullying,' in P.A. Linley, S. Harrington, and N. Garcea (Eds.) *Oxford Handbook of Positive Psychology and Work*, pp. 265–276, Oxford: Oxford University Press.

Harrow, J. (2002) 'New Public Management and Social Justice: Just Efficiency or Equity as Well?', in K. McLaughlin, S.P. Osborne, and E. Ferlie (Eds.) *New Public Management: Current Trends and Future Prospects*, pp. 141–159, London: Routledge, Taylor and Francis Group.

Health and Safety Executive (HSE) (2004) *Health and Safety Statistic Highlights, 2003/2004*, Merseyside, UK: Statistics Coordination Unit, Health and Safety Executive.

Health and Safety Executive (HSE) (2006) *Health and Safety Statistics Highlights, 2005/2006*, Merseyside, UK: Statistics Coordination Unit, Health and Safety Executive.

Huselid, M. (1995) 'The Impact of Human Resource Management Practices on Turnover, Productivity and Corporate Financial Performance', *Academy of Management Journal*, Vol. 38(3): 635–672.

Huselid, M., Jackson, S., and Schuler, R. (1997) 'Technical and Strategic Human Resource Management Effectiveness as Determinants of Firm Performance', *Academy of Management Journal*, Vol. 40(1): 171–188.

Jackall, R. (1988) *Moral Mazes: The World of Corporate Managers*, New York: Oxford University Press.

Keenoy, T. (1990) 'Human Resource Management: Rhetoric and Reality and Contradiction', *International Journal of Human Resource Management*, Vol. 1(3): 363–384.

Kersley, B., Alphin, C., Forth, J., Bryson, A., Bewley, H., Dix, G., and Oxenbridge, S. (2006) *Inside the Workplace: Findings from the 2004 Workplace Employment Relations Survey*, London: Routledge.

Kinnie, N., Hutchinson, S., and Purcell, J. (2005) 'Satisfaction with HR Practices and Commitment to the Organisation: Why One Size Does Not Fit All', *Human Resource Management Journal*, Vol. 15(4): 9–29.

Legge, K. (2005) *Human Resource Management: Rhetorics and Realities*, London: Palgrave Macmillan Publishers.

Leitch, S. (2006) 'Leitch Review of Skills: Prosperity for All in the Global Economy: World Class Skills', HM Treasury on behalf of HM Stationery Office, December.

Lepak, D.A., and Snell, S.A. (2005) 'The Human Resource Architecture: Towards a Theory of Human Capital Allocation', in S. Little and T. Ray (Eds.) *Managing Knowledge: An Essential Reader*, London: Sage Publishers.

Linden, R.C., and Maslyn, J.M. (1998), 'Multidimensionality of Leader-Member Exchange: An Empirical Assessment Through Scale Development', *Journal of Management*, Vol. 24: 43–72.

Marchington, M., and Wilkinson, A. (2005) *Human Resource Management at Work: People Management and Development*, London: CIPD.

Marchington, M., and Grugulis, I. (2000) 'Best-Practice' Human Resource Management: Perfect Opportunity or Dangerous Illusion?' *International Journal of Human Resource Management*, Vol. 11(6): 1104–1124.

Mathieson, H., and Lucas, R. (2007) *Employment Relations in North West England, Final report to the North West Region of the Advisory Conciliation and Arbitration Services (ACAS)*, Final Report 14th September 2007.

McCormack, A., and Scholarios, D. (2009) 'Recruitment', in T. Redman and A. Wilkinson (Eds.) *Contemporary Human Resource Management: Text and Cases*, Essex: Financial Times: Pearson Education Limited.

Meechan, F. (2018) *Compassion at Work Toolkit*, Alliance Manchester Business School, University of Manchester, www.researchgate.net/publication/322404 395_Compassion_at_Work_Toolkit

Meyer, J., and Allen, N. (1997) *Commitment in the Workplace*, London: Sage.

Miles, M.B., and Huberman, A.M. (1994) *Qualitative Data Analysis: An Expanded Source Book*, London: Sage Publications.

Monk, J. (1998) 'Trade Unions, Enterprise and the Future,' in P. Sparrow and M. Marchington (Eds.) *Human Resource Management: The New Agenda*, London: Pitman, pp. 171–9.

O'Donnell, M., and Shields, J. (2002) 'Performance Management and the Psychological Contract in the Australian Federal Public Sector', *Journal of Industrial Relations*, Vol. 44: 435–457.

Offerman, L.R. and Hellman, P.S. (1996) 'Leadership behavior and subordinate stress: A 360 degrees view', *Journal of Occupational Health Psychology*, Vol. 1: 382–390.

Peters, T., and Waterman, R. (1982) *In Search of Excellence*, New York: Harper and Row.

Pfeffer, J. (2005) 'Producing Sustainable Competitive Advantage through Effective Management of People', *Academy of Management Executive*, Vol. 19(4): 95–108.

Pilbeam, S., and Corbridge, M. (2006) *People Resourcing: Contemporary HRM in Practice*, Harlow: Prentice Hall, Financial Times, Pearson Education Limited.

Pinnington, A., and Edwards, T. (2000) *Introduction to Human Resource Management*, Oxford: Oxford University Press.

Poorkavoos, M. (2016) *Compassionate Leadership: What Is It and Why Do Organisations Need More of It?*, Roffey Park, Horsham, www.roffeypark.com/ research-insights/free-reports-downloads/compassionate-leadership/ (accessed 20th December, 2017).

Price, A. (2007) *Human Resource Management: In a Business Context*, New York: South-Western Cengage Learning.

Purcell, J. (2006) 'Best Practice and Best Fit: Chimera or Cul-de-sac?' *Human Resources Management Journal*, Vol. 9(3): 26–41.

Redman, T., and Wilkinson, A. (2009) *Contemporary Human Resource Management, Text and Cases*, London: Pearson Education.

Robinson, S. L., and Morrison, E.W. (1995) 'Psychological Contracts and OCB: The Effect of Unfulfilled Obligations and Civic Virtue Behaviour', *Journal of Organisational Behaviour*, Vol. 19: 289–298.

Rousseau, D.M. (2001) 'Schema, Promise and Mutuality: The Building Blocks of the Psychological Contract', *Journal of Occupational and Organisational Psychology*, Vol. 74: 511–541.

Saks, A.M. (2005) 'The Impracticality of Recruitment Research' in A. Evers, N. Anderson, and O. Voskuijl (Eds.) *Handbook of Personnel Selection*, Oxford: Blackwell, pp. 47–72.

Schein, E. (1965) *Organisational Psychology*, Englewood Cliffs, NJ: Prentice-Hall.

Storey, J. (1992) *Developments in the Management of Human Resources*, Oxford: Blackwell.

Storey, J. (2007) *Human Resource Management: A Critical Text*, 3rd Edition, London: Thomson Learning.

Strauss, G. (2006) 'Worker Participation: Some Under-Considered Issues', *Industrial Relations*, Vol. 45: 778–803.

Taylor, H., George, F., and Altman, Y. (2008) 'E-Mail at Work: A Cause for Concern? The Implications of New Communication Technologies for Health, Well-being and Productivity at Work', *Journal of Organisational Transformation and Social Change*, Vol. 5(2): 159–173.

Townley, B. (1994) *Reframing Human Resource Management*, London: Sage Publication.

Ulrich, D. (1997) *Human Resource Champions: The Next Agenda for Adding Value and Delivering Results*, Boston, MA: Harvard Business School Press.

Van Wanrooy, B., Bewley, H., Bryson, A., Forth, J., Freeth, S., Stokes, L., and Wood, S. (2011) 'The 2011 Workplace Employment Relations Study (WERS)', First Findings, commissioned by BIS, ESRC, ACAS, UKCES, and NIESR.

Wayne, S.J., Shore, I.M., and Liden, R.C., (1997) 'Perceived Organisation Support and Leader-Member Exchange: A Social Exchange Perspective', *Academy of Management Journal*, Vol. 40(1): 82–111.

White, M., Hill, S., McGovern, P., Mills, C., and Smeaton, D. (2003) 'High-Performance Management Practices, Working Hours and Work-Life Balance', *British Journal of Industrial Relations*, Vol. 41(2): 175–195.

Willmott, H. (1993) 'Strength is Ignorance; Slavery is Freedom: Managing Culture in Modern Organisations', *Journal of Management Studies*, Vol. 30(4): 515–552.

Wilkinson, A., Dundon, T., Marchington, M., and Ackers, P. (2004) 'Changing Patterns of Employee Voice: Case Studies from the UK and Republic of Ireland', *The Journal of Industrial Relations*, Vol. 46(3): 298–322.

Wood, S. (2008) 'Job Characteristics, Employee Voice and Well-Being in Britain', *Industrial Relations Journal*, Vol. 39(2): 153–168.

Wood, S., and de Menezes, L. (1998) 'High Commitment Management in the UK: Evidence from the Workplace Industrial Relations Survey and Employers WERS' Manpower and Skills Practices Survey', *Human Relations*, Vol. 51: 485–515.

Worline, M., and Dutton, J.E. (2017) *Awakening Compassion at Work: The Quiet Power That Elevates People and Organisations*, Oakland, CA: Berrett-Koehler Publishers.

4 Well-being at work
A review of the literature

Introduction

This chapter reviews the literature on employee well-being at work. The chapter discusses the historical development of HRM and Well-being research, and the multidimensional nature of workplace well-being that includes the individual, group dynamics in the employment relationship, and the organisational systems, polices, structures and climate. The chapter proposes a multidimensional well-being paradigm that is considered a relevant conceptualisation for employee well-being at work that can assist organisational leaders with effective people management and well-being strategies. The chapter concludes with a summary of the gap(s) in the literature.

The historical development of HRM and well-being research

The treatment of employees' stem from the history of HRM that can be traced back to the Industrial Revolution in England in the late eighteenth century (Redman and Wilkinson, 2009). Welfare paternalist employers such as Rowntree and Leverhulme concerned about the welfare of the workforce viewed health and education of employees as part of their responsibility (Pinnington and Edwards, 2000). In the early 1900s Frederick Taylor's scientific management was embraced, viewing teamwork and worker consultation as unnecessary and undesirable, with managers being responsible for task performance (Brewster et al., 2004). In contrast to scientific management, Elton Mayo introduced the 'Human Relations Movement' that focused on the 'human' side of management, viewing 'psychosocial factors' as important in understanding and influencing workplace performance (Ulrich, 1997). In the 1980s, Guest (2006) points out that the emergence of HRM in the USA was a stimulus of change, that came from a set of external pressures on industry resulting in increasing competition in national and international marketplace. This, combined with anxieties about slow productivity growth in American industries, was seen as a new approach in the 'search of excellence' (Lepak and Snell, 2005).

HRM as a management ideology replaced welfare-based personnel management (PM) and is distinctive with a strategic focus. It emphasises the alignment of HRM practices with business strategy and the effective deployment of people and skills to increase productivity, rather than emphasizing employees' personal interests (Legge, 2005). It is associated with the psychological contract (Rousseau, 2001; Guest and Conway, 2004) as it assumes that management will trust their workers and give them responsible and challenging assignments and workers will in turn respond with high motivation, commitment and performance (Guest, 2002).

Attempts to define HRM produced a polarisation of multiconceptual normative models of HRM (Guest, 2006) that predominantly focused on the contingency book that contributed to the best-fit school of HRM (Fombrun et al., 1984; Wood and Menezes, 1998), the universalistic book that contributed to the best-practice school of HRM (Legge, 2005; Storey, 2007), the Guest Model extended the others to include high quality and involvement of line management (Guest, 2006), and the Storey Model agreed with the basic assumptions and included key levers of managing culture (Storey, 2007). In essence, these developments in HRM have two significant implications in terms of the requirement to develop strategic credibility within organisations, and a shift in attitudes, behaviours and affiliations to fulfil the new role (Wright, 2005). The evolution of HRM in the United Kingdom (UK) promoted the introduction of a governing body for people management known now as the Chartered Institute of Personnel and Development (CIPD) (Storey, 2007). Furthermore, the government commissioned research by the Workplace Employment Relations Survey (WERS), to map the extent and use of a number of HR practices, the strategic location of HR through representative information, and until recently, employee well-being in British workplaces (Cully et al., 1999; Kersley et al., 2006).

Historically, the promotion of wellness in the human potential movement started in the 1960s in America (Cowen, 1991; Diener, 1984). Well-being is a complex construct that concerns optimal experience and psychological functioning (Ryan and Deci, 2001). Current research on well-being has been derived from two general perspectives: hedonic and eudaimonic. The hedonic approach focuses on happiness and views well-being in terms of pleasure attainment and pain avoidance (Diener, 1996; Diener et al., 2003; Ryff and Keyes, 1995). The evaluation of pleasure/pain continuum in human experience relates to subjective well-being which consists of life satisfaction, the presence of positive mood and the absence of negative mood that is often summarised as happiness (Eid and Larsen, 2008; Seligman and Csikszentmihalyi, 2000). By contrast, proponents of the eudaimonic approach disagree with the 'happiness' principle advocated by hedonism and focused on meaning and self-realisation. This approach views well-being in terms of the degree to which a person is fully functioning (Grant et al., 2007; Ryan and Deci, 2001; Ryff and

Keyes, 1995). This approach relates to psychological well-being as distinct from subjective well-being and includes aspects of autonomy, personal growth, self-acceptance and positive relatedness of human actualisation (Ryff and Keyes, 1995). According to Ryan and Frederick (1997) the fulfilment of these needs are essential for psychological growth, integrity, well-being and experiences of vitality. Ryan and Deci (2001) argue that the two views of well-being have given rise to different research foci and a body of knowledge that is in some areas divergent and in others complementary.

The growth in the field of well-being in the UK is evidenced by the expansion of interest academically, within organisations and government commissioned research on well-being from the Health and Safety Executive (HSE), Department of Health (DOH), Department of Works and Pensions (DWP), Economic and Social Research Council (ESRC), Health Work and Well-being Executive (HWWE), the Chartered Institute of Personnel and Development (CIPD) to name a few. These research were all geared towards gaining information and providing evidence on the promotion of the health and well-being of Britain's working age population, which has implications for the quality of working life, expenditure reduction, and bottom line for organisations and the national purse (Black, 2008; DOH, 2007; DWP, 2005, ESRC, 2006, 2010; HSE, 2007; HWWE, 2010).

Against this backdrop, what is interesting to note here is that the history of people management and well-being appears to have made a full circle, beginning with the people management approach from welfare paternalist employers, followed by the scientific management approach. The human relations movement focused on the human side of management, promoted the interest in psychological health and wellness. The emergence of HRM in the 1980s resulted in the shift from PM to HRM with a consequence of contrasting roles for HRM as a strategic partner versus an employee champion, which has implications for employee well-being in organisations. Thus, the growth of the fields of HRM and Well-being research are evident in the UK based on the expansion of interest from the government, academia and within organisations.

Employee well-being at work

The definition and meaning of work-related well-being is emergent with a number of competing meanings, making a precise definition of it open and can take many forms (Renwick, 2003, 2009). Proponents of employee well-being indicate that it is a complex concept with multiple dimensions (Diener et al., 2003; Grant et al., 2007; Ryan and Deci, 2001). Danna and Griffin (1999) emphasise work-related satisfactions and suggest that non-work related satisfactions are affected by work and general health. Warr (2002) argues that there is a need to go beyond 'satisfaction' to a more positive concept of well-being reflected in three dimensions: satisfaction, enthusiasm and contentment with their opposites of depression and anxiety (Holman, 2002; Wood, 2008). Peccei (2004) suggests that well-being at work concerns an overall sense of happiness, physical and mental health of the workforce (Currie, 2001; Graham, 2009). Wider aspects of well-being are reflected in questions about work satisfaction, work stress, work-life balance, job-related well-being, joy-filled workplaces and satisfaction with life as a whole (Bakke, 2005; Guest and Conway, 2004; Guest, 2002, 2006; Kersley et al., 2006).

Well-being is multifaceted, and for the purpose of this book employee well-being is defined as employee welfare that includes different domains that promotes an individual's well-being; the group interface between organisational social actors that promotes employee well-being; and organisational practices, polices, programmes and culture that strategically fosters and maintain positive work experiences and functioning for employees that promotes their well-being within the wider experience of organisational life and a healthy organisation (Baptiste, 2009). This definition invokes not just specific practices of HRM, wellness management programmes, health screening, or indeed fun programmes, but employees' 'holistic' functioning and organisational experiences within the employment relationship (Baptiste, 2007, 2009). In the context of well-being research, it has two major advantages over many other studies. First, it explores various aspects of the PC (i.e. the range or breadth of promises made, the fulfilment of promises, violation of promises and aspects of fairness and trust that form part of the wider concept of the PC) (Guest and Conway, 2004, 2009; Rousseau, 1995, 2001). Second, it explores a wide range of relevant outcomes (such as job satisfaction, organisational commitment, and several aspects of health and well-being that include anxiety, depression, irritation at work, physical health and self-rated sickness absence) (Guest, 2002; Warr, 2002).

The concept of employee well-being

The concept of employee well-being at work promotes the advantage to organisations of having a healthy workforce (Harter et al., 2002; MacDonald, 2005). The dynamics of well-being at work is essential to understand the different domains that affect the quality of life at work (Green and Whitfield, 2009). Personal well-being does not exist on its own or in the workplace but within a social context as individual lives are affected by social relations with organisational agents, lifestyle and employment changes (Tehrani et al., 2007; Guest, 2002). Employees' expect their employers to value, support and respect their efforts towards attainment of organisational objectives and as such are looking to employers to help them to achieve this, since a large proportion of their lives is spent at work. In support, Wilkinson et al. (2008) state that in order to ensure that employee well-being is promoted, it is important for employers to create a conducive environment that promotes a state of contentment that allows employees to flourish and achieve their full potential for the benefit of themselves and their organisation (Tehrani et al., 2007).

The meaning of work and well-being can have different meaning for individuals. Wilson (2010) suggests that work occupies a substantial proportion of most of our lives, can be a symbol of personal value, it can provide status, economic reward and potential. Echoing this view, Bolton and Houlihan (2007) state that working provides a sense of worth, dignity, and that people and employment structure our lives and shape the inequalities that we face (Terkel, 1977). Bolton and Houlihan (2007) further argue that maintaining dignity at work is something that workers from all walks of life struggle to achieve and can be attained through taking pride in productive accomplishments, and assistance against abusive bosses or bad management. Burke and Ng (2006) and Wilson (2010) highlight that employers, in particular, managers have the hierarchical power to influence, if not determine, the shape and degree of those inequalities in their organisation.

There is acknowledgement, however, that implementation of a well-being philosophy in the workplace may not be easy, and recognition that significant differences can exist between organisations in the degree to which their organisational cultures tolerate, facilitate, embrace, or embed well-being. More broadly, *individuals* are likely to differ in their attitudes regarding the importance, appropriateness, and perceived consequences of having well-being at work (Baptiste, 2009; Currie, 2001; Warr, 2002). These differences can be aligned to different groups of workers' having different psychological contracts (George, 2009). These tensions, along with questions about the underlying motivations of the well-being philosophy, can cause some employees to respond with cynicism and resistance (Fineman, 2006; Reichers et al., 1997). Perceptions of well-being at work may be dependent on employees' personal outlook, socialisation processes, gender, work experiences and personality characteristics – each accounting for varying attitudes and perceptions regarding the importance of workplace well-being (Grant et al., 2007).

Managerial practices can have implications on employee well-being and can lead to well-being tradeoffs or exchange, which is a common feature of organisational life (Weick, 1992). Echoing this view, Grant et al. (2007) point out that managers must often make tradeoffs in choosing between short-term profits and long term motivation (March, 1991). Grant et al. (2007) further argue that it is possible for tradeoffs to exist between differing dimensions of well-being by enhancing one aspect of well-being (i.e. psychological) while decreasing another aspect of well-being (i.e. physical). Proponents of well-being suggest that improvements in well-being can result if managers make changes in organisational contexts in terms of job redesign practices, reward, physical and social dimensions (Baptiste, 2009; Danna and Griffin, 1999; Hackman and Oldham, 1980). Moreover, Fried and Ferris (1987) state that when tasks are enriched to create feelings of meaningfulness, responsibility and knowledge of results, employees experience higher levels of job satisfaction. By contrast, Campion and McClelland (1993) point out that although work redesign practices can create job satisfaction they can also undermine employee health as the enriched job challenge stretches employees' skills to complete complex demanding work, which often leads to strain, fatigue, overload and increased risk of cardiovascular disease (Cooper et al., 2001). In essence, job enrichment can increase psychological well-being but decrease physical well-being due to well-being tradeoffs.

Employee well-being can also be increased by rewards and incentive compensation practices that can be both monetary and non-monetary to enhance employee performance (Danna and Griffin, 1999). Eisenberger et al. (1999) suggest that incentive compensation may lead to increased job satisfaction as employees might be pleased at the prospect of earning higher pay and recognise that effort can bring valued rewards (Jain et al., 2009). Although, incentive compensation may enhance the satisfaction of many employees, it can harm their interpersonal relationships. This can introduce inequality leading employees to compare with each other for earnings, eroding trust, cooperation, mutual support and helping. This can affect turnover, and reduce performance (Feraro et al., 2005; Munkes and Diehl, 2003). Therefore, rewards and compensation practices can have potential tradeoffs between psychological, material, social, and organisational well-being. Furthermore, improving relationships through team building can assist in increasing employee well-being by changing social dimensions of organisational context through improving interpersonal relations and cohesion at work (Katzell and Thompson, 1990). Interpersonal relationships and team building can have potential trade-offs for social and psychological well-being.

Multidimensional well-being paradigm

This book argues that there is a need to go beyond 'psychological', 'physical' and 'social' domains of well-being at work to a more 'holistic' conceptualisation of multidimensional well-being at work paradigm reflected in 16 domains: psychological, physical, mental health, intellectual, material/rewards, career, spiritual, financial, work/family, social, compassionate leadership, stakeholders, humanistic and fair practices, organisational financial, workplace well-being management and healthy work/organisation. These dimensions' attempt to overcome the limitations and better represent the notion of multidimensional well-being that can be an essential concept to understanding the individual perspective (i.e. the whole person), the group perspective (i.e. social actors and inter-relationships), and organisational perspective (i.e. humanistic HRM practices, workplace well-being management, healthy work/organisation context, and environment). The researcher argues that a multidimensional well-being model is a relevant concept that is practical for policy, practice and for the development of well-being theory from an HRM perspective. The summary of multidimensional well-being perspectives is in Table 4.1.

Individual well-being perspective

A number of workplace factors that can influence an individual's quality of working life and well-being at work is captured under the individual well-being perspective and includes nine key domains: psychological, physical, intellectual, mental health, material/rewards, career, spiritual, financial and work/family well-being.

Psychological well-being

The psychological dimension entails subjective experiences and functioning (Grant et al., 2007) involving positive or negative thoughts or feelings in an individual's judgement which influences a perception of stress, anxiety, happiness and other emotional states (Bakke, 2005; Baptiste, 2009; Guerrier and Adib, 2003; Haworth and Hart, 2007; Kersley et al., 2006; Robinson et al., 2004; Ryff and Keyes, 1995; Seligman and Csikszentmihalyi, 2000). The psychological well-being dimension takes into consideration similarities and differences of well-being existing amongst employee groups in organisations, job satisfaction, discrimination and fair treatment, and bullying and harassment. Well-being can be experienced differently by individuals and is captured by Burke et al. (2008) and CCOHS (2017) who highlight that similarity in work experiences exist for males and females that had similar work experiences, job satisfaction, and levels of psychological well-being (Emmons, 1991).

Another challenge that can affect the psychological well-being of employees is workplace bullying and harassment (Lewis and Rayner, 2003). It is now generally accepted that the definition of bullying contains the following elements: the experience of one or more negative behaviour(s) that is persistent, unwelcome, unwanted, or unsolicited, that violates a standard of conduct and is harmful to the target or victim. The behaviour may be deliberate or unconscious or a power imbalance between the victim and perpetrator resulting in a hostile working environment (CIPD, 2005, 2007, 2008; Peyton, 2003; Salin, 2003). In terms of its prevalence, the self-reported claims of bullying were revealed by WERS's 2004 survey which highlighted the main employee grievances involving bullying at work, work time practices, work allocation, pace of work, relationship with line managers, unfair treatment, pay and conditions, and annual leave. These elements were all higher in the NW than in the national standard (Forth and Stokes, 2006; Kersley et al., 2006).

Table 4.1 Summary of multidimensional workplace well-being perspectives

Perspectives	Well-Being Domains	Elements	Authors
Individual	Psychological	Job satisfaction, fulfilment, engagement, purpose in life, influence over job, psychological growth, competence, life satisfaction, happiness, contentment, sense of purpose, enjoyment, exciting and stimulating work, flexibility, feeling valued, positive emotional, coping with life, reducing individual working time arrangements, job demands, work control, psychological strain, commitment, personal choice, identity, organisational citizenship behaviour, self-congruence, integrity, fair treatment, realisation of human potential, anxiety, tense, calm, relaxed, worried, uneasy, depression, enthusiasm, pleasure, dignity at work, anti-bullying and discriminatory practices, equal opportunities, trust, desire for goals and challenges, desire for variety, need for clarity, opportunities for personal control, burnout, idealism and passion for job, distressed, cynical, discouraged, involvement, job security: piece of mind, confidence and self-respect	Perri (2007); Lewis and Purcell (2007); Kersley et al. (2006); Tehrani et al. (2007); Haworth and Hart (2007); Currie (2001); Guest (2002/2007); Baptiste (2008, 2009); Karasak and Theorell (1990); Podsakoff et al. (2000); Grant et al. (2007); Ryan and Deci (2001); Warr (2002)
	Physical	Physical and mental health, stress management, health and safety, safe working environment, physical comfort and security, fatigue, exhaustion, workloads, maintaining healthy and energetic bodies by making healthy choices about exercise and diet.	Danna and Griffin (1999); Karasak and Theorell (1990); WHO (1992); Warr (2002); HSE (2000); Currie (2001); Baptiste (2008a, 2009)
	Intellectual	Job design, appropriate education, training and development, management development, creativity, autonomy, mental agility from keeping our minds active, alert, open, curious and creative.	Currie (2001); Tehrani et al. (2007); Baptiste (2009); CCMD (2002)
	Mental Health	Work stress, long-term sickness absence, anxiety, depression, heart diseases, incapacity benefits, leaders and managers support for mental ill-health at work	CIPD (2019); Hesketh and Cooper (2014)

	Rewards/Material	Fair rewards strategies, non-cash benefits, money, pay schemes	Currie (2001); Baptiste (2009)
	Career	Devotion to career, profession, craft, occupation apart from the work environment, career development	Morrow (1983, 1993); Cohen (2003)
	Spiritual	The purpose, fulfilment and meaning that comes with having a sense of connection to those things that are larger than ourselves, religious well-being, meaning and purpose in life	CCMD (2002; Moss (2009); Freshman (1999)
	Financial	Financial needs, employee stress, right rewards and benefit choices, poor financial well-being	AEGON (2018),CIPD (2019)
	Work/Family	Work/life conflict, life changes, family time under pressure, psychological strain	Baptiste (2009); Currie (2001); Newall (2002)
Group	Social	Interpersonal relationships, fair treatment, trust, social support, reciprocity, leader-member exchange, cooperation, coordination, integration, social networks, bonding, communication, collaboration, team working, something that is done together and not something that we each possess, desire for supervisory support, the camaraderie that comes from maintaining a rich web of relationships with family, friends and colleagues, identification and sense of cohesiveness with other members of the organisation, individual's identification and sense of cohesiveness with other members of the organisation.	Baptiste (2008, 2009); Kramer and Tyler (1996); Grant et al. (2007); Sixsmith and Boneham (2007); Lewis and Purcell (2007); Tehrani et al. (2007): Perri (2007)
	Compassionate & Relational Leadership	Managers who are not judgemental, not too busy to be empathetic for another person's suffering, tolerating personal distress, being alive to the suffering of others, demonstrating care for people; taking appropriate action, encourage close relationships.	Poorkavoos (2016); Fryer (2013); Meechan (2018)
	Stakeholders	Collective, communal, community empowerment, relationship with stakeholders and counsellors, Stakeholders demands	Sixsmith and Boneham (2007); Delle (2007); Prilleltensky and Prilleltensky (2007); Baptiste (2009)

(Continued)

Table 4.1 Continued

Perspectives	Well-Being Domains	Elements	Authors
Organisational	Humanistic & Fair Practices	Reward strategies, working time arrangements, stress management, communication strategies, team working, positive relationships with managers and stakeholders, clarification and reduction in change initiatives, employee voice/involvement, equal opportunities, diversity management, bullying and harassment prevention, anti-violence, civility, respect, and trust	Baptiste (2009); Redman and Wilkinson (2009); Gould-Williams (2003); Kersley et al. (2006); Chechak and Csiernik (2014)
	Organisational Financial	Pay, budget limitation, financial difficulties, retirement plans and education, benefit plans, workplace financial education, material resources, financial health of an organisation	Haworth and Hart (2007); Perri (2007); Cartwright and Cooper (2009)
	Wellness Management	Health promotions (eye tests, healthy eating, gym, flu vaccinations, well-being days): employee support; and insurance protection initiatives	CIPD (2019); Putnam (2015) Willis (2014); ShapeUp (2011)
	Healthy Work/ Organisation	Provision of meaning and challenging work, provide opportunities to achieve personal aspiration while maintaining work life balance, safe working environment, provision of tools to get job done, ensuring culture fosters a positive working environment, absolution and praise culture, cultural empowerment, promoting social justice and human rights, clarification and reduction in change initiatives, selection, staff utilisation, role of executive leadership, ensuring the health of human capital, preventing absenteeism and turnover, a set of practices and not a state, performance, anti-harassment culture, biographic data on employees – lifestyles and interests, and equality and diversity management, and compassionate workplaces.	Adler and Kwon (2002); Baptiste (2007, 2009); CCOHS (2017); Kramer (1999); Tehrani et al. (2007); Delle (2007); Schabracq (2005); Perri (2007); Cartwright and Cooper (2009); Guest (2006); Poorkavoos (2016)

Likewise, one-third of NW workplaces had employment tribunal claims higher than the national average. For bullying and harassment, CIPD's (2008, 2009) report highlights that the proportion of people experiencing bullying and harassment in the workplace is higher for the public sector compared with the private sector or voluntary sector counterparts. Public sector staff are also more likely to experience violence or to have been threatened with violence, and women are marginally more likely than men to say they are experiencing bullying (CIPD, 2007, 2009). The effects of bullying behaviour have significant impact at the individual, team and organisational levels (Cooper and Marshall, 1976; Hoel et al., 2001). CIPD (2010) estimates that bullying costs UK employers £80 million lost working days annually and up to £2 billion in lost revenue via sickness absence, turnover, reduced productivity, formal and legal investigations, damage to employer branding, disturbance to working relationships, lower morale and commitment (CIPD, 2009). For individuals, the cost can be even higher, with lasting psychological and physical damage (CIPD, 2007).

Physical well-being

The key themes outlined by the physical well-being dimension include: physical health, work demands, increasing workloads, work stress, and sickness absence. The World Health Organisation (1999) identifies health as a key driver of socio-economic progress internationally (Grant et al., 2007). This view is echoed by the physical well-being dimension which relates to bodily health and functioning and influences employees' health by improving outcomes relating to cardiovascular disease, blood pressure, work-related stress and health and safety at work (Baptiste, 2009; Clarke and Cooper, 2004; Danna and Griffin, 1999; Grant et al., 2007; Karasek and Theorell, 1990). Thus, Tuomi et al. (2004) argue that changes in organisational practices and the demands of work are strongly associated with changes in employee physical well-being. Tuomi et al., further advocate that employee well-being can be improved with less uncertainty at work, decreasing mental and physical work demands, physical exercise, all of which have favourable effects (CCOHS, 2017).

Research shows that an estimated 137.3 million working days were lost due to sickness or injury in 2016 (ONS, 2016), and in 2014 over half of women and nearly two-thirds of men were overweight or obese (Health and Social Care Information Centre (HSCIC), 2016). In 2014, research conducted by HSCIC reveal that 58% of women and 65% of men were overweight or obese and obesity prevalence has increased from 15% in 1993 to 26% in 2014, with the net cost of obesity to the UK economy was 15 million in 2014 (HSCIC, 2016). Promoting good physical health and well-being among employees can reduce levels of obesity, sickness, increase energy levels and boost levels of concentration (Chen and Cooper, 2014). Research also shows that taking breaks, meditation, eating outside the office or in a staff room, lunch time walks gives employees a chance to unwind, move away from their desks that can help protect against musculoskeletal problems. Some organisations promote healthy eating and snacking, encourages cycling to work by providing bike racks so that employees have somewhere safe to chain their bikes; walking up the stairs instead of taking the elevators; physical challenges like walking or marathons for a charitable cause; encouraging contests among employees to encourage healthy living; encourage involvement of employees in company schemes soliciting ideas from employees for the improvement of their health and well-being; and sharing information with employees about the importance of physical well-being (Chen and Cooper, 2014; Health and Social Care Information Centre, 2016).

Intellectual well-being

Intellectual well-being explores creativity, agility and mental ability of individuals (Currie, 2001; CCDA, 2002). The key themes outlined by the intellectual well-being dimension include: coaching and mentoring. An organisation can facilitate the learning of all its members and continually transform itself focusing on facilitating the learning and development of its people to improve the overall functioning of the workplace. Grey (2005) and Thompson (2006) state that learning approaches and professional development adopted by organisations can include coaching and mentoring. According to CIPD (2010) coaching and mentoring have become, in the past decade, buzzwords in organisations and are important tools for supporting personal development. Central to this view, Grant and Spence (2010) argue that coaching interventions are primarily used to enhance goal attainment, positive psychology, and as a means of enhancing well-being to promote a flourishing workforce. For mentoring, Maellaro and Whittington (2009) claim that it is a technique for allowing the transmission of knowledge, skills and experience, in a supportive and challenging environment, to guide and develop the individual over a long-term. The development of intellectual well-being is captured by Thompson and Bates (2009) who advocate that the development of coaching and mentoring in organisations are essential to address well-being and performance (Wilkinson, 1998). In support, McGovern et al. (1997) state that looking after human capital is the key factor in organisational success and that looking after the well-being of staff in a nurturing and developmental way, facilitates employee development, being an example of 'best practice' which has implications for the reduction in absenteeism and turnover. Extending this view, Baptiste (2007) states that line managers have a central role in employee development and well-being and should be proactive instead of reactive to avoid employee dissatisfaction.

Mental health well-being

Mental ill-health is becoming a prevalent factor for employee sickness and absence. The CIPD's, 2019 health and well-being research reveal that mental ill-health is particularly prevalent in the public sector and is the main cause of long-term absence (followed by stress) and among the top causes of short-term absence (CIPD, 2019). Furthermore, nearly three-quarters of organisations in the public sector (72%) have experienced an increase in reported common mental health conditions over the past year, compared with just over half (53%) of private sector organisations (CIPD, 2019). Mental ill-health has prompted more organisations to have a policy that covers mental health to assist them to take action to manage mental health at work. Approaches used by organisations to manage mental health include: a phased return to work and/or other reasonable adjustments, increasing awareness of mental health issues across the workforce, access to counselling services and employee assistance programmes, provision of mental health first aid training, the use of mental health/well-being champions, organisational leaders encouraging an openness about mental health across the organisation, senior leaders and line managers promoting and supporting mental health (CIPD, 2019). Leaders and line managers are now encouraged to actively support people with mental ill-health through their actions and behaviour to avoid hindering organisational efforts. The CIPD's, 2019 research further reveal that just 44% of public sector organisations train managers to support staff with mental ill-health, although this is higher than the private sector, where 38% provide training. These figures show that we still have a long way to go but often training is curtailed or avoided due to budgetary constraints. Nevertheless, the commitment of senior leaders and managers to health and well-being is a key prerequisite for the success of any organisational programme or initiative (Hesketh and Cooper, 2014).

According to MacDonald (2005) and Silcox (2007) excessive pressure leads to stress which is linked to mental health conditions such as anxiety, depression and heart disease all of which have implications for absenteeism (Silcox, 2007; Warr, 2002). WERS's 2004 survey reveals that NW workplaces had days lost to sickness absence at 5.3%, slightly higher than the national average, with two-fifths of employees' agreeing that they never had enough time to get their job done, with a quarter agreeing that they worry a lot about work outside working hours (Forth and Stokes, 2006; Kersley et al., 2006). Another challenge faced by employees within organisations is increasing workloads and pressure at work, which can lead to work stress that can negatively impact health and productivity (CIPD, 2010; Jex, 1998). Stress and mental ill-health are major factors in human life that can influence people positively and negatively and as such the management of work-stress and mental health are crucial for both individual and organisational processes (Cooper et al., 2001;

Cooper and Robertson, 2001; HSE, 2007). Stress and mental health literatures advocate that managers and executives need to be positive, supportive and accommodating towards employees (Cartwright and Cooper, 2009; Chen and Cooper, 2014; CIPD, 2019; Hesketh and Cooper, 2014; William and Cooper, 1998). Thus, Schabracq (2005) argues that employees' mental health and well-being depends to an important degree on the extent to which leaders and mangers realise the functional reality of employees. This can be achieved through effective leadership and HRM interventions (Baptiste, 2007).

Public sector workers in particular report that their workloads were too much, from (38% to 48%) feeling under excessive pressure at work, and nearly a quarter (23%) saying they feel under excessive pressure every day compared with 13% a year ago. For private sector employees the results were (16% and 12%) (CIPD, 2010). MacDonald (2005) states that Warr's three-item index of 'work strain' shows a rise in average work strain between 1992 and 2001, which has implications for worker well-being. The approach to workplace stress in organisations has traditionally been dealt with by occupational health and psychological approaches like workplace counselling and employee assistance programmes (Mac-Donald, 2005). Likewise, other less acceptable approaches are adopted, which Thompson and Bates (2009) refers to as the 'ostrich approach'. This involves trying to pretend that the problems do not exist or that they are not important but Williams and Cooper (1999) point out that this is a very dangerous strategy that can seriously backfire.

Furthermore, Harvey et al. (2009) state that mental ill-health is now the leading cause of both sickness absence and incapacity benefits in most high-income countries, and as such, the rising economic and social costs make health at work an increasing priority for policy makers. However, ESRC (2006) advocates that these measures are reactive approaches to ill-health at work and there is need for a broader proactive approach to be introduced into the organisation through wellness programmes, to encourage attendance and reduce absenteeism. It is important to note here that this book goes a step further than 'wellness programmes' and suggests a multidimensional workplace well-being approach that includes: the individual, group, and the organisation have to be viewed holistically to enhance the employment relationship that can foster and maintain the quality of working life and employees' well-being.

Material/rewards well-being

Material/rewards well-being explores the working life experiences of individuals that pertain to reward strategies and functioning in the employment relationship (Baptiste, 2009; CIPD, 2007; Currie, 2001). Ulrich (1997) proposes that line managers need well-designed HR practices in their people management strategies in order to help motivate and reward employees in dealing with performance issues and work needs. CIPD (2010) report reveals reward strategies used in British workplaces, which include financial and non-financial schemes to motivate employees and reward high performers. Financial reward strategies used include pay schemes, performance related pay, bonuses, incentives, pensions and benefits. Non-financial strategies include recognition schemes (Kersley et al., 2006). Grint (2005) maintains that it is important for senior management to establish an appropriate organisational culture that supports, recognises and rewards people management behaviours. In essence, once employees perceive that their efforts are valued, respected and appreciated through various reward strategies this in turn can positively influence their perception of fairness, and overall well-being at work.

Career well-being

Career well-being is based on the concept of professionalism, namely the extent to which individual employees identify with their profession or occupation and endorse its values and behavioural intention toward his/her occupation (Blau, 2006; Cohen, 2003; Gould and Penley, 1984). Career well-being can represent an individual's motivation to work in a career he/she chooses or as a degree of centrality of one's career for one's identity (Gould, 1979). The conceptualisation of career well-being proposed in this book is identification and satisfaction with one's career and professional development and functioning, reflected in opportunities for advancement provided by the organisation. The key themes outlined by the career well-being domain include: career development opportunities, identification with an occupation, work-related stress on careers, and the individual's career responsibility. Holland (1997) advocates that people gravitate towards occupations and work environments congruent with their personal orientations, and the choice of an occupation is construed as an attempt to fulfil a desired way of life through one's work. Holland further argues that career choices reflect a person's self-perception regarding his or her abilities, values and personality along with assessment of how these individual's aspects fit with particular occupations (Cohen, 2003). Becker and Carper's (1956) work highlighted elements for identification with an occupation as an occupational title and associated ideology, commitment to task, commitment to particular organisations or institutional positions, and significance for one's position in the larger society. Some key requisites of work for employees are that work meets their professional needs, offers professional growth, satisfaction and the enhancement of their status (Cohen, 2003; George, 2009).

According to Baruch (2009) career choices, commitment and success at the individual level influence organisational interventions like career planning and management of work stress. In support, Clarke and Cooper

(2004) indicate the importance of understanding the specific impact of work-related stress on people's careers. This in turn can have implications for career well-being of individuals within organisations. Strickland (1997) and Gutherie et al. (1998) emphasise the need for organisations and individuals to acknowledge and act upon the increased importance for employees to self-manage their careers. This view is echoed by George (2009) who argues that the changing nature of work has led to perceived contract breach on the part of both the individual's profession and employing organisations and that twenty-first-century career management is seen as the individual's own responsibility, and one of the social domains in which individuals engage. The ideology of career management in organisations has changed and careers are no longer a long-term relationship between employers and employees (Blau, 2006; Cohen, 2003) but rather a series of beneficial transactions based on both organisational and individual needs (George, 2009). This can have implications for career management as perceived by employees and it can be regarded as an expectation that, if violated, can negatively affect the psychological contract, perceptions of fairness and ultimately well-being at work. Career well-being can dictate the relationship between affective and continuance commitment, job satisfaction, job involvement, enhanced performance, absenteeism, turnover intentions, and intentions to withdraw from the occupation (Cohen, 2003; Meyer and Allen, 1997; Randall and Cote, 1991).

Spiritual well-being

The spiritual domain of well-being relates to an internal coping resource satisfaction with one's life in relationship to God or a higher power and a perception of life as having meaning that nurtures and celebrates wholeness (Canadian Centre for Management Development, 2002; Fisher, 2005; Moss, 2009). The conceptual definition of spiritual well-being proposed in this study is satisfaction with one's religious well-being reflected in one's relationship with a Supreme Being, one's existential well-being, and one's sense of meaning and purpose in life. Krishnakumar and Neck (2002) argue that organisations demand more time, psychic energy, loyalty, and imagination from employees than ever before, but continue to treat them as if they were interchangeable parts.

Furthermore, Moss (2009) also contends that because of the emotional anxiety and complexities experienced at work, spirituality has been introduced as a profound way of looking at what is happening in the workplace. The notion of spirituality is not a management tool or theory used in an attempt to restore effectiveness and profitability to dysfunctional organisations, but as an invitation to explore challenges creatively and effectively and to suggest a more 'root and branch' approach that reflects the underlying values and aspirations (Fisher, 2005). Spiritual well-being relates to the problems that employees can experience in the workplace and spirituality can be used as a way to understand what is happening in the workplace as it relates to employees (CCMD, 2002). It can explore the extent to which issues such as meaning, purpose, and fulfilment are embedded and lived out within organisations. Freshman (1999) suggests that there is a link between spirituality and individual creativity, increased honesty and trust within the organisation, enhanced sense of personal fulfilment of employees, and an increased commitment to organisational goals (Burack, 1999; Wagner-Marsh and Conley, 1999).

Financial well-being

Financial well-being is a more neglected aspect of health and well-being consideration and few organisations have a financial well-being strategy that takes into account the needs of different employee groups (CIPD, 2019). The mental health and physical well-being of employees have been topics high on the agenda for many employers recently, and increasingly this is being joined by a third consideration – financial well-being (www. aegon.co.uk). The Centre for Economic and Business Research (CEBR) and AEGON (brand name for Scottish Equitable Plc.) state that financial well-being is about people having control over their finances, their ability to respond to financial unpredictability and unexpected financial expenses, and their ability to meet financial goals and make choices that allow them to enjoy life (www.aegon.co.uk). Key findings from research completed by CEBR and AEGON which surveyed 2,000 employees from diverse industry sectors about financial well-being found that 30% of employees agree they are just getting by financially but that large portions of the workforce live with significant money worries, with many people unable to manage an unexpected expense or worried about their savings. 41% of employees are concerned that the money they have now or will save will not last throughout retirement. 36% of employees do not think that they are in a position to handle a major unexpected expense financially, and 43% of employees usually have money left over at the end of the month, while nearly a third (31%) feel that their finances often or always control their life. The research further points out that there is a generational divide in financial well-being, in that, 40% of those under 35 years of age don't feel that they would handle an expected major expense, compared to 30% of those aged 55 or above. Financial worries are party seasonal, in that two in five (39%) of workers said they feel under more financial pressure than usual in November and December, while a quarter (24%) feel their finances are stretched more than usual in January and February (AEGON and CEBR, 2018). The CEBR and AEGON research found that causes of low financial well-being entails, low pay and insufficient pay rises (56%); high house prices (56%); high cost of living (excluding rent and house prices –50%); lack of understanding about managing money/budget (37%); insufficient pension provision (37%); low interest rates making savings less rewarding (34%); social pressure to spend/lead a certain lifestyle (34%); and high rental costs (48%) (AEGON and CEBR, 2018).

The financial well-being research further revealed that poor financial well-being costs UK employers GBP1.56 billion each year through absenteeism and presenteeism. Absenteeism account for GBP0.6 billion and Presenteeism accounts for GBP0.9 billion, with over 500,000 private sector workers have had to take time off in the last year due to their financial well-being, leading to a loss of over 4.2 million days of work (www.aegon.co.uk). London recorded the highest financial well-being score (52), while Wales recorded the lowest score (49), with North West England, the significant geographical location for the organisational cases mentioned throughout this book, scoring (50), with IT and Telecoms sectors recorded the highest financial well-being scores and Retail recorded the lowest, and employees are looking for help when it comes to understanding their benefits (AEGON and CEBR, 2018). AEGON points out that financial well-being scores are calculated by using four factors which include: first, *day-to-day control* over finances, including being able to pay bills on time and making ends meet. Second, *long-term goals*, being on track to meet financial goals, including paying off outstanding debt and saving for retirement. Third, *one-off* capacity to absorb a financial shock. And forth, *lifetime goals* and ability to make choices, and enjoy life (CCOHS, 2017).

The CIPD (2019) research states that poor financial well-being is a significant cause of employee stress in their organisation, absenteeism, mental ill-health, and suggest that if employees have the knowledge and skills to make the right financial choices, reward and benefit choices to meet their financial needs, this is likely to improve their well-being and productivity (CIPD, 2019). Research by CEBR and AEGON echoes this view and recommends that employers that communicate with employees about the benefits suggestion and to offer greater access to financial education for employees show higher financial well-being scores than those who don't (AEGON and CEBR, 2018). They further argue that employers can equip employees with tools to help them with financial future forecasting, including access to guidance on saving and investment (www.aegon.co.uk). The CIPD (2019) research states that the public sector is less active than private sector services organisations in regularly communicating reward policies to staff so they understand the benefits on offer and the choices available so that employees can assess how well their existing benefit offering is meeting their financial needs. Research by AEGON (2019) reveal that 21% of employees said that their employer does not currently provide information on how to make the most of the benefits on offer, but that they like them to do so. 7% of employees said that their employer offered face-to-face counselling and advice by specialised staff or external consultants.

Work/family well-being

The challenges of the changing world of work have a wide-ranging effect on work and family interaction which has major concerns for both employees and employers (Green and Tsitsianis, 2004; CIPD, 2006; MacDonald, 2005). Daniels and French (2006) argue that workers are experiencing life changes and aspirations and family time is coming under pressure, intensifying work-family conflict, resulting in psychological strains and ill-health (Cartwright and Cooper, 2009; Currie, 2001; Newall, 2002). Cooper et al. (2001) highlight that psychological strain experienced by employees as they strive for more of a balance between work and life mainly affects professionals and managerial workers who are increasingly pressured to work faster and longer hours (Baptiste, 2009; George, 2009).

According to Cooper and Quick (1999) it is essential for organisations to understand this conflict and implement family-friendly policies and wellness interventions that can help employees attain a better balance between work and life (Clutterback, 2003; Houston, 2005). Clutterback (2003) also regard work-life balance as being aware of different demands on time and energy, having the ability to make choices in the allocation of time and energy, knowing what values to apply to choices and making choices. The literature highlights the importance of work-life balance, working hours and well-being, advocating the benefits of a business case for organisations (CIPD, 2009, DWP, 2005; Guest and Conway, 2009; HWWE, 2010). Thus, long hours working can have negative implications for employees' health, fatigue and relationships. This can have implications for more accidents and errors, reduced satisfaction, psychological well-being and job performance (Houston, 2005; HSE, 2007, 2010).

Group well-being perspective

The group perspective of well-being entails three key domains: social, compassionate leadership and stakeholders well-being.

Social well-being

The social well-being domain identifies the relational experiences and functioning and focuses on the quality of interpersonal relationships with other people and communities, underpinned with fair treatment for employees (CCOHS, 2017; Grant et al., 2007; Renwick, 2003). The key themes outlined by the social well-being domain include: relationships, valued and supported, trust, blame culture and line management leadership. Stress management and leader-member exchange literatures show that the leader's impact is often incorporated into the broader situational variables of social support and supervisor-subordinate relationships experienced by employees within organisations (Cooper et al., 2001; Graen et al., 1982; Rhoades and Eisenberger, 2002). Thus, Baptiste's (2009) study reveals that management relationship behaviour, in the form of support and development of trust, can promote employee well-being with implications for policy and practice in organisations. Echoing this view, Renwick (2003) claims that HR managers are engaged in the process of enhancing employee well-being at work and also acting against it. Renwick further concludes that while there are advantages to employee well-being through adopting a strategic HR approach led by HR managers, the devolution of HR work to the line are numerous, and the potential costs to employee well-being are also significant. In essence, employee well-being must be addressed by organisations if future employee commitment to these organisations is to be secured.

In terms of self-reported relationships within organisations, WERS's 2004 survey reveals that in the NW 97% of managers agreed that management employee relations were good, whereas NW employees were less positive about the state of the employment relationship than their managers with 67% describing management-employee relations as good (Forth and Stokes, 2006; Kersley et al., 2006). It is also important for employees to feel valued and supported within the organisation that can have positive implications for their well-being. In support, Baptiste's (2007) research reveals that a culture of blame can promote negative well-being, and through this, promote fear, stifle creativity, and increase reluctance to take risks. Baptiste further concludes that being rewarded through praise and recognition, feeling valued, and being able to trust management are factors that can promote positive well-being at work.

The dynamics of leadership and well-being at work is usually influenced by line management which is well defined in the literature (Alban-Metcalfe and Alimo-Metcalfe, 2000; McGovern et al., 1997; Purcell and Hutchinson, 2007). It refers to a rational approach to organisational decision-making and is concerned with executing routines and maintaining organisational stability (Purcell and Hutchinson, 2007). McGovern et al. (1997) argue that line management action or support, and the quality of the relationship between employees and their immediate line manager, is also liable to influence perceptions not only of people management but of leadership and work climate, either positively or negatively. Echoing this view, Purcell and Hutchinson (2003) point out that employees' relationship with their line manager is especially important and powerful and can be seen in how line managers deliver HR practices, and how responsive they are to workers needs and in quality of leadership shown. Thompson and Bates (2009) advocate that leaders can affect the well-being of those who report to them, both individually and as a group. Central to this point, it is therefore essential for line managers to achieve the right balance in terms of communication, team working and leadership style adopted (McGovern et al., 1997). Cooper and Robertson (2001) suggest that leaders who are high on emotional intelligence are more likely to use the head-heart connection to make more healthy decisions from a logical decision-making process informed and guided by feelings. This ideology can be a stepping stone towards the enhancement of social well-being in organisations.

Compassionate and relational leadership well-being

Research shows that line management relationship is central to employee satisfaction, perception of fairness, support and employee well-being (Alban-Metcalfe and Alimo-Metcalfe, 2000; Baptiste, 2007; McGovern et al., 1997). Cooper and Robertson (2001) hold the view the leaders with high emotional intelligence are more likely to use the (head-heart connection) guided by feelings for decision making and functioning. This empathetic approach is associated with compassionate leadership that considers the key issue in creating healthier workplaces is through compassion and empathy at work, and in leadership more specifically (Meechan, 2018). Compassionate leadership is the opposite to toxic leadership, bullying bosses, psychopathic managers, and colleagues which are commonplace and frighteningly central in most research findings from employee surveys. However, despite these findings, most of us can relate to a time when we worked with a compassionate, empathetic leader or colleague and the difference this made to our sense of purpose, self-worth, empowerment, motivation, in the achievement of our personal and organisational goals, in a way that it enhanced our personal well-being, and ultimately our productivity. Given that employee well-being is now high on senior leaders' and management agenda it is now time to better understand the importance of developing the social and interpersonal skills of empathy and compassion to enhance their own and others well-being for the good of the organisation. Compassionate leaders should demonstrate empathy. Sinclair et al. (2016) state that empathy is widely understood as being able to resonate with someone else's shoes and feel with someone in their given circumstances, this can lead to people feeling recognised and valued. Meechan (2018) takes the ideology of empathy further by suggesting compassion, which relates to recognising the circumstances of another person or group of people and, critically, feeling compelled to take action to improve those circumstances. Armstrong (2011) asserts that compassion is a fundamental human condition, and it has been found to be the one concept which underpins all the world's major ethical, spiritual and religious traditions (Geotz et al., 2010). Meechan (2018) further claims that the outcome of compassion is improvement, this is why it is particularly important in a work context. Figley (1995) states that compassion process involves noticing the discomfort of the other person, being able to resonate with that discomfort and taking action to improve the circumstances of the other person.

Research from Roffey Park (Poorkavoos, 2016) has identified a compassion in the workplace model which highlights five key attributes of a compassionate individual at work to include: alive to the suffering of others, non-judgemental, tolerating personal distress, empathic, and appropriate action (Poorkavoos, 2016). If empathy and compassion are not demonstrated in the workplace it is likely to be associated with unethical practice (Dutton et al., 2006), leadership practices which lead to reduced employee well-being and reduced performance (Baptiste, 2007, 2009; Mathieu and Zajac, 1990), in certain service organisations like the health sector, a lack of compassion can lead to serious failings in basic standard of care which can lead to suffering and avoidable deaths, sexual exploitation, poor practices, putting profit over people, a lack of compassion for vulnerable and sick individuals and their families and much more can damage an organisation's reputation and leave long lasting psychological and physical scares in the lives of employees, patients and customers' well-being (Meechan, 2018). Meechan further argues that in workplaces lacking empathy and compassion occur on a daily basis. For example, managers are only interested in targets being delivered, with no interest in how that happens or in the people who deliver them; organisational change is implemented with no meaningful consultation with staff; people are dealing with wider life issues such as bereavement and illness and managers are insisting that those things should be kept separate from work; and people are expected to deliver more work with fewer resources due to budget cuts and pressure to increase profits. These practices can lead to staff feeling undervalued, unappreciated, de-humanised and pressurised, which generates suffering (Meechan, 2018). Figley (1995) state that suffering at work is a hidden cost to human capability. In support, Poorkavoos (2016) claim that employee suffering within an organisation incurs considerable financial, psychological and social costs.

There is growing evidence emerging to show the business case and positive benefits of empathy and compassion in practice. Avoiding unethical practice and poor productivity are strong enough arguments for ensuring empathy and compassion in organisations. Holt and Marques (2012) state that empathy is an essential aspect of twenty-first-century leadership and can no longer be ignored if we want to prevent continuation of ethic disasters in the business world. Research associated with transformational leadership has been found to be more ethical and more effective than other forms of leadership and is related to a number of positive work outcomes including improved relationships, motivation, job satisfaction, organisational commitment, creativity, safety, performance and well-being, improved communication, improved innovation, employee engagement, job satisfaction, higher organisational commitment, reduced absenteeism turnover, increase in patient satisfaction, reduction in serious incidents, positive emotions, lower heart rate and blood pressure, strengthen the immune system, decrease employees' psychological distress, improved employee performance, acts of altruism, kindness and care, sustains the sufferer through the grieving process and facilitates faster recovery, generate resilience in stressful times amongst staff, lower stress and greater resilience (Boyatzis et al., 2006; Lilius et al., 2008; Sinclair, 2016; Wang et al., 2013).

Poorkavoos (2016) identified a number of studies which demonstrate the positive benefits of compassion in the workplace. Lilius et al. (2008) state that those who experience compassionate leadership at work are more likely to report effective commitment to their organisation and to talk about it in positive terms. Compassion breeds compassion, and those who experience it are then more likely to demonstrate it towards others (Kanov et al., 2004), and supervisors who perceive that their organisation values their well-being are more likely to show supportive behaviour towards the people they manage (Dutton et al., 2006). Compassion at work connects co-workers psychologically and results in a stronger bond between them (Figley, 1995); people benefit by seeing compassionate acts being demonstrated in the workplace that has a rippling effect whereby the whole organisation can benefit which leads to relationships which are stronger and more positive and therefore more collaboration in the workplace (Dutton et al., 2006). When compassion is core to organisational values, there is a measurable increase in productivity and financial performance and well-being (Meechan, 2018; Poorkavoos, 2016).

Barriers to compassion is organisational culture, individual circumstances, and policy and procedures. Organisational culture that hinders compassion in the workplace entails pressure from senior management too focused on outputs, and managers not feeling empowered to make decisions themselves that enable them to be compassionate. Policy and procedures that hinders compassion in the workplace include HR policy too restrictive and not able to adapt to individual circumstances. When policies and procedures are followed to the letter, to the point where you can't see the real compassionate person. Individual circumstances that are a barrier to compassion in the workplace include: being too busy to stop and show care, low emotional intelligence, managers who genuinely don't care about their teams and focus only on getting the job done whatever the cost, being fearful of accidentally discriminating against a person, crossing unseen boundaries, and being seen as inconsistent (Meechan, 2018). Compassion in the workplace can be fostered in many levels in the workplace, at individual, team and organisational level. From an individual level, compassion can be fostered through *self-compassion*, which Neff (2013) defines as being open to and moved by one's own suffering, experiencing feelings of caring and kindness towards oneself, taking an understanding, non-judgemental attitude towards one's inadequacies and failures, and recognising that one's own experience is part of the common human experience (Neff, 2013). Organisations can develop leaders and people with empathy and compassion training and coaching. Kanov et al. (2004) state that compassionate leaders take pleasure in being able to foster the development and learning of those around them, and they use their own knowledge to support and help others through modelling and setting the tone in the organisation; engaging employees by truly listening to them valuing their wants, needs and contributions, and responding to these in the spirit of improvement; and setting vision and values for the organisation ensuring clarity and ownership for them throughout the organisation (Meechan, 2018). Compassion in organisations and teams promotes the culture of an organisation from shared values, assumptions, beliefs and practices which shape the behaviour of an organisation (Armstrong, 2011) and well-being of employees (Baptiste, 2007).

In order for the culture of an organisation to be compassionate, emphatic and compassionate approaches and practices needs to be embedded, through the demonstration of caring actions. For example, having a well-being strategy will be useless if there is a bullying and blame culture, incivility, disrespect, micro-managing, and self-interest because bullying and blame and these undesirable behaviours have a negative impact on employee well-being. Compassion, like well-being, needs to be weaved into the fabric of the organisation and can be done through organisational objectives, compassion fun games, coaching culture, reward and recognition, social networks and responding to suffering (Meechan, 2018). Therefore, compassionate leadership is an integral competence and skill that organisational leaders and managers should develop to promote employee well-being and foster effectiveness in the employment relationship and in organisations in the pursuit of healthy, 'WELL', and productive workplaces.

Stakeholder well-being

Stakeholder domain of well-being identifies collective, community empowerment, and quality relationships with stakeholders (Delle, 2007; Sixsmith and Boneham, 2007). The key themes outlined by the stakeholder well-being dimension include: relationships with external stakeholders, ethical practice and corporate social responsibility. Baptiste's (2009) study revealed that, in the public sector quality relationships between employees and counsellors, members of parliament, and customers are important for employees' well-being at work. Moreover, Baptiste (2009) advocates that organisations can convince their stakeholders that they are serious about good governance, ethical practice, and corporate social responsibility by demonstrating their commitment through HRM practices, fairness, compassionate leadership of leaders, line managers and employees throughout the organisation (Cox et al., 2006). Fair work practices and a culture that has compassion as a central thread of its practices and functioning, will deliver high quality service delivery to its customers and stakeholders, thereby enhancing organisational stakeholders' well-being and assist with building and maintaining strong relationships.

Organisational well-being perspective

The organisational perspective of well-being entails four domains: humanistic and fair practices, organisational financial, workplace well-being management, and work/organisational well-being. This perspective focuses on the interaction that occurs within the work organisational context which influences both individual and group experiences of the employment relationship.

Humanistic and fair practices

Literature states that humanistic and fair practices enhance employee commitment, job satisfaction, engagement and employee well-being (Guest, 2002; Kersley et al., 2006). Baptiste (2009) conducted research with senior managers in the public sector to find out which practices or organisational activities promoted their well-being at work (HSE, 2004). The research revealed that managers' well-being is strongly linked to eight organisational factors which include: working time arrangements, stress management, communication strategies, reward strategies, management development, team working, relationships with stakeholders and clarification and reduction in change initiatives (Cox et al., 2006). These are all associated with individual, group and organisational perspectives of the multidimensional well-being paradigm. Moreover, the importance of fair treatment and well-being was captured by Currie (2001) who claims that when people feel that they have been unfairly treated they experience a series of injustices, they feel hurt, slighted and in many cases frustrated because feelings of inferiority preoccupy the mind and dominate one's thoughts (Robertson et al., 2008). Currie also points out that the degree to which individuals are affected by unfair treatment varies, and perceived unfairness is a significant demotivator. In support, Newall (2002) argues that the victims of discrimination become alienated by the way they are treated, which ultimately affects the quality of their work life and performance. Employees may also become less amendable to accepting performance targets, resulting in rising absence rates, increase turnover and work-related stress (HSE, 2007; MacDonald, 2005; Wentling and Palma-Rivas, 1998).

One perceived dehumanised and unfair practice is that of bullying and harassment in the workplace. The literature highlights that bullying is a complex and multi-causal phenomenon influenced by the interaction between individuals' situational and organisational factors (Hoel and

Salin, 2003; Rayner and Hoel, 1997). From an individual perspective, bullying can take place between managers and employees and amongst subordinates. Situations like organisational downsizing and changes can influence bullying in organisations (Peyton, 2003). Moreover, Baptiste (2007) asserts that practices like praise and recognition, feeling valued and respected, feeling a sense of purpose, and the ability to trust management are factors that can promote a sense of fairness, support and consequently employee well-being that will positively influence the employment relationship between the employer and employee (HSE, 2004).

From an organisational perspective, organisations can be perceived by their employees as behaving as a bully, based on practices and procedures used to oppress, demean or humiliate the workforce (CIPD, 2008; Fineman, 2007). These can include external pressures from stakeholder groups; history and culture that can develop behaviours associated with institutionalised bullying (CIPD, 2009); senior team tactics resulting in harsh and uncaring actions (Salin, 2003); and process bullying involving oppressive organisational practices (e.g. withdrawal of overtime) that are employed so frequently and consistently that employees feel victimised by them (Hoel and Salin, 2003; Simpson and Cohen, 2004). Central to this view, Fineman (2007) points out that bullying and violence are the dark side of working life, are often hidden but invariably devastating for victims, leading to negative emotions such as discontent, rage, fear, anger, revenge and betrayal. In essence, these experiences may negatively affect the psychological contract, trust, fairness perceptions and ultimately well-being of employees within organisations (Guest and Conway, 2009).

Furthermore, CIPD research showed that 83% of organisations, 90% in the public sector have anti-bullying policies but highlighted that bullying is still happening (CIPD, 2009). However, despite research done in this area, bullying at work still remains an under-researched, under-reported and under-analysed phenomenon (Harrington and Rayner, 2010). Even further, there appears to be a 'silence' in the literature about employees' perspectives and reactions to their working life experiences relating to bullying at work and the effects of bullying at work to their well-being. This book seeks to contribute towards the debate in this area.

Organisational financial well-being

The key themes outlined by organisational financial well-being domain include: the challenges of economic changes, reformation due to modernisation, and expenditure reduction. The organisational financial domain can be as a result of adverse changes in the external environment due to tough economic conditions – resulting in reformation and expenditure reduction that is likely to have implications on the organisation's bottom line as well as the employees well-being. For example, at the time of writing this book the UK public sector in particular was facing challenges as a result of the recession, downsizing, expenditure reduction, continuous changes and budget limitations. Organisational Financial well-being has implications for all the other domains of well-being and underpins the holistic working life experiences of individuals as well as the financial health of the organisation. In support, Cartwright and Cooper (2009) state that organisational financial well-being is important for organisations and their members in order to be able to transform and adapt to changing circumstances more effectively than their competitors. They also point out that the success of an organisation is invariably judged on the basis of its financial performance and its ability to provide high-quality goods and services over time. Echoing this view, Bakke (2005) claims that joy-filled workplaces improve financial performance and ensure that employees have meaningful and enjoyable work in a healthy working environment (Baptiste, 2007, 2009; Currie, 2001; Newall, 2002). If the financial well-being of an organisation is not healthy and leaders and managers have to function with limited budgets and expenditure reduction ideology, these approaches have implications for job insecurity, increased workloads, job-related stress and strain, stress related absence and mental ill-health, which all will be perceived by employees as psychological contract breach and consequently negatively impact employees' well-being and performance.

Wellness management well-being

Organisations have adopted different approaches to workplace well-being and wellness management. There is a lot to be explored and discovered in the field of workplace wellness as organisational leaders have to consider workplace diversity, different generations at work, genders, diverse faiths, age groups, obesity-related disease, poor health conditions, mental ill-health, health care costs, are all as daunting as ever (CCOHS, 2017; Putnam, 2015). There is innovative thinking from other industries that are adopted for workplace wellness by applying promising practices from workplace wellness along with principles from related field like education, learning and development, organisational development, psychology, and even a discipline called 'design thinking' is drawn from to promote the overall culture of well-being at work through diverse programs (Putnam, 2015). According to CIPD's (2019) health and well-being research, most organisations take some action to promote employee well-being, but there remains considerable variation in how strategic and proactive approaches to wellness management are implemented. Some organisations have standalone well-being strategy, but most act on an ad hoc basis (CIPD, 2019). Wellness programs adopted by most organisations include: programme designed to promote mental health to a large or moderate extent through collective/social relationships, physical health and values/principles are commonly promoted, personal growth and good lifestyle choices. Programmes to promote financial well-being is also promoted through well-being benefits on offer by different organisations. Additional well-being management programmes include: health promotion, employee support, insurance/protection initiatives, lifestyle management programmes. *Health Promotions* entails: free eye tests, advice on healthy eating/lifestyle, in-house gym and/or subsidised gym membership, free flu vaccinations, health screening, programmes to encourage physical fitness, well-being days, regular on-site relaxation or exercise classes, access to complementary therapies (reflexology and message) (ShapeUp, 2011). *Employee Support*, provides access to counselling service, employee assistance programme, access to physiotherapy and other therapies, financial education (welfare loans for financial hardship), and stop smoking support (CIPD, 2019; Chen and Cooper, 2014; Dundon et al., 2004). *Insurance/Protection Initiatives*, can include private medical insurance, health cash plans, long-term disability/permanent health insurance, dental cash plans, group income protection, self-funded health plans/healthcare trust, personal accident insurance, and critical illness insurance (Willis, 2014). *Lifestyle Management Programme*, include weight control programme, fitness, wellness coaching, lunch & learns/onsite seminars, tobacco cession programmes, wellness resources, online programmes/ engagement platforms, drug/alcohol abuse programmes, stress management programmes and disease management (CIPD, 2019; Putnam, 2015).

Healthy work/organisational well-being

A healthy workplace is one that includes effective policies for dealing with all of the 'people' aspects of employment such as diversity and inclusion, communication and consultation, engagement and work-life balance (CIPD, 2019). The salient points outlined by the healthy work/organisational well-being domain include: diversity management, job security, job design, performance, and the promotion of a positive and healthy work environment. The UK workforce is multicultural and diverse in nature and, as highlighted by Newall (2002) organisations should pay attention to equal opportunities and diversity management in order to avoid inter-group hostility, frustration and prejudice in order to create a productive environment in which organisational goals are met efficiently and effectively by making best use of individual talent and potential (CIPD, 2010). Echoing this view, Wentling and Palma-Rivas (1998) state that companies that encourage diversity will be happier and healthier places in which to work, as diversity can lead to better work relationships, more effective team working, motivated employees and less conflict and misunderstandings between employees resulting in more satisfied and happy employees (Currie, 2001). Wright (2005) critiques this view and suggests that diversity can lead to increasing conflict, lowering morale, resulting in less effective teams and more dissatisfaction.

Moreover, Hellgren et al. (1999) point out that feeling comfortable at work is associated with a positive perception of the supportiveness of the organisational climate since insecurity is a key dimension of negative well-being. According to Tehrani et al. (2007) and Bakke (2005) the organisational domain of well-being can be exhibited by healthy institutions promoting an environment that makes work exciting, fulfilling, rewarding, stimulating and enjoyable. In support, Meechan (2018) argues that organisations that promote a compassionate culture that demonstrates support, caring, and empathetic culture are more likely to promote employee well-being and in turn enhanced performance. Moreover, Mowbray (2009) maintains that the relationship between individual well-being and personal performance is well established, indicating that people who feel well and valued perform better than those who feel ill. Mowbray also states that well-being and performance may be idiosyncratic and the environment in which individuals live and work has a major and significant influence on how individuals respond to their own feelings of well-being (MacDonald, 2005; Mowbray, 2009). Central to this view, Linley et al. (2010) state that an emotionally healthy workplace is achievement oriented, financially sound, has a solid customer base, emphasises cooperation over competition, enhances motivation and effort and can afford to be optimistic about its future (Currie, 2001; Dundon et al., 2004; MacDonald, 2005; Newall, 2002).

To this end, Baptiste (2009) explains that well-being has become one of the most important issues of the twenty-first-century world of work – a challenge not just for individuals in terms of their mental and physical health but for employers and governments who have started to assess its social and financial implications (Wainwright and Heaver, 2010). Echoing this view, O'Reilly (2009) advocates that well-being has now become a main concern than it was previously and should be embraced by organisations as a priority as it is a common sense approach to business. O'Reilly also contends that organisations that do not view employee well-being as important could find themselves marginalised in the future. Supporting this view, Grant et al. (2007) and Wainwright and Heaver (2010) state that contemporary organisations that foster well-being are perceived as employers of 'best practice' and are recognised by current and prospective employees as offering a desirable place to work.

Conclusion

This chapter reviewed literature that was considered relevant based on the variables studied in this book. The chapter reveals that the history and development of HRM and Well-being research have appeared to have come full circle as people management originated from the welfare philosophy and shifted ideologies for decades, resulting in focusing on welfare thinking in the twenty-first century, known now as employee well-being at work. This chapter developed a multidimensional workplace well-being perspective model, that highlights individuals, groups and organisation to give a better understanding of the diverse layers of workplace well-being that should be taken into consideration to facilitate positive employment relations, leader-member-exchange, perceived organisational support, justice perceptions, positive well-being, reduction in absences and mental ill-health and enhanced performance.

References

AEGON (Scottish Equitable Plc), and Centre for Economics and Business Research Report (CEBR) (2018) *Financial Well-Being in the Workplace: A Summary of the Aegon and Centre for Economic and Business Research Report*, www.aegon.co.uk/financialwell-being (accessed 1st January, 2019).

AEGON (Scottish Equitable Plc), and Centre for Economics and Business Research Report (CEBR) (2019) *The Challenges Physical Workers Face in Preparing for Retirement*, Aegon Retirement Readiness Survey 2018, Strategy and Sustainability, https://www.aegon.com/contentassets/e072709f2fc64309b77 8e61e6fba5acd/the-unique-retirement-challenges-of-workers-in-physically-demanding-jobs.pdf (accessed 20th October 2019).

Adler, P.S., and Kwon, S.W. (2002) 'Social Capital: Prospects for a New Concept', *Academy of Management Review*, Vol. 27(1): 17–40.

Alban-Metcalfe, R.J., and Alimo-Metcalfe, B. (2000) 'The Transformational Leadership Questionnaire (TLQ-LGV): A Convergent and Discriminant Validity Study', *Leadership and Organisation Development Journal*, Vol. 21: 280–296.

Armstrong, K. (2011) *Twelve Steps to a Compassionate Life*, London: The Bodley Head.

Bakke, D.W. (2005) *Joy at Work: A Revolutionary Approach to Fun on the Job*, Seattle: PVG Publishers.

Baptiste, N.R. (2007) 'Line Management Leadership: Implications for Employee Well-Being', in G.P. Clarkson (Ed.) *Developing Leadership Research, Chapters from the Northern Leadership Academy Fellow 2007 Conference*, pp. 229–238, Leeds: Leeds University Business School, Leeds University Press Financial Services.

Baptiste, N.R. (2008) 'Tightening the Link between Employee Well-Being at Work and Performance: A New Dimension for HRM', *Management Decisions*, Vol. 46(2): 284–309.

Baptiste, N.R. (2009) 'Fun and Well-Being: Insights from Senior Managers in a Local Authority', *Employee Relations*, Vol. 31(6): 600–612.

Baruch, Y. (2009) 'Stress and Careers', in C. Cooper, J. Campbell, and Q.M. Schabracq (Eds.) *International Handbook of Work and Health Psychology*, Oxford: Wiley-Blackwell.

Becker, H.S., and Carper, J.W. (1956) 'The Development of Identification with an Occupation', *American Sociological Review*, Vol. 32: 341–347.

Black, D.C. (2008) *Working for a Healthier Tomorrow*. London: TSO.

Blau, P.M. (2006) *Exchange and Power in Social Life: New Introduction by the Author*, 10th Edition, London: Transaction Publisher.

Bolton, S., and Houlihan, M. (2007) 'Beginning the Search for the H in HRM', in S. Bolton and M. Houlihan (Eds.) *Searching for the H in Human Resource Management: Theory, Practice and Workplace Context*, Basingstoke: Palgrave Macmillan.

Boyatzis, R.E., Smith, M.L., and Blaize, N. (2006) 'Developing Sustainable Leaders through Coaching and Compassion', *Academy of Management Learning and Education*, Vol. 5(1): 8–24.

Brewster, C., Mayrhofer, W., and Morley, M. (2004) *Human Resource Management in Europe: Evidence of Convergence?* London: Elsevier Butterworth Heinemann.

Burke, R.J., Koyuncu, M., and Fiksenbaum, L. (2008) 'Work Experiences, Satisfactions and Psychological Well-Being of Female and Male Managers in the Hospitality Sector in Turkey', *Journal of Opportunities International*, Vol. 27(6): 505–518.

Burke, R.J., and Ng, E. (2006) 'The Changing Nature of Work Organisations: Implications for Human Resource Management', *Human Resource Management Review*, Vol. 16: 86–94.

Burack, E.H. (1999) 'Spirituality in the Workplace', *Journal of Organisational Change Management*, Vol. 12(4): 280–291.

Campion, M.A., and McClelland, C.L. (1993) 'Follow-Up and Extension of the Interdisciplinary Costs and Benefits of Enlarged Jobs', *Journal of Applied Psychology*, Vol. 78(3): 339–351.

Canadian Centre for Management Development (2002) 'A Fine Balance: A Manager's Guide to Workplace Well-Being', CCMD Roundtable on Workplace Well-being, Canada.

Canadian Centre for Occupational Health and Safety (CCOHS) (2017) *Making the Case for Workplace Wellness Programs*, www.recyclingproductnews.com/article/26893/making-the-case-for-workplace-wellness-programs (accessed 20th November, 2017).

Cartwright, S., and Cooper, C.L. (2009) *The Oxford Handbook of Organisational Well-Being*, Oxford: Oxford University Press.

Chechak, D., and Csiernik, R. (2014) 'Canadian Perspectives on Conceptualizing and Responding to Workplace Violence', *Journal of Workplace Behaviour Health*, Vol. 29: 55–74.

Chen, P.Y., and Cooper, C.L. (2014) *Work and Well-Being: A Complete Reference Guide*, Vol. 3, Ed. P.Y. Chen and C.L. Cooper, UK: John Wiley & Sons Ltd.

CIPD (2005) *Bullying at Work: Beyond Policies to a Culture of Respect*, London: Chartered Institute of Personnel Development.

CIPD (2006) *Working Life: Employee Attitudes and Engagement*, Research Report, London: Chartered Institute of Personnel Development.

CIPD (2007) *Rewarding Work: The Vital Role of Line Managers, Change Agenda*, London: Chartered Institute of Personnel Development.

CIPD (2008) *Bully at Work and the 2007 Code of Practice*, London: Chartered Institute of Personnel Development.

CIPD (2009) *Harassment and Bullying at Work*, London: Chartered Institute of Personnel and Development.

CIPD (2010) *CIPD, IIP and HSE Join Forces to Issue Management Guidance to Help Employers Tackle Increasing Levels of Stress at Work as Recession Bites*, London: Chartered Institute of Personnel and Development.

CIPD (2019) *Health and Well-Being at Work, in Partnership with Simplyhealth*, London: Chartered Institute of Personnel and Development, Survey Report, April.

Clarke, S., and Cooper, C.L. (2004) *Managing the Risk of Workplace Stress*, London: Routledge.

Clutterback, D. (2003) *Managing Work-Life Balance: A Guide to HR in Achiev-ing Organisational and Individual Change*, London: CIPD.

Cohen, L., Manion, L., and Morrison, K. (2003) *Research Methods in Education*, 5th Edition, London: Routledge Falmer, Taylor and Francis Group.

Cooper, C.L., Dewe, P.J., and O'Driscoll, M.P. (2001) *Organisational Stress: A Review and Critique of Theory, Research and Application*, Newbury Park, CA: Sage Publications.

Cooper, C.L., and Marshall, J. (1976) 'Occupational Sources of Stress: A Review of the Literature Relating to Coronary Heart Disease and Mental Ill-Health', *Journal of Occupational Psychology*, Vol. 49: 11–28.

Cooper, C.L., and Quick, J.C. (1999) *Fast Facts-Stress and Strain*, Oxford: Health Press Limited.

Cooper, C.L., and Robertson, I. (2001) *Well-Being in Organisations: A Reader for Students and Practitioners*, Chichester: John Wiley and Sons Limited.

Cowen, E.L. (1991), In Pursuit of Wellness, *American Psychologist*, Vol. 46(4): 404–408.

Cox, A., Zagelmeyer, S., and Marchington, M. (2006) 'Embedding Employee Involvement and Participation at Work', *Human Resource Management Jour-nal*, Vol. 16(3): 250–267.

Cully, M., O'Reilly, A., Millward, J., Forth, S., Woodland, G., Dix, G., and Bryson, A. (1999) *British at Work: As Depicted by the 1998 Workplace Employee Rela-tions Survey*, London: Routledge Publishers.

Currie, D. (2001) *Managing Employee Well-Being*, Oxford: Chandos Publishing Oxford Limited.

Daniels, G., and French, S. (2006) 'The Growth of Work-Life Balance and Family-Friendly Policies and the Implications for Employment Relations', *Interna-tional Employment Relations Review*, Vol 12(2): 9–18.

Danna, K., and Griffin, R.W. (1999) 'Health and Well-Being in the Workplace: A Review and Synbook of the Literature', *Journal of Management*, Vol. 25(3): 357–384.

Delle, F.A. (2007) 'Individual Development and Community Empowerment: Suggestions from Studies on Optimal Experience', in J. Haworth and G. Hart (Eds.) *Well-Being: Individual, Community and Social Perspectives*, pp. 41–56, Basingstoke: Palgrave MacMillan.

Department of Health (2007) *Commissioning Framework for Health and Wellbe-ing*, London: DOH (www.dh.gov.uk/publications) March 2007.

Department of Works and Pensions (DWP) (2005) *Exploring How General Prac-titioners Work with Patients on Sick Leave*, Research Report 257, Department of Works and Pensions, June.

Diener, E., Oishi, S., and Lucas, R.E. (2003) 'Personality, Culture, and Subjective Well-Being: Emotional and Cognitive Evaluations of Life', *Annual Review Psy-chology*, Vol. 54: 403–425.

Diener, E. (1984) 'Subjective Wellbeing', *Psychological Bulletin*, Vol. 95: 542–575.

Diener, E. (1996) 'Traits Can Be Powerful, But Are Not Enough: Lessons From Subjective Well-Being', *Journal of Research in Personality*, Vol. 30: 389–399.

Dundon, T., Wilkinson, A., Marchington, M., and Ackers, P. (2004) 'The Mean-ing and Purpose of Employee Voice', *International Journal of Human Resource Management*, Vol. 15(6): 1149–1170.

Dutton, J.E., Worline, M.C., Frost, P.J., and Lilius, J. (2006) 'Explaining Compas-sion Organizing', *Administrative Science Quarterly*, Vol. 5(1): 59–96.

Economic and Social Research Council (ESRC) (2006) 'Health and Well-Being at Work of Working Age People', Seminar Series: Mapping the public policy landscape, Swindon: ESRC.

Economic and Social Research Council (ESRC) (2010) *Well-Being and Working Life: Towards an Evidence-Based Policy Agenda*, London: HSE/ESRC.

Eid, M., and Larsen, R.J. (2008) *The Science of Subjective Wellbeing*, London: The Guilford Press.

Eisenberger, R., Rhoades, L., and Cameron, J. (1999) 'Does Pay for Performance Increase or Decrease Perceived Self-Determination and Intrinsic Motivation?', *Journal of Personality and Social Psychology*, Vol. 77: 1026–1040.

Emmons, R.A. (1991) 'Personal Striving, Daily Life Events and Psychological and Physical Well-Being', *Journal of Personality*, Vol. 59(3): 453–472.

Ferraro, F., Pfeffer, J., and Sutton, R.I. (2005) 'Economics Language and Assumptions: How Theories Can Become Self-Fulfilling', *Academy of Management Review*, Vol. 30(1): 8–24.

Figley, C.R. (1995) *Compassionate Fatigue: Toward a New Understanding of the Costs of Caring*, compassion fatigue, Tulane University, www.researchgate.net/publication/232604330

Fineman, S. (2006) 'On Being Positive: Concerns and Counterpoints', *Academy of Management Review*, Vol. 31(2): 270–291.

Fineman, S. (2007) *Understanding Emotions at Work*, London: Sage Publishers.

Fisher, J. (2005) *Dimensions of Spirituality Christian Research Association*, www.cre.org.au/pages/00000072.cgi (accessed 12th June, 2010).

Fombrun, C., Tichy, N., and Devanna, M. (1984) *Strategic Human Resource Management*, New York: John Wiley and Sons.

Forth, J., and Stokes, L. (2006) 'A Regional Perspective on Employment Relations: Tabulations from the 2004 Workplace Employment Relations Survey', Report to the Advisory, Conciliation and Arbitration Services (ACAS), Final Report 8th September.

Freshman, B. (1999) 'An Exploratory Analysis of Definitions and Applications of Spirituality in the Workplace', *Journal of Organisational Change Management*, Vol. 12(4): 318–327.

Fried, Y., and Ferris, G.R. (1987) 'The Validity of the Job Characteristics Model: A Review and Meta-Analysis', *Personnel Psychology*, Vol. 40(2): 287–322.

Fryer, B. (2013) *The Rise of Compassionate Management (Finally)*, Boston, MA: Harvard Business School Blog Network.

George, C. (2009) *The Psychological Contract: Managing and Developing Professional Groups*, Work and Organisational Psychology, Berkshire: Open University Press.

Goetz, J.L., Keltner, D., Simon-Thomas, E. (2010) 'Compassion: An Evolutionary Analysis and Empirical Review', *Psychological Bulletin*, Vol. 136(3): 351.

Gould, S. (1979) 'Characteristics of Planners in Upwardly Mobile Occupations', *Academy of Management Journal*, Vol. 22: 539–550.

Gould, S., and Penley, L.E. (1984) 'Career Strategy and Salary Progression: A Study of Their Relationship in a Municipal Bureaucracy', *Organisational Behaviour and Human Performance*, Vol. 34: 244–265.

Gould-Williams, J. (2003) The importance of HR practices and workplace trust in achieving superior performance: a study of public sector organizations, *International Journal of Human Resource Management*, Vol. 14: 28–54.

Graham, C. (2009) *Happiness around the World: The Paradox of Happy Peasants and Miserable Millionaires*, Oxford: Oxford University Press.

Grant, A.M., Christianson, M., and Price, R. (2007) 'Happiness, Health or Relationships? Managerial Practices and Employee Well-Being Tradeoffs', *The Academy of Management*, Vol. 21(3): 51–63.

Grant, A.M., and Spence, G.B. (2010) 'Using Coaching and Positive Psychology to Promote a Flourishing Workforce: A Model of Goal-Striving and Mental Health', in P.A. Linley, S. Harrington, and N. Garcea (Eds.) *Oxford Handbook of Positive Psychology and Work*, Oxford: Oxford University Press.

Green, F., and Tsitsianis, N. (2004) 'An Investigation of National Trends of Job Satisfaction in Britain and Germany', *British Journal of Industrial Relations*, Vol. 43(3): 401–429.

Green, F., and Whitfield, K. (2009) 'Employees Experiences at Work', in W. Brown, A. Bryson, J. Forth, and K. Whitfield (Eds.) *The Evolution of the Modern Workplace*, Cambridge: Cambridge University Press.

Grey, C. (2005) *A Very Short, Fairly Interesting and Reasonably Cheap Book about Studying Organisations*, London: Sage Publications.

Grint, K. (2005) *Leadership: Limits and Possibilities*, Basingstoke: Management, Work & Organisations, Palgrave Macmillan.

Guest, D.E. (2002) 'Human Resource Management, Corporate Performance and Employee Well-Being: Building the Worker into HRM', *Journal of Industrial Relations*, Vol. 44(3): 335–358.

Guest, D.E. (2006) 'Human Resource Management-the Workers Verdict', *Human Resource Management Journal*, Vol. 9(3): 5–26.

Guest, D.E., and Conway, N. (2004) *Employee Well-Being and the Psychological Contract*, London: CIPD.

Guest, D.E., and Conway, N. (2009) 'Health and Well-Being: The Role of the Psychological Contract', in C. Cooper, J.C. Quick, and M. J. Schabracq (Eds.) *International Handbook of Work and Health Psychology*, pp. 9–23, London: Wiley-Blackwell Publication.

Guerrier, Y., and Adib, A. (2003) 'Work at Leisure and Leisure at Work: A Study of the Emotional Labour of Tour Reps', *Human Relations*, Vol. 56(11): 1399–1417.

Gutherie, J.P., Coate, C.J., and Schwoerer, C.E. (1998) 'Career Management Strategies: The Role of Personality', *Journal of Management Psychology*, Vol. 13(5/6): 371–386.

Hackman, J.R., and Oldham, G. R. (1980) *Work Redesign*, Reading, MA: Addison-Wesley Publishers.

Harrington, S., and Rayner, C. (2010) 'Look before You Leap or Drive Right in? The Use of Moral Courage in Response to Workplace Bullying', in P.A. Linley, S. Harrington, and N. Garcea (Eds.) *Oxford Handbook of Positive Psychology and Work*, pp. 265–276, Oxford: Oxford University Press.

Harter, J.K., Schmidt, F.L., and Hayes, T.L. (2002) 'Because-Unit-Level Relationship between Employee Satisfaction, Employee Engagement, and Business Outcomes: A Meta-Analysis', *Journal of Applied Psychology*, Vol. 87(2): 268–279.

Harvey, S.B., Henderson, M., Lelliott, P., and Hotopf, M. (2009) 'Mental Health and Employment: Much Work Still to Be Done', *The British Journal of Psychiatry*, Vol. 194: 201–203, doi:10.1192/bjp.bp.108.055111

Haworth, J., and Hart, G. (2007) *Well-Being: Individual, Community and Social Perspectives*, Basingstoke: Palgrave MacMillan.

Health and Safety Executive (2004) 'Managing Sickness Absence and Return to Work: An Employers' and Managers' Guide', *Health and Safety Executive*: 1–60.

Health and Safety Executive (2010) *New Workplace Well-Being Tool*, London: HSE.

Health and Social Care Information Centre (HSCIC) (2016) *Statistics on Obesity, Physical Activity and Diet: England 2016*, The National Statistics Publication, published 28th April, www.hscic.gov.uk

Health Work and Well-Being Executive (HWWE) (2010) www.workingforhealth. gov.uk/ (accessed 10th April, 2010) working in partnership with DOH, DWP, HSE, Welsh Assembly Government, and The Scottish Government.

Hellgren, J., Sverke, M., and Isaksson, K. (1999) 'A Two-Dimensional Approach to Job Insecurity: Consequences for Employee Attitudes and Well-Being', *European Journal of Work and Organisational Psychology*, Vol. 8(9): 179–195.

Hesketh, I., and Cooper, C.L. (2014) 'Leaveism at Work', *Occupational Medicine*, Vol. 64(3): 146–147, https://academic.oup.com/occmed/article/64/3/146/ 1439077

Hoel, H., and Salin, D. (2003) 'Organisational Antecedents of Workplace Bullying', in S. Einarsen, H. Hoel, D. Zapf, and C.L. Cooper (Eds.) *Bullying and Emotional Abuse in the Workplace: International Perspectives in Research and Practice*, pp. 203–218, London: Taylor and Francis.

Hoel, H., Rayner, C., and Cooper, C. (2001) Workplace Bullying, in C.L. Cooper and I.T. Robertson (Eds.) *Wellbeing in Organisations: A Reader for Students and Practitioners*, pp. 55–90, Chichester: John Wiley and Sons Limited.

Holland, J.L. (1997) *Making Vocational Choices: A Theory of Careers*, 3rd Edition, Englewood Cliffs, NJ: Prentice-Hall Publishers.

Holman, D. (2002) 'Employee Well-Being in Call Centres', *Human Resource Management Journal*, Vol. 12(4): 35–50.

Holt, S., and Marques, J. (2012) 'Empathy in Leadership: Appropriate or Misplaced? An Empirical Study on a Topic That Is Asking for Attention', *Journal of Business Ethics*, Vol. 105: 95–105.

Houston, D.M. (2005) *Work-Life Balance in the 21st Century*, New York: Palgrave Macmillan.

HSE (2007) *Workplace Health, Safety and Welfare: A Short Guide for Management*, London: Health and Safety Executive.

Jain, A.K., Giga, S.I., and Cooper, C. (2009) 'Employee Well-Being, Control and Organisational Commitment', *Leadership and Organisational Development Journal*, Vol. 30(3): 256–273.

Jex, S.M. (1998) *Stress and Job Performance: Theory, Research and Application*, Newbury Park, CA: Sage Publication.

Kanov, J.M., Maitlis, S., Worline, M.C., Dutton, J.E., Frost, P.J., and Lilius, J. M. (2004) 'Compassion in Organisational Life', *American Behavioral Scientist*, Vol. 47(6): 808–827.

Karasek, R.A., and Theorell, T. (1990) *Healthy Work: Stress, Productivity, and the Reconstruction of Working Life*, New York: Basic Books.

Katzell, R.A., and Thompson, D.E. (1990) 'Work Motivation: Theory and Practice', *American Psychologist*, Vol. 45(2): 144–153.

Kersley, B., Alphin, C., Forth, J., Bryson, A., Bewley, H., Dix, G., and Oxenbridge, S. (2006) *Inside the Workplace: Findings from the 2004 Workplace Employment Relations Survey*, London: Routledge.

Kramer, R.M., and Tyler, T.R. (1996) *Trust in Organisations*, London: Sage Publications.

Kramer, R.M. (1999) 'Trust and Distrust in Organisations: Emerging Perspectives, Enduring Questions', *Annual Review of Psychology*, Vol. 50(1): 569–598.

Krishnakumar, S., and Neck, C. (2002) 'The "What", "Why" and "How" or Spirituality in the Workplace', *Journal of Managerial Psychology*, Vol. 17(3): 153–164.

Legge, K. (2005) *Human Resource Management: Rhetorics and Realities*, London: Palgrave Macmillan Publishers.

Lepak, D.A., and Snell, S.A. (2005) 'The Human Resource Architecture: Towards a Theory of Human Capital Allocation', in S. Little and T. Ray (Eds.) *Managing Knowledge: An Essential Reader*, London: Sage Publishers.

Lewis, D., and Rayner, C. (2003) 'Bullying and Human Resource Management: A Wolf in Sheep's Clothing?', in S. Einarsen, H. Hoel, D. Zapf, and C.L. Cooper (Eds.) *Bullying and Emotional Abuse in the Workplace: International Perspectives in Research and Practice*, pp. 370–382, London: Taylor and Francis.

Lewis, S., and Purcell, C. (2007) 'Wellbeing, Paid Work and Personal Life', in J. Haworth and G. Hart (Eds.) *Wellbeing: Individual, Community and Social Perspectives*, Basingstoke: Palgrave Macmillan.

Lilius, J.M., Worline, M.C., Maltlis, S., Kanov, J., Dutton, J.E., and Frost, P. (2008) 'The Contours and Consequences of Compassion at Work', *Journal of Organisational Behaviour*, Vol. 29(2): 193–218.

Linley, P.A., Harrington, S., and Garcea, N. (Eds.) (2010) *Oxford Handbook of Positive Psychology at Work*, Oxford: Oxford University Press.

MacDonald, L.A.C. (2005) *Wellness at Work: Protecting and Promoting Employee Well-Being*, London: Chartered Institute of Personnel and Development.

Maellaro, R., and Whittington, J.L. (2009) 'Management Development for Well-Being and Survival: Developing the Whole Person', in C. Cooper, J. Campbell, and Q.M. Schabracq (Eds.) *International Handbook of Work and Health Psychology*, Oxford: Wiley-Blackwell.

March, J.G. (1991) 'Exploration and Exploration in Organisational Learning', *Organisational Science*, Vol. 2(1): 71–87.

Mathieu, J.E., and Zajac, D.M. (1990) 'A Review and Meta-Analysis of the Antecedents, Correlates and Consequences of Organisational Commitment', *Psychological Bulletin*, Vol. 108: 171–194.

McGovern, P., Gratton, L., and Hailey, H.V. (1997) 'Human Resource Management on the Line?', *Human Resource Management Journal*, Vol. 7(4): 12–29.

Meechan, F. (2018) *Compassion at Work Toolkit*, Alliance Manchester Business School, University of Manchester, www.researchgate.net/publication/322404395_Compassion_at_Work_Tooklit

Meyer, J., and Allen, N. (1997) *Commitment in the Workplace*, London: Sage Publications.

Morrow, P.C. (1983) 'Concept Redundancy in Organisational Research: The Case of Work Commitment', *Academy of Management Review*, Vol. 8: 486–500.

Morrow, P.C. (1993) *The Theory and Measurement of Work Commitment*, London: Greenwich Publication.

Moss, B. (2009) 'Spirituality in the Workplace', in N. Thompson and J. Bates (Eds.) *Promoting Workplace Well-Being*, pp. 141–153, London: Palgrave Macmillan.

Mowbray, D. (2009) *The Well-being and Performance Agenda*, www.the-stress-clinic.net (accessed 15th May, 2010).

Munkes, J.R., and Diehl, M. (2003) 'Matching or Competition? Performance Comparison Processes in an Idea Generation Task', *Group Processes and Intergroup Relations*, Vol. 6(3): 305–320.

Neff, K. (2013) 'The Development and Validation of a Scale to Measure Self-Compassion', *Self and Identity*, Vol. 2(3): 223–250.

Newall, S. (2002) *Creating the Healthy Organisation: Well-Being Diversity and Ethics at Work*, London: Thomson Learning.

Office for National Statistics (2016) *Sickness Absence in the UK Labour Market: 2016*, www.ons.gov.uk/employmentandlabourmarket/peopleinwork/labour productivity/articles/sicknessabsenceinthelabourmarket/2016 (accessed 1st May, 2019).

O'Reilly, S. (2009) *Well-Being: Recession Depression, Personnel Today, Human Resources News*, Strategy and Community, www.personneltoday.com/articles/2009/02/12/49385/well-being-recession-depression.html (accessed 12th June, 2009).

Peccei, R. (2004) 'Human Resource Management and the Search for the Happy Workplace', Erasmus Research Institute of Management, Rotterdam School of Management, Rotterdam School of Economics.

Pinnington, A., and Edwards, T. (2000) *Introduction to Human Resource Management*, Oxford: Oxford University Press.

Perri 6 (2007) 'Sense and Solidarities: Politics and Human Well-Being', in J. Haworth and G. Hart (Eds.) *Well-Being: Individual, Community and Social Perspectives*, Basingstoke: Palgrave Macmillan.

Peyton, P.R. (2003) *Dignity at Work: Eliminate Bullying and Create a Positive Work Environment*, London: Routledge Publishers.

Podsakoff, P.M., MacKenzie, S.B., Panie, J.B., and Bachrach, D.G. (2000) 'Organisational Citizenship Behaviours: A Critical Review of the Theoretical and Empirical Literature and Suggestions for Future Research', *Journal of Management*, Vol. 26(3): 513–563.

Poorkavoos, M. (2016) *Compassionate Leadership: What Is It and Why Do Organisations Need More of It?*, Research Chapter, Roffey Park, www.rof feypark.com

Prilleltensky, I., and Prilleltensky, O. (2007) 'Webs of Well-Being: The Interdependence of Personal, Relational, Organisational and Communal Well-Being', in J. Haworth and G. Hart (Eds.) *Well-Being: Individual, Community and Social Perspectives*, Basingstoke: Palgrave Macmillan.

Purcell, J., and Hutchinson, S. (2007) Front-Line Managers as agents in the HRM performance causal chain: theory, analysis and evidence. *Human Resource Management Journal*, Vol. 17(1): 3–20.

Putnam, L. (2015) *Workplace Wellness That Works: 10 Steps to Infuse Well-Being and Vitality into Your Organisation*, Hoboken, NJ: John Wiley and Sons.

Randall, D.M., and Cote, J.A. (1991) 'Interrelationships of Work Commitment Constructs', *Work and Occupation*, Vol. 18: 194–211.

Rayner, C., and Hoel, H. (1997) 'A Summary Review of Literature Relating to Workplace Bullying', *Journal of Community and Applied Social Psychology*, Vol. 7: 181–191.

Redman, T., and Wilkinson, A. (2009) *Contemporary Human Resource Management, Text and Cases,* London: Pearson Education.

Reichers, A.E., Wanous, J. P., and Austin, J.T. (1997) 'Understanding and Managing Cynicism about Organisational Change', *Academy of Management Executive,* Vol. 11(1): 48–59.

Renwick, D. (2003) 'HR Managers, Guardians of Employee Well-Being?', *Personnel Review,* Vol. 32(3): 341–359.

Renwick, D. (2009) 'The Origins of Employee Well-Being in Brazil: An Exploratory Analysis', *Employee Relations,* Vol. 31(3): 312–321.

Rhoades, L., and Eisenberger, R. (2002) 'Perceived Organisational Support: A Review of the Literature', *Journal of Applied Psychology,* Vol. 87(4): 698–714.

Robinson, D., Perryman, S., and Hayday, S. (2004) *The Drivers of Employee Engagement,* p. 2, Institute of Employment Studies Report No. 408, Brighton: IES.

Robertson, I.T., Tinline, G., and Robertson, S. (2008) 'Enhancing Staff Well-Being for Organisational Effectiveness', in R.J. Burke and C.L. Cooper (Eds.) *Building More Effective Organisations: HR Management and Performance Practice,* Cambridge: Cambridge University Press.

Rousseau, D.M. (1995) *Psychological Contracts in Organisations: Understanding Written and Unwritten Agreements,* Thousand Oaks, London: Sage Publications.

Rousseau, D.M. (2001) 'Schema, Promise and Mutuality: The Building Blocks of the Psychological Contract', *Journal of Occupational and Organisational Psychology,* Vol. 74: 511–541.

Ryan, R.M., and Deci, E.L. (2001) 'On Happiness and Human Potentials: A Review of Research on Hedonic and Eudaimonic Well-Being', *Annual Review of Psychology,* Vol. 51: 141–166.

Ryan, R.M., & Frederick, C.M. (1997) 'On Energy, Personality, and Health: Subjective Vitality as a Dynamic Reflection of Well-Being', *Journal of Personality,* Vol. 65: 529–565.

Ryff, C.D., and Keyes, C.L.M. (1995) 'The Structure of Psychological Well-Being Revisted', *Journal of Personality and Social Psychology,* Vol. 69: 719–727.

Salin, D. (2003) 'Ways of Explaining Workplace Bullying: A Review of Enabling, Motivating and Precipitating Structures and Processes in the Work Environment', *Human Relations,* Vol. 56(10): 1213–1233.

Schabracq, M.J. (2005) 'Well-Being and Health: What HRM Can Do about It', in R. Burke and C. Cooper (Eds.) *Reinventing HRM: Challenges and New Directions,* pp. 187–206, London: Routledge Taylor Francis Group.

Seligman, M.E.P., and Csikszentmihalyi, M. (2000) 'Positive Psychology: An Introduction', *American Psychologist,* Vol. 55: 5–14.

ShapeUp (2011) *Employer Wellness Survey: Understanding How Large, Self-Insured Employers Approach Employee Wellness,* Providence, RI: ShapeUP, Inc.

Silcox, S. (2007) 'Health Work and Well-Being: Rising to the Public Sector Attendance Management Challenge', *ACAS Policy Discussion Chapter,* (6), May.

Simpson, R., and Cohen, R. (2004) 'Dangerous Work: The Gendered Nature of Bullying in the Context of Higher Education', *Gender, Work and Organisation,* Vol. 11(2): 163–186.

Sinclair, S., Beamer, K., Hack, T.F., McClement, S., Bouchal, S.R., Chochinov, H.M., and Hagen, N.A. (2017) 'Sympathy, Empathy and Compassion: A Grounded Theory Study of Palliative Care Patients' Understandings, Experiences, and Preferences', in *Palliative Medicine,* Vol. 31(5): 437–447.

Sixsmith, J., and Boneham, M. (2007) 'Health, Well-Being and Social Capital', in J. Haworth and G. Hart (Eds.) *Well-Being: Individual, Community and Social Perspectives*, pp. 75–92, Basingstoke, Palgrave MacMillan.

Storey, J. (2007) *Human Resource Management: A Critical Text*, 3rd Edition, London: Thomson Learning.

Strickland, R. (1997) 'Self-Development in a Business Organisation', *Journal of Managerial Psychology*, Vol. 11: 30–39.

Tehrani, N., Humpage, S., Willmott, B., and Haslam, I. (2007) *What's Happening with Well-Being at Work?*, Change Agenda, London: Chartered Institute of Personnel Development.

Terkel, S. (1977) *Working*, Harmondsworth: Penguin Publishers.

Thompson, N., and Bates, J. (Eds.) (2009) *Promoting Workplace Well-Being*, London: Palgrave Macmillan.

Thompson, N. (2006) *Promoting Workplace Learning*, Bristol: Policy Press.

Tuomi, K., Vanhala, S., Nykyri, E., and Janhonen, M. (2004) 'Organisational Practices, Work Demands and the Well-Being of Employees: A Follow-Up Study in the Mental Industry and Retail Trade', *Occupational Medicine*, Vol. 54: 115–121.

Ulrich, D. (1997) *Human Resource Champions: The Next Agenda for Adding Value and Delivering Results*, Boston, MA: Harvard Business School Press.

Wagner-Marsh, F., and Conley, J. (1999) 'The Fourth Wave: The Spirituality-Based Firm', *Journal of Organisational Change Management*, Vol. 12(4): 292–301.

Wainwright, D., and Heaver, E. (2009) 'Can a Better Working Life Cut Sickness Absence Costs', in ESRC (Ed.) *Well-Being and Working Life: Towards an Evidence-Based Policy Agenda*, ESRC Seminar Series Mapping the Public Policy Landscape, London: ESRC.

Warr, P. (2002) *Psychology at Work*, Suffolk: Penguin Group Books.

Weick, K.E. (1992) 'Agenda Setting in Organisational Behaviour', *Journal of Management Inquiry*, Vol. 1(3): 171–182.

Weng, H.Y., Fox, A.S., Shackman, A.J., Stodola, D.E., Caldwell, J.Z., Olson, M.C., Rogers, G.M., and Davidson, R.J. (2013) 'Compassion Training Alters Altruism and Neural Responses to Suffering', *Psychological Science*, Vol. 24(7): 1171–1180.

Wentling, R.M., and Palma-Rivas, N. (1998) 'Current Status and Future Trends of Diversity Initiatives in the Workplace: Diversity Experts' Perspective', *Human Resource Development Quarterly*, Vol. 9(3): 235–253.

Wilkinson, A., Bacon, N., Snell, S., and Redman, T. (Eds.) (2008) *The Sage Handbook of Human Resource Management*, London: Sage Publication.

Williams, S., and Cooper, L. (1999) *Dangerous Waters: Strategies for Improving Well-Being at Work*, Chichester: John Wiley and Sons.

Williams, W., and Cooper, C.L. (1998) 'Measuring Occupational Stress: Development of the Pressure Management Indicator', *Journal of Occupational Health Psychology*, Vol. 3: 306–321.

The Willis Report (2014) *The Willis Health and Productivity Survey 2014*, Willis North America, Inc, Brookfield Place, New York, USA.

Wilson, F. (2010) *Organisational Behaviour and Work: A Critical Introduction*, Oxford: Oxford University Press.

Wilkinson, A. (1998) 'Empowerment: Theory and Practice', *Personal Review*, Vol. 27(1): 40–56.

Wood, S. (2008) 'Job Characteristics, Employee Voice and Well-Being in Britain', *Industrial Relations Journal*, Vol. 39(2): 153–168.

Wood, S., and de Menezes, L. (1998) 'High Commitment Management in the UK: Evidence from the Workplace Industrial Relations Survey and Employers WERS' Manpower and Skills Practices Survey', *Human Relations*, Vol. 51: 485–515.

World Health Organisation (WHO) (1992) *Basic Document*, 39th Edition, Geneva: WHO.

Wright, T.A. (2005) 'The Role of "Happiness" in Organisational Research: Past, Present, and Future Directions', in P.L. Perrewe and D.C. Ganster (Eds.) *Research in Occupational Stress and Well-Being*, Vol. 4, pp. 221–264, Amsterdam: JAI Press.

Part II

The workers' voice

HRM practices, line management leadership and well-being at work

5 Exploring employees quality of working life through observations and documentary analysis in the public sector

Introduction

This chapter presents the findings from field observation and analysis of company documents that contributes towards answering objectives one and two of this study (see Table 5.2). Data collection was done when New Labour was in government over the period 2005 to 2007 which has implications for the study. The observations of the working environment were made by observation of the 'social actors' in the organisation. This chapter is discussed in the first person for emphasis. The analysis of documents reveals what can be expected from the public sector adherence to 'best practice' standards. This is discussed in the context of work environment, partnership working, pay and reward strategy, communication and health safety and welfare management. The chapter concludes with a summary of the key themes discussed.

Field observations

The field observation began with communication and interaction with the HR director, her personal assistant, and informants who provided relevant 'trivia' or details that helped to construct the story (Van Maanen, 1994) of the working life realities of employees in an NPM environment. Field observations made during the pilot and main studies are discussed in the following sections.

Pilot questionnaire and interview observation

The pilot questionnaire was controlled by the HR director's personal assistant as I had no access to employees. The chapter questionnaire with self-posted envelopes was delivered to this gatekeeper (discussed in Chapter 5) and my observation reveals that the council was not liberal in exposing their employees to a researcher although access was granted to conduct the study. At the beginning of the pilot interview phase, I was provided with a small office at the end of the HR department between the chief executive and senior managers' offices to interview respondents.

Once again, I had no control over where the interviews were to be held and this created tensions and challenges that were viewed as salient and given additional consideration in the field notes. The following explains my experience:

> I was escorted into an extremely large open plan office by the personal assistant to the HR director. The office was divided into two main sections, dividing the room equally into two main halves with a pathway in the middle of the two sections stretching from north to south of the office. The location of the office where the interviews were to be kept was the north end of the office and we entered from the south end and as I followed the personal assistant I observed that employees were tightly fitted into this open-planned office layout. They were all working; some typing, some using computers, others reading documents and writing, some searching in drawers and cabinets, and some talking on the phone. As we walked towards the allocated office, I observed some employees observing us with curious expressions on their faces; others pretended not to look but observed what was happening; and yet others appeared not to notice. There was a strange and uncomfortable silence in what appeared to be a tense atmosphere as we walked towards the office. The journey felt like 30 minutes but in reality took no more than two minutes.
>
> (Field notes, 31st July 2006)

When I arrived at the allocated office, I observed that the environment was not conducive for keeping anonymity and confidentiality. This experience was also noted as salient and provided clearer insight of the work environment atmosphere; it is outlined here:

> The room was very small and was located between two offices. The first office to the right belonged to the CEO of the council and the office to the left was occupied by some senior managers. The walls of the office appeared to be delicate and I presumed that sounds could be heard easily from this office as I was able to hear some senior managers talking. There was a glass peep hole in the middle of the door to the office where the interviews were held which also contributed to hindering confidentiality and anonymity. Control of the choice of interview candidates was done by the PA to the HR director and a sheet with the names of candidates and the allocated interview times was given to me fifteen minutes after I arrived. The candidates were mixed according to their job roles and gender and comprised of senior managers, managers, and the PA's for both the HR director and the CEO. As the interviews commenced, managers appeared relaxed as compared to employees who appeared to be slightly uneasy. All candidates appeared almost rehearsed as responses to

questions were fundamentally positive and when asked about challenges faced the majority commented that the council was doing an excellent job. However, one candidate from the list was not available and another employee took her place, who was not originally on the list. There was a great contrast in the responses to questions with this employee compared with the other respondents on the list. The employee that was not originally on the list of interview candidates' responses highlighted positive and negative issues and explored her personal experiences within the council. During the interview she kept asking to be reassured in a silent almost whispering voice that the information given will be kept private and confidential. Once this reassurance was given she continued to open up and discussed issues with what appeared to be with great ease as compared to the other candidates. The setting was almost relaxed but there was still an atmosphere of tension.

(Field notes, 31st July 2006)

My personal impression and feelings from this observation was that a 'controlled and tense' working environment existed. This assumption was substantiated when I was not allowed to have control over how data was collected and which participant could be interviewed. There were instances at the beginning where I had an opportunity to put forward my views about how the research should be conducted but my views were not taken on board as the process was handled in the way the HR Director felt was appropriate. This experience can be associated to a less obvious form of bullying where powerful agents insist that their way of doing things is always right without discussion (CIPD, 2005; HSA, 2007). I wondered whether employees' experiences were the same. This assumption was further demonstrated by an email received from the HR Director after the interim report from the pilot study was submitted.

Observation of email communication from the HR Director

On 16th April 2007, I received an email from the HR Director giving feedback from the strategic leadership team. The email reveals themes of: bureaucracy, control, tension, hesitation, reluctance to take risks, lack of trust, managerialist instead of employees' perspectives. The HR Director said in the email:

I presented your findings on the Council Human Resources employees to our Strategic Leadership team meeting on Wednesday and they were well received and pointed to some issues for us to address. We will be taking forward the research with our teams to see how we can improve our own performance against the indicators. I am really sorry to tell you that we did not conclude our discussions on your proposed full study. There are some concerns about overlaps between your study and some work that we are in the process of commissioning in terms of an employee survey and there were concerns that we could not afford to be going out to employees with broadly similar studies in a very short space of time. At this stage therefore, we are not saying that your full study cannot go ahead but we will need to consider carefully our options. There is a possibility that we could ask you to cover the key questions in our proposed survey but if we do that we would need to firm up with you when we could have the results and in what format etc. as these results do need to feed in to our strategic plans within Directorates. If you are interested in working with us in this way then I would have to arrange for you to meet with our Head of Organisational Development and Learning and other key players in the development of our employee survey and therefore inevitably there would be further delays I am afraid. I will understand if you feel that this would make your study too difficult and /or the timeliness would not suit so please let me know if you are no longer interested in pursuing your study with our organisation.

(Field notes, HR Director's Email, dated 16th April 2007)

From this email it appeared that the council's strategic leadership team was reluctant to move forward with the main study in keeping with the original research aims and objectives which were initially reviewed and approved by the HR Director. One can deduce that perhaps the Council leadership team was somewhat reluctant and fearful that the findings may not fit into their strategic plans but may instead open a Pandora's box, which would reveal 'evils' that the leadership team were not prepared for or equipped to handle given the continuous challenges and changes faced in this complex and NPM work environment. Instead the 'ostrich' approach was adopted and I found myself having to re-negotiate the terms and conditions of access for the main study in an effort to avoid access termination. After several discussions with the HR Director, she agreed to extend access with the original research objectives with a specific condition that the questionnaire had to be re-designed electronically. This was another hoop that I was able to jump through in the research process. I was still unsure of my position given the sensitivity of 'access' within the organisation, but I was able to negotiate through the gatekeeper to have a letter prepared from the HR Director of the council confirming that access was received. This letter was not included in this book to maintain the confidentiality of the case organisation.

Observation from the main data collection

Twenty-seven respondents were interviewed (see Table 5.6) in a more relaxed environment as a result of re-negotiating alternative accommodation. At the commencement of the interviews, it was observed that both managerial and non-managerial employees appeared anxious and reluctant to answer questions. A depiction of this salient point was observed as follows:

> It's 9:15am and I keep looking at the clock on the wall in one of the small conference rooms assigned for the interviews. The ergonomic design and decoration of the room was professional and created a relaxed atmosphere. There was a pitcher of water with two glasses in the middle of the table, I sat on one side of the table and ensured that there was enough room for the employee to sit on the opposite side of the table. My writing pad for note taking is in front of me, along with the interview schedule, consent form and the digital recorder to record the interview. The room was well ventilated and well lit. There was a solid door which gave privacy once closed. It was a beautiful sunny morning in Manchester; the sun was peering through one of the windows of the office. The employee eventually showed up at 9:25am apologising for being late as she walked into the room. She appeared as though she has been rushing as there were small beads of perspiration on her forehead. I offered her some water which she accepted. I thanked her for agreeing to be interviewed and allowed a few more minutes to ensure that she was relaxed before I began to give a brief introduction of who I was and the nature of the research. She listened attentively nodding her head at intervals showing her understanding of issues mentioned. The interview commenced with an open question which allowed the employee to discuss generally about her experiences within the council. Then the interview questions narrowed in scope to discuss specific issues. At this point, the employee paused, and inquired whether the information given will be kept private and confidential with a concerned look on her face. She was reassured that all information shared with me will be kept confidential and will not be disseminated in any way that will identify her. After sharing this, I observed that she appeared more relaxed and continued talking.
>
> (Field notes, 28th July 2007)

Similarly, interviews with managerial employees also revealed some hesitation, caution and a lack of openness. An example of an interview with a manager was noted as important to support this point: –

> A mature female manager who was smartly dressed was very curious about the questions to be asked. She made several enquiries before the interview began and after her questions were answered she appeared to be satisfied with the responses given and the interview commenced. She answered general questions confidently giving examples to support comments made and appeared very open and the interview progressed well. The questions narrowed from general

to specific about her working experiences within the council and her relationship with her line manager and his/her responsiveness to the promotion of her well-being. At this point, there was an apparent reluctance to answer the questions asked by giving irrelevant and broad responses. Puzzled by these responses the questions were rephrased but the same responses were received. I rephrased the question again and asked the manager to talk about her management/leadership style and it was observed that her body language immediately changed as she appeared more relaxed to discuss issues. She smiled and began to answer the questions asked confidently. I questioned this behaviour and was curious to find out more about its source.

(Field notes, 9th October 2007)

The preceding observations reveal a super-ordinate theme of a less obvious bullying culture existing with sub-themes of control, hesitation, reluctance, lack of trust, employees appearing anxious, lack of openness, and managerialist perspective as opposed to an employee's perspective.

The following section adds another layer to the picture and discusses the analysis of documents.

Analyses of company documents

Company documents were collected over the period July to December 2007 and added yet another layer to the 'text'. Looking through the documentation it revealed what can be expected from policy documents that were linked to the high commitment HRM practices and employee well-being[1] adopted in this study. The council strategic perspectives towards HRM policy documents are drawn from 'best practice' employment legislation standards. According to Guest (1990) the approach to the management of human resources usually adopted in the public sector is aligned to traditional/conservative strategy.[2]

Human resources (HR) policies adopted by the council are typical in their nature, and were written by the council's HR officials and other associated governmental institutions for senior managers, managers and employees. All documents collected and reviewed were dated between 2001 to 2007. They were considered reliable as they were received from the HR department and implemented via partnership working which is central to all HR policies discussed in this research. What is of interest is whether the council would have considered high commitment HRM policies as important if they were not governed by employment legislation and 'best practice' governing bodies.

The analysis of the documents is discussed under five key themes: nature of the work environment, partnership working, pay and rewards strategy, communication, and health, safety and welfare management.

Nature of the work environment

The work environment of local government is influenced by external and internal factors. Externally, global, political and socio-economic changes have implications for management and employees' experiences within organisations. Internally, the modernisation agenda has implications for budget limitations, workforce transformation, efficiency savings and enhanced service delivery, increasing workloads and work-related stress (Noblet et al., 2006). The council's corporate business plan 2006–2009 advocates that the council has a duty to demonstrate value for money and to actively engage with the modernisation agenda and view its employees as vital to the attainment of these goals and vision[3] (Corporate Business Plan, 2006). The documentation also reveals that the council view the involvement of employees as critical and ensuring that employees continue to have the right skills to enable them to deliver quality services is an important priority for the council.

Partnership working

This section discusses the analysis of policy documents that relates to partnership working and includes: job security, recruitment and selection, internal recruitment, learning and development, team working and rewards. As part of its endeavour to become a 'best practice' employer the council professes to promote job security and recognises that due to operating procedures in times of budget constraints or capability issues, employees may no longer be able to continue working in their current positions (Recruitment and Selection Policy, 2006; Redeployment Policy, 2003). As such, 'redeployment policy' caters for the redistribution or alternative employment in the first instance before redundancy or dismissal, which is in keeping with 'best practice' standards outlined by CIPD (2009a). The policy document was written to ensure that the council demonstrated value for money and engaged with the modernisation agenda (Redeployment Policy, 2003).

In terms of promoting high commitment and employee well-being this policy document is geared to facilitate commitment and well-being through the provision of an alternative employment option. This can be done via internal recruitment which can mitigate against redundancy and dismissal which has been brought to the forefront due to the economic recession that is affecting job security (CIPD, 2010). However, employee-centred practices like the redeployment policy and avoidance of redundancy and dismissal are not likely to prevail when it comes to choices between the economic bottom line and 'employees' interests at the level of senior management and strategic decision making. However, employees' reactions from the questionnaire survey confirm the council espousal of job security as both managerial and non-managerial employees agreed that their jobs were secured.

Documentary evidence revealed that the council espoused to recruit and select candidates that were most likely to succeed in assisting them to deliver effective services and business aims (Recruitment and Selection Policy, 2006). The recruitment and selection policy was produced to ensure that appropriate people were in the appropriate roles to deliver effective services and business aims and it was written to support management in the recruitment and selection process as the council views the 'effective recruitment and selection of employees as a key management activity' (Recruitment and Selection, 2006). The council holds the view that if recruitment and selection is done properly it can reduce expenditure via e-recruitment and recruitment campaigns. This policy is linked to the 'best-practice' standard outlined by (CIPD, 2007, 2009b) and can be effective in promoting high commitment and employee well-being. It can also be used as a vehicle for the promotion of equal opportunity, diversity, employer branding, and allow the council to be able to attract, recruit, develop and retain talented individuals (Human Resource Strategy, 2006).

The economic interest of expenditure reduction and efficiency savings is likely to supersede the 'human' interest when it comes to recruitment and selection. This has become evident from proposals of recruitment freezes and redundancies in both public and private organisations as a result of the economic recession. Employee reactions to the recruitment and selection policy adopted by the council show agreement that a rigorous selection process was used to select new recruits and that new positions were filled with people from inside the organisation.

Reviewing the learning and development framework policy document revealed the council commitment to assisting employees in delivering quality services by adopting a learning culture (Learning and Development Framework, 2003). The document highlighted the need for employees to be competent and capable for service delivery, performance, continuous improvement, communication and organisational development – underpinned by a lifelong learning philosophy in keeping with Investors in People standards (Learning and Development Framework, 2006). Learning and development is an important HRM practice that can facilitate commitment, professional development, career advancement, and employee well-being (Redman and Wilkinson, 2009). However, in a recession and with the expenditure reduction proposed by the NPM philosophy, emphasis on learning and development can be shrouded and re-prioritised to enable the council to meet its targets, and continue to deliver high quality services with limited resources. From a practice perspective, employees' reactions were positive as they agreed that they were provided with sufficient opportunity for training and development.

Team working is a salient HR practice that is associated with partnership working and well-being at work. The analysis of the document revealed that partnership working facilitates efficient inter-departmental working and espoused that the council increasingly works in a collaborative way with a range of partners to deliver services across the borough (Pulling Together -Team Working Policy, 2007). Partnership working is encouraged due to cost minimisation, enhanced service delivery, and changing customer and employee expectations. The policy has been written to promote the importance of partnership working internally and externally (Human Resource Strategy, 2006). Team working can be affected when organisations function in an environment of constant change and restructuring (Bach, 1999; Morphet, 2008). This view was echoed by respondents who completed the questionnaire and agreed that team working was strongly promoted in the council.

Pay and reward strategies

The analysis of the pay and rewards strategy document reveals that reward systems enable the council to recruit, retain and motivate people within the constraints of affordability (Pay and Reward Policy, 2002). The document reveals that the council rewards creativity and innovation through different praise and recognition initiatives. This enables the council to reward employees, enhance motivation and retain a skilled and flexible workforce whilst achieving value for money in service delivery and developing a total reward environment (Pay and Reward Policy, 2002). This policy is linked to Equality Act (2010) that refers to fair pay in the public sector codes of practice (HM Treasury, 2010). The council view of a total reward system entails: work-life balance strategies, and single status in pay. The council views these as being attractive to employees and can reduce overheads for the organisation as well as redesign jobs. This can allow the council to be more productive and can potentially offset some of the cost of single status. The pay and reward strategy can be used to promote high commitment and well-being (Gould-Williams, 2004). The tensions and challenges of limited finances can curtail these practices. From a practice perspective, respondents' views from the questionnaire, employees disagreed that they were adequately rewarded for the amount of effort they put into their jobs.

Communication

As part of the council's endeavour to become a 'best-practice' employer the council introduced a 'Communication Strategy' to establish and maintain 'clear, efficient and regular two-way channels of communication with external audiences and staff to encourage an environment of trust and loyalty in which work is supported, aspirations to excellence are valued and achievements are celebrated' (Communication Strategy, 2003). The analysis of the document reveals that communication supports councillors, stakeholders, partners, and local national government bodies in their work. The ongoing changing environment of the council requires effective and clear communication and training and leadership for managers to implement effectively. The document also reveals that the council views communication as important for the following reasons: to raise awareness of the services provided, to listen to and involve people in decisions that are important to them, to ensure that they are accountable for and provide a wider understanding of what is done, and to encourage consultation and partnership working (Communication Strategy, 2003; Human Resource Strategy, 2006). This policy is likely to have implications for commitment, collaboration, involvement/participation, voice and employee well-being (Marchington and Wilkinson, 2005).

By contrast, economic interest can supersede human interest in such a complex NPM environment that has to make efficiency savings and are operating with limited budgets. From a practice perspective, employees' reactions differed to that espoused by the council. Employees disagreed that management involves them in decision making that affects them; employees also disagreed that managers provided them with the chance to comment on proposed changes, or responded to their suggestions and effectively deals with problems at the workplace. However, employees did agreed that the council keeps them informed about business issues on how well it is doing.

Health, safety and welfare management

The analyses of documents reveal that a relationship exists between 'best-practice' approaches to health, safety and wellness at the council and employee well-being (Dignity at Work Policy, 2004; Human Resource Strategy, 2006; Managing Stress Policy, 2003; Managing Sickness Absence Policy, 2005; The Reporter, 2006; Well-being News, 2007; Work-Life Balance Policy, 2005). These policies drew from the Workplace (Health, Safety and Welfare) Regulations 1992 which cover a wide range of basic health, safety and welfare issues[4] that apply to most workplaces (HSE, 2007a).

A. Managing stress

Documentary evidence from the 'stress management policy' reveals that the council recognises that workplace stress is a health and well-being issue and acknowledges the importance of identifying and reducing workplace stressors by conducting risk assessment to eliminate and control risks from stress (Managing Stress Policy, 2003). HSE (2007b) states that work-related stress is a major cause of occupational ill health, poor productivity and human mistakes that can result in sickness absence, high turnover and possible increase in accidents due to human error. The council also espoused to provide training for all managers and supervisory staff in good management practices to promote effective leadership in developing a positive and understanding style of management. The understanding style of management is supported by Meechan (2018) views, which claims that compassionate leadership allows leaders and line managers to be empathetic, caring and understanding to the feelings and needs of others with the view of taking action for improvement to support people that are suffering. Leaders and line managers in the Council, can support employees, by providing confidential counselling and other approaches for employees affected by stress caused by either work or external factors. The stress management policy can assist the council in enhancing employee commitment and well-being through monitoring workloads and other workplace stressors. Workplace stress in the public sector is commonplace given the nature and the complexity of the organisation (CIPD, 2019). It is envisaged that it is likely to increase given the recent proposals by the new coalition government to reduce public sector spending and implementation of further changes. Therefore, it is envisaged that this can have implications for rising stress levels.

The Health and Safety Executive's (HSE, 2007b) Management Standards approach to risk assessment has been professed to be adopted by the council. However, employees' reactions to these were mixed. *Work Demands*, managerial and non-managerial employees disagreed that they had difficulty balancing work and non-work commitments and worked extended hours. However, managerial employees agreed that they worked under pressure as compared to their non-managerial counterparts. *Control*, managerial employees agreed that they were satisfied with the scope for using their initiatives as compared to their non-managerial counterparts. *Support*, both managerial and non-managerial employees agreed that their immediate supervisor supports them in getting the job done. For *Relationships* and *Role*, there was overall agreement that good relationships existed with their immediate boss/manager, and that they were satisfied with the work they did. Finally *Change*, both managerial and non-managerial employees disagreed that their manager provided everyone with a chance to comment on proposed changes. In contrast, both managerial and non-managerial employees agreed that they were kept updated with proposed changes.

B. Sickness absence management

The analysis of the sickness absence policy document reveals that the council views the prime duty of management is to ensure continuity of service to service users (Managing Attendance-Sickness Absence Policy and Procedure, 2005). The council also espoused the view that employees are the most important resource and that management are concerned that employees are able to attend work regularly and are able to contribute effectively (Managing Attendance-Sickness Absence Policy and

Procedure, 2005). The council espoused to be committed to the health and well-being of all employees by ensuring a consistent approach to managing attendance and sickness absence (Silcox, 2007). The council view is that effective monitoring and management of attendance will improve the health and morale of the workforce. This can enhance the quality of service provision, identify and address factors in the workforce which may be affecting employee attendance, establish a culture of high attendance and reduce costs. From a practical perspective, employees self-reported sickness absence over the last 12 months reveals reasons for absence ranging from flu to pregnancy. However, 23% of respondents reported that their sickness absence was as a result of work-related stress resulting in 11 to 20+ days absence at the Council (Managing Attendance-Sickness Absence Policy and Procedure, 2005).

C. Dignity at work

The analysis of documents revealed that the council view all forms of harassment and bullying as unacceptable and will not tolerate such behaviour (Dignity at Work Policy, 2004). The policy revealed that the council is committed to a safe, healthy and productive work environment through the elimination of harassment and bullying and it is an employee's right to be treated with dignity at work (HSA, 2007). This policy is aligned to various legislations[5] that facilitate best-practice codes of conduct (CIPD, 2009b) where employees have a vital role to play in the implementation and support of the policy. Management and supervisors are required to take early and appropriate action to safeguard a stress free working environment. The council view harassment as 'people abusing their powers over others in different ways'. The council view bullying under two categories: obvious[6] and less obvious[7] bullying (Dignity at Work Policy, 2004). From a practical perspective, both managerial and non-managerial employees highlighted experiencing less than obvious bullying. This was reflected as both groups disagreed that management responded to suggestions from employees, and dealt with problems at the workplace.

D. Work-life balance

The analysis of documents revealed that the Work-life balance strategy adopted by the council led to flexible working as a significant tool in achieving business objectives and employee commitment (Work-Life Balance Policy, 2005). This 'best practice' approach to work-life balance as outlined by (CIPD, 2009c) is that it can promote potential benefits to organisations outlined in the business case. The council professed that work-life balance can facilitate improvements in access to services and service delivery, stimulate the work environment for employees to feel valued and establish the council as an employer of choice (Work-Life Balance Policy, 2005). From a practice perspective, both managerial and non-managerial employees agreed that they were satisfied with flexible working time arrangements; arrangements to support employees to manage their work-life balance, and that the council helped employees to achieve a balance between work and life.

E. Wellness initiatives

The council profess to have adopted the wellness management 'best-practice' standards outlined by HSE, HWWE, Investors in People, and Price Waterhouse Coopers geared towards promoting employee well-being (HSE, 2007a; PwC, 2008). These policy standards underpin New Labour government commitment to improve the health and well-being of people of working age (Black, 2008; HSE, 2007a; PwC, 2008). The analysis of the human resource strategy policy revealed that the council introduced certain wellness initiatives[8] to promote the health and well-being of workers to reduce workplace stress (Human Resource Strategy Policy, 2006). The wellness initiatives adopted by the council were linked to some practices adopted by other organisations in the UK, USA, Canada and Europe (PwC, 2008) as well as practices adopted by other metropolitan borough councils in Greater Manchester (www.lga.gov.uk). It is important to note here that with the exception of the case organisation, the other nine local government organisations did not have a formal health and well-being policy that was strategically aligned to business processes. Instead, these local authorities appeared to have adopted a piecemeal approach to wellness management which was being used as a short-term stress management strategy. This view was substantiated by the HR director of the council who held the view that the organisation adopted 'best practice' standards with respect to the promotion of employee health and well-being. However, in reality the organisation was at an 'embryo stage' in wellness management, and the wellness initiatives implemented were not evaluated to ascertain their effectiveness, but instead centred on principal aspects of the employment relationship. This was also corroborated by employees' meaning given to and their perspectives of their well-being which did not relate to wellness initiatives and programmes, but instead focused on key factors that influenced their experiences and well-being at work. These factors and themes are uncovered in more detail in the remaining chapters in this book.

Conclusion

This chapter adds the first layer of text of the data collection process in this study and contributed to answering objectives one and two. The salient points observed entailed the existence of a controlled and tense working environment, that was observed by employees' hesitation and resistance to respond openly. Bureaucracy and managerial focus was also evident in the NPM working environment which had implications for an anti-trust and bullying climate. Policy documents analysed were in keeping with 'best practice' high commitment employment standards and wellness management. However, employees' reactions to that which was espoused by the council were mixed. Employees' reactions and perceptions about their working life experiences and well-being will be developed in detail in future chapters.

Notes

1 Redeployment policy, recruitment and selection, training and development, communication strategy, partnership working, rewards, work-life balance, stress management, sickness absent management and wellness initiatives.
2 This is one of carrying on as before, with personnel policies centring around administrative efficiency and cost minimisation. This may be selected because it is considered to be working effectively, because the external pressures are not sufficiently strong to merit a reappraisal or because the company lacks the resources to know-how to try anything else (Guest, 1990).
3 To achieve a cleaner, greener, safer, stronger borough for the local community through promoting a strong and responsible economy, safe and healthy communities, protecting and promoting the environment and heritage, developing learning communities, improve performance.
4 Management of Health and Safety at Work Regulations 1999; Provision or use of work equipment regulations 1998; Manual handling operations regulations 1992; Personal protective equipment at work regulations 1992; Health and Safety (Display Screen Equipment) Regulations 1992; The work at height regulations 2005; heat stress in the workplace; preventing slips and trips at work; workplace transport safety etc. (HSE, 2007).
5 Discrimination law covering harassment 2006; Employment rights Act 1996; Health and Safety Act 1974; Human Rights Act 1998; Protection from Harassment Act 1997; Breach of Contract; and Common Law rights to take care of the safety of workers.
6 Obvious bullying involves using strength and power to coerce other by fear, attempting to make others toe the line by singling out, demeaning and devaluing, a culture that endorses a 'macho' style management, never listening to another's point of view etc.
7 Making life difficult for those who have the potential to do the job better than the bully does, deliberately ignoring or excluding individuals from activities, keeping individuals in their place by blocking their promotion, refusing to delegate because bullies feel they can't trust anyone but themselves etc.
8 The council embarked on a number of initiatives designed to increase the well-being of all its employees: a health care scheme entitled 'healthsure'; facilities for hearing loss; the launching of a well-being awareness campaign called 'healthwise challenge'; an internet survey used to raise awareness promote and monitor awareness of physiotherapy services, smoking cessation etc.; daily well-being messages posted on the staff intranet; stepwise competition to predict the number of steps taken weekly; well-being workout that encouraged employees to progress in exercises, healthy eating and stopping for a lunch break; stress busters; fast track physiotherapy service; counselling service; and occupational health services.

References

Bach, S. (1999) 'Personnel Managers: Managing to Change', in S. Corby and G. White (Eds.). *Employee Relations in the Public Services: Themes and Issues*, 1st Edition, Routledge Publishers, London, pp. 22–38.

Black, D.C. (2008) *Working for a Healthier Tomorrow*, London: TSO.

CIPD (2005) *Bullying at Work: Beyond Policies to a Culture of Respect*, London: Chartered Institute of Personnel Development.

CIPD (2007) *Recruitment, Retention and Turnover Survey*, London: Chartered Institute of Personnel and Development.

CIPD (2009a) *Redundancy*, London: Chartered Institute of Personnel and Development.

CIPD (2009b) *Recruitment: An Overview*, London: Chartered Institute of Personnel and Development.

CIPD (2009c) *Work Life Balance*, Fact Sheet, London: Chartered Institute of Personnel and Development.

CIPD (2010) *Employee Outlook Recovery Yet to Reach the Workplace*, Quarterly Survey Report, Spring 2010, London: Chartered Institute of Personnel Development.

CIPD (2019) *Health and Well-Being at Work, in Partnership with Simplyhealth*, London: Chartered Institute of Personnel and Development, Survey Report, April.

Communication Strategy (2003) *Policy Document Received from the Case Local Government Organisation in North West of England*, September 2008.

Corporate Business Plan (2006) *Policy Document Received from the Case Local Government Organisation in North West of England*, September 2008.

Dignity at Work Policy (2004) *Policy Document Received from the Case Local Government Organisation in North West of England*, September 2008.

Gould-Williams, J. (2004) 'The Effects of High Commitment HRM Practices on Employee Attitude: The Views of Public Sector Workers', *Public Administration*, Vol. 82(1): 63–81.

Guest, D. (1990) 'Human Resource Management and the American Dream', *Journal of Management Studies*, Vol. 27(4): 377–397.

Health and Safety Authority (2007) *Bullying at Work*, www.hsa.ie/eng/Topics/Bullying_at_Work/ (accessed 20th May, 2010).

Health and Safety Executive (HSE) (2007a) *Workplace Health, Safety and Welfare: A Short Guide for Management*, London: Health and Safety Executive.

Health and Safety Executive (2007b) *Managing the Causes of Work-Related Stress: A Step-by-Step Approach Using the Management Standards*, 2nd Edition, London: HSE.

Human Resources Strategy Policy (2006) *Policy Document Received from the Case Local Government Organisation in North West of England*, September 2008.

Learning and Development Framework (2003) *Policy Document Received from the Case Local Government Organisation in North West of England*, September 2008.

Learning and Development Framework (2006) *Policy Document Received from the Case Local Government Organisation in North West of England*, September 2008.

Managing Attendance-Sickness Absence Policy and Procedures (2005) *Policy Document Received from the Case Local Government Organisation in North West of England*, September 2008.

Managing Stress Policy (2003) *Policy Document Received from the Case Local Government Organisation in North West of England*, September 2008.

Marchington, M., and Wilkinson, A. (2005) *Human Resource Management at Work: People Management and Development*, London: CIPD.

Meechan, F. (2018) *Compassion at Work Toolkit*, Alliance Manchester Business School, University of Manchester, www.researchgate.net/publication/322404395_Compassion_at_Work_Tooklit

Morphet, J. (2008) *Modern Local Government*, London: Sage Publications.

Noblet, A., Rodwell, J., and McWilliams, J. (2006) 'Organisational Change in the Public Sector: Augmenting the Demand Control Model to Predict Employee Outcomes under New Public Management', *Work and Stress*, Vol. 20(4): 335–352.

Pay and Reward Policy (2002) *Policy Document Received from the Case Local Government Organisation in North West of England*, September 2008.

PricewaterhouseCoopers (2008) *Building the Case for Wellness*, www.workingfor health.gov.uk (accessed 20th July, 2010).

Pulling Together – Team Working Policy (2007) *Policy Document Received from the Case Local Government Organisation in North West of England*, September 2008.

Recruitment and Selection Policy (2006) *Policy Document Received from the Case Local Government Organisation in North West of England*, September 2008.

Redeployment Policy (2003) *Policy Document Received from the Case Local Government Organisation in North West of England*, September 2008.

The Reporter (2006) *Policy Document Received from the Case Local Government Organisation in North West of England*, September 2008.

Silcox, S. (2007) 'Health Work and Wellbeing: Rising to the Public Sector Attendance Management Challenge', *ACAS Policy Discussion Paper*, (6), May.

Van Maanen, M. (1994) *Researching Lived Experience: Human Science for an Action Sensitive Pedagogy*, Michigan: Althouse.

Well-Being News (2007) *Policy Document Received from the Case Local Government Organisation in North West of England*, September 2008.

Work-Life-Balance Policy (2005) *Policy Document Received from the Case Local Government Organisation in North West of England*, September 2008.

6 Tough times
Well-being in a period of restricted resources in the public sector

Modernisation in the public sector and New Public Management

One of the aims of the last Labour government in the UK (1997–2010) was to transform and modernise the public sector through the introduction of New Public Management (NPM) (Bach, 2002; Bach et al., 2005; Dibbens et al., 2007). The transformation agenda has also been embraced by the new coalition government that took office in May 2010. Central to the NPM is a transformation of the nature of work in public sector organisations resulting in new approaches to the delivery of goods and services with an emphasis on improved efficiency (Beaumont et al., 2007). Public sector organisations are now expected to emulate 'best practice' in the private sector in relation to people management. This involves taking a more proactive and strategic approach rather than focusing on reactive administration. This in turn has led to changes in the function of human resources (Kessler and Coyle-Shapiro, 2000; Harris, 2007; Diffenbach, 2009; Truss, 2008). NPM is concerned with improving the efficiency and performance of employees through tighter control of resources, changes in organisational structures, the use of targets, standards and control systems. But the aim is to develop a high commitment workforce of motivated, productive and entrepreneurial people (Gould-Williams, 2004; Diffenbach, 2009; ONS, 2007).

To be a 'good employer' within NPM means to attract and retain talented business-like people and not, as the public sector traditionally aspired to, that is, to provide careers and jobs for life. NPM is also concerned with looking for new ways of delivering services as efficiently and cheaply as possible. Whilst some argue that high commitment 'best practice' HRM practices within the public sector have been shown to increase job satisfaction of employees (Gould-Williams, 2004), others argue that, whatever the rhetoric, within a context where delivering 'value-for-money' means cost reductions, constant re-organisations and work intensification, employees are left feeling stressed, de-motivated and insecure (Baptiste, 2009; Diffenbach, 2009; Massey and Pyper, 2005). This chapter explores the reactions of managerial and non-managerial employees in an English local government authority to HRM practices, working life and particularly to the adoption of 'best practice' employee well-being initiatives. It contributes to a small but growing body of research which attempts to evaluate HRM practices by focusing on employees' views (Gibb, 2001; Grant and Shields, 2002; Guest, 2002). We explore how HRM practices and well-being initiatives are perceived by managerial and non-managerial employees within an environment in which they are struggling with limited resources, budget cuts and increased workloads. The research highlights the discrepancies between the intended effects of policy initiatives and the way in which they actually impact on people's working lives.

Human resource management and well-being at work

Over the past decade, there has been much interest in the notion of 'best practice' HRM sometimes referred to as 'high performance work systems' (Keenoy, 1990; Appelbaum et al., 2000), 'high commitment' (Guest, 2001; Boxall et al., 2007) or 'high involvement' (Wood, 1999) practices. Research on HRM has focused on identifying a particular set of high commitment HRM practices that, it is suggested, are able to improve employee and organisational performance and the bottom line for all organisations (Legge, 1995; Huselid et al., 1997; Marchington and Wilkinson, 2005). There is no agreement as to which HRM practices actually constitute 'best practice' and the debate is ongoing with researchers using ranges between 7 and 28 practices (Becker and Gerhard, 1996; Huselid et al., 1997; Wood, 1999; Gould-Williams, 2007, 2004). But those HRM practices commonly held to be associated with high worker satisfaction include trust, team working, involvement/participation, employee voice, fair rewards, job security, job design, equal opportunities, family-friendly and anti-harassment practices (Guest, 2002; White et al., 2003; Gould-Williams, 2004). These practices overlap with those which form the well-being at work agenda. Within this way of thinking it can be argued that there is a 'business case' for employee well-being in the same way that it can be argued there is a 'business case' for diversity (The Workplace Engagement Specialist, 2011).

But there are mixed opinions about whether the move towards high performance HR practices in the public sector is actually improving employee well-being. There is a debate about how far the public sector has actually adopted the 'best practice' HR model. Truss (2008) and Harris (2007) argue that, rather than the new 'best practice' model replacing the 'traditional' model of HRM, the high performance practices have been grafted on to existing HR functions. This leaves the HR function having to cope with the ambiguities and tensions of managing multiple roles. Whilst HR, as a function, inevitably has to balance several competing roles, the high performance approach is about privileging 'business competitiveness rather than employee comfort' (Ulrich, 1998: 126). One role which the HR function has traditionally played, especially in the public sector, is that of 'employee champion' or 'guardian of employee well-being' (Renwick, 2003); that is, as the interest group which pushes forward the interests of employees when management decisions are being made. Harris's (2007) research within the public sector suggested that this employee champion role was being lost. HR staff saw their role primarily as being about providing a service for line managers and no longer saw that they had a responsibility for 'employee well-being'. Similarly, employees no longer felt that HR was concerned about them. In essence, this has implications for well-being at work in the public sector.

Well-being has become one of the most important issues of the twenty-first-century world of work – a challenge not just for individuals, in terms of their mental and physical health, but for employers and governments who have started to assess its social and financial implications (Baptiste, 2009). The definition and meaning of work-related well-being is emergent with a number of competing meanings, making a precise definition of it open as it can take many forms (Ryan and Deci, 2001; Renwick, 2003). Grant et al. (2007) distinguish between three dimensions: the psychological dimension (satisfaction, attitudes and emotions in relation to work); the physical dimension (relating to employees' health and safety at work); and the social dimension (relating to interpersonal relationships, team work and management style). However, Baptiste (2009) argues for a broader more holistic definition with ten domains: psychological, physical, intellectual, material, career, spiritual, social, stakeholders, financial and organisation. This definition invokes not just specific practices of 'wellness' programmes, health screening, or indeed fun programmes, but employees' physical, emotional and psychological needs, material conditions and the wider experience of fulfilment and functioning at work. Well-being, then, is about the development of a 'healthy workforce'. It is important to define this in broad terms and recognise that well-being at work is affected by social interaction and functioning at work (DWP, 2006).

The well-being of employees may be influenced by a raft of different organisational policies and practices that will include practices that prevent staff from suffering harm at work, (e.g. stress management, health and safety, anti-bullying and harassment, and discrimination practices) but also practices that may positively promote health and satisfaction (e.g. 'wellness' and fun at work programmes). It is also affected by very narrow initiatives (e.g. whether there is a healthy eating option in the canteen) but also by broad issues such as organisational culture. The notion that 'good' employers should concern themselves with the health and welfare of the workforce dates back to at least the eighteenth century with paternalistic employers such as Roundtree and Leverhulme (Pinnington and Edwards, 2000; Redman and Wilkinson, 2009). But there are several reasons why well-being initiatives have moved up the agenda especially within public sector organisations in recent years.

Firstly, there have been pressures from government. Essential to New Labour's policies was the espousal of wellness initiatives and health and safety 'best practice' standards for the promotion of the health and well-being of the working age population (Black, 2008; HWWE, 2010). These policies were not just about the improvement of the quality of life for its own sake as stress and ill-health place significant costs on the UK economy (Dibbens and James, 2007; MacDonald, 2005). Thus, the average days absent through sickness are significantly higher for workers in the public sector than in the private sector (Silcox, 2007; HSE, 2009). Well-being at work initiatives have also been promoted as a strand within 'best practice' high commitment HRM. For example, well-being is one of the dimensions which is used within Sunday Times 'Best places to work' awards (www.bestcompanies.co.uk).

Within the critical management literature, there is scepticism about the extent to which the well-being initiatives which form part of high commitment HRM actually improve well-being. Critical theorists obviously want to engage with the project of humanising work and improving the well-being of those at work but see the main barrier to this as the way in which power is institutionalised within organisations, privileging some and disadvantaging others (Fineman, 2006). At best, critical theorists view prescribed well-being programmes as, Fineman (2006: 283) points out, 'somewhat hit-and-miss instruments of affective liberation and positive experience, held principally within the purview of management, they can sustain oppressive power imbalances and resituate or recolor employee grievances'.

Similarly, Marchington and Grugulis (2000) argue that 'high commitment' HRM policies constitute 'nice' rhetoric but 'harsh' realities as they strengthen rather than weaken management control. Indeed, one impact of NPM is a strengthening of the ideology of the 'manager' and the belief that public sector organisations can only be run by 'managers' (Deem and Brehony, 2005; Diffenbach, 2009). The previous discussion does not take into account the economic context in which well-being initiatives are being introduced. But in the public sector in the late 2000s, when the research reported in this chapter was conducted, there was pressure to manage with reduced resources. Finding ways of 'doing more with less' is also, of course, part of the NPM philosophy. Restructuring, cuts, redundancies and the intensification of work have been argued to have a negative effect on employee well-being in that they increase uncertainty and work related stress (Noblet et al., 2006; Noblet and Rodwell, 2009). It may be argued that well-being initiatives are even more important in these circumstances to ensure that people are supported through stressful changes and the morale of those who will be remaining in the organisation is maintained (PwC, 2008). But the tensions and ambiguities in relation to the role of the HR function becomes even more pointed if HR specialists are, on the one hand, being seen as the people managing redundancies and restructuring and, on the other, as the 'guardians of employee well-being.'

This chapter starts from the premise that, to understand how well-being initiatives work in practice, it is necessary to look beyond the rhetoric of policies and to try to understand the way in which these practices impinge on the lived experiences of employees within an organisation (DWP, 2006). It is also timely to explore the ways in which they affect managerial and non-managerial employees who are also coping with restricted resources and financial cuts.

Methodology

This chapter is based on a case study conducted within a local authority in the North West of England. The authority is located in an urban region and is one of the most socially polarised in the country. The case study was conducted during 2005–2007 when a Labour government was in power both nationally and within the authority studied. A strategy of the New Labour government was to implement funding reductions in keeping with the modernisation agenda. The authority was selected as appropriate to study because it professed to have adopted well-being policies and practices to establish employee well-being at work, a positive attendance culture and enhance staff welfare. A number of different types of data were collected. The authority's written HRM policy and procedure documents were analysed. Field notes were written and analysed of the researcher's experience conducting research within the authority. Finally, a series of focused semi-structured interviews were conducted with managerial and non-managerial employees exploring their experiences of HRM practices and well-being initiatives. This chapter will draw particularly on these interviews (Ricoeur, 1981). The process of gaining access was met with challenges and tensions and required the researcher having to jump through several 'hoops' of tailorised processes, controlled systems, and a series of negotiations before access to employees was granted. Even further, the researcher had to begin a new process of negotiations with employees to get people to talk honestly about their working life experiences and well-being at work.

Twenty-seven semi-structured face-to-face interviews were conducted with managerial and non-managerial employees (15 managers and 12 employees) with the aim of understanding their experiences of HRM practices and well-being initiatives. Purposive sampling was used to ensure that all departments within the council were reflected in the study. All twenty-seven informants were Caucasian; (23 respondents) aged 40–59 years, and (four respondents) aged 20–39 years. They were all well-educated up to master's degree for managerial employees and HND/C for non-managerial employees; the majority (i.e. 25) worked full time and reported a range of incomes[1] and held a variety of tenures with the organisation.[2]

The interview approach was collaborative where information was exchanged between the informant (i.e. employee) and the researcher in both directions and the emphasis was on listening to what the informant said as opposed to guiding and controlling the conversation (Cohen et al., 2000; Morse, 1991). A retrospective approach was used to solicit narratives of experiences from informants asking them to talk about their experiences and as such, the first question asked was open ended 'what is it like to work for the council?' This was followed by probing questions focusing on eliciting narrative data, as opposed to explanations or opinions until the employees' experiences were fully described (Lyons, 2000; Ray, 1994; Smith and Osborn, 2003). Each interview lasted between 60–90 minutes and was tape-recorded, transcribed verbatim and analysed using hermeneutic phenomenological analysis (HPA) (Van Maanen, 1994).

The interview schedule covered two broad topics: (1) understanding of well-being at work; and (2) views on well-being initiatives in the organisation. Both managerial and non-managerial employees were asked to respond in relation to their own experiences and priorities as employees, rather than from an espoused practice point of view. Initial transcripts were reviewed through immersion in the data to establish an orienting Gestalt that drove later coding. Interviews were coded line-by-line, necessary for thematic analysis. Concepts, themes and sub-themes were identified. Half of the transcripts were coded separately by an independent researcher to identify emerging themes, and the resulting coding match of 85% provides evidence of reliability in the coding process (Silverman, 2005). Final themes were also verified by informants to ensure they appropriately captured the meaning that the informant sought to convey.

Findings

At the time when the data were collected, the authority was going through a process of *change, restructuring and reduction of resources*, which, managers acknowledged, was having an impact on morale and well-being. The HR Director explained:

> People come to work because they want to contribute to society and in particular the council, but they also come to work because it pays their mortgage and their bills so when there is a discussion around budget reduction and one of the consequences may be deletion of post, in my own department people have written to me expressing anxiety and concern in terms of what they have heard mainly from the grape vine rather than my mouth, yes it will affect people's morale and well-being, but is how we manage and reassure people and how we take them forward is important. So managing that process and taking staff along with us and reassuring them and putting the whole information as transparently as we can is quite important.

It is not unique to this council, in any organisation that is going through financial difficulties it will impact on morals and well-being.

(HR director, Female, Age 40–49 years,
Tenure 6–10 years)

It is important to note here that the HR director highlighted areas of managing processes, reassuring staff, communication and transparency as key themes to reduce employees' anxiety and enhance their morale in this complex environment. It is ironic that there is no mention of using wellness initiatives to promote and maintain employee morale and well-being.

At the same time, analysis of the council's policy documentation confirmed the adoption of high commitment HRM practices and well-being initiatives. The HRM policy documents were informed by 'best practice' employment legislation standards. The human resources policies adopted by the council were typical of those adopted across other authorities, and were written by the council's HR officials and other associated governmental institutions for senior managers, line managers and employees. The documents covered such topics as partnership working, the adoption of recruitment, selection and retention strategies in keeping with talent management, and communication strategies with external and internal audiences to facilitate an environment of trust and loyalty, as well as health, safety and wellness management strategies.[3]

The HR director commented specifically on the reasons for introducing the well-being initiatives was related to the reduction in absence levels, improvement in health, and the business case for well-being. The *well-being programme initiatives* used included: smoking cessation schemes, crèche facilities, medical checks, healthy food and water in the canteen, cycling to work, yoga, occupational health, learning days etc. She explained:

The Well-being programme is being promoted because it will reduce our absence levels by 10.6 days per year downwards and was introduced to try and improve employees health in terms of healthy foods in the canteen, cycling to work, walking more and not using our cars as much, staff counselling service, messages etc. . . . they are all linked to the business plans of central government view that we are going to work longer because we are going to live longer.

(HR director, Female, Age 40–49 years,
Tenure 6–10 years)

Although the reasons for introducing well-being programmes relates to an economic, moral, health and business case perspective; it is interesting that the HR director described these initiatives in terms of an agenda to keep employees 'fit' for work rather than as a mechanism to promote and maintain employee well-being and morale. She had also not considered evaluating these initiatives for their effectiveness in promoting well-being at work or its strategic alignment with the council's corporate business plans. Instead she assumed that these programmes would be effective in reducing absenteeism levels and enhancing the health and well-being of the workforce.

The reality of working life

The impact of budget reduction was echoed by managerial employees. Their responses to the initial question 'what it is like to work here?' reflected the realities they faced, including *challenges with money, protecting their resources, budgeting and staffing restrictions, avoiding redundancies, having to promote efficiency savings, manage staff anxieties*, at the same time trying to find the balance to ensure that their services contribute to the greater good of the community. One manager explained,

> Money, is something that is constantly on my mind – 'how can I protect my resources, both my staff and my budget, to try and avoid people losing their jobs'. You've also got to think about efficiencies and savings – 'how can we do things better, how can we do it cheaper with fewer resources?' . . . and sometimes that's a difficult balance.
> (Manager, Male, Age 40–49 years,
> Tenure less than 5 years)

The salient point of limited resources was echoed by the non-managerial employees who claimed that '*limited resources*' resulted in *increasing workloads* affecting their stress levels. One employee discussed her experience:

> The challenges are meeting all these targets and the offices are really crappy offices . . . it's not been painted in about 15 years, the floors are filthy, got stairs up and down, there's not enough technical equipment all that sort of thing is a nuisance . . . we are expected to do more work with less.
> (Employee, Female, Age 50–59 years,
> Tenure 6–10 years)

Limited resources were perceived to negatively affect the work-life balance of employees. Although flexible working initiatives had been formally adopted, employees indicated that they experienced *challenges with managing work and life*. One manager commented:

> Although there is a fair amount of work-life balance, heavy workloads and working under lots of pressure at work hinders the balance

between work and life. This also affects morale and the fact that there is no recognition also affects morale and satisfaction with work and life . . . the workloads needs to be addressed through increased (resources), and greater efficiency in management leadership.

(Manager, Female, Age 40–49 years,
Tenure 11–15 years)

One employee described having nightmares about how she could manage her workload. She stated,

This is a struggle for me as I have lots of nightmares about work and thinking about how things are at work – this affects my work-life balance. The workloads and stress at work are other issue that affects my work-life balance . . . there need to be a more structured way to do the job

(Employee, Female, Age 30–39 years,
Tenure less than 5 years)

One persistent theme across several interviews was about the *existence of bullying* as a part of employees' experience of working life. Respondents spoke of their personal experiences of being bullied or knowledge of others who experienced or were experiencing bullying. These experiences resulted in feelings of inadequacy and removal of dignity, which all had implications for well-being. One manager described bullying between peers. She commented,

I was a new home support manager and there were other more experienced home support managers there I did feel intimidated by some of them as they made it very clear that they were much more experienced than me and I was the new girl on the block. I did feel quite intimidated as everything I did was 'no you've done that wrong, you should have done it like this or why do you think you did' . . . it was almost like negative comments all the time.

(Manager, Female, Age 50–59 years,
Tenure 16–20 years)

Another employee gave a personal account of bullying within her department and how the knowledge that others were being bullied affected her psychological well-being and mental health. She commented,

I recognise the difference between somebody being a bit difficult to work with and people being quite serious, nasty persecuting bullies . . . bullying is absolutely dreadful, I've never experienced anything like it in my life. There are quite a number of people on medication for depression as a result of the bullying which was perverse, horrific and really upsetting and seeing people that you care about being absolutely squashed on a daily basis was terrible.

(Employee, Female, Age 30–39 years,
Tenure less than 5 years)

Limited resources affected *trust, team working, status differences, bureaucracy and autonomy*. One manager felt that the emphasis on hierarchy and status differences affected her effectiveness at work. She explained her experience of how certain meetings were arranged:

There is a kind of hierarchy that exists here and I find it very, very strange, I do not know why it should exist here but it feels like there is quite a lot of layers and I do not really understand what they are there for and there are things that seem to have more to do with status than usefulness so, there are meetings that are available to people because they are a certain grading rather than because they need to have that information for their job. I find that very peculiar and misguided.

(Manager, Female, Age 50–59 years,
Tenure 11–15 years)

The preceding view regarding a bureaucratic environment is echoed by another employee who likened her experiences to 'Chinese Whispers'. She said:

It's a case of you can't do anything without asking your manager, who then has to go and ask his manager, who asks her manager who asks his manager and before you know where you are it's gone through six people and what you actually originally wanted has come out as completely something else because its 'Chinese Whispered' up the chain and it comes out with a result and you think 'what's that all about, I didn't ask that.

(Employee, Female, Age 50–59 years,
Tenure 6–10 years)

What is striking about the informants' responses is the mismatch between the formal HR policies and practices, where the rhetoric of high commitment, 'best practices' are espoused and adopted, compared with the actual working realities and experiences of managers and employees within the local government organisation, who described a culture where managers and employees were *stressed with high workloads* and demands, the organisation was *hierarchical, bureaucratic*, with an evident *status differential* existing between senior and less senior employees. The reality of working life experiences of the employees also included *challenges balancing work and life* due to the *heavy workloads and work-related stress*. Employees also highlighted their perceptions of a *widespread culture of bullying* (from management) existed, and there was a *lack of trust, team working, and autonomy*. The findings reveal that managers and employees' working life realities were particularly different to what the HR director suggestions and organisational policies espoused to do. There is a disconnect with the HRM practices and wellness programmes that are implemented to promote employee well-being and enhanced performance, when employees are experiencing negative well-being as a result of dysfunctional social actions and actors throughout the NPM environment where the focus was on expenditure reduction and doing more with less. It seems almost silly that the well-being ideology adopted was associated with physical well-being only with suggestions like (healthy eating campaigns or smoking cessation programmes) instead of being aligned to strategic business objectives that look more closely into individuals, groups, and the organisational well-being with the view of taking action towards development, absence and stress reduction, positive well-being and enhanced service delivery and performance.

Understanding well-being at work

Respondents were asked how they understood well-being at work. The factors identified include: happiness and job satisfaction, reasonable workloads, mental health, valued and supported, flexibility, duty of care and compassion, financial well-being, motivation, empowerment, healthy organisational environment, reward strategies, fair treatment, work-life balance, stress management, career advancement and communication. It is important to note here that employees' perspectives and understanding of well-being at work were not associated with the espoused wellness management programmes that are adopted by 'cutting edge companies'. Instead they focused on the material aspect of the employment relationship.

One manager's account touched on the key factors mentioned earlier. He commented,

> To get the balance right between work and life and the expectation of the organisation to support this balance . . . health and safety, feeling valued as an individual, career progression, flexibility, fairness with reward . . . a duty of care to ensure that people are able to function at their maximum potential and being fully informed about what could benefit employees.
>
> (Manager, Male, 50–59 years,
> Tenure 11–15 years)

This view is echoed by non-managerial employees' meanings. One employee said,

> It is about how you feel in your surroundings and the workloads and the stress associated with work . . . provided with safety equipment

to do the job to ensure that you get satisfaction with the work done . . . being rewarded for work done and feeling happy and healthy at work . . . not being stressed that affects your health.

(Employee, Female, Age 30–39 years,
Tenure less than 5 years)

Perspectives on well-being initiatives

Respondents were also asked about what they thought about the well-being initiatives being introduced in the organisation. The interviews highlighted the discrepancies between the intended effects of policy initiatives and the way in which they actually impact on people's working lives. Non-managerial employees associated well-being initiatives with *unfair treatment at work*.

One employee likened her experiences of well-being initiatives to management not *providing 'time off' for the take-up of wellness initiatives*, the information about well-being initiatives *not effectively communicated*, and employees *lacking spare time to partake in these initiatives due to heavy workloads*. She explained,

> Initiatives like yoga, occupational health, learning at work shouldn't be coming out of my time . . . that's my time and that's a big thing. . . . People don't like doing things because they feel they may lose their hours . . . so initiatives that do take place during working hours are not well attended. . . . I think senior managers should allow some time off (say one or two hours) to encourage staff to get involved and take up these initiatives . . . staff are reluctant because they do not feel they've got management authority . . . and also they are aware that it might creep into their personal time.
>
> (Employee, Female, Age 40–49 years,
> Tenure less than 5 years)

However, comments from a manager emphasised a practical perspective on how non-work initiatives can promote well-being. He said:

> I think if I had a shower at work it would be very helpful so I can cycle more. It's more important than you think, I am a great believer in physical exercise and mental health and if you can combine the two so that as you're cycling at the beginning of your day; you're thinking about the day ahead and thinking what you need to do and gearing yourself up, and vice versa on your way back . . . getting your exercise and dealing with the pressures of the day is important. . . . So I actually think it's a very healthy thing to do, so facilitating that more is good . . . I've always said, they (*the council*) should give free

sessions at the sports centres for things like swimming and what have you. If it was free for council staff, you'd get a lot more people using it.

(Senior manager, Male, Age 40–49 years,
Tenure under 5 years)

This comment highlighted '*cycling to work, shower at work, free sessions at the sports centre, and swimming*' relates to opportunities to engage in wellness programmes that are not directly related to work but can positively promote mental health and well-being, and consequently enhanced performance. However, few employees mentioned that physical well-being was central to their overall well-being at work and wellness initiatives were raised less frequently, and assigned notably less importance than more material aspects of employment relations such as heavy workloads, work-life balance challenges, bullying at work, trust, and stress management. One can deduce that wellness programmes appear to have a much lower priority for these employees. This suggests that when the emphasised material aspects of employment relations and well-being at work are fulfilled (e.g. management trust, work-life balance, reduced workloads, fair rewards, stress management, perceived organisational support, line management leadership, allocated time to participate in organisational wellness initiatives etc.) then employees are more likely to place value on initiatives and programmes generally advocated by 'ministers of wellness management' such as therapies, messages and play/fun activities.

Taken as a whole, these managerial and non-managerial employees' comments touched on serious challenges faced from an individual, group and organisational perspectives. For these respondents it would seem that material issues like adequate resources, reasonable workloads, satisfaction with work-life balance, avoidance of bullying at work, trust and stress management are of fundamental importance to the promotion of their well-being (see Table 6.1). To go further, 'well-being initiative programmes' are not likely to be readily embraced when these employees are faced with the daily challenges they described, nor are wellness programmes perceived by respondents as particularly high on their list of concerns, in their own right.

Discussion

According to Diffenbach (2009) there are inconsistencies, and even hypocrisies, within NPM. For example, he argues (2009: 905):

The principles of empowerment and subsidiarity are announced while at the same time more hierarchical structures and tailorised processes, formalized surveillance, and control systems are being implemented.

This study illustrates these inconsistencies. The analysis of documents showed that this Local Authority had adopted the practices and philosophies of New Public Management (NPM) including practices such as controlled delegation, increased emphasis on user orientation and the measurement of performance which are the recognised characteristics of NPM (Harrow, 2002). The local government organisation had also adopted the rhetoric of 'best practice' high commitment HRM including well-being initiatives. But the council was also responding to a mandate to improve its efficiency and reduce its expenditure and this was resulting in reductions in budgets and service cuts, workforce transformation by merging departments for greater efficiency and capital asset reduction, the introduction of flexible working initiatives and partnership working. These changes had implications for workloads, work pressure, and work related stress (Armstrong and Brown, 2001).

Despite the espousal of well-being policies aimed at reducing absenteeism and promoting a happier and more stress-free workforce, the managers and employees interviewed did not feel that their well-being was being promoted. Rather, the picture was of beleaguered managerial and non-managerial employees needing recognition of their very real day-to-day concerns. Employees *working life realities* were of limited resources, heavy workloads, work-life balance challenges, bullying at work, and a distrustful environment within which these managers and employees functioned. The respondents' depiction of their working life and meaning of well-being in local government in North of England is precisely echoed by Studs Terkel's depiction of work (1977: 1):

> Work is, by its very nature, is about violence – to the spirit as well as to the body. It is about ulcers as well as accidents, about shouting matches, as fistfights, about nervous breakdown as well as kicking the dog around. It is above all (or beneath all), about daily humiliations. To survive the day is triumph enough for the walking wounded among the great many of us.

Terkel argues that work has been affected by significant changes taking place over the decades, but certain factors have stayed the same. This is evidenced by the employees' depiction of their working life experiences and well-being. It also reveals that the search for happiness centres on 'what lies beneath the melting ice' of employees' evaluation of the employment relationship, the quality of their working lives and well-being at work.

The working life realities affected managerial and non-managerial employees differently. Managerial employees were challenged with having to find a balance between resource restrictions and having to deal with increasing workloads, protecting their budgets, promoting efficiency savings, staffing limitations, redundancies, changing organisational priorities, service delivery, managing staff anxieties while, at the same time, trying to manage their own work-life balance. Non-managerial employees were challenged with increased workloads, work-related stress, anxieties from budget reduction, fears of redundancy, bullying at work, unfair treatment, and functioning in poor work accommodation with inadequate equipment. Tuomi et al. (2004) state that changes in organisational practices and the demands of work are strongly associated with changes in employee physical well-being. In support, Baptiste (2009) and MacDonald (2005) suggest that the negative effects on the level of stress and pressure experienced by employees have implications for the psychological and physical well-being of workers.

This case study illustrates how well-being initiative programmes do not necessarily deliver what they profess (PwC, 2008). Rather it indicates that employees' own understanding and definition of well-being is associated with the material aspect of the employment relationship (see Table 6.1) where employees' defined their well-being at work from an individual, group and organisational perspective. These perspectives are associated with psychological, physical, reward, career, financial and mental health well-being. The group perspective is associated with compassionate leadership well-being, and the organisational perspective is associated with practices aligned with fostering a healthy work environment. In support, well-being proponents argue that emotional experiences construct individuals' reality of happiness and well-being (Ryan and Deci, 2001; Grant et al., 2007). Literature advocates that physical and mental health and experiencing a safe working environment are areas that can reduce work stress which in turn can promote well-being (MacDonald, 2005; Noblet and Rodwell, 2009; HWWE, 2010). In essence, these material aspects of the employment relationship have to be addressed before the philosophy of 'well-being at work' can have meaning or relevance. It is hard to imagine that employees would welcome yoga classes, messages and other organised employee assistance programmes and activities that would encroach even more into their already busy schedules. Therefore, serious consideration is required to address the factors that promote employee well-being at work rather than more prescriptions of wellness programmes.

In conclusion, it can be argued that these managerial and non-managerial employees, and perhaps more generally, employees in similar contexts have some way to go before they self-actualise and are fulfilled in their well-being at work. It will take moving away from superficiality, tick boxes ideology, to embrace 'hard' but essential issues like 'walking the talk' by showing genuine interest in what really promotes employee well-being at work from an employee's perspective. It will take a further step for public sector employees, given resource restrictions, and the complexities and daily challenges faced before they can welcome managerially led well-being programme activities. The mantra of 'working hard,' is evident for public

Table 6.1 Employees' understanding and definition of well-being at work in a new public management environment

Perspective	Well-Being Domain	Themes
Individual	Psychological	Job satisfaction
		Happiness
		Sense of purpose
		Motivation
		Spare time
	Physical	Showers at work
		Free subscriptions to the gym and swimming
		Cycling to work
	Reward/Material	Fairly rewarded
	Career	Career advancement
	Financial	Fair benefits
	Mental Health	Mentally healthy and empowered
Group	Compassionate Leadership	Fair treatment
		Feeling valued and supported
		Team working
		Trust
		Autonomy
		Duty of care
		Empathy
Organisation	Work/Organisation Practices	Reasonable workloads
		Work-life balance
		Stress management
		Communication and collaboration
		Anti-bullying culture
		Removal of status differentials
		Safe working environment
		Removal of hierarchy and bureaucracy
		Time off to take-up organisational wellness initiatives
		Healthy organisational environment

sector employees, as for so many contemporary professionals; however, the Utopian state of 'well-being at work' is likely to remain a dream for the future rather than a reality of their current work. Further, in the context of the further cuts to public expenditure currently being imposed by the current UK government (HM Government, 2010; Richardson, 2010) the challenge for public sector organisations to genuinely improve the well-being of their employees becomes even greater.

Notes

1 £10,001–£20,000 = six respondents; £20,001–£30,000 = nine respondents; £30,001–£40,000 = five respondents; £40,001–£50,000 = four respondents; £50,001–£60,000 = one respondent.

2 Less than 5 years (11 respondents); 6–10 years (6 respondents); 11–15 years (3 respondents); 16–20 years (4 respondents) and 21–25 years (3 respondents).

3 Management of Health and Safety at Work Regulations 1999; Provision or use of work equipment regulations 1998; Manual handling operations regulations 1992; Personal protective equipment at work regulations 1992; Health and Safety (Display Screen Equipment) Regulations 1992; The work at height regulations 2005; heat stress in the workplace; preventing slips and trips at work; workplace transport safety etc. (HSE, 2007).

References

Appelbaum, E., Bailey, R., Berg, P., and Kalleberg, A. (2000) *A Manufacturing Competitive Advantage: The Effects of High Performance Work Systems on Plant Performance and Company Outcomes*, New York, NY: Cornell University Press.

Armstrong, M., and Brown, D. (2001) *New Dimensions in Pay Management*, London: Chartered Institute of Personnel Development (CIPD).

Bach, S. (2002) 'Public Sector Employment Relations Reform under Labour: Muddling through on Modernization?', *British Journal of Industrial Relations*, Vol. 40(2): 319–339.

Bach, S., Kessler, I., and White, G. (2005) 'Employment Relations and Public Services "Modernisation" under Labour', *Personnel Review*, Vol. 34(6): 626–633.

Baptiste, N.R. (2009) 'Fun and Well-Being: Insights from Senior Managers in a Local Authority', *Employee Relations*, Vol. 31(6): 600–612.

Beaumont, P., Pate, J., and Fischbacher, M. (2007) 'Public Sector Employment: Issues of Size and Composition in the UK', in P. Dibben, P. James, I. Roper, and G. Wood (Eds.) *Modernising Work in Public Services: Redefining Roles and Relationships in Britain's Changing Workplace*, Basingstoke: Palgrave Macmillan.

Becker, B., and Gerhard, B. (1996) 'The Impact of Human Resource Management on Organisational Performance: Progress and Prospects', *Academy of Management Journal*, Vol. 39(4): 779–801.

Black, D.C. (2008) *Working for a Healthier Tomorrow*, London: TSO.

Boxall, P., Purcell, J., and Wright, P. (Eds.) (2008) *The Oxford Handbook of Human Resource Management*, Oxford: Oxford University Press.

Cohen, M.Z., Kahn, D.L., and Steeves, R.H. (2000) *Hermeneutic Phenomenological Research: A Practical Guide for Nurse Researchers*, London: Sage Publications.

Deem, R., and Brehony, K. (2005) 'The Case of New Managerialism in Higher Education', *Oxford Review of Education*, Vol. 31(2): 213–231.

Department for Work and Pensions (2006) *A New Deal for Welfare: Empowering People at Work, CM 6730, Stationery Office*, London, w.dwp.gov.uk/welfarereform/docs/A_new_deal_for_welfare-Empowering_people_to_work-Full_Document.pdf (accessed 19th July, 2009).

Dibben, P., and James, P. (2007) 'Introduction: Is "Modern" Necessarily Better?', in P. Dibbens, P. James, I. Roper, and G. Wood (Eds.) *Modernising Work in Public Services: Redefining Roles and Relationships in Britain's Changing Workplace*, pp. 1–2, Basingstoke: Palgrave MacMillan.

Dibbens, P., James, P., Roper, I., and Wood, G. (2007) *Modernising Work in Public Services: Redefining Roles and Relationships in Britain's Changing Workplace*, Basingstoke: Palgrave Macmillan.

Diffenbach, T. (2009) 'New Public Management in Public Sector Organisations: The Dark Sides of Managerialistic "Enlightenment"', *Public Administration*, Vol. 87(4): 892–909.

Fineman, S. (2006) 'On Being Positive: Concerns and Counterpoints', *Academy of Management Review*, Vol. 31(2): 270–291.

Gibb, S. (2001) 'The State of Human Resource Management: Evidence from Employees' Views of HRM Systems and Staff', *Employee Relations*, Vol. 23(4): 318–336.

Gould-Williams, J. (2004) 'The Effects of High Commitment HRM Practices on Employee Attitude: The Views of Public Sector Workers', *Public Administration*, Vol. 82(1): 63–81.

Gould-Williams, J. (2007) 'HR Practices, Organisational Climate and Employee Outcomes: Evaluating Social Exchange in Local Government', *International Journal of Human Resource Management*, Vol. 18(9): 1627–1647.

Grant, D., and Shields, J. (2002) 'In Search of the Subject: Researching Employee Reactions to Human Resource Management', *Journal of Industrial Relations*, Vol. 44(3): 313–334.

Grant, A., Christianson, M., and Price, R. (2007) 'Happiness, Health or Relationships? Managerial Practices and Employee Well-Being Tradeoffs', *The Academy of Management*, Vol. 21(3): 51–63.

Guest, D. (2001) 'Human Resource Management and Performance: A Review and Research Agenda', *International Journal of Human Resource Management*, Vol. 8(3): 263–276.

Guest, D. (2002) 'Human Resource Management, Corporate Performance and Employee Well-Being: Building the Worker into HRM', *Journal of Industrial Relations*, Vol. 44(3): 335–358.

Harris, L. (2007) 'The Changing Nature of the HR Function in UK Local Government and Its Role as "Employee Champion"', *Employee Relations*, Vol. 30(1): 34–47.

Harrow, J. (2002) 'New Public Management and Social Justice: Just Efficiency or Equity as Well?', in K. McLaughlin, S.P. Osborne, and E. Ferlie (Eds.) *New Public Management: Current Trends and Future Prospects*, pp. 141–159, London: Routledge and Taylor & Francis Group.

Health and Safety Executive (2009) *Health and Safety Statistics 2008/2009*, London: HSE.

Health Work and Well-Being Executive (HWWE) (2010) www.workingforhealth. gov.uk/ working in partnership with DOH, DWP, HSE, Welsh Assembly Government, and The Scottish Government (accessed 10th April, 2010).

HM Government (2010) *The Coalition: Our Programme for Government*, May, Ref No. 401238/0510, London: Crown Copyright, www.hmg.gov.uk/programme forgovernment (accessed 20th July, 2010).

Huselid, M., Jackson, S., and Schuler, R. (1997) 'Technical and Strategic Human Resource Management Effectiveness as Determinants of Firm Performance', *Academy of Management Journal*, Vol. 40(1): 171–188.

Keenoy, T. (1990) 'Human Resource Management: Rhetoric and Reality and Contradiction', *International Journal of Human Resource Management*, Vol. 1(3): 363–384.

Legge, K. (1995) 'HRM: Rhetoric, Reality and Hidden Agendas', in J. Storey (Ed.), *Human Resource Management: A Critical Text*, pp. 33–61, London: Routledge Publishers.

Lyons, E. (2000) 'Qualitative Data Display: Data Display Model', in C. Fife-Schaw (Ed.) *Research Methods in Psychology*, pp. 269–280, London: Sage Publications.

MacDonald, L.A.C. (2005) *Wellness at Work: Protecting and Promoting Employee Well-Being*, London: Chartered Institute of Personnel and Development.

Marchington, M., and Grugulis, I. (2000) 'Best-Practice' Human Resource Management: Perfect Opportunity or Dangerous Illusion?', *International Journal of Human Resource Management*, Vol. 11(6): 1104–1124.

Marchington, M., and Wilkinson, A. (2005) *Human Resource Management at Work: People Management and Development*, London: The Chartered Institute of Personnel and Development.

Massey, A., and Pyper, R. (2005) *Public Management and Modernisation in British*, Basingstoke: Palgrave Macmillan.

Morse, J.M. (1991) 'Qualitative Nursing Research: A Free-for-All?', in J.M. Morse (Ed.) *Qualitative Nursing Research: A Contemporary Dialogue*, pp. 14–22, 2nd Edition, Newbury Park, CA: Sage Publication.

Noblet, A.J., and Rodwell, J.J. (2009) 'Integrating Job Stress and Social Exchange Theories to Predict Employee Strain in Reformed Public Sector Contexts', *Journal of Public Administration Research and Theory and Advance Access*, Vol. 19(1): 555–524.

Noblet, A.J., Rodwell, J., and McWilliams, J. (2006) 'Organisational Change in the Public Sector: Augmenting the Demand Control Model to Predict Employee Outcomes under New Public Management', *Work and Stress*, Vol. 20(4): 335–352.

Office of National Statistics (ONS) (2007) *First Release: Public Sector Employment*, Quarter 1, 13th June, London.

Pinnington, A., and Edwards, T. (2000) *Introduction to Human Resource Management*, Oxford: Oxford University Press.

PricewaterhouseCoopers (2008) *Building the Case for Wellness*, www.working forhealth.gov.uk (accessed 20th July, 2010).

Ray, M.R. (1994) 'The Richness of Phenomenology: Philosophic, Theoretic, and Methodologic Concerns', in J.M. Morse (Ed.) *Critical Issues in Qualitative Research Methods* (pp. 117–133), Thousand Oaks, CA: Sage Publications.

Redman, T., and Wilkinson, A. (2009) *Contemporary Human Resource Management: Text and Cases*, London: Prentice Hall and Financial Times.

Renwick, D. (2003) 'HR Managers, Guardians of Employee Well-Being', *Personnel Review*, Vol. 32(3): 341–359.

Richardson, D. (2010) 'Austerity Measures Hit North West of England', *World Socialist Web Site, International Committee of the Fourth International (ICFI) Publishers*, www.wsws.org/articles/2010/aug2010/nort-a18.shtml (accessed 10th August, 2010).

Ricoeur, P. (1981) *Hermeneutics and the Human Science*, New York: Cambridge University Press.

Ryan, R.M., and Deci, E.L. (2001) 'On Happiness and Human Potentials: A Review of Research on Hedonic and Eudaimonic Well-Being', *Annual Review of Psychology*, Vol. 51: 141–166.

Silcox, S. (2007) 'Health Work and Well-Being: Rising to the Public Sector Attendance Management Challenge', *ACAS Policy Discussion Chapter*, No. 6, May.

Silverman, D. (2005) *Doing Qualitative Research: A Practical Handbook*, 2nd Edition, London: Sage Publications.

Smith, J.A., and Osborn, M. (2003) 'Interpretative Phenomenological Analysis', in J.A. Smith (Ed.) *Qualitative Psychology: A Practical Guide to Research Methods*, London: Sage Publications.

Terkel, S. (1977) *Working*, Harmondsworth: Penguin Publishers.

Truss, C. (2008) 'Continuity and Change: The Role of the HR Function in the Modern Public Sector', *Public Administration*, Vol. 86(4): 1071–1088.

Tuomi, K., Vanhala, S., Nykyri, E., and Janhonen, M. (2004) 'Organisational Practices, Work Demands and the Well-Being of Employees: A Follow-Up Study in the Mental Industry and Retail Trade', *Occupational Medicine*, Vol. 54: 115–121.

Ulrich, D. (1998) *Delivering Results: A New Mandate for Human Resources Professionals*, New York: Harvard Business Review.

Van Manen, M. (2016) *Researching Lived Experience: Human Science for an Action Sensitive Pedagogy*, Routledge Taylor & Francis Group, London and New York.

White, M., Hill, S., McGovern, P., Mills, C., and Smeaton, D. (2003) 'High-Performance' Management Practices, Working Hours and Work-Life Balance', *British Journal of Industrial Relations*, Vol. 41(2): 175–195.

Wood, S. (1999) 'Human Resource Management and Performance', *International Journal of Management Reviews*, Vol. 1(4): 367–374.

The Workplace Engagement Specialist, The Sunday Times 'Best Companies to Work for' in the UK, www.bestcompanies.co.uk/Overview.aspx (accessed March, 2011).

7 Leadership and well-being at work

Implications for job satisfaction, service delivery and performance

The global market

The rising dependencies on the global market have, and continue to place an ever-increasing burden on those of working age in the delivery of products and services. In turn, this has had an adverse effect on the health and well-being of workers, resulting in high cost to business and the public purse (MacDonald, 2005). For example, public sector absence levels (and associated costs) are now estimated to be nearly ten days per employee every year (DWP, 2005); with stress and other mental health conditions now being the leading causes of employee absence (CIPD, 2007). Moreover, the issue of employee well-being at work has increasingly attracted government attention, as employment continues to change (DWP, 2005), and concentration on problems such as absenteeism and accidental injury is giving way to a broader vision of what a healthier, happier and more productive workforce can achieve in terms of higher performance and productivity (DWP, 2005; ESRC, 2006). Therefore, the fundamental principle outlined by policymakers is that all working-age people have the opportunity to make the maximum contribution to their organisations while enjoying a safer, more satisfying and healthier working life (DWP, 2006). This vision has been embraced by cutting-edge companies that have invested deeply in the well-being of their workforce and is now reaping the benefits, as it appears that well-being at work is increasingly being recognised as an essential factor in determining organisational success (Peccei, 2004; Tehrani et al., 2007; Warr, 2002). Similarly, organisational leadership has multiple effects on the performance of businesses, directly and indirectly, through the impact of success on employee well-being at work.

Despite the appeal for such initiatives, recently there has been relatively little research devoted to gaining an in-depth understanding of the relationship between leadership practices, well-being at work, and performance (Dibbens et al., 2007). This is certainly true for employees' well-being at work within the public sector, even though government dissatisfaction with public sector performance and failure to deliver services was contributable primarily to a shortage of leadership and perceived lack of innovation (Pratt et al., 2007). Given the impact that management implementation of people management practices can have on employees (Guest, 2002; Pfeffer, 2005; Purcell and Hutchinson, 2003) and given the considerable changes which have occurred in the public sector over the past decade and are still happening, this is a fascinating and essential area of investigation. While the issue of employee well-being at work has reached a new level of importance in the minds of managers, there is still little evidence that attention has been paid to the relationship between leadership and employee well-being at work in the public sector. Research within this area remains relatively untapped. With this in mind, this study aims to begin to address this gap.

The dynamics of leadership and well-being at work

Line management is well defined in the literature (McGovern et al., 1997; Purcell and Hutchinson, 2003, 2007), and refers to a rational approach to organisational decision-making as well as a concern with executing routines and maintaining organisational stability. There is clear evidence that line managers' roles in people management (and in management generally) have broadened while maintaining their traditional supervisory duties (McConville and Holden, 1999), but they may not transmit the articulated values of top management, as instead, they reflect the informal culture of the firm (Truss, 2001). Therefore, people management practices perceived or experienced by employees will be enacted by line managers and can include HR duties of selecting, appraising, developing, communicating, employee involvement, consultation, team working, etc., which are all linked to leadership behaviours (Purcell and Hutchinson, 2007) which aim to influence employee attitudes and behaviour and are also likely to affect absenteeism, presenteeism and performance. Similarly, line management action or support, and the quality of the relationship between employees and their immediate line manager is also liable to influence perceptions not only of people management, but leadership and work climate, either positively or negatively (McGovern et al., 1997). Therefore, management practices are aligned with leadership amelioration through adaptive leadership where openness to change, flexibility and 'thinking outside the box' are commonplace. Glover et al. (2002) support this view and claim that adaptation allows a flexible approach to sharing information and resources, decisions and leadership.

Moreover, leadership has been widely researched in the literature (Alban-Metcalfe and Alimo-Metcalfe, 2000; Bakke, 2005; Pratt et al., 2007; Purcell and Hutchinson, 2007) but Grint (2005) suggests that leadership is concerned with direction setting, with novelty and is intrinsically linked to change, movement, relationships, morality and persuasion. For example, good leadership starts with a person's character, which is essential to creating a fun place to work (Bakke, 2005). Arguably, the essential character trait of a leader is the embracing of the principles and values of humility, willingness to give up power, courage, integrity, love and passion for the people, values and mission of the organisation (Grint, 2005).

The concept of employee well-being at work promotes advantages to organisations of having a healthy workforce (MacDonald, 2005). Therefore, the dynamics of well-being at work is pivotal in the understanding of the different domains that affect the quality of life at work. Peccei (2004) suggests that well-being at work concerns an overall sense of happiness, physical and mental health of the workforce (Currie, 2001). However, the more restricted concern in this chapter is for job-related well-being that is, individuals' feelings about themselves and their job. Warr (2002) argues that job-related well-being refers to people's satisfaction with their jobs regarding facets like pay, colleagues, supervisors, working conditions, job security, training opportunities, involvement, team working and the nature of the work undertaken. Therefore, if employees are working in a stress-free and physically safe environment, this can be exciting, rewarding, stimulating, enjoyable and Bakke (2005) proposes that joy-filled workplaces improve financial performance.

Personal well-being does not exist on its own or in the workplace, but within a social context (CIPD, 2007). Thus, individual lives are affected by social relations with organisational agents, lifestyle and employment changes (Guest, 2002). However, despite these shifts Tehrani et al. (2007) suggest that people still have the same basic physical and mental needs for social support, feeling valued, physical safety, health and a feeling that they can cope with life. With this in mind, employees are looking to employers to help them to achieve this, since a large proportion of their lives are spent at work. In order for employers to assist employees with their well-being at work, they will need to embrace and embed distributive leadership (Wilkinson, 2007) by creating an environment to promote a state of contentment, which allows an employee to flourish and achieve their full potential for the benefit of themselves and their organisation (Tehrani et al., 2007).

The HRM Performance literature makes a clear link between the employee experiences of people management as well as the formation and modification of attitudes towards the employing organisation and the job, and the encouragement these provide to engage in certain types of discretionary behavior (Purcell and Hutchinson, 2007). These behaviors and experiences are associated with employee beliefs and attitudes towards their employer, which is reciprocated through behavior as seen in organisational commitment and job satisfaction (Gallie et al., 2001). Employees' relationship with their line manager is especially important and influential and can be seen in how line managers deliver HR practices, as well as how responsive they are to worker needs and in the quality of leadership shown (Purcell and Hutchinson, 2003).

The people management activities engaged in by line management have a twin aspect of leadership behaviour and the application of HR practices as argued by Purcell and Hutchinson (2003) and implies a symbiotic relationship. Ulrich (1997) purports that line managers need well-designed HR practices in their people management strategies to help motivate and reward employees and deal with performance issues and work needs. The way, and the extent to which line managers enact these practices are influenced by their leadership behaviour (Grint, 2005) and that of senior management in establishing an appropriate organisational culture that supports, recognises and rewards people management behaviours. Kinnie et al. (2005) point out those employees are likely to be influenced both by the people management practices they experience and by their managers' leadership behaviour. Therefore, poorly designed or inadequate policies can be rescued by good management behaviour in much the same as good HR practices can be negated by poor line manager behaviour or weak leadership.

Research methods

In the present study, data were collected using semi-structured interviews with employees at the local government organisation in the North. Twenty-six interviews were conducted from a diverse range of employees with each interview lasting (45–60 minutes), tape-recorded and transcribed verbatim. The research investigated the subjective perceptions of senior managers, managers, senior officers, and clerical/secretarial staff regarding their views concerning line management leadership on employee well-being at work. This local authority was chosen to represent a variety of other local authorities in the North West. Employees were interviewed with an aim of gaining information about their experiences of line management leadership and implications for employee well-being and performance at work. The interview data were analysed using Interpretative Phenomenological Analysis (IPA) (Smith and Osborn, 2003; Smith, 2006). IPA is committed to the detailed exploration of the personal experience of an individual's world and engagement with participants' account in such a way to encourage an insider perspective. The objective of the analysis is to obtain an insight into another person's thoughts and beliefs about the phenomenon under investigation (Willig, 2001).

The interview schedule comprised open-ended questions. This allowed the interviewer to have an element of control over the questions posed, although it permitted some findings and explanations to arise unexpectedly. The interviews were conducted face to face and the interview process was collaborative and emphasised the role of the participants as the primary experts, thus keeping with the aims of IPA research. There were four lines of exploration which comprised the schedule. These include initial questions on employees' views and experiences about working for the organisation and the individual meaning of the job. The main purpose of the interview was to explore employees' views and experiences of line management leadership and its effects on employee well-being at work. Therefore, a key question in the schedule was presented as follows: 'Can you tell me your views about your line managers' leadership practices and how it has affected you personally?' Another question was: 'How responsive is your line manager to the promotion of your well-being at work?' These relationships were explored from the researchers' interpretation of the data extracted from the interviews. That is, the researcher interpreted the language discourse constructed by participants' interpretation of their reality. The discussion was centred on employees' personal experiences of work, line management leadership and their interpretation of well-being at work.

Results and discussion

The interview findings reflect individuals' own experiences about their place of work. As the participants give their portrayals of their views and experiences: their thoughts, feelings, behaviours as well as situations, events, places, and people connected with these experiences are discussed. On occasions, the explanations of experiences were different but yet familiar to others in similar situations. The findings will be discussed from both a positive and negative viewpoint in the context of three perspectives: (1) the work organisation, (2) the meaning of the job and (3) the people. Within these three perspectives, the study highlighted five superordinate themes that emerged from the analysis. These dimensions (Blame Culture; Rewards; Trust in Management; Support; and Communication) are discussed in the following sections.

The work organisation

Blame culture

Participants expressed their enjoyment for their jobs within the organisation and felt that fundamentally the organisation was honest in its vision to focus on employee perspectives, commitment, and satisfaction by creating opportunities for career development, training and flexibility for greater organisational effectiveness. It was also reported that individual experiences of the work organisation varied depending on their line manager:

> I think they're quite honest and it's quite pleasing that they are trying to drive things from the employees' perspective.
>
> (P1)

> My experiences have varied depending on my manager. I'm on my fourth job with the Council. I would admit that I enjoy it sufficiently to stay and the opp-opportunities with the Council. I would agree that I enjoy it enough to stay and the opportunities have been interesting.
>
> (P2)

Nevertheless, the participants expressed the fact that the reality of their experiences has been different from the rhetoric that was promoted by the organisation. The most prevalent experiential dimension in the interviews was the experience of a blame culture. This theme emerged in every interview, although the meaning of 'blame culture' in defining the experience differed significantly across respondents. The blame culture that existed within the organisation acted as a catalyst that promoted fear and the reluctance to take a risk and implement change.

It was further reported that managers' inability to lead and avoidance of responsibility for decision-making, resulted in fault finding, mutual suspicion and lack of trust amongst employees for managers. Rhode (2006) suggests that culture is a result of a complex learning process that is influenced by leader behaviour. Schein (2004) further expresses that culture and leadership are two sides of the same coin and neither can be understood by itself because leadership creates and changes cultures:

> I think there's still an inherent culture of blame. The biggest thing that I fear is the reluctance to take any risks: trying to do something different, try and go out of the system, try and go out of the box. The danger then is if it goes wrong, senior management will just say: 'Well, what are you playing at? You shouldn't be doing that.' However, if it goes right, nobody says a thing, 'Oh, right, that's what you get paid for.'
>
> (P3)

> They have this vision of what should be achieved, but they don't know how to do it. Therefore, they say, 'You go and make sure we get there, but that's your responsibility. You achieve that and let me know how it goes at the end,' and 'When we get there, we'll have a meeting and decide how you should have done it.'
>
> (P4)

In another group of participants for whom 'blame culture' seemed to define the experience, the meaning was from more a 'Them and US' perspective that negatively affected team working, not only amongst employees but also within the management structures themselves. The apparent lack of team working promoted negative attitudes among employees who were not prepared to be team players and displayed negative discretionary behaviour, which in turn is likely to affect service delivery and performance:

I think sometimes even the staff below us have an attitude that conveys this sentiment: 'Oh tell us what you want, and we'll get on with it' – begrudgingly. I think the higher up it gets, the further it gets. It's not necessarily a team where we're all in the same club, and we're all trying to get on with it. It's, 'Look, that's your responsibility, you get on with it.'

(P5)

I do feel certainly with my line manager that there was an obvious kind of 'them and us' sort of situation, which I find irritating.

(P6)

The second perspective (the meaning of the job) and emerging theme (rewards) in this study is suggested by respondents' answers to the question asking them to describe what their job meant to them personally.

The meaning of the job

Rewards

The most common aspect of this theme expressed by more than half of the respondents interviewed related to having a career focus and drive, which has now been reduced as a result of other interests and not feeling adequately rewarded and valued in the job. Respondents noted that the job was no longer challenging and this contributed to employees having different interests. Similarly, other participants expressed challenges with their jobs as a result of having a negative relationship with their line managers, which impacts negatively on their well-being at work and what the job means to them:

Well, the job used to be everything . . . my career and that was my focus. But in the last few years, I think it's probably dropped in significance. I don't feel rewarded, particularly from the job that I'm doing. In certain respects, it's possibly too easy now . . . and I don't think it's as challenging as it used to be. I've got other interests that have surpassed that now, and the job is almost a way of paying for those.

(P7)

I feel quite bored and demotivated at the moment, which is a bit of a shame considering that I feel passionate about my job. Therefore, I am quite cross that my relationship with my manager makes me feel so demotivated about my job.

(P8)

The commitment of participants was tied to their careers, which seemed to be the predominant and motivating factor for most participants.

However, organisational commitment and loyalty were affected due to the lack of praise and recognition for good work. Similarly, respondents noted that the existing work climate does not motivate and cultivate excellence among professional staff who is looking to progress in their jobs:

> I'm not reluctant to change jobs and I'm going to go where I think is going to be best for me career-wise.
>
> (P9)

> You know, you can do part of a job, and people will react to it like: 'Right, okay.' You can do an excellent job, and people react to it: 'Right, okay.' Sometimes, people get away with a lousy job, and the response is: 'Yeah, okay.' It doesn't seem to have the real impact unless you make a real clangour for what your case is.
>
> (P10)

Respondents expressed satisfaction with the actual jobs they did but desired to have more praise, recognition and rewards for good work done. Respondents state that teamwork is working, and managers are looking after their self-interest, and personal goals reduced their trust and satisfaction levels. Respondents indicated that their satisfaction would be improved through improved motivation by having defined goals and objectives, feeling valued and being intellectually challenged:

> At the moment, I am not satisfied at all really; I'm entirely cheesed off. To me, satisfaction is feeling valued and challenged. I don't feel very intellectually challenged at the moment, and that will make a huge difference.
>
> (P11)

The third and final perspective (the people) and emerging themes (trust in management; support; and communication) in this study are suggested by respondents' answers to questions asking them: (1) how line management leadership practices affected employees individually and (2) to describe how responsive their line managers were to the promotion of their well-being at work.

The people

Trust in management, support and communication

The most common aspect of having trust in management and being supported was expressed by more than two-thirds of respondents who suggested that their line managers treated them fairly and with respect. In contrast, others noted that they were not fairly treated by their line managers. Moreover, respondents also expressed that they were not certain whether they can fully trust their line managers. Support received was embraced but was regarded as being toothless, controlled and stifling autonomy:

> My manager is fair. I think that's the important thing. Yes, I think we've got a sort of genuine respect for each other, but then I'm never really sure whether I can fully trust him.
>
> (P9)

> Yes, I think my manager will support me, but it is toothless. My manager will back me up on certain things, or try and back me up at a meeting, but then not back that up with anything substantial.
>
> (P10)

> My manager directs the work that we're going to do so I suppose that's how he supports me regarding the work programme, which we're going to follow. However, I don't find that very supportive. I'd much prefer to be able to determine some of that work within the work programme.
>
> (P4)

Communication was another major theme that emerged as a role that managers play in promoting the well-being of employees at work. Most respondents noted that feedback was very important to their well-being, but some felt that feedback received was relatively unhelpful, and in some instances, employees got feedback in response from other comments. Similarly, there also existed a reduction in communication between management and employees, with communication flow being inadequate in certain instances:

> Yes, I receive feedback, but it tends to be a reaction from some other comment, so it's entirely unhelpful in certain respects, and it does leave you bewildered sometimes.
>
> (P13)

> Not having helpful feedback has changed my focus.
>
> (P7)

> I used to communicate and talk to my manager quite a lot. Now, I can't be bothered. I'm just going to do my job, and if he says something, okay I'll do it, but I try to not have that much communication with either of them now.
>
> (P12)

> I'm not sure about good communication flow; messages can be quite succinct. Almost to the point of tactlessness.
>
> (P5)

In another group of respondents where communication described their experience of management response to the promotion of their well-being at work, they noted that they appreciated the managers' knowledge as well as skills, and indicated that this contributed to the promotion of well-being at work. It was also noted that development for management was pivotal. In contrast, other respondents indicated that their managers' inability to be an effective problem solver and change management agent, hindered their well-being at work. It is suggested that management should develop people skills regarding listening, fewer time constraints, support and promoting autonomy, which all promote well-being at work:

> Management could do with some development. My manager is one of those cases where he is a perfect policy person and capable regarding his specialist area, as he knows his stuff and can interpret well. He's got that.
>
> (P13)

> I don't think my manager is very good regarding how he works around problems and change management, but in the public sector, this is a difficult skill.
>
> (P11)

> I don't think managers are going to be able to change their spots. I think if they listen more and have fewer time constraints, this will help the quality of my work life and well-being at work.
>
> (P12)

> Perhaps being a bit more responsive to me. . . . I would like more responsibility. I want to develop. I'd like to be left alone to get on with some more stuff, be More creative about it. My manager knows all of this but still doesn't take on board, which is extremely frustrating.
>
> (P13)

These explanations can be termed a 'Continuum of Well-Being Influence,' which stems from leadership practices. This highlights a variety of experiences that can affect individual well-being at work, either positively or negatively. It was clear that there was a strong association between line management leadership practices and blame culture, rewards, trust, support, and communication. The investigation sheds light on these associations by showing that line management leadership has been more influential in affecting employees' attitudes, behaviour and performance, which have implications for well-being at work. This relationship is illustrated in Figure 7.1.

Discussion and conclusion

The study found that a culture of blame promoted negative well-being at work (i.e. promoted fear, stifled creativity, reluctance to take risks, etc.),

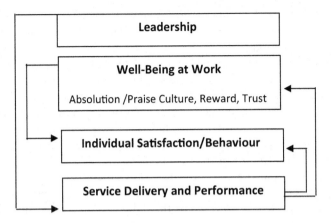

Figure 7.1 Leadership and well-being influence model

which are consequences of leadership practices adopted that is likely to hinder organisational success. Moreover, it can also reduce morale, and job satisfaction and eventually performance (Warr, 2002). In contrast, a culture of absolution and praise can be adopted instead of 'blame' to promote positive well-being to enhance service delivery and performance. Being rewarded through praise and recognition and feeling valued was seen as factors that promote well-being at work. The leadership practices adopted by management will dictate how these factors are promoted. Trust in management influences positive organisational outcomes. Once employees can distinguish trust in public sector management from alternative organisational factors such as procedural fairness and commitment, this, in turn, can improve efficiency and effectiveness (Albrecht and Travaglione, 2003). Perceived support from line management leadership facilitates social exchanges between management and employees. Once initiated by organisations, this shows the extent to which the organisation values employees' general contributions and cares for their well-being at work. With this in mind, once employees perceive that organisations value and deal equitably with them, they will reciprocate these 'good deeds' with positive work attitudes and behaviours (Guest, 2002). Communication and people skills are vital to the promotion of well-being at work. An open climate of communication, fairness, and equity in organisational policies and procedures, in addition to perceived organisational support and satisfaction with the job are significant determinants of effective leadership.

The development of line management leadership practices can promote well-being at work, which in turn can enhance the effectiveness of service delivery and performance within local authority organisations in the North. The implication of this study for line managers can thus contribute to developing the well-being of a public sector workforce which is more committed, satisfied, happy, valued and which is more positively predisposed towards organisational change. Moreover, despite the mediating effects of well-being not being fully evidenced, leaders and practitioners can use the model in (Figure 7.1) to frame and focus organisational assessments and intervention. Therefore, line managers, practitioners, policy makers and leaders throughout the North can use the model to target their 'followers' (employees) to develop well-being at work, which in turn can be used to influence organisational commitment, attitudes to change and turnover intentions. Similarly, this can have far-reaching effect by empowering and promoting distributive leadership that can be used as a catalyst to uproot the talents of existing leaders and unlock the leadership potential that has lain dormant. Once this sea of leadership talent has been unleashed, it gives access to promoting employee well-being at work: the 'key' that opens the door to enhanced leadership and performance in the North.

References

Alban-Metcalfe, R.J., and Alimo-Metcalfe, B. (2000) 'The Transformational Leadership Questionnaire (TLQ-LGV): A Convergent and Discriminant Validity Study', *Leadership and Organisation Development Journal*, Vol. 21: 280–296.

Albrecht, S., and Travaglione, A. (2003) 'Trust in Public-Sector Senior Management', *International Journal of Human Resource Management*, Vol. 14(1): 76–92.

Bakke, D.W. (2005) *Joy at Work: A Revolutionary Approach to Fun on the Job*, Seattle: PVG Publishing.

Chartered Institute of Personnel Development (CIPD) (2007) *Rewarding Work– the Vital Role of Line Managers, Change Agenda*, London: CIPD.

Currie, D. (2001) *Managing Employee Well-Being*, Oxford: Chandos Publishing Oxford Limited.

Department for Work and Pensions (2005) *Exploring How General Practitioners Work with Patients on Sick Leave*, Research Report 257, June, London: Department of Works and Pensions.

Department for Work and Pensions (2006) *A New Deal for Welfare: Empowering People at Work*, CM 6730, London: Stationery Office, www.dwp.gov.uk/ welfarereform/docs/A_new_deal_for_welfare-Empowering_people_to_work-Full_Document.pdf (accessed 19th July, 2010).

Dibbens, P., James, P., Roper, I., and Wood, G. (2007) *Modernising Work in Public Services: Redefining Roles and Relationships in Britain's Changing Workplace*, Basingstoke: Palgrave Macmillan.

Economic and Social Research Council (2006) *Health and Well-Being at Work of Working Age People*, Seminar Series: Mapping the Public Policy Landscape, Swindon: Economic and Social Research Council.

Gallie, D., Felstead, A., and Green, F. (2001) 'Employer Policies and Organisational Commitment in Britain 1992–1997', *Journal of Management Studies*, Vol. 38(8): 1081–1101.

Glover, J., Friedman, H., and Jones, G. (2002). 'Adaptive Leadership: When Change Is Not Enough (Part One)', *Organisation Development Journal*, Vol. 20(2): 15–32.

Grint, K. (2005) *Leadership: Limits and Possibilities*, Basingstoke: Management, Work & Organisations, Palgrave Macmillan.

Guest, D. (2002) 'Human Resource Management, Corporate Performance and Employee Well-Being: Building the Worker into HRM', *The Journal of Industrial Relations*, Vol. 44(3): 335–358.

Kinnie, N., Hutchinson, S., and Purcell, J. (2005) 'Satisfaction with HR Practices and Commitment to the Organisation: Why One Size Does Not Fit All', *Human Resource Management Journal*, Vol. 15(4): 9–29.

MacDonald, L.A.C. (2005) *Wellness at Work: Protecting and Promoting Employee Well-Being*, London: Chartered Institute of Personnel and Development.

McConville, T., and Holden, L. (1999) 'The Filling in the Sandwich: Managers in the Health Sector', *Personnel Review*, Vol. 28(5/6): 406–424.

McGovern, P., Gratton, L., and Hailey, H.V. (1997) 'Human Resource Management on the Line?', *Human Resource Management Journal*, Vol. 7(4): 12–29.

Peccei, R. (2004) 'Human Resource Management and the Search for the Happy Workplace', Erasmus Research Institute of Management, Rotterdam School of Management, Rotterdam School of Economics.

Pfeffer, J. (2005) 'Producing Sustainable Competitive Advantage through Effective Management of People', *Academy of Management Executive*, Vol. 19(4): 95–108.

Pratt, J., Plamping, D., and Gordon, P. (2007) 'Distinctive Characteristics of Public Sector Organisations and the Implications for Leadership', *Northern Leadership Academy*, The Centre for Innovation in Health Management.

Purcell, J., and Hutchinson, S. (2003) *Bringing Policies to Life: The Vital Role of Front Line Managers in People Management*, London: CIPD.

Purcell, J., and Hutchinson, S. (2007) 'Front-Line Managers as Agents in the HRM-Performance Causal Chain: Theory, Analysis and Evidence', *Human Resource Management Journal*, Vol. 17(1): 3–20.

Rhode, D.L. (2006) *Moral Leadership: The Theory and Practice of Power, Judgment, and Policy*, CA: Jossey-Bass Publisher, A Wiley Imprint, San Francisco: CA.

Schein, E.H. (2004) *Organisational Culture and Leadership*, CA: Jossey-Bass Publisher: San Francisco.

Smith, J.A. (2006) *Qualitative Psychology: A Practical Guide to Research Methods*, London: Sage Publication.

Smith, J.A., and Osborn, M. (2003) 'Interpretative Phenomenological Analysis', in J.A. Smith (Ed.), *Qualitative Psychology: A Practical Guide to Research Methods*, London: Sage Publications.

Tehrani, N., Humpage, S., Willmott, B., and Haslam, I. (2007) *What's Happening with Well-Being at Work?*, Change Agenda, London: Chartered Institute of Personnel Development.

Truss, K. (2001) 'Complexities and Controversies in Linking HRM with Organisational Outcomes', *Journal of Management Studies*, Vol. 38(8): 1121–1149.

Ulrich, D. (1997) *Human Resource Champions: The Next Agenda for Adding Value and Delivering Results*, Cambridge, MA: Harvard Business School Press.

Warr, P. (2002) *Psychology at Work*, Suffolk: Penguin Group Books.

Wilkinson, D. (2007) 'Distributed Leadership Briefing Chapter', in *The Centre of Innovation in Health Management*, Maurice Keyworth Building, University of Leeds, UK: North Leadership Academy.

Willig, C. (2001) *Introducing Qualitative Research in Psychology: Adventures in Theory and Method*, Buckingham: Open University Press.

8 Workplace well-being or fun initiatives

Perspectives from senior managers in the public sector

Fun at work

Fun at work. Play culture. Humour. Laughter. Skiing trips. Weekends in Spain. Fishing trips. Boozy barbecues. Award ceremonies. Hula hoop marathons. Mummy fashion shows. Wild-wacky activities. How do these terms fit into the manager's glossary in the twenty-first-century world of work, with its profoundly changing character as well as the shifting and uncertain environment (Burke and Ng, 2006)? What do they deliver to organisations facing the challenges of globalisation, cost efficiency, profit maximisation and, more recently, global recession? Historically fun has not been readily associated with the workplace, but a growing body of evidence suggests that fun at work can enhance quality of work life, reputation, performance, employee development programmes, diversity initiatives, communication, group cohesiveness, enthusiasm, satisfaction, creativity, generate fewer human resource problems and employee retention (Ford et al., 2004; Guerrier and Adib, 2003; Jeffcoat and Gibson, 2006; Karl and Peluchette, 2006; Karl et al., 2007; Newstrom, 2002). Such claims are also being championed by business writers, who advocate that 'people should love coming to work' (Bakke, 2005) and that creating a workplace culture of fun is pivotal to enhancing employee motivation and productivity, reducing stress and increasing customer satisfaction (Kersley et al., 2006). Indeed, there are many parallels between the claims of advocates of both workplace fun and well-being initiatives.

What is of particular interest to the discussion presented here is whether the same philosophy can be extended to the public sector. The UK public sector, as with many public sectors worldwide, continues to undergo significant reform processes around efficiency and costs. The push towards new public management (NPM) has led to considerable changes within funding models, governance structures, and initiatives such as joint procurement, and joint public service delivery (Morphet, 2008; Noblet et al., 2006). In particular, local government reforms tend to focus on improved management of resources and redefinition of roles and responsibilities (Noblet et al., 2006). All these changes place additional demands on public sector employees, leading to an increase in the stresses they face, relative to their normal work (Morphet, 2008). And, of course, public sector employees are at times subject to intense scrutiny by their stakeholders, who may regard recourse to 'fun' as a poor use of the public purse. In this context, it is not at all clear whether a fun culture can thrive or deliver all that is espoused, and the fun at work literature has made a little comment on its applicability to differing contexts, not least the public sector.

There is an acknowledgement, however, that implementation of a fun philosophy in the workplace may not be easy, and recognition that significant differences can exist between organisations in the degree to which their organisational cultures tolerate, facilitate or reward fund (Aldag and Sherony, 2001; Plester, 2009). More broadly, individuals are likely to differ in their attitudes regarding the importance, appropriateness, and perceived consequences of having fun at work (Karl et al., 2007). These tensions, along with questions about the underlying motivations of the fun philosophy, can cause some employees to respond with cynicism and resistance (Fineman, 2006; Warren, 2005). Whether employees find fun at work appropriate or not is dependent on their personal outlook, socialisation processes, work experiences and personality characteristics – each accounting for varying attitudes and perceptions regarding the importance of workplace fun (Aldag and Sherony, 2001).

Thus, while many supporters of fun have argued that fun can and should be infused into every workplace (Ford et al., 2004), more account is needed of the complexities of diverse organisational cultures, structures, and employment relations practices, as well as the day-to-day realities faced by contemporary employees, including managers themselves. Research is needed to expand this literature, particularly as it pertains to the public sector. To this end, this article takes local government as its setting. Based on findings stemming from research with 12 senior managers about their own experiences as employees, it will be argued that the promotion of well-being at work is a more pivotal requirement and perhaps a precursor to workplace fun, in place of the narrow focus on organised activities proposed by 'ministers of fun' (Ford et al., 2004; Karl and Peluchette, 2006; Karl et al., 2005). In so doing, it is intended that the research findings presented here will contribute to the emerging debate on workplace fun by shining a light on its under-explored relationship with well-being.

Well-being and fun at work

Well-being has become one of the most important issues of the twenty-first-century world of work – a challenge not just for individuals, regarding their mental and physical health, but for employers and governments who have started to assess its social and financial implications. Well-being is multifaceted, and for this chapter employee well-being is defined as employee welfare which includes material conditions, and the wider experience of organisational life. This definition invokes not just specific practices of 'wellness' programmes, health screening, or indeed fun programmes, but employees' physical, emotional and psychological needs including issues of stress, anxiety, insecurity, exhaustion, and depression (Kersley et al., 2006). In support, Grant et al. (2007) state that well-being is the overall quality of an employee's experience and functioning at work (Warr, 2002). The concept of employee well-being at work promotes the advantages to organisations of having a healthy workforce and is pivotal to understandings of the different domains that affect the quality of life at work (Baptiste, 2008a). Personal well-being does not exist in isolation, but within a social context (Tehrani et al., 2007) and individual lives are affected by social relations with organisational agents, lifestyle and employment changes (Kersley et al., 2006). Contemporary organisations that foster well-being are perceived as employers of 'best practice' and are recognised by current and prospective employees as offering a desirable place to work (Grant et al., 2007). While well-being at work is being promoted as a potential avenue for providing meaning and fulfilment at work, the factors that foster well-being at work have attracted limited empirical research.

Although not formalised within a well-being framework, the philosophy of 'fun at work' is also embraced as a means of promoting employees' satisfaction through organised activities (Karl and Peluchette, 2006). Experienced fun is the extent to which a person perceives the existence of fun in their workplace (Karl et al., 2007). In support, a recent analysis of the Sunday Times 'Best Companies to Work For' (Bolton, 2006) notes that fun at work environment is treated as one of the distinguishing factors of a caring approach to employees, and is claimed to enhance superior performance. Taylor and Bain's (2003) research exposes perhaps a darker side to fun programs, and highlights that for some employees' fun is regarded as a smokescreen disguising real conflicts. Other researchers go further in finding exhortations to be fun expressions, reserving autonomy in when people do and do not have fun (Warren, 2005). On the other hand, some employees may embrace the introduction of fun activities into the workplace, seeing them as a welcome release from a stressful job (Ford et al., 2004). The middle ground for fun programs, as argued by Fineman (2006), is likely to be characterised by a mixture of reactions – with compliance, discomfort or feeling used on the one hand, and temporary light-heartedness or relief from repetitive work on the other. This ambivalence may mean that the fun philosophy faces challenges, and even curtailment, where occasions of stress, anxiety, anger, pessimism, and unhappiness within work life are silenced or marginalised (Fineman, 2006).

The results that fun at work would appear to aim to achieve include relaxed, engaged (even happy!) employees as an immediate factor in the enrichment of the quality of working life. However, deeper questions must be asked about whether the invocation to fun can be a false route to happiness and well-being. Where the fun literature focuses on performance-related outcomes through fun initiatives, well-being at work focuses on the organisational climate and work arrangements that hold the potential for making employees happier and healthier as a primary goal, with acknowledged implications for effort, contributions, and productivity. Grant et al. (2007) argue that employee well-being comprises three dimensions:

1   The *psychological* dimension is where employees' well-being is shaped by experiences of satisfaction with their job and lives. In support, Haworth and Hart (2007) argue that these subjective experiences entail pleasure, the balance of positive and negative thought and feelings in an individual's judgement, which influences a perception of stress, anxiety, happiness, and other emotional states.
2   The *physical* dimension involves influencing employees' health regarding improvement of outcomes relating to cardiovascular disease, blood pressure, workplace health and safety (Danna and Griffin, 1999), and work stress (Karasek and Theorell, 1990).
3   The *social* dimension focuses on the quality of interpersonal relationships and the dimensions of fair treatment for employees (Renwick, 2002) regarding the trust, social support, reciprocity, leader-member exchange, cooperation, coordination, and integration (Keyes, 1998).

Organisations that embrace employee well-being appear then to prioritise the protection and promotion of employee satisfaction (Baptiste, 2008a; Tehrani et al., 2007), embracing a praise and rewards culture, trust (Baptiste, 2008b), fulfilment and health (Bakke, 2005; Danna and Griffin, 1999).

However, a closer look at the realities of managerial work shows the challenges that such an approach can face. Managers have certain distinct functions as compared to owners of the organisations or its employees. In the contemporary business environment, managers increasingly need to focus on cost management and competitive strategies. Clark and Salaman (1998) observe that the key characteristics of management work emerging from studies over the last 40 years include brevity, spontaneity, fragmentation and discontinuity, adaptation to circumstances, unreflective thinking or actions, and a focus on immediacy, doing, and on tangible, concrete activities. Moreover, senior managers' daily realities are inundated with social and moral problems in corporate life (Jackall, 1988), often further challenging espoused rationality and efficiency. In these contexts, senior managers may find it difficult to embrace and instigate 'fun at work' initiatives, and it is a worthy question to explore the degree to which managers' own experience of work can be characterised by fun.

As with any other group of employees, for senior managers. Material aspects of the employment relationship are key to their well-being. This chapter, therefore, seeks to explore workplace fun through the window of 'well-being at work' as it relates to senior managers. There has been little research done in the area, and this chapter begins to address the gap. The next section discusses the methodological approach adopted, followed by the findings, discussion and conclusion.

Methodology

This research is part of a larger study investigating employees' experiences of HRM practices and how such experiences have contributed to their well-being at work in the local government context. A local authority was chosen in the North West of England. This authority professed to have adopted well-being policies and practices to establish fun and well-being, a positive attendance culture, promote fun at work and enhance staff welfare. This present study focuses on a particular group within the local authority – i.e. senior managers – and their experiences of the relationship between fun and well-being. As has been noted, limited empirical research has been done on this demographic. In-depth, face-to-face interviews were conducted with senior managers with the aim of understanding their experiences of working life and the meanings they attach to their well-being at work. Purposive sampling was used to ensure that all departments within the council were reflected, and six male and six female managers participated in the study. All 12 were Caucasian, aged from 30 to 59 years, had attained qualifications of a first degree and above, worked full-time, reported a range of incomes between £30,000 and £50,000, and held a variety of tenures with the organisation:

- 0–5 years (five respondents)
- 6–10 years (three respondents)
- 11–20 years (two respondents)
- 21–25 years (two respondents)

Interviews lasted for 60–90 minutes, and were tape-recorded, transcribed verbatim and analysed using hermeneutic phenomenological analysis (HPA) (Van Manen, 1990). The study commenced with an initial question: 'Can you tell me what it is like to work here?' The interview schedule covered three broad topics:

1 Defining individual well-being at work
2 Why well-being at work as defined by the respondent was important
3 What things they would like to see improved at the council to promote their well-being at work

Managers were asked to respond based on their own experiences and priorities as employees, rather than from an espoused practice point of view. Initial transcripts were reviewed through immersion in the data to establish an orienting Gestalt that drove later coding. Interviews were coded line-by-line, necessary for thematic analysis. Concepts, themes, and sub-themes were identified. Half of the transcripts were coded separately by an independent researcher to identify emerging themes, and the resulting coding match of 85% provides evidence of reliability in the coding process (Silverman, 1993). Final themes were also verified by informants to ensure they appropriately captured the meaning that the informant sought to convey.

Data is presented in this chapter in two forms:

1   Rich descriptions and meanings drawn from interview texts
2   Graphical data display

Table 8.1 indicates salient points raised in the interviews (Lyons, 2000). While no statistical significance is claimed, the tabular representation of themes has been structured on the assumption that a theme cited by a larger number of interviewees has more importance to the respondents as a whole (Miles and Huberman, 1994). The resulting patterns provide an enriched understanding of the factors pertinent to the relationship between employee well-being and fun in local government.

Findings

Managers' perception of the initial question 'What is it like to work here?' reflected realities faced and included themes that relate to budget pressures, workplace stress, and stakeholder relationships. Managers' perceptions of well-being at work were explored through interpretation of the discourse constructed by informants. All three dimensions of well-being (psychological, physical and social) emerged in managers' responses without prompting, as illustrated in Table 8.1. Stemming from this, informants' reports of working life and conditions that fostered their well-being were clustered into eight categories:

1   Working time arrangements
2   Stress management
3   Communication strategies
4   Reward strategies
5   Management development
6   The team working
7   Relationships with stakeholders
8   Clarification and reduction in change initiatives

The following findings are organised according to the initial question and the three interview topics.

Table 8.1 Managers' interpretations of well-being at work

Multifaceted Nature of Employee Well-Being	Individual Definition of Well-Being	Importance of Well-Being	Improvements in Well-Being
Psychological Well-being	• Work-life Balance • Recognition and Rewards • Appreciation • Honesty • Transparency • Confidence • Competence • Happiness • Empowerment • Fun at Work • Job Satisfaction • Relaxed Environment • Job Enrichment • Autonomy	• Sense of Belonging • Commitment • Intellectual Challenge • Job Satisfaction • Purpose and Identity • Making a difference • Job Enrichment • Appreciation • Recognition • Performance • Encouragement • Flexible Working • Retention • Career Development	• Work-life balance • Clear and reduced priorities • Creativity and Innovation • Develop management competencies • Rewards and Recognition • Reduction in working hours • Reduction in Anxiety • Trust • Home Working
Physical Well-being	• Safe Environment • Work Stress • Physical and Mental Health • Health and Safety	• Stress Reduction • Health and Safety	• Stress Management • Therapies to de-stress
Social Well-being	• Support from HR • Team Working • Feedback • Avoiding Bullying • Reduce Absenteeism • Attendance culture • Retention	• Team Working • Retention • Avoiding Bullying • Support from Manager	• Team Working • No Evening Meetings • Communication • Relationships

Working life realities

The most prominent points cited by managers, interpreted as those most frequently mentioned, were budget pressures, heavy workloads, staffing issues, fragmented teams and stakeholder relationships. Illustrating this, one manager stated:

> It's very good. I think a lot of effort is made to look after us. The policies are automatically in place and my team and I particularly benefit from flexible working. On the other hand, I think it's patchy, and some of the operational teams are very stretched, and we're

swamped. There are budget pressures and staffing pressures. My team is down here, and I'm at another location. There are some disadvantages regarding some banter and the bouncing ideas off each other. . . . There are tensions between sections and departments inevitably, and we try to break that down as much as possible. I think for a long time we had a bit of a silo mentality that, 'We're in this section and this is what we do.' I mean in a large organisation there's going to be tensions and difficulties, but I don't think we're any worse than anybody else. . . . Not understanding, misunderstanding, fighting your corner which you know many managers have had a history of that, haven't they? You know, they've got to make sure things are for their benefit, and you get used to that.

(Female manager, aged 50–59 years,
tenure 11–20 years)

Another senior manager built this picture further, highlighting external pressures on his work in particular. He said:

Local government is a bit of a mystery to people I think. The perception of it is entered on this town hall clerk ethos, and we're all pushing bits of chapter and pushing pens. However, it still sometimes feels like we're in an environment where we are fighting off all sort of attacks from customers who aren't happy with the service; from members who might be outside counsellors, who might have had unhappy constituents, MPs doing the same . . . dealing with staffing issues takes a lot of time here because we try to do things properly. At times it could feel a bit cumbersome, or still, sometimes it will all clash, and the days of feeling that it's a job for life have gone with budget problems. However, you still get the public sector ethos in parts of what you do. It always can depend on what job you do within the council, but there's still that motivation, 'Well I'm doing something that is benefiting the people of the community.'

(Senior manager, male, age 40–49 years,
tenure under 5 years)

Such descriptions give a strong flavour of the working realities for these senior managers and suggest that their working context offers little by way of fun.

Managerial work and well-being

When asked to define individual well-being at work from a personal point of view, the most significant aspects cited by these managers were the work-life balance, stress management, and a sense of purpose. For example, one assistant director invoked all three, as she shared her definition:

It's about the balance between work and life in a nutshell really, and obviously not feeling stressed at work. Work-life balance is a huge bonus for me now. I can work mainly from home now, and it's a big help. It is a big help. That's probably one reason why I wouldn't necessarily look for another job just now because the work-life balance is quite good. I can work around things to suit my other demands. Also, I think stress is a problem at the council, and I don't think many people want to admit it. Stress affects people coming to work or not coming to work and results in poor attendance. The issue of stress needs to be looked at because a lot of people suffer from anxiety.

(Assistant director, Female, Age 40–49 years,
Tenure 6–10 years)

Another male manager had this to say:

To me, my well-being at work is not waking up in the morning and thinking, 'Oh God, I have to go to work. I hate my job.' I guess I'm lucky in the fact that I have always had jobs that I have quite enjoyed doing. I never really had a job that is routine, so new things happen all the time. If I ever get to the stage where I think, 'I am not going to work tomorrow,' I will go and look for another job. I think it is all about the ethos of the organisation, and the freedom to get on and do your job without being bullied or abused.

(Manager, Male, Age 40–49 years,
Tenure 6–10 years)

It is clear that for these managers the material dimensions of their working experience are keenly felt, and have a significant effect on their sense of well-being. How important is that well-being, and what does it mean to them? When this question was put to respondents, it became evident that the attitudes of these managers towards their psychological well-being were complex, and the influence of individual characteristics such as personality, age, and previous working experiences in local government suggests itself. Their comments on 'the importance of well-being at work' tended to invoke further ingredients of well-being, and again, according to frequency noted, the most important of these was an opportunity to make a difference, work-life balance, support from management, and feeling valued. The following quote illustrates the emphasis put on making a difference:

I suppose it is most important to know that what you do counts; that what you do is making a difference; that there is a purpose to your working life; that you're not just turning up and hitting the keyboard for a few hours, so that at the end of the day when asked, 'What did you do today?' you say, 'The same thing I do every day,' and when asked, 'What is that?' your response is, 'I'm not sure.' Instead, you can say that you have had a good day and you have achieved something and made a difference. What you do is essential, and to do that you have to be valued, you need to be rewarded, you need to be part of a team. You need to know that your work is going somewhere and doing things, but not just things for the sake of it. At the end of your career, you need to be able to look back and say, I did this. I did that.'

(Senior manager, Male, Age 40–49 years,

Tenure 6–10 years)

Another manager spoke more directly about the importance of well-being to her at work, and what that represented. She explained:

Without flexible working and support from my manager, it makes the job harder. I can't imagine working in any environment without the support of my manager; that's probably the most important thing. It would make me want to look elsewhere for a job. If you don't get that reinforcement that you're doing a good job – if you don't get that support for the decisions that you make, it can make your working life unbearable.

(Manager, Female, Age 50–59 years,

Tenure 11–20 years)

To develop an understanding of managers' experiences further, the research explored suggestions from respondents on how their well-being could be enhanced. Managers were asked: 'Can you tell me what things you would like to see improved in the Council to promote your well-being?' A key example cited was the communication climate, as the following comments testify:

I would like to see something that improves upward communication. The reason why I say this is because it's linked to creating an environment where staff will be able to say what they want. Staff should be able to share their wacky ideas about fun and well-being without thinking, 'I would be disciplined for wacky ideas.' This environment creates some job satisfaction and therefore will improve people's well-being because you would want to come to work. It's better to think that you work for an organisation that allows you to experiment and do things differently, and if you get it wrong, then what is stressed is that you learned from it, rather than thinking, 'Do, I want to take the risk? If I do, I might be on my own.'

(Director, Male, Age 40–49 years,

Tenure under 5 years)

Some aspects of this director's comments relate to the promotion of a culture that encourages open communication, that would support 'wacky' ideas and more creative thinking. While it can be speculated that a fun work environment would allow such a culture to be more readily embraced, it is not clear that fun has a cultural fit with this environment, nor that fun at work ethos is the only means of promoting the creativity and involvement that is being aspired to.

Continuing the communication theme, another manager shared her perception of how improvements in this area would promote her well-being. She explained:

> Communication with staff from above needs to be filtered down much better. When they have these corporate meetings, these 'thinking out of the box' and samples of staff attend these meetings. it's the division that causes problems. However, when staff knows that they are appreciated, you'll get the best out of them. If you don't do that, you will never get the best out of them, and you'll get more absences. They need to communicate better with the staff and improve things. They need to offer staff things that will enhance their well-being like therapies that will help them to de-stress. Offer them the opportunity to do things that are not necessarily work-related. There should be a promotion for those who are doing high-levelled jobs like myself. Allow us to work from home or promote us. Encourage managers not to look at it as a bad thing and allow flexible working hours. For me, coming into the office from 9:30am to 10:00am is perfect for me.
>
> (Manager, Female, Age 50–59 years,
> Tenure under 5 years)

An issue raised in the preceding comments, 'offering staff things to enhance their well-being like therapies, opportunities to do things that are not necessarily work-related' invokes aspects of the 'fun at work' philosophy. However, although certainly mentioned, such initiatives were raised less frequently and assigned notably less importance than more material aspects of employment relations such as work-life balance, stress management, and team working. It is fair to say that such ingredients appear to have a much lower priority for these managers. This suggests that only when the more material aspects of well-being are fulfilled is their value in the initiatives advocated by 'ministers of fun,' such as therapies and play activities. However, comments from another manager raise a different, more practical, perspective on how non-work initiatives that can promote well-being and possibly fun could be enhanced. He said:

> I think if I had a shower at work it would be beneficial and I could cycle more. It's more important than you think. I am a great believer in physical exercise and mental health. If you can combine the two so that while you're cycling at the beginning of the day, for example, you're thinking about your day and gearing yourself up and doing

the same on your way home, would certainly, be beneficial. Getting your exercise and dealing with the pressures of the day is important. It's a healthy thing to do, so facilitating more of that is good. . . . I've always said that they [the Council] should give free sessions at the sports centres for things like swimming and other activities. If it were free for Council staff, you'd get a lot more people using it.

(Senior manager, Male, Age 40–49 years,
Tenure under 5 years)

Returning to the theme of work organisation related improvements that would contribute to well-being, another such example was the desire for more conducive working patterns:

Somehow we have to persuade the members that we can't have evening meetings; they must meet during the daytime. Persuade them that the best place to make decisions is when officers are not tired after having worked for maybe 12 hours before the meeting starts, because it's not just me but my director, and my team leaders and my lawyers going to those meeting in the evenings as often as once a month and even more frequently sometimes. I don't think it's the best place to make decisions. Also, I don't think it's helpful to my team and my lawyers to be there at 10.00 pm or 11.00 p.m. I don't think it's the best decision-making time for the Council either. That is the first thing I will say can be removed to improve my well-being at work. In addition, they should perhaps look at the possibility of rewarding staff as well.

(Assistant director, Female, Age 40–49 years,
Tenure 6–10 years)

Another director had similar comments to make. He explained:

Improve the relationship with some of our stakeholders because of some of them are having a disproportionate impact on me and the rest of the organisation. We need a bit more clarity about our priorities and need to narrow down our priorities, rather than wanting to do everything. . . . Stress management, rightly or wrongly, is becoming a massive problem in society and the public sector and it's significant. . . . If we can do some more work with regards to developing staff and managers' capacities to be able to recognize and manage stress and respond positively to signs of stress, it will benefit everyone's well-being in the organisation.

(Director, Male, Age 40–49 years,
Tenure 6–10 years)

Taken as a whole, these managers' comments touched on serious challenges faced by an individual and organisational perspective. For these respondents, it would seem that material issues like a relationship with stakeholders, clarification and narrowing down of change priorities, stress management, and management development are of fundamental importance to the promotion of their well-being. To go further, 'fun initiatives' are not likely to be readily embraced when managers are faced with the daily challenges they describe, nor is fun perceived by respondents as particularly high on their list of concerns.

Discussion

The study shows that in this local authority, despite the espousal of well-being policies aimed at promoting a happier and more stress-free workforce, none of these managers were having much fun. Instead, it indicates beleaguered managers, needing recognition of genuine day-to-day concerns. This is reflected in managers' responses to working life realities regarding budget and staffing pressures, team working, and stakeholder relationships within which these managers function. The results highlight a silence in fun at work literature around the conditions of fun and indicate that experiences of well-being at work are strongly associated with material aspects of employment relations, which have to be addressed before the philosophy of 'fun at work' can have meaning or relevance. It is hard to imagine that these managers would welcome organised fun activities that would encroach even more into their already busy schedules. Therefore, serious consideration is required to address the factors that promote employee well-being rather than more prescriptions to have fun. The articulated individual definitions of well-being (Table 8.1) indicated important points associated with the psychological perspective of well-being to include work-life balance, reward strategies, management development, trust, and autonomy.

In support, well-being proponents argue that emotional experiences construct individuals' reality of happiness and well-being (Ryff and Keyes, 1995; Kersley et al., 2006). This was consistent across all managers. The salient points that focused on the physical perspective entailed health and safety and work stress. Managers responded similarly for each question asked. The literature advocates that physical and mental health and experiencing a safe working environment are areas that can reduce work stress, which in turn can promote well-being (Danna and Griffin, 1999; Karasek and Theorell, 1990). Prominent points identified concerning the social perspective involved support, team working, feedback, avoidance of bullying and reduction in absenteeism.

In support, Keyes (1998) denotes that all qualities of employees' relationships with other people and communities within the organisation provide opportunities for interpersonal relationships (Grant et al., 2007). Advocates of fun propose that employee 'happiness' can result from 'fun activities,' which in essence is rhetoric when considering the reality faced by these managers in their daily working lives.

Managers' responses to the importance of well-being seemed to be essentially associated with the psychological perspective, noting the importance of a sense of purpose and belonging, reward strategies, support, work-life balance, and performance, all of which shape employees' satisfaction with their jobs and lives (Tehrani et al., 2007). These crucial points were cited by all managers. Similarly, the physical and social perspectives were reflected by the same issues discussed previously.

Subsequently, managers had much to say on the topic of improvements in their well-being. Each was concerned with fulfilment and realisation of their human potential. The psychological perspective for improvements touched on issues previously discussed and also included the effect of clarification and reduction in the volume and frequency of change initiatives. The physical aspect noted problems discussed earlier, and the social perspective noted previous factors and also included communication strategies, relationships, and discontinuance of evening meetings with members. These points resonate with the views of Grant et al. (2007)

Figure 8.1 Organisational factors that foster well-being to enable fun

regarding the importance of social support, cooperation, coordination and integration to be associated with relational interactions.

Overall, the often highly bureaucratic and slow-to-change culture of public sector organisations (Noblet et al., 2006) is likely to be less tolerant of 'fun', as this can bring about heavy scrutiny from stakeholders. In this context, fun initiatives can be perceived as yet another program to drain more effort out of already overworked employees. While these findings concern the employment experiences of local government managers, a moderate generalisation can be made for managers and employees more broadly (Williams, 2002, p. 211). The findings also point to the need for balance between ideals of 'workplace fun' and human needs (Fineman, 2006).

In conclusion, it can be argued that these senior managers, and perhaps more generally, employees in similar contexts have some way to go before they self-actualise and are fulfilled in their well-being at work. It will take a further step, given the complexities and daily challenges faced, before they can welcome managerially led fun activities. The mantra of "working hard" is evident for these managers, as for so many contemporary professionals; however, the Utopian state of 'fun at work' is likely to remain a subjective phenomenon in the pursuit of happiness for the foreseeable future.

References

Aldag, R., and Sherony, K. (2001), 'A Spoonful of Sugar: Some Thoughts on "Fun at Work"', *Current Issues in Management*, Vol. 1(1): 62–76.

Bakke, D.W. (2005) *Joy at Work: A Revolutionary Approach to Fun on the Job*, New York, NY: Penguin.

Baptiste, N.R. (2008a) 'Tightening the Link between Employee Well-Being and Performance: A New Dimension for HRM', *Management Decision*, Vol. 46(2): 284–309.

Baptiste, N.R. (2008b) 'Line Management Leadership: Implications for Employee Well-Being', in G.P. Clarkson (Ed.) *Developing Leadership Research, Chapters from the Northern Leadership Academy Fellow 2007 Conference*, Leeds: Leeds University Press Financial Services.

Bolton, S. (2006) 'The UK's Best Could Do So Much Better', *Personnel Today Magazine*, 7th March.

Burke, R.J., and Ng, E. (2006) 'The Changing Nature of Work Organisations: Implications for Human Resource Management', *Human Resource Management Review*, Vol. 16: 86–94.

Clark, J., and Salaman, G. (1998) 'Telling Tales: Management Gurus' Narratives and the Construction of Managerial Identity', *Journal of Management Studies*, Vol. 35(2): 137–161.

Danna, K., and Griffin, R.W. (1999) 'Health and Well-Being in the Workplace: A Review and Synbook of the Literature', *Journal of Management*, Vol. 25(3): 357–384.

Fineman, S. (2006) 'On Being Positive: Concerns and Counterpoints', *Academy of Management Review*, Vol. 31(2): 270–291.

Ford, R.C., Newstrom, J.W., and McLaughlin, F.S. (2004) 'Making Workplace Fun More Functional', *Industrial and Commercial Training*, Vol. 36(3): 117–120.

Grant, A., Christianson, M., and Price, R. (2007) 'Happiness, Health or Relationships? Managerial Practices and Employee Well-Being Tradeoffs', *The Academy of Management*, Vol. 21(3): 51–63.

Guerrier, Y., and Adib, A. (2003) 'Work at Leisure and Leisure at Work: A Study of the Emotional Labour of Tour Reps', *Human Relations*, Vol. 56(11): 1399–1417.

Haworth, J., and Hart, G. (2007) *Well-Being: Individual, Community and Social Perspectives*, Basingstoke: Palgrave Macmillan.

Jackall, R. (1988) *Moral Mazes: The World of Corporate Managers*, New York, NY: Oxford University Press.

Jeffcoat, K., and Gibson, J.W. (2006) 'Fun as Serious Business: Creating a Fun Working Environment as an Effective Business Strategy', *Journal of Business and Economic Research*, Vol. 4(2): 29–34.

Karasek, R.A., and Theorell, T. (1990) *Healthy Work: Stress, Productivity, and the Reconstruction of Working Life*, New York, NY: Basic Books.

Karl, K.A., and Peluchette, J.V. (2006), 'How Does Workplace Fun Impact Perception of Customer Service Quality', *Journal of Leadership and Organisational Studies*, Vol. 13(2): 2–13.

Karl, K.A., Peluchette, J.V., Hall-Indiana, L., and Harland, L. (2005) 'Attitudes towards Workplace Fun: A Three Sector Comparison', *Journal of Leadership and Organisational Studies*, Vol. 12(2): 1–17.

Karl, K.A., Peluchette, J.V., and Harland, L. (2007), 'Is Fun for Everyone? Personality Differences in Healthcare Providers' Attitudes toward Fun', *Journal of Health and Human Services Administration*, Vol. 49(4): 409–447.

Kersley, B., Alpin, C., Forth, J., Bryson, A., Bewley, H., Dix, G., and Oxenbridge, S. (2006) *Inside the Workplace: Findings from the 2004 Workplace Employment Relations Survey*, London: Routledge.

Keyes, C.L.M. (1998) 'Social Well-Being', *Social Psychology Quarterly*, Vol. 61(2): 121–140.

Lyons, E. (2000) 'Qualitative Data Display: Data Display Model', in C. Fife-Schaw (Ed.) *Research Methods in Psychology*, pp. 269–280, London: Sage Publications.

Miles, M.B., and Huberman, A.M. (1994) *Qualitative Data Analysis: An Expanded Source Book*, London: Sage Publications.

Morphet, J. (2008) *Modern Local Government*, London: Sage Publications.

Newstrom, J.W. (2002) 'Making Work Fun: An Important Role for Managers', *SAM Advanced Management Journal*, Vol. 67(1): 4–21.

Noblet, A.J., McWilliams, J., Teo, S.T.T., and Rodwell, J.J. (2006) 'Work Characteristics and Employee Outcomes in Local Government', *International Journal of Human Resource Management*, Vol. 17: 1804–1818.

Plester, B. (2009) 'Crossing the Line: Boundaries of Workplace Humour and Fun', *Employee Relations*, Vol. 31(6): 584–599.

Renwick, D. (2002) 'HR Managers, Guardians of Employee Well-Being', *Personnel Review*, Vol. 32(3): 341–359.

Ryff, C.D., and Keyes, C.L.M. (1995) 'The Structure of Psychological Well-Being Revisited', *Journal of Personality and Social Psychology*, Vol. 69: 719–727.

Silverman, D. (1993) *Interpreting Qualitative Data: Methods for Analysing Talk, Text and Interaction*, London: Sage Publications.

Taylor, P., and Bain, P. (2003) '"Subterranean Worksick Blues": Humour as Subversion in Two Call Centres', *Organisation Studies*, Vol. 24(9): 1487–1509.

Tehrani, N., Humpage, S., Willmott, B., and Haslam, I. (2007) *What's Happening with Well-Being at Work?*, Change Agenda, London: Chartered Institute of Personnel and Development.

Van Manen, M. (1990) *Researching Lived Experience: Human Science for an Action Sensitive Pedagogy*, New York, NY: State University of New York Press.

Warr, P. (2002) *Psychology at Work*, Harmondsworth: Penguin.

Warren, S. (2005) 'Humour as a Management Tool? The Irony of Structuring Fun in Organisations', in U. Johannson and J. Woodilla (Eds.) *Irony and Organisation: Epistemological Claims and Supporting Field Stories*, pp. 174–199, Copenhagen: Copenhagen Business School, Liber.

Williams, M. (2002) 'Generalization in Interpretative Research', in T. May (Ed.) *Qualitative Research in Action*, London: Sage Publications.

9 Work, quality of working life and job meaning

A well-being experience in the public sector

The global economy and New Public Management

In the middle of the twenty-first century, the British economy experienced recessionary challenges which resulted in financial turmoil, a fall in output, employment and the decline in labour productivity (Van Wanrooy et al., 2011). Both private and public sector organisations were affected by the recession with a pattern of unstable growth and uncertainty. Public sector organisations in particular were stretched further to endure the challenging financial crisis which places a tighter squeeze and pressure on there already limited resources within a New Public Management (NPM) environment. The key principles and political context of the NPM has been applied to the public sector because of funding limitations and the growing expenditure due to technological progress and an aging population (Simonet, 2013). Simonet (2013) further states that NPM theory reforms can be traced to the neoliberal ideas of the early 1980s, economic shocks, and the desire for governments to balance their budgets. Boyne (2002) and Dibbens et al., (2007) state that the NPM ideology and the way decisions are made with respect to declining budgets, increasing demands for service and productivity, and human resources activities have implications for human resources management, working life and well-being at work for public sector employees.

The public sector has been the centre for continuous politically sensitive reform that has been underpinned by the NPM approach that focuses on the move from hierarchical formalised approach, with an emphasis on avoiding mistakes and application of rules (Butterfield et al., 2005). It also involves the existence of bureaucracy and red tape (Bozeman, 1993, 2000) to espousal of decentralisation, values of innovation, enterprise and management problem solving (Clarke et al., 2000; McLaughlin et al., 2008). Other features involve a shift towards value for money, supported by techniques of performance management, budgeting, costing, balance scorecard and key performance indicators (Jackson and Lapsley, 2003). The modernisation of the public sector consequently affected, and still affects, public sector workers in the areas of declining public service ethos (Needham, 2007), increasing criticism of the quality of public services and failure to meet citizens expectations (Dibbens and James, 2007), work intensification and delivery of public services (Noblet et al., 2006a), pay and rewards (Folger and Cropanzano, 1998), fairness and equity (Harrow, 2002; Marsden, 2007), employment security (Dibben, 2007), increased absenteeism, mental health challenges, financial well-being, presenteeism and leaveism (CIPD, 2019; Hesketh et al., 2014), and even less discussed employee well-being (Baptiste, 2007, 2009; Emmott, 2006).

The challenges of limited resources in the public sector have diminished the confidence and trust in government, which in turn is likely to erode the morale and well-being of public sector employees (Anderson and Bateman, 1997). Berman et al. (2010) assert that rebuilding trust is an important challenge facing the public sector at all levels. Central to this view, Pate et al.'s (2007) research reveals a relative distrust of senior management in the public sector. Research from the CIPD's Health and Well-being at work survey reveal that employees noted that relationships with management was the second major cause of work-related stress, and mental ill-health, which in turn have implications for negative well-being, absenteeism, presenteeism and leaveism behaviours in the public sector (CIPD, 2019).

The crisis of work

The implications of reform changes, restructuring, downsizing in the public sector resulted in closing departments, discontinuation of services, with numerous employees facing layoffs and organisational changes and restructuring, requiring the delivery of more efficient services and performance within minimum budget levels. This situation created what Braverman (1999) referred to as 'a crisis work environment' (20). This represents the workplace turning into a stressful environment that threatens to destroy the health and, in some cases, the lives of working people. Braverman further argues that some of the causes of stress derive from unions and company management embattling and mistrusting the other, human resources and employee relations departments overwhelmed by the demands of unrelenting organisational change, and domestic challenges spilling into the workplace. Such environments foster control over limited resources, competition and uncertainty that set people against one another, pushing many past their limits, and for many workers, these conditions have turned the workplace into a place of desperation, isolation and despair (Braverman, 1999; Tehrani, 2012).

The sources of stress on organisational systems represent multiple and complex issues that can originate from the work situation itself and from outside the work environment, deriving from the community and family (Braverman, 1999). Pauchant and Mitroff (1992) and Dibbens et al. (2007) argue that leaders in crisis-prepared organisations understand that stress, which directly affects the people in their companies, can derive from diverse sources. This stress will have a direct impact on the health and well-being of their people and the success of their businesses (Baptiste, 2008). Pauchant and Mitroff (1992) further posit that crisis-prepared organisations would have systems to alert them to stressors and danger signs that could trigger workplace bullying and harassment, and mistreatment (Hanrahan and Leiter, 2014). Workplace mistreatment or incivility starts with personal experience of being left out of a meeting, not being asked to sit in on a call relevant to your work, catching a co-worker slip out an exaggerated sigh as you express your opinion, and outward rude remarks, are some of the meanings and incidents that can be used to define our interpersonal experiences of incivility (Hanrahan and Leiter, 2014). Workplace incivility relates to the negative, harmful and inappropriate behaviours that can occur in the workplace. Anderson and Pearson (1999) argue that workplace incivility should be viewed as a social interaction as involving and influencing the instigator, the targets or recipients, any observers, and the social context in which the interaction occurs. Anderson and Pearson define workplace incivility 'as low intensity deviant behaviour with ambiguous intent to harm the target, in violation of workplace norms for mutual respect. Uncivil behaviours are characteristically rude and discourteous, displaying a lack of regard for others' (457); as well as acts of inappropriate behaviours that had a clear intent to cause harm and falls under a large scope of antisocial behaviours that brings harm, or is intended to bring harm to an organisation, its employees, or it's stakeholders (Anderson and Pearson, 1999; Giacalone and Greenberg, 1997). Researchers also looked at how these less intense behaviours of ambiguous intent were related to the more serious acts of aggression and violence (Anderson and Pearson, 1999). Incivility in the workplace interferes with the ability of individuals, groups, and entire organisations to meet their full potentials and positive well-being. Individuals, groups and organisations that can counteract the dysfunction of mistreatment or incivility in the workplace may recover positive employee well-being and productivity that workplace incivility often impact employee's health and well-being and the bottom line (Hanrahan and Leiter, 2014).

The relentless pace of change, both inside the workplace and in society, continues to cause stress and disruptions that affect individuals and the work organisations they inhabit, causing a loss of job security for employees at all levels (Baptiste, 2008). Furthermore, with respect to the public sector, greater increased service delivery performance pressure causes stress levels to heighten for many employees, creating mounting concerns about limited resources, bullying and harassment and conflict within the workplace. Braverman (1999) suggests that the signs of an organisation in crisis might involve a single employee submitting a claim for stress, complaining of harassment, or reporting domestic abuse (HSE, 2008).

The employment relationship provides a context in which employers can act effectively to evaluate and resolve the threat to safety, personal health, and financial health as well as to prevent and stop the damage of bullying and violence in the workplace (Namie and Namie, 2011). A workplace can thrive only when its members feel positively connected and when employees at all levels trust the organisation as a whole (Baptiste, 2008; Cvenkel, 2018). When one mismanages change and trauma, people at all levels of the organisation become nervous, unsure of their duties, and hesitant of their interdependence concerning others in the structure, which results in critical breakdowns in trust and communication (Baptiste, 2008; Chechak and Csiernik, 2014; Cvenkel, 2018). Chechak and Csiernik (2014) further argue that within the employment relationship, when a breakdown of trust and communication occurs, people suffer in silence rather than reaching out for help; moreover, managers and supervisors hide worrisome or explosive situations rather than bringing them to the attention of their supervisors. Braverman (1999) posits that without trust in an organisation's system, people do not communicate. Without communication, no early warning may occur; therefore, no opportunity will exist to take action to correct the error (Baptiste, 2009).

Consequently, stresses affecting contemporary workplaces manifest directly in system-level crises, involving breakdowns in communication between workers and management, loss of morale and loyalty to the company, and the failure of systems designed to deal with conflict resolution, fairness, and physical security (Dibbens et al., 2007; Pauchant and Mitroff, 1992). From an individual perspective, increasing alienation, stress and helplessness lead inevitably to dysfunctional, disruptive and even dangerous behaviours (e.g., violence or bullying and harassment).

Methodology

The methodological approach adopted is a case study that draws from an Interpretivism paradigm of Hermeneutic Phenomenology using semi-structured interviews and focus groups with managerial and non-managerial employees from a local government organisation in North West England. Twenty-seven semi-structured interviews were completed with a diverse range of managerial and non-managerial employees from different departments in the public sector local government organisation. Each interview lasted 60–75 minutes, tape-recorded and transcribed verbatim. The two focus groups lasting 45–60 minutes, one with managers only and the second with non-managerial employees only. The interviews and focus groups, explored the subjective perceptions of managerial and non-managerial employees regarding their views concerning their experiences of work, working life realities, and the meaning of their jobs in the local government organisation.

The interview and focus group data were analysed using the phenomenological interpretative approach to analyse the qualitative data, assisted with repeated immersion into the data as a whole, leading to the categorisation into themes as described by (Giorgi, 1985; Thorne et al., 1997). Narrative analysis was also used to assist with the analysis of the qualitative data retrieved from semi-structured interviews and focus groups. Thorne et al. (1997) point out that one of the foundations of knowledge from human subjects includes that, although shared aspects of experience exist, each person lives that experience from an individual perspective generated by unique life events. Thorne et al. (1997) further argue that one could use interpretative description research to explore the uniqueness of each person's experience while identifying the aspects of the phenomenon, familiar to everyone.

The interpretative description is uniquely suited to explore sensitive issues, such as workplace well-being in the public sector, where the knowledge of workplace well-being may seem familiar to all. However, the experience of work and the quality of working life from the perspective of individuals' historical accounts of events, can have a profound effect on each and by extension the organisation, families, and communities associated with them. The interviews and focus group schedules comprised open-ended questions. This allowed the interviewer to have an element of control over the questions posed, although it permitted some findings and explanations to arise unexpectedly. The interview and focus group processes were collaborative and emphasised the participants as the primary experts in keeping with the aims of the Interpretative research approach. There were crucial lines of exploration comprising the interview and focused groups schedules. These include primary questions on respondents' views and experiences of work, the quality of working life, and the meanings of their job. The relationship between these questions was explored from the researcher's interpretation of the data extracted from the interviews and focus groups. That is, the researcher interpreted the language discourse constructed by participants' interpretation of their reality.

Exploring lived experiences

The semi-structured interviews and focus groups findings reflect individuals' own experiences about the quality of their working life realities, and the meaning of their jobs in the public sector organisation (e.g. the Council) in North West England. This chapter presents the findings from 27 semi-structured interviews and two focus groups conducted with public sector managerial and non-managerial employees to explore these workers voice as it relates to their working life realities, and consequently how these experiences have impacted on their well-being at work and performance. The chapter is presented in two main sections: (1) working life realities and (2) the meaning of the job to employees.

Informants were asked to respond in relation to their own experiences and priorities as employees, rather than from an espoused practice point of view. Van Maanen (1994) and Cohen et al. (2000) argue that individual employees have different experiences of their working environment and interpret the meaning of their experiences differently. Van Maanen (1994) and Cohen et al. (2000) further state that the notion of 'difference' recognises that there is more than one valid form of representing human experience, behaviours, activities, perspectives, insights and priorities. Purposive sampling was used to ensure that all departments within the local government organisation (the Council) were represented and as such, 15 managerial employees (Male = 8, Female = 7) and 12 non-managerial employees (Male = 3, Female = 9) participated in the study. All 27 were Caucasian; (23 respondents) aged 40 to 59 years, and (4 respondents) aged 20–39 years. They were all well-educated up to master's degree for managerial employees and diploma/certificate (HND/C) for non-managerial employees. The majority of respondents (i.e. 25) worked full time and reported a range of incomes[1] and held a variety of tenures with the organisation.[2]

The findings show mixed responses (i.e. similarities and differences) between managerial and non-managerial employees'. Data is presented in two forms: rich descriptions and meanings drawn from interview texts, and graphical data display. Tables 10.1 to 10.4 indicate salient points raised in the interviews (Miles and Huberman, 1994). While no statistical significance is claimed, the tabular representation of themes has been structured on the assumption that a theme cited by a larger number of interviewees have more importance to the respondents as a whole (Miles and Huberman, 1994). The resulting patterns provide an enriched understanding of the factors employees consider pertinent to the employment relationship, their quality of working life and the meaning employees' give to their job in local government. A 'road map' of the structure of the chapter is outlined in Table 9.1.

Working life realities

The question asked to trigger reflection on this category was 'can you tell me what it is like to work here?' Respondents were also prompted using subsequent questions based on issues raised as well as exploring good things and challenges experienced within the local government organisation. The findings clustered into four super-ordinate themes the impacted the individuals, groups and the organisation, which include restricted

Table 9.1 Employees' perspectives of their working life realities and the meaning of their jobs in local government

Sections	Key Themes
1 Working Life Realities	**Restricted Resources** (i.e. budgets and staff) Redundancy & Anxiety Efficiency Savings
	Workplace Stress Heavy Workloads Pressurised Environment Doing More with Less Stress Sickness Absence
	Job Insecurity Government Grant Funding Instability Talent Brain Drain Anxiety & Depression Presenteeism & Retention
	Bureaucracy and Control Red Tape Control & Lack of Autonomy Nepotism
	Constant Change and Instability Persistent Restructuring Time Limitation Re-alignment of Resources
	Bullying and Psychological Violence Humiliation Blame Culture Incivility Mental Ill-health Persecution
	Lack of Trust Them and Us Culture Tensions between Teams Hierarchical & Status Differentials Fighting off Attacks & Protecting Limited Resources
	Excessive Emails Hinders Communication & Relationships Building Controls workday & Increase workloads
	Job Dissatisfaction & Public Sector Ethos Unhappy Employees & Lack of Career Ambition Lack of Enthusiasm for Work & Demotivation
	Dilapidated Office Environment Limited Budgets Inadequate Technical Equipment
	Work-Life Balance Flexible Working Arrangements Support for employees with dependent children

Sections	Key Themes
	Professionally Stimulating and Engaging
	Contribute Professionally
	Not routine or repetitive
	Job Design
	Financial Stability
	Pays Mortgage
	Pays Bills and Rent
	Facilitate Life Enjoyment
	Community Contribution
	Helping People
	Engaging Others
	Making a Difference
2 The Meaning of the Job	**Confidence and Self Esteem**
	Sense of Purpose
	Fulfilment and Gratitude
	Sense of Purpose
	Thankfulness
	Accomplishment
	Career Advancement
	Enhance Experience
	Formal Qualifications
	Professional Development
	Identity
	Relationships
	Internal Stakeholders
	External Stakeholders
	Social Engagement
	Personality of Line Manager
	Politics
	Close Proximity to Home
	Can walk to work

resources and controlled work environment, workplace incivility and mistreatment, relationships and work-life balance. The prominent points cited by respondents as those most frequently mentioned are highlighted below.

Restricted resources and controlled work environment

Restricted resources

The findings reveal critical issues managerial employees experienced within their working life realities which include: challenges with money, protecting their resources budgeting and staffing restrictions, avoiding redundancies, having to promote efficiency savings, manage staff anxieties, at the same time trying to find the balance to ensure that their services contribute to the greater good of the community. They also have to avoid the deletion of positions as employees' jobs are important to ensure that individuals are able to pay their mortgage, bills and have financial stability (financial well-being). These tensions are likely to affect the psychological contract, mental health, and well-being of mangers. One manager's depiction of his working life experiences highlighted some of these salient points. He shares,

> Money, is something that's constantly on my mind – 'how can I protect my resources, both my staff and my budget, to try and avoid people losing their jobs'. You've also got to think about efficiencies and savings – 'how can we do things better, how can we do it cheaper with fewer resources?' . . . and sometimes that's a difficult balance. . . . . Budget restrictions are challenging because people come to work to contribute to society and the Council in particular but they also come to work because it pays their mortgage and their bills so when there is a discussion around budget reduction and one of the consequences may be deletion of post, causes anxiety amongst employees . . . yes it will affect people's morale and well-being.
>
> (Manager, Male, Age 40–49 years,
> Tenure less than 5 years)

Workplace stress

Managers and non-managerial employees all mentioned that they have heavy workloads which results in increased stress and a pressurised working environment of having to do more with less. The work-related stress experienced by employees has an impact on stress-related sickness absence at the Council. One manager comments:

> Some staff, particularly the operational staff are stressed and our sickness absence levels show this as it is high. Staff like the home carers and some others can be work-related, like back pains, that sort of thing. Some people are working with people with incredibly challenging behaviour and so you have to think about that and the wear and tear of this, and sometimes the physical assault of that . . . staff in these positions are offered Counselling and other support.
>
> (Manager, Female, Age 40–49 years,
> Tenure 6–10 years)

Job insecurity

Managerial and non-managerial employees highlighted job insecurity as a factor that is part of their working life realities with the Council. The respondents relate job insecurity to budget restrictions and government grant funding, worrying, staff anxiety, retention issues, talent and brain drain. One manager states:

> Mostly, we have job security, if you have a permanent position, because the Council is committed to avoid compulsory redundancies, but this is associated with budgets. However, the Council is committed to keeping jobs and I have seen this in practice. What is more worrying, and it's not the Council's fault, it is the Government's fault, with grant funding. A lot of positions are time limited and temporary. That's the problem.
>
> (Manager, Female, Age 50–59 years,
> Tenure 21–25 years)

Another manager echoes the view of government grant funding as being problematic for job security, retention and talent management. She said:

> Government grant funding is an extreme challenge. I have got three members of staff, two-part time admin and a full time other officer whose funding is the national training strategy grant which ends in March. Now I don't really know what's going to happy come September it's only six months away so you really need to start planning. And what do I do? And the staff have started to get very twitchy and anxious. The big danger is one of the admin people have already gone. She's got herself another job that is permanent, and she's fine. I would have liked to keep her as she is very good at her job . . . you know these sort of things is problematic, but that isn't the Council, that is Government funding.
>
> (Manager, Female, Age 40–49 years,
> Tenure 11–15 years)

Yet another manager discussed the challenges of job insecurity at the Council and relate this to work-related stress, worry, anxiety, depression, lack of enthusiasm, negative well-being, presenteeism, limited time to complete projects, work-related stress, lack of commitment, and challenges with accuracy and productivity. He said:

> Limitations in budgets can affect job security, well-being and performance. It can go both ways. I have an employee who is at the beginning of a one-year contract and is working so hard to get the project plan and other things in place because she knows that there's limited time. I am hoping that at the end of it there might be an extension to the contract. I have no idea. It's a different pot of money. She is working her socks off, she is working exceptionally hard over and above

her hours. However, there is another member of staff who's okay but she is a bit dispirited because of what is going to be the end of her contract. While she is not a problem, the enthusiasm is not there . . . she is anxious. So naturally of accuracy and productivity can drop off a bit.

(Manager, Female, Age 40–49 years, Tenure 11–15 years)

Another manager spoke about job insecurity being devastating to employees placed in the situation of not being able to continue in a role due to budget limitation. Challenges such as this can affect an individual's mental health, stress levels, psychological, physical and financial well-being. He states:

Well, I think job security is perplexed and upsetting, but it's part of life and you get used to it. Luckily, I have always managed to have people whose contracts ended go back into something else, I have had some disappointed but I've have never actually made somebody totally redundant at the end of a project. I've never had to say 'well, that's it, you've got nothing left' but other managers have not been that lucky. I had somebody that had been on a secondment to me and desperately didn't want to go back to her previous post and when it came to renewal, instead of having three posts, I had two. I interviewed everybody and this person didn't get it and she was devastated, absolutely devastated, and I found that I was upset about it. I felt unnaturally responsible for it. I mean your logic tells you that you have done everything you can but you know when somebody's that unhappy it's not nice.

(Manager, Male, Age 50–59 years,
Tenure 16–20 years)

Employees perspective about job insecurity differed to that of managerial employees as it relates to permanent staff. In contrast to managerial employees' perspectives, employees highlighted the negative attitudes and behaviours that are associated with the perception of having a job for life, which can result in a laisser-faire attitude towards the job and organisation. In turn, these negative attitudes and behaviours can cause more passionate employees to feel depressed and demotivated. One employee claims:

Oh yes definitely, job security is good for permanent staff. I would have to moon the Chief Executive Officer at a Board Meeting or something like that to get dismissed . . . it's just ridiculous. But that's not helpful when people are so secured in their jobs because you also get negative attitudes and behaviours from people because they know that their jobs are secure and this contributes to feelings of depression and sickness I think.

(Employee, Female, Age 40–49 years,
Tenure 6–10 years)

Bureaucracy and control

Other salient features of employees' experiences of the work environment were highlighted by respondents as bureaucracy, control and lack of autonomy. One employee likened her experiences to 'Chinese Whispers' – she said,

> It's a case of you can't do anything without asking your manager, who then has to go and ask his manager, who asks her manager who asks his manager and before you know where you are it's gone through six people and what you actually originally wanted has come out as completely something else because its Chinese Whispered up the chain and it comes out with a result and you think 'what's that all about, I didn't ask that.
>
> (Employee, Female, Age 50–59 years,
> Tenure 6–10 years)

The preceding view was echoed by a manager from Adults and Communities who described his experiences as 'red tape' and bureaucratic structures and administration. He states,

> The Council still has a bit of red tape . . . not in my directorate but as you get further and wider there's issues between different directorates and different teams and how they operate . . . a scenario where somebody would do something wrong instead of having a word with them very often the manager would go to their manager, who goes to the manager of the manager that goes across to their manager and comes back down and its takes weeks to actually get back to the point to tell someone they've done something wrong . . . . by which time it's been blown out of all proportion.
>
> (Manager, Male, Age 30–39 years,
> Tenure less than 5 years)

An employee work experience also entails the existence of bureaucracy and red tape. He said,

> Bureaucracy! That's one of the downside of local government, bureaucracy far too much of it, if you want some money you have to jump through about 30 hoops and hoops are increasing and getting smaller and it's just a tremendous awash with bureaucracy, it's dreadful, far too much red tape that's something we definitely have to improve.
>
> (Employee, Male, Age 40–49 years,
> Tenure 11–15 years)

Another employee states that the challenge of working for the Council is associated with a bureaucratic organisational structure along with nepotism in management. He said,

There's a lot of bureaucracy and red tape to get anything done, and there does appear to be some kind of nepotism in some managerial posts.

(Employee, Male, Age, 40–49 years,
Tenure 6–10 years)

Constant change and instability

Another managerial employee shared that continuous changes to services, persistent restructuring, heavy workloads, and budget constraints are central to her working life reality at the council, and she likened here experiences to 'shifting sand' that has implications for her well-being at work. She comments,

It's almost like shifting sands all the time, when a new director comes in they bring new ideas and new things they want to see happening, new changes and that brings very little stability within the council as we are always asked to make changes to our services. . . . There is always re-structuring going on within services and that's unsettling . . . so for me personally my work loads are too heavy and although it has been recognised budgetary constraints does not allow that to change.

(Manager, Female, Age 50–59 years,
Tenure 16–20 years)

Another manager likened his experience of constant organisational changes to increased workloads, anxiety, time limitation, the need for more staff and capacity, and realignment of existing resources. He states:

Change initiatives is giving me a bit more work. I do understand some of the need for change and I have the capacity intellectually, it's just the time capacity that I am concern with. I also believe that they could provide just a bit more staff . . . a little bit more capacity would do it. There is also re-alignment within existing resources. . . . I am having to think about all of this

(Manager, Male, Age 50–59 years,
Tenure 21–25 years)

The view of continuous change is echoed by employees who claim that continuous changes result in increasing workloads that affects employees' stress levels, without appreciation for the extra work done. One employee discussed her experience likening it to increasing stress and pressure. She said:

Continuous changes have contributed to my stress levels, it is just the pressure I have been put under . . . no help, no thank you and you have to do this extra work as well and you can't get anything wrong, it's just crazy, absolutely crazy.

(Employee, Female, Age 50–59 years,
Tenure 20–25 years)

Dilapidated office accommodation

Employees revealed that due to the challenges faced with budget limitations and having to do more with less, also has a negative impact on their workplace accommodation. One employee shares,

The challenges are meeting all these targets and the offices are really crappy offices . . . it's not been painted in about 15 years, the floors are filthy, got stairs up and down, there's not enough technical equipment all that sort of thing is a nuisance.

(Employee, Female, Age 50–59 years,
Tenure 6–10 years)

Excessive emails

Some managers highlighted that they received an excessive amount of emails daily that contributed to their workloads and stress. One manager says:

There are too many emails to be honest that you have to keep on top of, and it makes me feel frustrated.

(Manager, Male, Age 30–39 years,
Tenure less than 5 years)

Another manager's experience of excessive emails echoes this view as he relates it to controlling his work day and hinders communicating in other ways as well as relationship building in the Council. He commented,

Emails is the nuisance of my life in a lot of respects, and it controls my whole working day now. . . . I attend manager's conferences and the biggest issues is always emails there's too many and it should be cut down . . . you send an email instead of going and talking to people or picking up the phone. . . . I think emails has stopped people communicating in other ways – verbally and face to face which hinders relationships in the Council.

(Senior manager, Male, Age 40–49 years,
Tenure under 5 years)

Job dissatisfaction and public sector ethos

Respondents shared their experiences about what it is like to work for the Council. The views highlighted by employees' experiences are varied and are dependent on the department worked. Themes that emerged include, unhappy employees, lack of career ambition and depressed about job. She said:

> There is a kind of feeling really in the public sector that you are not necessarily working with the happiest bunch of people. You tend to feel that quite a lot of people are here just because they haven't got aspirations to be anywhere else. I think this is probably the thing. This can be demotivating to be honest why people feel a bit depressed about being here. . . . I don't really feel so much like that in my current department. It's people that I meet at meetings share this with me.
>
> (Employee, Female, Age 40–49 years,
> Tenure less than 5 years)

Another employee echoes the view of public sector employees' not being passionate about their jobs, and relates this experience to having a sense of purpose, retention and desire to be in a more stimulating and engaging environment. She states:

> My husband and I both work for the Council and he told me that now is the time to move to an environment that's a bit more uplifting rather than feeling quite run-down. My husband is going to leave for the private sector and he just can't wait to be surrounded by people who are just a bit more enthusiastic about being at work . . . so this is also influencing me as well to move to the private sector where there is people who think there is a purpose to work other than sitting it out to your retirement.
>
> (Employee, Female, Age 20–29 years,
> Tenure less than 5 years)

The preceding findings that relate to *restricted resources and controlled working environment* reveal the challenges that both managerial and non-managerial employees experienced daily as their working life realities in the local government organisation in North West England. The challenge and pressure of working with restricted limited budgets, has a negative impact on workplace stress, increased workloads, job insecurity, manage staff anxieties and constant changes, in a bureaucratic and controlled working environment. In support, Thompson and Bates (2009) and Tehrani (2012) says that a crisis work environment represents the workplace turning into a stressful environment, overwhelmed by the demands of unrelenting organisational change that threatens to destroy the health and, in some cases the lives of working people, turning the workplace into a place of desperation, isolation and despair. The findings also reveal that managers highlighted having to find the difficult balance of efficiency savings and delivering high quality services to the community, re-alignment of existing resources to facilitate restructure changes, staffing capacity to support project development and completion, and excessive emails controlling their time and day's productivity. In contrast, employees shared their experiences of having to work in dilapidated office conditions with inadequate equipment in a pressurised environment that requires more from them with little to no appreciation.

Workplace incivility and mistreatment

Bullying and psychological violence

The findings reveal the existence of an inherent bullying environment within the context of the local government organisation. Respondents' perspectives reveal an awareness of bullying and psychological violence, existing within the organisation either from the perspective of personal experiences of bullying or knowledge of others who experienced or are experiencing bullying. The analysis of Council HRM policy documents reveal the existence of a 'Dignity at Work' policy and the Council espousal and commitment not to tolerate such behaviour in keeping with 'best practice' standards and employment legislation. However, irrespective of a dignity at work policy, respondents claim to experience bullying and psychological violence within the organisation. Kelly (2005) argues that organisational changes have resulted in increased control for managers and a reduction in the power of employee voice when bullying behaviour occurs. Organisational downsizing frequently increases internal competition and workload, creating higher pressure, anxiety, powerlessness and a lower threshold for aggressive behaviour (Peyton, 2003).

Both managerial and non-managerial employees profess to have experienced bullying or some undignified and uncivil behaviour at work or know of someone who has. The findings show managerial employees experiencing more bullying at work as compared to non-managerial employees. The bullying behaviour professed existed between peers, as well as between manager and employees. Bullying and uncivil behaviours existed between managerial peers resulting in intimidation is captured in one manager's experience. She commented,

> I was a new home support manager and there were other more experienced home support managers there I did feel intimidated by some of them as they made it very clear that they were much more experienced than me and I was the new girl on the block. I did feel quite

intimidated as everything I did was 'no you've done that wrong, you should have done it like this or why do you think you did' . . . it was almost like negative comments all the time.

(Manager, Female, Age 50–59 years,
Tenure 16–20 years)

Another manager described his bullying and psychological violence experience with his line manager as humiliating, uncivil, blaming culture, with allegations of being called a liar, Them and Us culture and not apologising when wrong. He claims,

There was an issue that cropped up . . . I was taken into an office with my manager and saw a much senior manager who was very ferocious and bullish in his office and accused me of being a liar. And I thought 'oh gosh, twenty years of working and I've never been spoken to like that' . . . so I stood my ground and said you know 'I don't take very kindly to being called a liar'. . . . Another senior member of staff had to go and call her member of staff to prove the point that I was a liar . . . another member of staff came in and proved the point that I wasn't a liar and she went bright red but failed to apologise, which is always a bit annoying . . . it's a bit above them to apologise.

(Manager, Male, Age 40–49 years,
Tenure 6–10 years)

In contrast, non-managerial employees also shared their experiences of being bullied at work and gave a personal account of her experience as well as describing how the knowledge of others being bullied affected her psychological and mental well-being. She likened the experience as persecution. She comments,

I feel much better than I did when I felt that I was in an environment where we were bullied, that was absolutely horrific. I recognise the difference between somebody being a bit difficult to work with and people being quite serious, nasty persecuting bullies . . . bullying is absolutely dreadful, I've never experienced anything like it in my life. There are quite a number of people on medication for depression as a result of the bullying which was perverse, horrific and really upsetting and seeing people that you cared about being absolutely squashed on a daily basis was terrible. There was a poem that goes *'first they came for the Communists and I did not speak up because I was not a Communist'* . . . that's what it felt like there, it was really odd and eventually it did get around to you, so people who sat and said nothing, you thought, 'well just keep awake because one day it will be your turn to and they'll persecute you and make you feel absolutely miserable'.

(Employee, Female, Age 30–39 years,
Tenure 6–10 years)

The findings reveal an environment where bullying, psychological violence and incivility were evident in the Council, which is echoed by the just-quoted respondents' accounts of their working experiences. These accounts also captured the existence of 'blaming, incivility, humiliation, Them and US culture, being called a liar, persecution, and psychologically violent environment. These behaviours are likely to create greater challenges and anxieties amongst employees given the increasing workloads and work pressures which have implications for work-related stress, mental ill-health, the psychological contract breach, and well-being at work. Salin (2003) argues that a constantly changing high stressed environment can lead to greater risk of bullying as employees seek to improve their own position at the expense of their colleagues. Echoing this view, Simpson and Cohen (2004) indicate that changes result in managers adopting autocratic styles of management to meet increasingly aggressive targets. Anderson and Pearson (1999) point out that workplace incivility include deviant behaviours that are harmful to an organisation or its individual members, and also violates the norms that have been established within the organisation (Robertson and Bennett, 1997).

Relationships

Lack of trust

Both managerial and non-managerial respondents highlighted a lack of trust exists from within the Council with managerial colleagues, line managers and with external stakeholders of the Council. Managerial respondents highlighted that tensions exists between departments affecting team working and trust, silos mentality, Them and Us culture, and managers protecting their limited resources.

One manager shares her views and said,

> There are tensions between sections and departments inevitably and we try and break that down as much as possible and I think for a long time we had a bit of a silo mentality that 'we're in this section and this is what we do'. . . . In large organisation there's going to be tensions and difficulties . . . not understanding, misunderstanding, fighting your own corner which a lot of managers have had a history of.
>
> (Manager, Female, Age 50–59 years,
> Tenure 11–20 years)

Another manager likened his experience of a lack of trust to the negative perceptions and attacks on Council officers by diverse external stakeholders. He states,

> Local government is a bit of a mystery to people and the perception of it is a town hall clerk ethos and we're all pushing bits of paper and pushing pens. But it still sometimes feels like we're in an environment where we are fighting off all sort of attacks from customers who aren't happy with the service, from members who might be outside councillors who might have had unhappy constituents, and Members of Parliament (MPs) doing the same.
>
> (Manager, Male, Age 40–49 years,
> Tenure less than 5 years)

Another manager's experience of a lack of trust was likened to the existence of a hierarchy and status difference throughout the organisation. She explained her experience of how certain meetings were arranged. She explains,

> There is a kind of hierarchy that exists here and I find it very strange, I do not know why it should exist here but it feels like there is quite a lot of layers and I do not really understand what they are there for and there are things that seem to have more to do with status than usefulness so, there are meetings that are available to people because they are a certain grading rather than because they need to have that information for their job. I find that very peculiar and misguided.
>
> (Manager, Female, Age 50–59 years,
> Tenure 11–15 years)

In contrast, non-managerial employees' perspectives of a lack of trust are associated with the existence of a 'Them and Us culture', a lack of harmonisation, conflicts, autocratic and target-oriented leadership approach. One employee's view captures these themes as she explores her experience. She explains,

> I feel though that there is still a feeling within the council that it is a Them and Us situation in terms of the bosses and the workers . . . the management are coming from one side and the workers are coming from another side and there is a lot of conflict going on there . . . two sides locking against each other a lot of the time and management just saying things in terms of targets and how they can get the most out of the workers is sometimes an approach that is still taken even today rather than looking at things more holistically.
>
> (Employee, Female, Age 40–49 years,
> Tenure 21–25 years)

Another employee likened his experiences of a lack of trust in the Council to centralisation, control, not taking risks, lack of confidence in employees' ability to do the job, a lack of autonomy and budget restrictions. He said,

> Trust is not at all promoted and is lacking because of centralisation, it's about control, not taking risks and if you trust people to do things you have to trust they are capable of doing their jobs and making decisions that can affect change . . . if these changes actually costs money . . . it always comes down to money at the end of the day, then you've lost control of a particular budget, you've lost control of the way something has been done . . . so trust isn't something that is readily available.
>
> (Employee, Male, Age 40–49 years,
> Tenure 11–15 years)

Trust is vitally important for psychological contract breach and well-being. Helliwell and Wang (2010) state that trust is widely seen as an essential element in any social setting and without trust people are loath to reach out and to make the social connections that underpin any collaborative action which needs to be matched with trustworthiness. The possible benefits and consequences of trust relates to the economic effects, physical health, subjective well-being, and an individual evaluation of the quality of life (Helliwell and Wang, 2010; Knack, 2001; Kawachi et al., 2007).

Work-life balance

Flexible working arrangements

In contrast, from a positive perspective, there are similarities existing between managerial and non-managerial employees' perspectives as it relates to working for the council. Both groups of respondents' state that the council is a good place to work with an 'employee focus' evidenced through the introduction of working time arrangements and wellness management initiatives to assist with workplace stress and the promotion of the physical and mental health of the employees. This view is captured by a manager's account of working for the council. She commented,

> Generally, it's very good; I think a lot of effort is made to look after us. The policies are automatically in place and I and my team particularly benefit from flexible working which is a good experience. . . . I think it's patchy and some of the operational teams are very stretched and we're very busy. But I think generally, in terms of staff care, we are quite well cared for.
>
> (Manager, Female, Age 50–59 years,
> Tenure 11–15 years)

Another employee echoes the view that the Council is a good employer that looks after the welfare of staff and also highlight benefits such as flexible working as a positive benefit for working at the Council despite the constant changing environment. He commented,

> I quite like working for the council. . . . I've had a lot of different experiences in terms of change and changing management structures but I don't think it's a particularly bad local authority as such it's been okay and I quite enjoy working here especially with the fringe benefits like flexible working for individuals with dependent children.
> (Employee, Male, Age 40–49 years,
> Tenure 11–15 years)

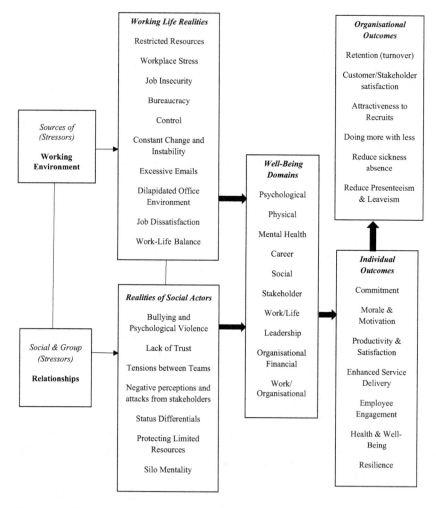

Figure 9.1 Working life realities and well-being: an employee's perspective

The findings reveal that both managerial and non-managerial employees held similar positive perspectives in terms of their working life experiences at the Council as it relates to the provision of work-life-balance opportunities through flexible working arrangements to assist employees with stress management due to heavy workloads and constant changing environment. Flexible working arrangements is likely to promote employee well-being as supported by Cooper et al. (2001) that state mental anxiety experienced by employees as they strive for more of a balance between work and life mainly affects professionals and managerial workers who are increasingly pressured to work faster and more extended hours (Baptiste, 2009; George, 2009). Further, Cooper and Quick (1999) states that it is essential for organisations to understand this conflict between work and life and implement family-friendly policies and wellness interventions that can help employees attain a better balance between work and life (Clutterback, 2003; Houston, 2005).

The meaning of the job

Delving deeper into employees' experiences of their working life realities, and its' implications for their well-being at work, respondents were asked to discuss *what their job meant to them?* The meaning of the job revealed a super-ordinate theme of identity-work-life-integration. The meaning of the job for management employees relates to, professionally stimulating and engaging, financial stability, a sense of purpose that promotes confidence and self-esteem, gratitude and fulfilment, career advancement, relationships and the job in close proximity to home.

Professionally stimulating and engaging work

One manager's explanation of the meaning of his job relates to being satisfied from the challenges of the job. He states:

> I am satisfied to be able to contribute professionally, the job is satisfying because it is not routine or repetitive and I am satisfied with the challenges of the job, it stretches me and I enjoy my work.
>
> (Manager, Male, Age 40–49 years,
> Tenure 6–10 years)

In contrast, employees reveal that their jobs are boring and does not motivate them. One employee shares her views,

> My current job is not particularly challenging. I feel quite bored and demotivated at the moment, which is a shame considering its diversity and equality and it's an area that I feel really passionate about.
>
> (Employee, Female, Age 30–39 years,
> Tenure 6–10 years)

Financial stability

Another manager revealed that his job allowed her to enjoy financial well-being and stability. She says:

> The job pays the mortgage and provides financial stability and allows me to pay my bills which feeds into other areas of life.
>
> (Manager, Female, Age 50–59 years,
> Tenure, less than 5 years)

Confidence and self esteem

Another manager relates the meaning of the job as contributing to her self-esteem, confidence and feeling valued, and a sense of purpose. She states,

> I get a sense of worth and self-esteem and it increases my confidence and gives me a sense of purpose knowing that I can make a difference.
>
> (Manager, Female, Age 50–59 years,
> Tenure 20–25 years)

Career advancement

Yet another manager likened the meaning of his job to career advancement. He comments,

> My job means a lot to me because when you have put that effort into getting qualified and building up that level of experience then doing another degree later in your life then the career becomes more and more important. It defines you some of the time rather than you defining it so it is pretty important.
>
> (Manager, Male, Age, 40–49 years,
> Tenure 6–10 years)

In contrast, *non-managerial employees* meaning given to their jobs relate to financial stability, community engagement, and for the greater good of the community.

Financial stability and community contribution

One employee's response captures the themes of financial stability, relationships through social interaction and community contribution. She said,

> The job pays my bills, I enjoy the social interaction and it means a lot to me because I feel I'm helping people in the community as I was born in this borough.
>
> (Employee, Female, Age 50–59 years,
> Tenure 11–15 years)

Echoing this view another employee's meaning of the job highlights community empowerment, and that the job is close proximity to home. He indicated,

> One of the reasons why I work at the council is that I enjoy enabling people and another main reason for coming to work and staying with the council is that it is local, I can walk to work it only takes me 25 minutes.
>
> (Employee, Male, Age 50–59 years,
> Tenure less than 5 years)

Gratitude and fulfilment

Yet another employee likened the meaning of her job to fulfilment and gratitude. She said

> For me, I didn't stumble on this job, I came through the bureau unto this job and I do every day thank God that this particular opportunity came at that particular time in my life and it does mean a lot to me.
>
> (Employee, Female, Age 30–39 years,
> Tenure less than 5 years)

Relationship

Some employees relate the meaning of their job to the relationship with their line manager, the manager's personality, and political agendas. One employee's view captures these themes. She says:

> So I feel quite crossed that my relationship with my manager makes me feel so demotivated about my job. I don't know if it's just him or the politics around the diversity agenda.
>
> (Employee, Female, Age 40–49 years,
> Tenure 6–10 years)

The findings reveal that both managerial and non-managerial employees held similar perspectives in what their job meant to them as it relates to *financial stability, and community contribution* that are associated with psychological, intellectual, financial and stakeholder well-being. In contrast, managerial employees' views of what their job mean to them are associated with psychological, intellectual, and career well-being (i.e. professionally stimulating and engaging, career advancement, and confidence and self-esteem). Non-managerial employees' views of what their job means to them relates with psychological, physical, spiritual, social, and compassionate leadership well-being (i.e. relationships with stakeholders, non-repetitive job, social interaction, gratitude and fulfilment, the job is in close proximity to home, and relationship with their line manager). The meaning both employee groups gave to their jobs are captured by HSE (2008) and Steger and Dik (2010) argue that meaningful work arises when people have a clear sense of self, an accurate understanding of the nature and expectations of their work environment and understand how to transact with their organisations to accomplish their work objectives. They further point out that the comprehension of the self in work provides the foundation for people to develop a sense of purpose and mission about their work. They claim that this motivates engagement, well-being and performance and helps individuals to transcend their own immediate interests to achieve their contributions to their organisation and the greater good.

In summary, the preceding findings reveal respondents working life realities are expressed through four super-ordinate themes: restricted resources and controlled work environment, workplace incivility and mistreatment, relationships, and work-life balance. The meaning of employees' jobs was expressed through one super-ordinate theme, identity-work-life equilibrium. The discussion, as it relates to employees working life realities as well as the meaning of the job, paints a picture of the organisation environment through the voices of different groups of social actors (i.e. managerial and non-managerial employees). Moreover, it provides the rationale as to why it is essential for employee well-being to be researched, understood, and viewed as a strategic objective that is to be included in senior management business plans and implemented at the Council and all organisations alike. The themes mentioned are vital to managerial and non-managerial experiences within this local government organisation. These challenges or stressors are likely to jeopardise employees' perception of the psychological contract, perceived organisational support, employer-employee relationship, justice perceptions and consequently well-being which in turn can affect individual and organisational outcomes. To this end, it is essential to gain a better understanding of the 'worker's voice' and the meanings given to explain their working life realities and the meanings attached to their jobs and well-being at work experiences.

The multidimensional well-being nature of employees' working life realities and meaning of their jobs are outlined in the working life and meaning of job model[3] that emerged from managerial and non-managerial employees' perspectives of their experiences at work and the meanings they give to their jobs in local government, is illustrated in Table 9.2. Given the working life experiences of respondents, the question of whether employee well-being can be effectively promoted in a New Public Management environment with budgetary restrictions and the drive towards efficiency savings and enhanced services are actually attainable? The findings reveal that the material aspects of employment relations, budget limitations, constant changes, bureaucracy, the controlled work environment, workplace stress, heavy workloads, excessive emails, the

Table 9.2 Multidimensional well-being: employees' perspectives of working life realities and meaning of the job

Multidimensional Nature of Employee Well-Being at Work	Working Life Realities at the Council	Meaning of the Job
Psychological Well-Being	Wellness Programmes Powerlessness Lack of Appreciation Lack of Support Fear of making mistakes Lack of Enthusiasm and Motivation	Confidence Self-Esteem Sense of Purpose Feeling Valued
Physical Well-Being	Heavy Workloads Workplace Stress	Ability to walk to work
Intellectual Well-Being	-	Professionally stimulating and engaging work
Mental Health Well-Being	Bullying and Psychological Violence Workplace Stress Increased Pressure Heavy Workloads Managing Staff Anxieties Depression Mental ill-health Powerlessness Fear of making mistakes	–
Material/Rewards Well-Being	-	-
Career Well-Being	-	Career Advancement
Spiritual Well-Being	-	Gratitude and Fulfilment
Financial Well-Being	-	Financial Stability
Work/Family Well-Being	Flexible Working Arrangements	-
Social Well-Being	Excessive Emails Poor Relationship Building Tensions between Teams	Relationship with Manager Politics
Compassionate Leadership Well-Being	Lack of Trust Blame Culture Them and Us Culture Relationship with Line Manager	–
Stakeholders Well-Being	Community Contribution Lack of Trust Attacks from Stakeholders	Community Contribution
Humanistic and Fair Practices	Managing Redundancies Deletion of Jobs Nepotism Status Differentials Humiliation Incivility Lack of Dignity	–

(Continued)

Table 9.2 Continued

Multidimensional Nature of Employee Well-Being at Work	Working Life Realities at the Council	Meaning of the Job
Organisational Financial Well-Being	Restricted Resources (budget and staffing) Financial Instability Budgetary Constraints Balancing Fewer Resources	–
Work/Organisation Well-Being	Efficiency Savings Job Insecurity Constant and Continuous Change Constant Restructuring Bureaucracy and Control Red Tape Deprived Office Accommodation Changing Management Structures Inadequate tools and equipment to function effectively	–

lack of trust, removal of bullying and psychological violence, job security, career advancement and financial stability have to first be addressed before employees can begin to experience a 'crisis-free' and respectful quality of working life and consequently enjoy positive well-being at work in the local government environment (HSE, 2008).

Moreover, organisational leaders, managers, HR & Health and Safety practitioners, and policymakers in local government organisations and private sector industries can draw from this research to better understand the meanings that employees give to their jobs as well as their perspectives that relates to the quality of their working life and the stressors and drivers that contributes negatively and positively to their well-being in a NPM work environment. This knowledge can be used to target factors to prevent or minimise workplace individual, group and organisational stressors that have a negative impact on employee well-being, service delivery, performance and turnover intentions. Similarly, this can have far-reaching effect by empowering and promoting well-being, leadership, respectful and civil employment relations in a public sector environment. The findings from this study can assist public sector organisational leaders to better understanding the factors that hinder and promote employee well-being and performance to that they can in turn prevent the high price of 'crisis' attached to individuals, organisations, community and the society as a whole, for doing nothing.

Notes

1 £10,001–£20,000 = six respondents; £20,001–£30,000 = nine respondents; £30,001–£40,000 = five respondents; £40,001–£50,000 = four respondents; £50,001–£60,000 = one respondent.
2 Less than 5 years (11 respondents); 6–10 years (6 respondents); 11–15 years (3 respondents); 16–20 years (4 respondents) and 21–25 years (3 respondents).
3 Multidimensional Nature of Employees' Working Life Realities are associated with the individual, group, and the organisation, and relates to psychological, mental health, work/family, social, compassionate leadership, stakeholder, humanistic and fair practices, and organisational financial well-being, as well as work/organisation. The meanings employees gave to their jobs ae associated the individual and groups and relates to psychological, physical, career, spiritual, financial and stakeholder well-being.

References

Anderson, L.M., and Bateman, T.S. (1997) 'Cynicism in the Workplace: Some Causes and Effects', *Journal of Organisational Behaviour*, Vol. 18: 449–469.

Anderson, L.M., and Pearson, C.M. (1999) 'Tit for Tat? The Spiraling Effect of Incivility in the Workplace', *Academy of Management Review*, Vol. 24(3): 452–471.

Baptiste, N.R. (2007) 'Line Management Leadership: Implications for Employee Well-Being', Developing Leadership Research, Papers from the Northern Leadership Academy Fellow 2007 Conference, Edited by G.P. Clarkson, Leeds University Business School, Leeds University Press Financial Services, Leeds, pp. 229–238.

Baptiste, N.R. (2008) 'Line Management Leadership: Implications for Employee Well-Being at Work', Developing Leadership Research: Papers from the Northern Leadership Academy Fellows 2007 Conference, Leeds University Business School, Leeds University Press, Leeds, UK.

Baptiste, N.R. (2009) 'Fun and Wellbeing: Insights from Senior Managers in a Local Authority', *Employee Relations*, Vol. 31(6): 600–612.

Berman, E.M., Bowman, J.S., West, J.P., and Van Wart, M.R. (2010) *Human Resource Employment Relations in the Public Services*, London: Routledge.

Boyne, G.A. (2002) 'Public and Private Management: What's the Difference', *Journal of Management Studies*, Vol. 39(1): 97–122.

Bozeman, B. (1993) 'A Theory of Government "Red Tape"', *Journal of Public Administration Research and Policy*, Vol. 3: 273–303.

Bozeman, B. (2000) *Bureaucracy and Red Tape*, Upper Saddle River, NJ: Prentice Hall.

Braverman, M. (1999) *Preventing Workplace Violence: A Guide for Employers and Practitioners*, London, England: Sage Publications.

Butterfield, R., Edwards, C., and Woodall, J. (2005) 'The New Public Management and Managerial Roles: The Case of the Police Sergeant', *British Journal of Management*, Vol. 16: 329–341.

Chechak, D., and Csiernik, R. (2014) 'Canadian Perspectives on Conceptualizing and Responding to Workplace Violence', *Journal of Workplace Behavior Health*, Vol. 29: 55–74.

CIPD (2019) *Health and Well-Being at Work, In Partnership with Simplyhealth*, London: Chartered Institute of Personnel and Development, Survey Report, April.

Clarke, J., Gewirtz, S., and McLaughlin, E. (Eds.) (2000) *New Managerialism, New Welfare?*, London: Sage Publications.

Clutterback, D. (2003) *Managing Work-Life Balance: A Guide to HR in Achieving Organisational and Individual Change*, London: CIPD.

Cohen, M.Z., Kahn, D.L., and Steeves, R.H. (2000) *Hermeneutic Phenomenological Research: A Practical Guide for Nurse Researchers*, London: Sage Publications.

Collins, J.C., Baase, C.M., Sharda, C.E., Ozminkowski, R.J., Nicjolson, S., Billotti, G.M., Turpin, R.S., Olson, M., and Berger, M.L. (2005) 'The Assessment of Chronic Health Conditions on Work Performance, Absence and Total Economic Impact for Employers', *Journal of Occupational and Environmental Health*, Vol. 47: 547–557.

Cooper, C.L., and Quick, J.C. (1999) *Fast Facts-Stress and Strain*, Oxford: Health Press Limited.

Cooper, C.L., Dewe, P.J., and O'Driscoll, M.P. (2001) *Organisational Stress: A Review and Critique of Theory, Research and Application*, Newbury Park, CA: Sage Publications.

Cox, T., Griffiths, A.J., and Rail-Gonzalez, E. (2000) *Work-Related Stress*, Luxembourg: Office for Official Publications of the European Communities.

Cox, T., MacLennan, S., and N'Dow, J. (2014) 'Cancer, Work and the Quality of Working Life: A Narrative Review', in P. Chen and C. Cooper (Eds.) *Work and Wellbeing, a Complete Reference Guide*, Oxford, UK: John Wiley and Sons.

Cvenkel, N. (2018) 'Employee Well-Being at Work: Insights for Business Leaders and Corporate Social Responsibility', in Edited by S. Seifi and D. Crowther (Eds.) *Stakeholders, Governance and Responsibility, Developments in Corporate Governance and Responsibility*, Volume 14, pp. 71–90, SRRNet Social Responsibility Research Network.

Dibben, P. (2007) 'Employment Security and Job Insecurity in Public Services: Two Sides of the Same Coin?', in P. Dibben, P. James, I. Roper, and G. Wood (Eds.) *Modernising Work in Public Services: Redefining Roles and Relationships in Britain's Changing Workplace*, Basingstoke: Palgrave Macmillan.

Dibben, P., and James, P. (2007) 'Introduction: Is 'Modern' Necessarily Better?' in P. Dibbens, P. James, I. Roper, and G. Wood (Eds.) *Modernising Work in Public Services: Redefining Roles and Relationships in Britain's Changing Workplace*, Palgrave Macmillan: Basingstoke, pp. 1–2.

Dibbens, P., James, P., Roper, I., and Wood, G. (2007) *Modernising Work in Public Services: Redefining Roles and Relationships in Britain's Changing Workplace*, Basingstoke: Palgrave Macmillan.

Emmott, M. (2006) 'Employee Attitudes in the Public Sector', in *Reflections on Employee Well-Being and the Psychological Contract*, London: Chartered Institute of Personnel and Development.

Folger, R., and Cropanzano, R. (1998) *Organisational Justice and Human Resource Management*, London: Sage Publications.

George, C. (2009) *The Psychological Contract: Managing and Developing Professional Groups*, Work and Organisational Psychology, Berkshire: Open University Press.

Giacalone, R.A., and Greenberg, J. (Eds.) (1997) *Antisocial Behaviour in Organisations*, Thousand Oaks, CA: Sage Publishers.

Giorgi, A. (1985) *Phenomenology and Psychological Research*. Pittsburgh, USA: Duquesne University Press.

Hanrahan, M., and Leiter, M.P. (2014) 'Workplace Mistreatment: Recent Developments in Theory, Research and Interventions', in P. Chen and C. Cooper (Eds.) *Work and Wellbeing, a Complete Reference Guide*, Oxford, UK: John Wiley and Sons.

Harrow, J. (2002) 'New Public Management and Social Justice: Just Efficiency or Equity as Well? in K. McLaughlin, S.P. Osborne, and E. Ferlie (Eds.) *New Public Management: Current Trends and Future Prospects*, pp. 141–159, London: Routledge and Taylor & Francis Group.

Health and Safety Executive (2008) *Working together to Reduce Stress at Work: A Guide for Employees*, www.hse.gov.uk (accessed 10th May, 2019).

Helliwell, J.F., and Wang, S. (2010) 'Trust and Wellbeing', *NBER Working Paper Series 15911, National Bureau of Economic Research*, Cambridge, MA.

Hesketh, I., Cooper, C., and Ivy, J. (2014) 'Leaveism and Work-Life Integration: The Thinning Blue Line?', *Policing*, Vol. 9(2): 1–12.

Houston, D.M. (2005) *Work-Life Balance in the 21st Century*, New York: Palgrave Macmillan.

Jackson, A., and Lapsley, I. (2003) 'The Diffusion of Accounting Practices in the New Managerial Public Sector', *International Journal of Public Sector Management*, Vol. 16(5): 359–372.

Kawachi, I., Subramanian, S.V., and Kim, D. (Eds.) (2007) *Social Capital and Health*, New York: Springer.

Kelly, D.J. (2005) 'Review of Workplace Bullying: Strengthening Approaches to a Complex Phenomenon', *Journal of Occupational Health and Safety: Australia and New Zealand*, Vol. 21(6): 551–564.

Knack, S. (2001) 'Trust Associational Life and Economic Performance', in J.F. Helliwell and A. Bonikowska (Eds.) *The Contribution of Human and Social Capital to Sustained Economic Growth and Wellbeing*, pp. 172–202, Ottawa: Human Resources Development Canada and OECD.

Marsden, D. (2007) 'Pay and Rewards in Public Services: Fairness and Equity', in P. Dibben, P. James, I. Roper, and G. Wood (Eds.) *Modernising Work in Public Services: Redefining Roles and Relationships in Britain's Changing Workplace*, Basingstoke: Palgrave Macmillan.

McLaughlin, K., Osborne, S.P., and Ferlie, E. (2008) *New Public Management: Current Trends and Future Prospects*, London: Taylor and Francis Group.

Miles, M.B., and Huberman, A.M. (1994) *Qualitative Data Analysis: An Expanded Source Book*, London: Sage Publications.

Namie, G., and Namie, R.F. (2011) *The Bully Free Workplace: Stop Jerks, Weasels, and Snakes from Killing Your Organization*, Upper Saddle River, NJ: John Wiley & Sons.

Needham, C. (2007) 'A Declining Public Sector Ethos?', in P. Dibben, P. James, I. Roper, and G. Wood (Eds.) *Modernising Work in Public Services: Redefining Roles and Relationships in Britain's Changing Workplace*, Basingstoke: Palgrave Macmillan.

Noblet, A., Rodwell, J., and McWilliams, J. (2006a) 'Organisational Change in the Public Sector: Augmenting the Demand Control Model to Predict Employee Outcomes under New Public Management', *Work and Stress*, Vol. 20(4): 335–352.

Pate, J., Beaumont, P., and Stewart, S. (2007) 'Trust in Senior Management in the Public Sector', *Employee Relations*, Vol. 29(5): 458–468.

Pauchant, T.C., and Mitroff, I.I. (1992) *Transforming the Crisis-Prone Organization: Preventing Individual, Organizational and Environmental Tragedies*, San Francisco, CA: Jossey-Bass.

Peyton, P.R. (2003) *Dignity at Work: Eliminate Bullying and Create a Positive Work Environment*, London: Routledge Publishers.

Salin, D. (2003) 'Ways of Explaining Workplace Bullying: A Review of Enabling, Motivating and Precipitating Structures and Processes in the Work Environment', *Human Relations*, Vol. 56(10): 1213–1233.

Simonet, D. (2013) 'The New Public Management Theory in the British Health Care System: A Critical Review', *Administration & Society*, 147(7): 1–25.

Simpson, R., and Cohen, R. (2004) 'Dangerous Work: The Gendered Nature of Bullying in the Context of Higher Education', *Gender, Work and Organisation*, Vol. 11(2): 163–186.

Steger, M.F., and Dik, B.J. (2010) 'Work as Meaning: Individual and Organisational Benefits of Engaging in Meaning Work', in P.A. Linley, S. Harrington, and N. Garcea (Eds.) *Oxford Handbook of Positive Psychology and Work*, pp. 131–142, Oxford: Oxford University Press.

Tehrani, N. (2012) *Workplace Bullying: Symptoms and Solutions*, London, England: Routledge and Taylor & Francis Group.

Thompson, N., and Bates, J. (eds.) (2009) *Promoting Workplace Wellbeing*, London: Palgrave Macmillan.

Thorne, S., Kirkham, S.R., and MacDonald-Emes, J. (1997) 'Interpretive Description: A Noncategorical Qualitative Alternative for Developing Nursing Knowledge', *Research in Nursing and Health*, 20: 169–177.

Van Maanen, M. (1994) *Researching Lived Experience: Human Science for an Action Sensitive Pedagogy*, London: Routledge Taylor and Francis Group

Van Wanrooy, B., Bewley, H., Bryson, A., Forth, J., Freeth, S., Stokes, L., and Wood, S. (2011) *The 2011 Workplace Employment Relations Study: First Findings*, The Workplace Employment Relations Study (WERS), Oxford: Oxford University Press.

10 Employees' reactions to HRM practices and well-being in the public sector

Introduction

The rising dependencies on workers to deliver products and services at a speedy rate has had a negative effect on the health and well-being of workers, resulting in the high cost to business and the public purse (Cox and Jackson, 2006; MacDonald, 2005). In the case of the public sector, reform has resulted in cutbacks and the shifting focus centred on cost reduction to the human condition, particularly around efficiency (Crouch, 2004). Another driver of change in the public sector is the notion of New Public Management (NPM) which advocates the transfer of various management styles and business practices from the private sector (Beaumont et al., 2007). Central to the NPM is a transformation of the nature of work in public sector organisations (Torres and Pina, 2002) resulting in new approaches to the delivery of goods and services with greater efficiency (Morphet, 2008). This has influenced changes in human resources (HR) role impacting on the function's ability to act as an 'employee champion' due to reduced employee contact and more fragmented HR roles (Harris, 2007; Kessler and Coyle-Shapiro, 2000).

NPM is concerned with improving the efficiency and performance of employees through tighter control of resources, changes in organisational structures, the use of targets, standards and control systems (Dibben et al., 2007; McLaughlin et al., 2008). But the aim is to develop a high commitment workforce of motivated, productive and entrepreneurial people (Clarke et al., 2000). Whilst some argue that high commitment 'best practice' HRM practices within the public sector have been shown to increase employees' job satisfaction (Gould-Williams, 2004; Silcox, 2007), others argue that whatever the rhetoric, within a context where delivering 'value-for-money' means cost reductions, constant re-organisations and work intensification, employees are left feeling stressed, de-motivated and insecure (Baptiste, 2008, 2009; Noblet and Rodwell, 2009).

High commitment 'best practice' HRM are associated with the success of employee well-being at work and yet little is known about how employees, the principal subjects of HRM reacts to its practice (Gibbs, 2001; Grant and Shields, 2002; Guest, 2002; Silcox, 2007). Despite the appeal for such research, until recently there has been relatively little research devoted to gaining an in-depth understanding of employees' reactions to HRM practices, working life and well-being at work in the public sector (Torres and Pina, 2002). Given the impact that management implementation of people management practices can have on employees (Guest, 2002; Pfeffer, 2005; Purcell and Hutchinson, 2003; Silcox, 2007) and given the considerable changes, which have occurred in the public sector over the past decade and are still occurring, this is an essential area of investigation. This chapter present findings from public sector managerial and non-managerial employees to better understand the relationship between employees' reactions to high-commitment HRM practices, the quality of working life and well-being at work.

Theoretical debates in HRM and high performing organisations

The dominant prescriptive stream of research within the field of HRM has explored the link between HRM and organisational performance (Gould-Williams, 2003; Guest, 1998, 1999; Huselid et al., 1997) and is an essential determinant of the organisational success which distinguishes high-performing organisations (Boxall et al., 2007). Over the past decade, there has been much interest in the notion of 'best practice' HRM sometimes referred to as 'high performance work systems' (Appelbaum et al., 2000; Keenoy, 1990), 'high commitment' (Guest, 2001; Marchington and Wilkinson, 2005) or 'high involvement' (Bakke, 2005; Wood, 1999).

Research on HRM focuses on a particular set of high commitment HRM practices that are suggested to be able to improve employee and organisational performance and the bottom line for all organisations (Guest, 2001; Huselid et al., 1997; Marchington and Wilkinson, 2005; Purcell, 1999). There is no agreed assumption as to which HRM practices actually constitute 'best practice' and the debate is ongoing with researchers using ranges between 7 and 28 practices (Becker and Gerhard, 1996; Gould-Williams, 2003, 2004; Wood, 1999). HRM practices associated with high worker satisfaction include trust, team working, involvement/participation, employee voice, fair rewards, job security, job design, equal opportunities, family-friendly and anti-harassment practices (Gould-Williams, 2004; Guest, 2002; White et al., 2003). The 'bundles' of high commitment HRM practices that signal management dedication towards employee engagement and well-being is drawn from Pfeffer (2005) and are now widely recognised and universally accepted, and have been modified by Marchington and Wilkinson (2005) for the UK context. These include (1) employment security and internal labour markets, (2) selective hiring and sophisticated selection, (3) extensive training, learning and development, (4) employee involvement, information sharing and worker voice, (5) self-managed teams/team working,

(6) high compensation contingent on performance, and (7) reduction of status differentials and harmonisation (Redman and Wilkinson, 2009).

By contrast, HRM is also disdained as a blunt instrument to bully workers' and is associated with increased job intensity, reduced security and high levels of worker anxiety (Grant and Shields, 2002; Guest, 2002). In an effort to demonstrate value in organisations, human resource professionals (HRPs) should adopt seemingly contrasting roles of both the strategic partner and employee champion (Storey, 2007; Ulrich, 1997). There are many debates around such conceptualisations and typologies and the particular challenge of HRM positioning itself as a business partner (Storey, 2007). Likewise, there are conflicting debates about HRM role of an employee advocate which places HRPs in an impossible situation of attempting to simultaneously champion employees while being part of the management team (Ulrich, 1997). Such a conflict has resulted in the criticism of the philosophy and components of HRM for creating an environment in which bullying can remain unchallenged, allowed to thrive, or actually encouraged in an indirect way, thus becoming a source of bullying itself (Harrington and Rayner, 2010; Lewis and Rayner, 2003).

Proponents of the critical stream claim that HRM views the worker purely as a resource or commodity to be exploited for the benefit of the organisation (Keenoy, 1990; Legge, 1995; Willmott, 1993). HRM is also viewed as another management initiative to secure greater control and reinforcement of management prerogatives, raising the spectre of inhuman resource management (Grant and Shields, 2002). Yet other researchers claim that HRM looms as a 'wolf in sheep's clothing', that in practice HRM has not worked, performance has not been significantly enhanced, and workers and management remain locked into their conflicting positions (Keenoy, 1990; Legge, 1995).

The third stream of HRM literature is employee-focused literature which is one of the central focuses of this study. Proponents of this stream of literature argue that there is a neglect of workers' reactions to HRM and attempts to re-centre the employee as the primary subject of HRM (Browning and Edgar, 2004; Gibb, 2001; Grant and Shields, 2002; Guest, 2006; Legge, 1995; Wilkinson et al., 2004). The reactions of employees' to HRM practices have attracted little scholarly attention and even less research have been conducted into the effects of those practices on employee well-being (Baptiste, 2008, 2009; Gibb, 2001; Grant and Shields, 2002; Guest, 2002). Researchers' further argue that studies linking HRM and performance never go beyond considering workers' as subjects of HRM, instead employees' are left disenfranchised – their verdict on HRM being seriously ignored (Gallie et al., 2001; Guest, 1999, 2002). Yet other researchers' point out that the growing body of employee-focused literature fails to provide an adequate basis for understanding the association between HRM and the employee. It also ignores inputs from employees' and believes that the dearth of research into employee reactions leaves us unable to evaluate HRM (Browning and Edgar, 2004; Gibb, 2001; Guest, 2006).

Furthermore, there is a lack of clarity as to whether or not employees' are as enthusiastic about the model as their employers, since their views are not accorded the same space (Gibb, 2001; Grant and Shields, 2002). However, Grant and Shields (2002) and Gibb (2001) also point out that attempts to assess employee reactions are affected by conceptual and methodological limitations. Where large-scale surveys of HRM do exist they generally fail to appraise employees' reactions to HRM, and employee presence is mostly incidental rather than fundamental, leaving us unable to evaluate HRM. This led to a strong call for the 'employee voice' to be heard in HRM research (Fiorito, 2002; Guest, 2001). Research findings reveal a mixed but overall positive picture of the state of HRM highlighting positive results, suggesting employees 'like' for HRM which contradicts the views that HRM is 'talked up' by management and is ineffectual (Guest, 2006; Renwick, 2003, 2009). Guest also suggests that the greater number of HR practices used are more likely to enhance a more positive psychological contract, greater satisfaction, fairness of treatment, trust in management and lower levels of work pressure (Guest and Conway, 2004; Guest, 2006). Gibb's study found that employees report areas of strengths and weaknesses of HRM and highlighted strengths to include the provision of training and development, rewards and levels of personal motivation (Baptiste, 2008; Gibb, 2001).

By contrast, weaknesses of HRM in employees' estimation existed in the management of staffing levels, aspects of recruitment and retention, levels of morale, and a reduction in the worker's voice (Black, 2008; Gibb, 2001). It also include a more responsive management, insufficient line management commitment (Baptiste, 2007, 2009; Browning and Edgar, 2004), unfairness, inconsistency in the application of HRM policies (Bryson et al., 2006), and poor communication (Baird, 2002). According to O'Donnell and Shields (2002) HRM practices are likely to meet with negative employee reactions where they are incompatible with employees' prior experience and expectations, and where they conflict with the underlying, as opposed to espoused, organisational values. Therefore, O'Donnell and Shields (2002) suggest that, however configured, 'best-practice' HRM is likely to fall short of its own criteria for success, unless it is attuned to existing employees' perceptions of the employment relationship.

Social exchange and the employment relationship

Social exchange behaviour originated from Homans (1961), Gouldner (1960), and Blau (1964) as a dominant theoretical framework that is used in literature to interpret behaviour and to examine the employment relationship as exemplified by research on the psychological contract (George, 2009; Guest and Conway, 2004; Rousseau, 1995), perceived organisational support (Coyle-Shapiro and Conway, 2005; Eisenberger et al., 1986), leader member exchange (Graen et al., 1982), and organisational justice (Cropanzano, 1993) and its consequences on employee attitudes and behaviours (Bakke, 2005).

Social exchange theories are used in this study as a lens to explain employees' perspectives and reactions to HRM practices, working life and well-being at work. The employment relationship when viewed from a social exchange perspective can be categorised as consisting of social and/or economic exchanges (Aryee et al., 2002). The situation and conditions that are likely to lead to adverse employee responses, such as workplace stressors and negative well-being, are those that are likely to evoke strong feelings of inequality and unfairness (Cropanzano and Folger, 1991). By contrast, positive employee attitudes depend on employees' perceptions of how much the employing organisation cares about their well-being and values their contribution (Coyle-Shapiro and Conway, 2005). Proponents of social exchange suggest that organisations treatment of its employees' is with the expectation that such treatment will be reciprocated in kind (Blau, 1964; Gouldner, 1960; Homans, 1961). Trust is regarded as a critical factor underpinning social exchanges in an act of initiating social exchange relationships (Aryee et al., 2002; Blau, 2006). Central to this view, WERS's 2004 survey reveals that British employees are becoming less trusting of their managers and employers (Kersley et al., 2006) and this situation appears to be worse in the public sector (Albrecht and Travaglione, 2003).

Employees' perception of how the organisation cares about them and values their well-being (Denier et al., 2003) is a view that is consistent with social exchange theory (Blau, 1964) as managers signal their desire to engage in social exchange relationships with employees (Eisenberger et al., 1986; Renwick, 2003, 2009). There is evidence showing that HR practices and the climate in which they are introduced signal the extent to which organisations value and care for employees (Gould-Williams, 2007). Some commentators are concerned that high exchange relationships are leading to adverse worker outcomes, such as reduced quality of life and increased work-related pressure (Green, 2006; Marchington and Grugulis, 2000). The majority of studies in this field have been undertaken in the private sector, the extent to which public sector experience mirrors that of the private sector is unknown.

These limitations are of particular relevance given that 'New' Labour attempts to reform and the new coalition government is now attempting to reform and improve public service delivery through the modernisation agenda, a regime based on the assumption that private sector management practice will have similar effects in public sector organisations

(Morphet, 2008). Thus, this study focuses on the exchange relationships between workers and their immediate line manager as we better understand employees' reactions to HRM practices in the public sector.

Methodology

This research is part of a larger study investigating employees' evaluation of HRM practices, working life and how such experiences have contributed to their well-being at work in the local government context. A local authority was chosen in the North West of England. This authority professed to have adopted high commitment HRM practices, which they espoused that the HRM practices has establish a positive attendance culture, promote fun at work and enhance staff welfare. This present study focuses on particular groups within the local authority: senior managers, managers, professionals, associate professional and clerical/secretarial staff regarding their views concerning their reactions to HRM practices in this public sector organisation. Local government was considered an appropriate context to analyse the relationship between employees' reactions to HRM practices, and consequently well-being at work. This is in keeping with best value regimes placing a statutory duty on local government organisations to review the processes used in delivering services in an attempt to enhance the effectiveness and efficiency of service provision and performance.

The local government authority is located in an urban region and is one of the most socially polarised in the country. The case study was conducted during 2005–2007 when a Labour government was in power both nationally and within the local government case authority studied. A strategy of the New Labour government was to implement funding reductions in keeping with the modernisation agenda. The local government case authority was selected as appropriate to study because it professed to have adopted HRM policies and practices to establish employee well-being at work, a positive attendance culture and enhance staff welfare. A number of different types of data were collected. The authority's written HRM policy and procedure documents were analysed. A series of focused semi-structured interviews were conducted with managerial and non-managerial employees exploring their experiences of HRM practices. This chapter will draw particularly on these interviews but will also present some findings from the questionnaire survey. The process of gaining access to the organisation was met with challenges and tensions and required the researcher having to jump through several 'hoops' of taylorised processes, controlled systems, and a series of negotiations before access to employees were granted. Even further, the researcher had to begin a new process of negotiations with employees to get people to talk honestly about their experiences and reactions to the HRM Practices that were implemented at the local government organisation.

The decision to use an electronic questionnaire was based on the single alternative given to the researcher by the local government organisation to have access to employees. The electronic questionnaire was uploaded on the staff intranet of the local authority and a database link was created to accommodate participants' responses. A final question was added to the questionnaire requesting employees who were interested in taking part in the interviews to respond. Saunders et al. (2009) state that only employees who are interested in the research topic and consider it important will be willing to devote their time to be interviewed. An incentive prize draw was offered to assist with response rates. Self-selection non-probability sampling was adopted as outlined by Sheehan and Hoy (2004) who state that web-based surveys and emails are used by researchers for data collection and these methods collect broad-based data from individuals who self-select to respond to surveys that are posted on web sites. However, Punch (2005) argues that limitations can be overcome by combining them with interviews, as interviews with selected respondents also allow a dynamic investigation within the sample. Follow-up reminders were posted on the staff intranet that resulted in 106 usable questionnaires being returned.

Twenty-seven semi-structured face-to-face interviews were conducted with managerial and non-managerial employees (15 managers and 12 employees) with the aim of understanding their experiences of HRM practices and its impact on their well-being. Purposive sampling was used to ensure that all departments within the council were reflected in the study. All twenty-seven informants were Caucasian; (23 respondents) age 40–59 years, and (4 respondents) age 20–39 years. They were all well-educated up to master's degree for managerial employees and HND/C for non-managerial employees; the majority (i.e. 25) worked full time and reported a range of incomes[1] and held a variety of tenures with the organisation.[2]

The interview approach was collaborative where information was exchanged between the informant (i.e. employee) and the researcher in both directions and the emphasis was on listening to what the informant said as opposed to guiding and controlling the conversation (Bolton, 2006). A retrospective approach was used to solicit narratives of experiences from informants asking them to talk about their experiences and as such, the first question asked was open ended 'what do you understand by the term human resources management?' This was followed by probing questions focusing on eliciting narrative data, as opposed to explanations or opinions until the employees' experiences were fully described (Smith and Osborne, 2003). Each interview lasted between 60 and 90 minutes and was tape-recorded, transcribed verbatim and analysed using hermeneutic phenomenological analysis (HPA) (Van Mannen, 1990).

The interview schedule covered three broad topics: 1) understanding of HRM Practices; 2) which HRM Practices are important; 3) and which HRM practices employee would like to be improved. Both managerial and non-managerial employees were asked to respond in relation to their own experiences and priorities as employees, rather than from an espoused practice point of view. Initial transcripts were reviewed through immersion in the data to establish an orienting Gestalt that drove later coding. Interviews were coded line-by-line, necessary for thematic analysis. Concepts, themes and sub-themes were identified. Half of the transcripts were coded separately by an independent researcher to identify emerging themes, and the resulting coding match of 85% provides evidence of reliability in the coding process (Silverman, 1995; Williams, 2002). Final themes were also verified by informants to ensure they appropriately captured the meaning that the informant sought to convey.

This chapter presents the findings from the questionnaire survey. The quantitative aspect of the research is the leanest part of the study and is used to provide statistical corroboration and reinforcement of some of the relationships that exist between managerial and non-managerial respondents found in the qualitative part of the study. In this context, this chapter presents the additional findings that show that there is a statistically significant difference that exists between managerial and non-managerial as well as male and female employees' perspectives of HRM practices, work and well-being based on the sample size. The quantitative section of this chapter is structured under four core areas: the demographics of the respondents; the differences between managerial and non-managerial employees as well as male and females; and the relationships that exist between the variables and neutral responses received.

The independent variables in this study are the HRM practices. The study focuses on 11 HRM practices that are generally accepted and forms the core (i.e. job security, internal labour market, rigorous recruitment and selection, opportunities for training and development, involvement in decision making, informed about business issues, opportunities to express own views, team working, formally designed teams, adequately rewarded, and removal of status difference between management and staff encouraging harmonisation). Respondents were asked to indicate the extent to which they agree or disagree with these 11 statements relating to HRM practices using a five-point Likert scale. According to Meyer and Allen (1997) employees' perceptions of 'reality' are likely to influence their performance more so than formal policy documentation. Hence, the importance of collecting employees' individual perception of and reactions to the HRM practices they are subjected to.

The dependent variables in this study are employee commitment, job satisfaction, work-life balance, work pressures, support and trust in

management, and line management leadership which collectively constitute employees' attitudinal experiences of working life which can affect
their 'well-being at work' (Renwick, 2003; 2009). Commitment is frequently associated with an exchange relationship between the employer
and employee (Cohen, 2003). The commitment scale adopted for this
study is from Cook and Wall's (1980) British Organizational Commitment Scheme (BOCS) that discusses the identification, involvement and
loyalty of employees towards the organisation. The concept of job satisfaction was adopted from WERS 2004 survey (Kersley et al., 2006)
and focuses on employees being satisfied with eight categories (i.e. sense
of achievement, scope of using initiative, influence over job, pay, job
security, training received, the work they do and involvement in decision
making).

Work-life balance satisfaction was also adapted from WERS 2004
survey, which assesses employees' reactions to HRM practices that promote satisfaction with work-life balance amongst employees. Measures
of work strain were adopted from WERS 2004 survey (Black, 2008; Kersley et al., 2006). These measures focused on work strain experienced
by employees based on the responsibilities of their job (Renwick, 2003).
Measures of supervisory support were adopted from social exchange
theory (Blau, 2006). These measures focus on the employees' perception that the organisation cares about their well-being at work. Measures of employee trust in management were based on items adopted
from the (Cook and Wall's, 1980) trust scale. These measures focused
on good relations and management concern for employees' best interests. Measures of line management leadership were adopted from WERS
2004 survey (Kersley et al., 2006). These measures focused on manager-
employee relationship within employee relations (Renwick, 2009). The
findings that are linked to the qualitative aspect of the research are discussed and the section concludes with a summary of the key principles
discussed.

Respondents demographic characteristics

The key demographics from respondents that are considered important
for this study are summarised in Table 10.1 using occupational and personal characteristics.

It is evident that the majority of respondents work full-time, and have
been working for the local government (i.e. Council) for less than five
years. The majority of respondents worked between 30 to 48 hours
weekly. The occupational groups are diverse and are divided into two
main groups (i.e. managerial and non-managerial) for ease of reference.
What is interesting to note is the high percentage of respondents in the
occupational group that responded with the 'Other' category (18.5%).

Table 10.1 Summary of demographic characteristics

Characteristics	Demographics
Occupational Characteristics	
1. Employment Contract	73% Full-Time
	17% Part-Time
	10% Temporary/Contract
2. Tenure	54% worked less than 5 years
	31% worked 6–15 years
	15% worked 16–26+ years
3. Hours Worked	82% worked 30–48 hours' weekly
	18% worked 10–29 hours' weekly
4. Directorates/Department Worked	Chief Executive (3.8%)
	Business Services (25.5%)
	Environment and Economy (19.8%)
	Adults and Communities (25.5%)
	Children and Young Persons (22.6%)
	'Other' Category (2.8%)
5. Occupational Groups	Assistant Director (2%)
	Manager (21%)
	Professional (17%)
	Associate Professional/technical (9.4%)
	Clerical and Secretarial (22.6%)
	Social Care (5.7%)
	Education (3.8%)
	'Other' Category (18.5%)
Personal Characteristics	
6. Gender	Female (81%)
	Male (19%)
7. Ethnicity	95% White Ethnic Group
	5% Ethnic Minority Groups
8. Age	54% aged 30–49 years
	29% aged 50–60+ years
	17% aged 20–29 years
9. Income	81% earned between £10,001 and £30,000
	10% earned above £30,001
	9% earned below £10,000
10. Education	60% educated to degree level and above
	40% educated to GCSE to HNC/D level
11. Self-Reported Absence over 12 months	23% absence was due to work-related stress
	77% various illness and reasons

Likewise, the majority of respondents were women, from the Caucasian ethnic group aged between 30 to 60 plus years, with income between £10,001 to £30,000. Respondents were all educated to degree level and above. Twenty-three per cent of self-reported absence over the last 12 months was associated with work-related stress.

Differences between managerial and non-managerial as well as male and female employees

Proposition 1 There is a significant difference between managerial and non-managerial employees' views of HRM practices, social exchange constructs and well-being characteristics

The results answer proposition 1 and reveal that there are statistically significant differences that exist between managerial and non-managerial employees in terms of work-life balance, perceived support, work demands, job satisfaction, and employee commitment. Table 10.2 summarises these differences and managerial employees were less satisfied with the balance between work and family life (Mean 2.88, SD 1.152) as compared to non-managerial employees (Mean 3.38, SD 1.148; $t(104) = -2.164$, $p = .033$). Reactions to perceived support, managerial employees were statistically significantly different in their views about being very motivated in their jobs (Mean 3.64, SD 1.055) compared to non-managerial employees (Mean 3.08, SD 1.172; $t(104) = 2.522$, $p = .013$). Managerial employees agreed that they worked under pressure (Mean 3.48, SD 1.131) as compared to non-managerial employees (Mean 2.92, SD 1.117; $t(104) = 2.486$, $p = .014$). Managerial employees agreed that they were satisfied with the scope for using their initiative (Mean 3.55, SD 1.041) compared to non-managerial employees (Mean 2.92, SD .981; $t(104) = 3.136$, $p = .002$). Managerial employees were more in agreement that their work made a contribution to the good of the organisation and would be pleasing to them (Mean 4.33, SD .570) as compared to non-managerial employees (Mean 4.09, SD .526; $t(104) = 2.181$, $p = .03$).

Overall managerial and non-managerial employees reacted positively in agreement to the existence of HRM practices within the organisation. They disagreed that management involved people when making decisions that affected them, and that they were adequately rewarded for the amount of effort they put into their job. Managerial employees disagreed that the Council tried to fill new positions with people from inside the organisation as compared to non-managerial employees who were in agreement. Both managerial and non-managerial employees agreed that work-life balance initiatives have been adopted by the Council and that they received support. However, both employee groups disagreed that they trust management to look after their best interests. This was evident from both groups' reactions to line management leadership. They disagreed that their manager provided everyone with a chance to comment on proposed changes; and that management responds to suggestions from employees and deals with problems at the workplace.

Table 10.2 Summary of statistical significance differences, mean, standard deviation and T-test for managerial and non-managerial, and male and female employees

ITEMS	Total = 106 M=42/ E=64		Mean		SD		T-Test	P-Value
Managerial and Non-Managerial Employees Work-Life Balance	M	E	M	E	M	E	t	Sig.
18. I am satisfied with the balance between work and family life	42	64	2.88	3.38	1.152	1.148	−2.164 (M<E)	.033*
Perceived Support and Trust in Management								
30. I am very motivated in my present job	42	64	3.64	3.08	1.055	1.172	2.522 (M>E)	0.13*
Work Demands								
33. I work under pressure	42	64	3.48	2.92	1.131	1.117	2.486 (M>E)	0.14**
Job Satisfaction								
35. I am satisfied with the scope for using initiative	42	64	3.55	2.92	1.041	.981	3.136 (M>E)	.002**
Employee Commitment								
41. To know that my own work had made a contribution to the good of the organisation would please me	42	64	4.33	4.09	.570	.526	2.181 (M>E)	.03**
Male and Female Employees Work-Life Balance	M N=20	F N=86	M	F	M	F	t	Sig.
17. I am satisfied with arrangements to support employees to manage their work life balance	20	86	2.95	3.58	.999	1.153	−2.259 (M<F)	.03**
18. I am satisfied with the balance between work and family life	20	86	2.70	3.29	1.129	1.157	−2.066 (M<F)	.04**
Perceived Support and Trust in Management								
29. I trust management to look after my best interests	20	86	2.25	2.85	.967	1.090	−2.257 (M<F)	.03**

Both groups disagreed that they experienced work demands but managerial employees agreed that they worked under pressure compared to non-managerial employees. Overall, both groups were positively satisfied with their jobs with the exception of pay as both managerial and non-managerial employee groups were dissatisfied with their pay. Managerial employees were satisfied with the scope for using their initiative compared to non-managerial employees who disagreed. In terms of commitment, both groups showed effective commitment to the organisation with the exception of managerial employees who did not display continuance commitment.

Proposition 2 *There is a significant difference between male and female employees' views of HRM practices, social exchange constructs and well-being characteristics*

The findings also answer proposition 2 and show that there is a statistically significant difference that exists between male and female employees' reactions as it relates to work-life balance and perceived support. Males (Mean 2.95, SD .999) as compared to their female counterparts (Mean 3.58, SD 1.153; t(104) = −2.259, p = .03) disagreed that they were satisfied with arrangements to support employees to manage their work and life. Males also disagreed (Mean 2.70, SD 1.129) that they were satisfied with the balance between work and life as compared to their female counterparts (Mean 3.29, SD 1.157; t(104) = −2.066, p = .04). Likewise males (Mean 2.25, SD .967) as compared to females (Mean 2.85, SD 1.090; t(104) = −2.257, p = .03) were less trusting of management to look after their best interests. The statistically significant differences between males and females are beyond the remit of this book but are relevant for future research from a gender perspective. These statistically significant differences can be interesting for future study.

Overall, both male and female respondents positively agreed to the existence of HRM practices in the organisation with the exception of management involving people when making a decision that affects them and being adequately rewarded for the amount of effort they put into their jobs. Males disagreed that they are provided with opportunities to express their own views compared to their female counterparts. Responses that were not statistically significant as it relates to work-life balance and perceived support were positive. Likewise, both groups disagreed and were dissatisfied with line management leadership with males disagreeing that managers kept everyone up to date with proposed changes as compared to their female counterparts who were in agreement. Males disagreed that they had difficulty balancing work and non-work commitments and work extended hours compared to females. However, both groups agreed that they worked under pressure. Males and females reacted positively to job satisfaction in terms of scope for using initiative, influence over their jobs and satisfaction with the work they did. However, males disagreed that they were satisfied with the sense of

Table 10.3 Correlation analysis: average scores for HRM practices, social exchange constructs and employee well-being characteristics

Correlations	Mean	SD	1	2	3	4	5	6	7
HRM Practices									
1. Average HRM Practices	3.21	.654	1						
Social Exchange									
2. LM Leadership	2.88	.974	.704**	1					
3. Perceived Support	3.42	.806	.537**	.592**	1				
4. Employee Commitment	3.54	.612	.461**	.419**	.465**	1			
Employee Well-being Characteristics									
5. Work-Life Balance	3.44	.964	.486**	.410**	.280**	.442**	1		
6. Job Satisfaction	3.11	.763	.669**	.493**	.535**	.500**	.479**	1	
7. Work Demands	2.81	.934	–.299**	–.279**	–.206*	–328**	–.663**	–315**	1

Total (N = 106) *Statistically significant at the 0.05 level

** Statistically significant at the 0.01 level

*** Statistically significant at .001 level

achievement they got from their job compared to females. Both employee groups disagreed that they were satisfied with their pay. Males and females were committed to the organisation but males were least likely to show continuance commitment compared to their female counterparts.

Bivariate inter-correlation analysis

Proposition 3 The relationships between HRM practices and social exchange constructs can influence employee well-being characteristics

The results answer proposition 3 and reveal that there is a statistically positive relationship that exists between HRM Practices and Social Exchange that can influence Well-being characteristics based on the sample size. This relationship is shown in Table 10.3.

Statistical significant difference between the variables in the study

Proposition 4 Statistically there is no difference that exists between managerial and non-managerial employees and male and female views of HRM practices, social exchange constructs and employee well-being characteristics

The results indicate a null hypothesis. The findings reveal that there are statistically significant differences that exist between managerial and non-managerial as well as between male and female employees' perspectives and reactions to HRM practices, social exchange and employee well-being.

Employees neutral responses

The findings show high levels of neutral responses from respondents that were mixed (Table 10.4). It is assumed that high neutral responses may imply and be associated with 'hesitation' and 'concealment' from employees. This may be as a result of employees who did not want to be too negative, by stating 1 or 2 or too positive, by stating 4 or 5 and chose to state neutral instead. Neutral responses are central to an observed 'controlled' working environment and the existence of 'fear' and a 'lack of trust'. Managerial employees as well as females responded neutrally to employee voice, management responding to suggestions, and dealing with problems at work. Non-managerial employees had higher neutral responses than managerial employees. These related to internal recruitment, involvement in decision making, team working, trust, motivation, commitment, scope for using initiative and work pressure. Non-managerial employees who were males answered neutrally to experiencing work-life balance.

Findings linked to the qualitative section of the research

The findings from the quantitative study that are linked to the qualitative section of the research are associated with the variables outlined in Table 10.4. The 'hesitation', 'fear', 'lack of trust' and 'concealment' behaviours displayed by respondents was evident during the interviews and observation made that a 'controlled', 'fearful' and 'lack of trust' working environment existed. This was also observed in the qualitative aspect of the research. The higher neutral responses were more associated with non-managerial employees as compared to managerial employees. The key themes highlighted in the quantitative findings that are corroborated and reinforced in the qualitative findings relate to: internal recruitment, involvement, voice, team working, trust, line management leadership, work-life balance, work demands and motivation and commitment. These themes are all associated with employees working life experiences and their reactions to HRM practices, social exchanges within the employment relationship and consequently employee well-being. The findings reveal that there is a statistically significant difference that exists between managerial and non-managerial employees as it relates to work-life balance, motivation, work demands, job satisfaction, and employee commitment. Likewise, statistically significant differences also exist between males and females as it relates to work-life balance and trusting management to look after their best interests.

The preceding section presents the findings from the questionnaire survey which is considered the leanest part of the study. The findings

Table 10.4 Summary of employees' neutral responses

Variables in the Study	Employees' Responses	Themes
HRM Practices		
Internal Recruitment	Non-Managerial	Internal
Rigorous recruitment and	Employees	Recruitment
selection	Females	Involvement
Involvement in decision making		Team Working
Team Working		
Social Exchange		
Line Management Leadership		
Manager provides everyone	Managerial	Voice
with a chance to comment on	Employees	Responding to
proposed changes	Females	suggestions and
Managers respond to		problems at work
suggestions from employees		
Manager deals with problems		
at the workplace		
Perceived Support/ Trust in Management		
Trusting managers to look after	Non-Managerial	Trust
my best interests	Employees	Motivation
I am very motivated in my	Females	
present job		
Employee Commitment		
Proud to tell people that you	Non-Managerial	Sense of Belonging
work for the council	employees	Pride
Feeling part of the council	Females	
Employee Well-Being		
Work Life Balance		
Satisfied with arrangements to	Non-Managerial	Work-Life Balance
support employees to manage	Employees	
their work-life balance	Males	
The council helps employees		
achieve a balance between		
work and life		
Job Satisfaction		
Satisfied with the scope for	Non-Managerial	Creativity and
using initiative	employees	Innovation
Work Demands	Females	
Working under pressure	Non-Managerial	Work Pressure
	employees	
	Females	

were used to provide statistical corroboration and reinforcement to some of the relationships that exist between managerial and non-managerial respondents' views found in the qualitative part of the study. The chapter covered four core areas: the first reviewed the respondent's demographics. These are likely to be consistent with employee demographics in the public sector. This section also highlighted that statistically significant differences exist between managerial and non-managerial employees that relates to work-life balance, perceived support, work demands, job satisfaction and employee commitment. The second salient point entails an interesting finding of a statistically significant difference existing between male and female employees as it relates to work-life balance and trust in management. The gender statistical difference further debate is beyond the remit of this book but may be used in future research. Thirdly, the findings confirmed the there is a statistically positive relationship that exists between HRM practices and social exchange that influence employee well-being characteristics. Finally, the high level of neutral responses may imply the existence of a 'controlled', 'fearful' and 'anti-trust' work environment. This was also observed to exist in the organisation during the collection of data by the researcher. The next section discusses the findings from the semi-structured interviews and its implications for the academic literature.

Employees reactions to HRM practices

Respondents were asked questions to trigger reflection on their experiences of HRM[3] practices in the organisation. Respondents' reflections as it relates to their understanding of HRM are reflected through the theme, Communication. HRM practices that are most important to respondents are clustered into are clustered into 21 themes: flexible and fair recruitment and selection strategies, fair internal recruitment, clarify and simplify discipline and grievance procedures, team working, involvement in decision making, employee voice, harmonisation and status differential, pay and rewards, absence management, career development opportunities, management performance evaluation, HR Support, return the 'human' back to HRM, recognition and appreciation, succession planning, health and safety office ergonomics, equality in training and development, coaching and mentoring, reduction in bureaucracy, improve flexible working to reduce dispersed teams and reduction in change processes.

Understanding of HRM

The findings reveal varied responses to the Council's espousal of 'best-practice' HRM as they relate to the understanding of HRM, the importance of HRM and improvement in HRM which are discussed throughout this chapter. Respondents understanding of HRM practices are associated with four super-ordinate themes which include; talent management, work-life balance and equality. The improvement in HRM practices at the local government organisation is associated with three key salient themes, which include; fairness at work, trust, and equal opportunities.

Respondents perspectives regarding their understanding of HRM related to a wide range of people management practices that include recruitment and selection, disciplinary practices, training and development, succession planning and diversity. One manager shares his view:

> I think human resources management is incredibly wide and is often interpreted as sort of recruitment and selection and disciplining. I think we need to be sharper on the whole workforce development aspect, the whole planning, succession planning, and diversity policies.
> (Manager, Male, Aged 50–59 years,
> Tenure 11–15 years)

Employees had similar views to managers regarding their understanding of HRM. Furthermore, employees understanding of HRM touched on unfair and bullying practices such as termination of employment. One employee shares her views and says:

> Human resources management . . . well I suppose it's like the spectrum of things from recruitment and selection and trying to retain people and develop people in posts, and you know all the stuff around people management in terms of discipline and capability . . . all stuff that I see that they're the poorest at except trying to get rid of people.
> (Employee, Female, Age 30–39 years,
> Tenure 0–5 years)

The preceding findings reveal similarities between managerial and non-managerial employees with respect to their understanding of HRM practices in the local government case organisation. Managerial employees fundamentally viewed HRM as a strategic partner with a set of tools or practices that can be used to assist them with the management and performance of people in the workplace. Although employees understanding of HRM was similar to managers, they viewed HRM practices as 'a stick' that is used for bullying, mistreatment, and unfairness in the workplace. Literature supports this finding as Grant and Shields (2002) and Cooper et al., (2001) point out that HRM is despised as a blunt instrument to bully workers' and is associated with increased job intensity, reduced security and high levels of worker anxiety (Guest, 2002). Furthermore, Harrington and Rayner, 2010) also criticises the strategic approach to HRM and argues that the philosophy and components of HRM creates an environment in which bullying can remain unchallenged, allowed to thrive, or actually encouraged in an indirect way, thus becoming a source of bullying itself (Harrington and Rayner, 2010; Lewis and Rayner, 2003). For the non-managerial employees in this research, HRM is certainly not viewed as a strategic partner, or employee champion or advocate but instead, HRM is viewed as workplace unfairness and mistreatment.

Important HRM practices

Respondents were asked to share their perspectives regarding which HRM practices are important to them and why? The findings reveal five salient themes that include sustainability, work-life balance, performance management, workforce development and communication.

Succession planning

Some managers highlighted succession planning as a key HRM practice that is important. Their perspectives touched on training and development opportunities, equal opportunities, fair treatment, budget restrictions, and pressure of meeting targets. One manager states:

> I like to think that there are good development opportunities at the Council by and large for most staff. Well it's never absolutely equal is it? We try very hard and we have very big targets under legislation to meet and so staff with certificates like NVQ, those sort of staff don't tend to get on the conferences and those developmental opportunities. There isn't the capacity and the budget to do things such as succession planning as you might wish to do . . . you know grooming people to become the managers in the future. For example, a social worker for instance, contacted me and said 'I want to go on a management course'. 'Well, no, sorry. You would need to be in a management position. As soon as you are in a management position, we would put the effort in there', and that is not always the best.
> (Manager, Male, Age 50–59 years,
> Tenure, 11–15 years)

Flexible working arrangements

Most managers expressed that the Council implemented flexible working arrangements to assist with workplace stress and pressures. One manager states,

> HR big initiative is around home and flexible working. We do a lot around that, all my staff had the option of having the ability to work from home. Nobody had to. Everybody chose to eventually as it rolled out, and they have to work from home twenty percent of the

time, which we are very flexible about. Some people work more than that and some people just about manage that. I manage by doing it first thing in the morning . . . it's very rare that I can carve out a whole day to stay at home and work. Sometimes it would be wonderful and you can rattle through a phenomenal amount of work, but I do my emails the first thing in the morning and avoid the traffic into work, and I often pick bits up at night, and make sure that I prepare for the next day.

(Manager, Female, Age 50–59 years,
Tenure 11–15 years)

Other managers raised some concerns regarding 'the new ways of working' that are associated with flexible working arrangements at the Council and likened it to fragmented team working, reduced brain-storming, hinders relationship building, hinders team interaction and performance, contribute towards silos working. One manager shares:

There are some disadvantages to the new ways of flexible working. My team are down here, and I am at a different location. My training rooms are in the Council so there are some disadvantages in terms of some of the banter and the bouncing ideas off each other. So you have to manage that differently. We have slightly more team meetings and we try to arrange more social events than we used to because we don't all see each other, because somebody's working at home, somebody's working here, somebody's there, we are 'hot desking'. . . you don't just flop back at your desk and it's the same people around you all the time. That's a little bit of a disadvantage I have to say. But generally, its flexible and people have gotten used to it.

(Manager, Male, Age 40–49 years,
Tenure 5–10 years)

Like managers, employees also held the view that flexible working arrangements was a nice HRM practice implemented at the Council. They embraced the idea that they can work from home in their pyjamas, financial well-being benefit, avoid the drive to work, enhanced employee commitment and retention. One employee says:

I signed up for flexible working and have been working from home two days a week for the last two years. In my previous post I had much more flexible working and was hardly ever in the office because my role generally required me to be out of the office. Flexible working is worth a couple of thousands to me to be honest on my salary. I really like that flexibility of not having to look particularly glamorous today, not having to bother to put any makeup on or wash my hair or even get changed out of my pyjamas, and not having to drive to work through the traffic. I absolutely love it. Flexible working is one of the reasons why I stayed at the Council to be honest, is having good access to home working.

(Employee, Female, Age 30–39 years,
Tenure 6–10 years)

Performance management

Managers revealed that managing performance within their departments among their direct reports is important. They further argue that managing performance is challenging due to flexible working and some teams being displaced in different departments or are working from home. Themes of communication through emails and phone, support, supervision, commitment, motivation, and assertive direction were also revealed. One manager shares:

I manage performance carefully! I have a system in place where my direct report keeps in touch. I email and phone staff all the time. Supervision is very important, and by and large I know what's going on. The whole thing is based on trust and that works very well until somebody who is affected and then you have to manage things more tightly. You may have a staff who is not as motivated or as committed at certain points. Sometimes that staff may need a bit of support and sometimes its Supervision or direct instructions, 'I need that report by then and not then', that sort of thing.

(Manager, Male, Age 50–59 years,
Tenure 20–25 years)

Training and development

Managers expressed that training and development is very good at the Council and is important to them as training provides opportunities for advancement and is a prerequisite for working in certain positions. One manager commented:

I have had plenty of training. I have done my advance award which included a Masters. I've done the Advance Practice Teaching because it was necessary for my job and I had to do my level 5 Strategic Management . . . good quality stuff. I am not good at computers and it doesn't interest me at all so I would have preferred not to do the ECDL but I did it and I passed. It was right, I should have done it for all sorts of reasons, and I did.

(Manager, Male, Age 50–59 years,
Tenure 20–25 years)

One management respondent associates training and development to staff motivation, career and professional development which she views as important to her. She commented,

> Training and development policy is used a lot in performance management and to motivate staff so this is why training is most important to me. . . . I think if there are skills that you think you need to do a better job, the Council values you in terms of things like training which is available almost at your very doorstep . . . adequate training is very important to assist in my personal and professional development.
>
> (Manager, Female, Age 40–49 years,
> Tenure 0–5 years)

Employees' also reflected on their experiences of training and development throughout the Council, and reveals graduate training, accessibility into management training courses, red tape, and dissatisfied employees. One employee state:

> I would like to see some more permanent engagement in graduate training. They are only just dipping their toes into the idea of modern apprenticeships for example in terms of encouraging younger people in . . . the training here is not that great, but the IT training is good . . . there is training that is geared towards spring boarding an officer grade person into a Manager grade. The staff survey that was done last year says that we're (*employees*) are the most depressed out of everybody in the organisation. So they invented a course to try and inspire us to get to Manager grade, but I cannot get on this course . . . so it's the perversity of the things that they try and introduce to motivate people who are depressed to get access to management training, but you cannot get on the course, it just drives me nuts. But I actually find it funny and I just shrug my shoulders now and go 'hmm you know it's just the Council, it will always be like this.'
>
> (Employee, Female, Age 30–39 years,
> Tenure 0–5 years)

Communication

Managers highlighted that communication is good throughout the Council, and diverse communication methods are used to keep managers and staff updated with everything. One manager commented:

> It's improving all the time. We communicate reasonably well within my department. From an organisational perspective, we sent out a questionnaire to everybody and all staff gets a copy of the corporate in-house magazine. Quite a lot comes up in emails and on the bulletin boards. We get the service managers and team managers to

cascade information down to teams. I feel I have immediate access, but then possibly that's because of my position. I can just nip along the corridor and talk to the Director if I want to. And I share an office with the Services Director who use to be the Senior Assistant Director, and the other Heads of Services, because we don't have individual offices, we work flexibly. We have hot desks, we totally embraced it.

(Manager, Female, Age 40–49 years,
Tenure 6–10 years)

Employees' perception of communication methods used to disseminate information throughout the Council was similar to the managers account. However, employees' experiences of communication were different to the managers as they felt that too much information was circulated and that employees did not have the time to read everything given their current workloads in the Council, constant changes, communicate information that staff would be interested in, improvements in exit interviews data collection, talent retention, and reduction in bureaucratic change processes. One employee comments:

The Council is much better at cascading information down now through managers' briefings and we do get quite a lot of information by the way of employee publications and this HR bulletins and stuff. There is so much stuff to read anyways, you know that you just don't really have time to read it when it turns up. I scan through the stuff that's relevant to my work but I don't really pay that much attention as things are just never going to change, I don't think. I would like to see information about attracting the best people for the job, have a decent induction for example, we should actually monitor why people choose to leave the organisation and I can't believe that there were no exit interview questions collated anywhere centrally to be examined in any way shape or form. When you think about how much it cost to recruit and develop someone, it is important to know why the 'knowledge' walks in somebody's head when they leave. You should want to know why people are leaving and try to hang on to them . . . but there is an awful lot of stuff that needs changing but it just does not seem to happen with any kind of particular pace and this is frustrating and annoying.

(Employee, Male, Age 50–59 years,
Tenure 11–15 years)

Improvements in HRM practices

All respondents were asked about the improvements that they would like to see with respect to HRM practices in the local government organisation that would improve and impact their well-being at work and performance. The results highlighted ten key salient points, which include rigid recruitment and selection strategies, grievance and disciplinary procedures, team working, involvement in decision making and employee voice, harmonisation and status differentials, pay and rewards, absence management, career development opportunities, management performance evaluation and HR support.

Rigid recruitment and selection strategies

Some employees' reactions to HRM practices in the local government organisation touched on issues relating to management training, inflexible recruitment and selection strategies, bureaucratic processes, controlled approaches to recruitment and selection, unfair internal recruitment practices and career advancement opportunities, risk avoidance, lack of trust, and retention. An employee's comment captures these points. She said:

> I don't think that management training is very good at the Council and I think some of it's to do with the way that people are recruited in the public sector. It's really interesting, they all went to a management conference this last week where they had some kind of big motivational speaker and my manager was going on about how they should recruit for new employees. . . . I believe that people should be recruited for the fact that they're dynamic and talented, and I thought, 'great, that's really nice'. However, in the public sector we have a prescriptive kind of 'person specification' that you have to meet to get an interview in the first place, and then you've got to answer the questions around them at the interview, so you can never ever recruit people just on the basis of the fact that you think they got potential, they have to always meet this checklist, and tick these boxes . . . that is one of the major problems with the public sector! Then you get managers who kind of meet these checklists, who are not necessarily that dynamic, they can't take a chance on people, and that means that you don't necessarily get the best people in the job in the first place and people are here who are enthusiastic and they would like to carve out a career, like me. I feel like unless I have done my ten years, I can't get into a higher position or I have to move somewhere else, as I am not encouraged to stay on . . . so I think this is quite a big problem in the public sector.
>
> (Employee, Age 30–39 years,
> Tenure 0–5 years)

Another employee's reactions to HRM practices at the Council captures recruitment and selection strategies that he likened to talent wasting, age discrimination, career advancement and retention intentions. He said:

Recruitment and selection processes at the Council is really bloody annoying to be honest. I think it's wasting of talent really . . . when I sit in meetings and they're saying 'oh we're really struggling to get people under twenty-five working here' and I think, 'well, I am not surprised!'. You know, if you are under twenty-five, you will say to yourself, 'well, I'm going to be stuck at a really low grade for ages until they deem I'm kind of old enough and wise enough to move up'. And I know that they are not supposed to judge you on age but they blatantly do. There is that kind of like young girl, young man type of mentality I think. So, yeah, it does make me think that I might have to move out to get on really.

(Employee, Male, Age 25–30 years,
Tenure 0–5 years)

Another manager likened HRM and more particularly recruitment and selection process as an irregular process and service to managers at the Council. She also highlighted that cases takes too long to process, bureaucracy, lack of control over new hiring decision, assigning HR representatives to respective cases, timely induction and onboarding, better management support and efficiency. She said:

I think the policies are fine by and large, however the practice is a bit patchy. My feeling is that cases falls through the cracks, so you think that you are dealing with person X to do with a post, and then suddenly, it's changed to person Y, and there might be a bit of a time lag. . . . I have had one or two problems with that. For instance, I was very crossed with how the last appointment was handled, I had an opening for a year's contract position and required the person urgently and she was available so we had to hit the ground running, and I couldn't appoint her because I didn't have the second reference and I kept writing to HR, and eventually the post holder contacted her second reference, who has never been contacted by HR and yet I have been pushing. So we wasted a month. Things like that irritates me greatly, you can imagine. There are quite a few bits like that. But then on the other hand, I've got someone who has been very ill and been on long-term sick and the HR manager that's dealing with that has been superb, quick to respond and get things done. But it's patchy. I think the recruitment process is patchy and the efficiency is patchy.

(Manager, Female, Age 40–49 years,
Tenure 11–15 years)

In contrast, employees' perspectives on recruitment and selection at the Council is associated with unfairness with internal recruitment. Employees perceive unfairness exists in the recruitment and selection strategy at the Council that hinders career advancement which leaves employees feeling demotivated and depressed thinking that their career has been curtailed or derailed. One employee shares:

> There seem to be some kind of rule that says that you have to have an open recruitment outside the Council without considering internal candidates and this makes people feel not good enough. Some people don't want to go any further than what they're been recruited for and that's absolutely fine and I completely respect that. But there are lots of people who turn up and they're quite honest about the fact that they are looking to progress but there isn't any effort to do that. When roles do come up, people aren't really encouraged to apply for them, so people get frustrated and demotivated about that. Then you will hear them say that they are finding it difficult to recruit that they will have interviews where there are literally just two candidates to interview and you just think 'am I so crap that they don't want to interview me in a pool of two' essentially you know that's really demotivating . . . so I think that they are really short-sighted about the way they look at developing people.
>
> (Employee, Female, Age 40–49 years, Tenure 6–10 years)

The findings reveal that the local government organisation had a rigid, bureaucratic and controlled approach to the recruitment and selection processes. Respondents found that they were treated unfairly and not given equal opportunities for internal recruitment and the younger employees were subjected to age discrimination for career advancement opportunities and recruitment into more senior positions. Managers had a lack of control over the hiring process and had to rely on sporadic support from HR to get new hires into positions that was often a lengthy process that lacks efficiency. Improvements in induction and onboarding were highlighted by both managerial and non-managerial employees claiming their intentions to leave the organisation in search for career advancement because they lost confidence, motivation and trust that things will improve. Bakke (2005) and Black (2008) state that recruitment is the most critical human resource function for organisational survival or success (DWP, 2006). CIPD research findings suggest the importance of organisations harnessing talent, is by ensuring selection processes that enhances the value individuals perceive, enhance feelings of self-awareness, confidence and motivation to perform (Dibben, 2007; Currie, 2001).

Disciplinary and grievance procedures

Managers' reactions to HRM practices that should be improved touched on issues of disciplinary and grievance procedures, cost associated with a proactive approach to disciplinary and grievance procedures, clarification and simplification of the grievance and disciplinary process, expense to the public purse and time consuming, diverts attention from service users. One manager's reactions echo these points. He says:

> I have very mixed feelings about the discipline and grievance process having gone through a situation with a member of staff who, dealing with successive grievances, went to stage two, went to stage three, went to employment tribunal, and at no result. I felt that somebody should have been sitting down and saying 'this is a huge amount of public money. . . . I think we need to stop'. Things went on a bit too far. I don't think that we are proactive enough about this. I would never want us to be a hefty culture where one wrong move and you're out. I would always want to listen and understand, but we do get serial complainers and serial grievances. They take up a phenomenal amount of time and public money, which diverts from service users. I'd be quite critical on some of that. I don't know how you get around it all but I think we do need to be a bit sharper around that.
>
> (Manager, Male, Age 50–59 years,
> Tenure 11–15 years)

Team working

Some managers raised the issues of tensions existing between teams in some sections and departments in the Council. Silo mentality, and Them and Us culture were also highlighted. One manager says:

> There are tensions between some sections and departments inevitably. We try and break that down as much as possible. There are management conferences and within the directorates we try and have meetings across the different service areas. I think for a long time we had a bit of a silo mentality that 'we're in this section and this is what we do' . . . the directorates have amalgamated and they're smaller, there are a smaller number of Service Directorates. I think it's improving. In any large organisations there's going to be tensions and difficulties but I don't think we are any worse than anybody else.
>
> (Manager, Female, Age 40–49 years,
> Tenure 11–15 years)

Another manager's reflections of team working revealed that tensions do exists between teams and shared her perspectives as to why this challenge exists. Themes of misunderstanding, territorial behaviour, self-interests, a lack of trust, protect limited resources, and incomplete projects. She shares:

> I think the causes of all the tension between departments is that people not understanding, misunderstandings, fighting your own corner

which a lot of managers have had a history of that. They have got to make sure, they got their own bet, and you get use to that and maybe don't move forward.

(Manager, Female, Aged 40–49 years,
Tenure 6–10 years)

Managers highlighted the challenges experienced with team working due to flexible working arrangements that were implemented to reduce workplace stress, and assist with budgetary limitations. Managers' highlighted Employee awards, dispersed workforce, difficulty in holding regular team meetings, and team development as challenges of team working at the Council. One manager shares his experience:

I think that team working could be promoted more, things like employee awards is difficult to address and this is very much a team thing. Investors In People (IiP) puts a lot of expectation around team meetings and we're very hot on that. However, I don't know if it works as well in all parts of the Council as when you have got very dispersed workforce, team working becomes difficult. For example, our home carers, it's very difficult to hold a lot of team meetings with them, and they have group supervision and less team meetings . . . they have regular meetings but it is much more difficult. There is still that ethos of working in a team. I think all local authorities (*Local Government*) could do a bit more about team working. We can look into 'what is the model of good team development?' That sort of thing, we don't have that kind of focus at this time.

(Manager, Male, Age 40–49 years,
Tenure 6–10 years)

Generally, employees held the view that team working does not really exists throughout the Council and highlights that team working exists based on your line manager. Organisational team working, silo working, team working embraced by employees to buffer and protect themselves against bullying and workplace incivility from their line manager. One employee shares her experience:

I think team working is dependent on where you are. I don't feel that there is very much team working at all where I am now. It's just a very strange thing. I am in a team of two with myself and my manager, but what we are trying to achieve is for the benefit of a lot of teams across the organisation so I suppose it's essentially change management. But you don't really feel that the Council sees itself as a team in the round. People are in their own little silo where they see themselves as a very small little team or a larger service directorate so they don't see the bigger picture or the greater good in this case.

When I was working in Social Care, the people that were on my level was very good at working together in a team and some of that was because the management was so bad, this united us against the 'evil' – that was the management in that particular bit of the organisation. We still meet up actually, just to marvel at how bad that experience was.

(Employee, Female, Age 30–39 years,
Tenure 11–15 years)

Both managerial and non-managerial employees agree that team working should be improved at the Council. They both agreed that tensions exist between teams and directorates resulting in silo mentality and a perceived 'them and us' culture across departments and direetorates. This division perception was as a result of a lack of trust, misunderstandings, self-interests and managers protecting their already limited resources. Trust is regarded as a critical factor underpinning social exchanges in an act of initiating social exchange relationships (Aryee et al., 2002; Blau, 2006). Central to this view, WERS's 2004 survey reveals that British employees are becoming less trusting of their managers and employers (Kersley et al., 2006) and this situation appears to be worse in the public sector (Albrecht and Travaglione, 2003). Teams were dispersed due to the 'new ways of flexible working' which added another layer of difficulty to have regular team meetings and team development initiatives. Non-managerial employees purport that the Council has to first see the strategic importance of organisational team working before the culture of team working can be embraced throughout the organisation. Furthermore, employees view of team working is based on their experiences with their line managers. Team working was embraced by employees to protect them from injustices from their line manager's bullying and mistreatment of employees. Cropanzano and Folger (1991) state that situations and conditions that are likely to lead to adverse employee responses, such as workplace stressors and negative well-being, are those that are likely to evoke strong feelings of inequality and unfairness (Cropanzano and Folger, 1991).

Involvement in decision making and employee voice

Managers perspectives on involvement in decision making and the ability to express their views and voice were all positive. They held the view that they had the opportunity to express their views and be listened to at different levels to make a contribution. One manager shares:

Oh yes, I feel comfortable with the team that I am in, with the heads of services and being able to express my views. I am on a slightly different level to them but my views are always listened to and

welcomed and I contribute to other people's businesses and projects
. . . and I feel very comfortable.

(Manager, Male, Age 50–59 years,
Tenure 11–15 years)

Employees held a different view to managers regarding involvement
in decision making and employee voice. Salient points highlighted by
employees include, employee representative groups, corporate social
responsibility, the Council viewed as an attractive employer, and employees not asked about their views regarding the development of policies and
the assessment and impact of these policies. One employee's comment
supported this perspective. She said:

As an individual, I am not really involved in decisions about stuff.
Only recently, the Council had employee networks like LGBT and
they've just set up a Carers LGBT group for Lesbian, Gay, Bi, and
Trans and for disabled employees. There are four kind of employee
networks and I think they're really started to get going in the last
eighteen months so this is the first kind of tangible evidence I can see
of people being consulted on their opinions about their experiences
within the Council and how policies should be developed to make
their experience better and to make the Council look more attractive
to people in the community. These employee representative groups
are very small groups but what about everybody else in the organisation, you know there are other people with opinions and experiences
that might be worth comparing. So, yes I don't feel that I am asked
personally about my views regarding the development of policies,
and they should be doing that as they supposed to be assessing the
impact of these policies.

(Employee, Female, Age 20–25,
Tenure less than 5 years)

Harmonisation and status differentials

Some managers held the view that some areas of the Council there is
differential, hierarchical, bureaucratic and red tape exists. The discussion also reveals, status differentials, and them and us culture exists. One
manager points out:

Yes, in some areas it's more hierarchical than others. In some departments, very hierarchical and you have to go through the layers but
I think we are much more informal in my department but yes, there
is a differential. And sometimes there needs to be some distance.
Some differential which assures that balance. As a manager you can't
be one of the crowd completely, but nor should you be aloof and

inaccessible. I think you do need some differential, and that balance can be difficult particularly for new managers, and for managers like myself. I was a staff development officer for a long time, and then I became the manager, so I started to manage my ex-peers.

(Manager, Female, Age 30–39 years,
Tenure 15–20 years)

Employees also agree that there is the existence of status differentials at the Council. Employees also highlighted themes equal opportunities, respect, fear, Them and Us culture, Unfairness and Incivility at work. One employee comments:

Yes, definitely, status differential does exist. It's annoying when you know that they're (*managers*) are not necessarily that much better than you. I think that's quite frustrating when you know it's only a matter of time when I can be in that position. I think that you should treat everybody with some respect when you're at work. Just because you are a manager you've got the God-given right to be uncivil, and some people really do seem to assume that as soon as they're on X-grade, that they got a right to be rude to people but it doesn't hurt to be pleasant to people, and you will probably get much better results than being really rude and obnoxious and difficult. I see that some people are really in awe of some of the really senior figures in the organisation, and I have heard people say 'oh they spoke to me' or 'they asked me to do something' or some people jump into action if you copy some very senior managers into an email then people know that you mean business, then they will jump . . . but that's quite concerning. I can deal with people at that level, they're less frightening to me than the majority of people. I do feel certainly with my line manager, not necessarily with the last one but with this manager, there is a very clear kind of 'them and us' sort of situation.

(Employee, Female, Age 40–49 years,
Tenure 11–15 years)

Pay and rewards

Managers held diverse views regarding pay and rewards but most managers' perspectives were that they could be rewarded more for the work that they do given their responsibilities. One manager shares;

Considering the extra work that I have taken on as extras, I should be rewarded. I have gotten one increment as an honorarium at the moment but an honorarium isn't the most satisfactory way of doing it.

(Manager, Male, Age 40–49 years,
Tenure 6–10 years)

Employees views on pay and rewards highlighted appreciation and recognition for a job well done as important to employees along with financial remuneration. One employee shares:

> I am not terrifically well paid working here but I think the pay is fine. My pay is reviewed each year and I received a double increment this time and that's nice, it's more than I was expecting. However, I would like just informal feedback, which doesn't take much for somebody to say to you 'well done, that was a really good job'. It happened to me once when the chief executive walked up to me at a conference and said 'well done' for something, and it knocked me off my feet and I am not someone who's struck for words very often as you can tell, but I was just very surprised, but it was really nice. I really like that sort of appreciation. It's all very well to financially reward people, I would be lying if I say that is not nice, but sometimes it's just nice to be recognised for a job well done. I don't think that we are that good at that within the organisation either in terms of just saying 'oh you know well done and thanks for that', you know . . . I worked at another organisation before I joined the Council and it was common practice there to recognise people for a good job. After completing a project, the director wrote to people thanking them for a good job and they were absolutely shocked . . . you know the expressions on people's faces when they got the letters, it was fantastic. Most people said 'I didn't even know that he thought I existed'. It just shows you that actually sometimes you don't need to give people money it's just a bit of recognition and I don't necessarily think we get that really in the public sector.
>
> (Employee, Female, Age 50–59 years,
> Tenure, 20–25 years)

Absence management

Managers shared their experiences of the implementation of the Absence Management policy has assisted them to reduce increasing employee absence, but the rigidity and harshness of the absence management policy is like bullying and unfairness for people who are truly on long-term sick. One manager shared her views:

> Absence Management by and large is fine. Where it seems a bit draconian is at the first stages with the meetings and occupational health getting involved. It certainly stopped the odd person that takes the odd days off. Where it is difficult is when you got somebody who's really ill and its long-term sickness, the standard letters highlighting 'final warning' can be rigid and harsh. I think we need this policy

and procedure as it is a way of monitoring and managing it and our absence levels have improved a bit since it started.

(Manager, Female, Age 30–39 years,
Tenure 5–10 years)

Another manager echoes this view that absence management has reduced employee absence levels and claims that it also prevents presenteeism, lack of employee commitment, and employees avoiding workplace obligations, like meetings claiming to be working from home. He shares:

I know in the past there has been huge absences that have never been tracked and people have been off. . . . I have heard about it but I have never experienced it, but people have been off for a very, very long periods of time and it's drifted and drifted. Well, again, public money, you know. But managing it, they've sifted the ones that says 'oh I don't feel great, I'll just have a day off'. I think it's stop some of that. For e.g. I had an argument with one of my staff, her supervisor was away and she rang me to tell me that she could not come to a couple of meetings because she wasn't feeling great, but she was insisting that she wasn't going off sick, she was going to work from home. And I said to her 'if you are not well enough to come to meetings that are scheduled, you're off sick'. And she was getting distressed about it. She said 'no, no, no, I always just take it as – I work from home, and I work well'. And I said, 'well if you are not fit to be at the scheduled meetings, you are off sick'. . . . It's a grey area there and again it's a judgement call and sometimes being strict about it.

(Manager, Male, Age 50–59 years,
Tenure 6–10 years)

Career development opportunities

Most employees' highlighted career development as an HRM practice that should be improved. They also pointing out the importance of mentoring and coaching, performance evaluation, succession planning, and retention. One employee shares:

Career development would be a really big help. I carved out a career for myself by spotting things I think are interesting and being obviously the best person to recruit on the day for them, which is astonishing as an internal person, because internal recruitment almost never happens. But it would be quite nice to know where I am going to go from here. I would like to get some mentoring and coaching from somebody more senior or from my manager about some ideas about where I am at and where I am going to go next. Sometimes it's about being honest about the fact that perhaps there isn't anywhere to go within the organisation and maybe it would be a benefit if I went somewhere else for a bit . . . and we don't really have that . . . that would be quite helpful.

(Employees, Male, Age 30–39 years,
Tenure less than 5 years)

Managers echo employees regarding the lack of career advancement opportunities at the Council and likened this experience to unfair treatment as it relates to the absence of career development opportunities at the Council and having to leave the organisation to access promotional opportunities. One manager said:

It's not just this council I think most councils have always got a phrase that 'if you want to get up and if you want to move up in the council, you move out' . . . and you find that a lot of senior management – that the only way they'll progress is by moving to a different council . . . certain authorities like to see that they're bringing in something new and fresh all the time, you know a new innovation.

(Manager, Male, Age 40–49 years,
Tenure 6–10 years)

In contrast, non-managerial employees highlighted that they would like to see improvements in career prospects, and training opportunities. One employee shares:

Career development would be a really big help. . . . Yes, career prospects definitely, being given opportunities to be trained up to other jobs within the council, having that opened out to employees I think would be really helpful.

(Employees, Female, Age 40–49 years,
Tenure less than 5 years)

Both managerial and non-managerial employees held the view that there is an absence of career advancement opportunities in the Council. There is a lack of succession planning, coaching and mentoring, and performance evaluation to provide feedback and guide employees on how they can accomplish, train and prepare for the next career level. Both managerial and non-managerial employees view the lack of career opportunities as unfair treatment and bullying.

Management performance evaluation

Management respondents explore suggestions for improvement in management performance evaluation. Additional themes mentioned include;

coaching and mentoring, bureaucratic tick-box process, disregard for health and safety ergonomic matters in the workplace fitting for the user's needs, and unprofessional facilitation of management performance evaluation. This was captured by one manager's account of her experiences. She explained,

> A thing I do find hugely unsatisfactory, is what the Council calls 'one-to-one' and some departments it's called supervision . . . it is done at a very poor standard and all I can see is a bunch of tick boxes and I am never asked in depth about my work, I could be doing anything . . . I am always asked if there are any health and safety issues and when I point out that the screen's too small or the chair's not good or carpet comes off at the end, none of those would ever be taken any notice of. . . . I just feel again it's a thing that you tick the boxes. . . . I just feel it's not real . . . in terms of one-to-one it feels like there's no practice, there's no preparation gone in . . . it's just an exercise – it's about nothing.
>
> (Manager, Female, Age 40–49 years,
> Tenure 21–25 years)

HR support

Managerial employees reveal that HRM practices that help them to be able to manage effectively in the public sector NPM environment are important to them. One manager's views highlighted recruitment and selection, flexibility and support, prompt onboarding, interpretation of HRM policies, improvements in equal opportunities and efficiency, time delays with HR support provided, time delays to complete service supports to managers, management training and interpretation of the policies, and removal of mechanisms to improve process time, and efficiency and performance, and heavy workloads. She said:

> To be able to manage you need to be able to recruit well and you need to have that flexibility and support to get the person into the post quickly, this process can sometime take too long . . . that's where I really want the support, to get the person into the new position as soon as possible, and to have some flexibility around this . . . interpretation of the policy is a bit better now. I would like to see improvement with equal opportunities and the efficiency around that would be good. The time taken if you do have difficulties is a problem. You may get a grievance in or whatever, and something has happened, generally HR is good but they're stretched so there can be a time lapse . . . it's just some of the HR mechanisms that should be looked at.
>
> (Manager, Female, Age 50–59 years,
> Tenure 20–25 years)

Yet another manager likened support to that which is received from the HR department during recruitment and selection process. She associates the support as mechanistic and suggests a more personable supportive approach should be implemented instead of an anonymous email system. She comments,

> Managers are required to take a bigger lead in sickness monitoring, disciplinary and recruitment. . . . My job role is increasingly busy and I need to have that support and specialist knowledge from HR as back up, it does worry me. . . . I would contact HR for advice but that's sort of been diluted but I would like to have two named people who I knew were linked to my service and they'd come down and help us and provide support . . . sometimes you call HR and not know who you're talking to and it can be a different person every single time. . . . They have this process now where you have to email the corporate name – 'HR First' and it goes into a big pile which is allocated to people which really does not help because as a manager with time constraints trying to set up a stage three long-term sickness absence meeting and it's not allocated to an HR representative . . . . it's less supportive than it used to be . . . if they went back to the way it was (allocated representatives) that would really help rather than going to an anonymous email system.
>
> (Manager, Female, Age 50–59 years, Tenure 16–20 years)

Employees also touched on the notion of bureaucratic, improving outcomes for people and equal opportunities as being important to them. One employee said:

> The whole agenda in local government is obviously immensely bureaucratic rather than trying to improve outcomes for people who are having a rubbish time . . . and I don't really feel that kind of filling and ticking the boxes in the way to achieve equality for people.
>
> (Employee, Female, Age 30–39 years, Tenure less than 5 years)

Both managerial and non-managerial employees held the view that the HR support requires improvement at the Council. Given that the HR department is centralised at this local government organisation, presented additional challenges for the delivery of efficient support to line managers and departments. Managerial employees highlighted that HR support is too mechanistic and time consuming and a more 'human focus' to the support provided to managers to assist them with people management initiatives instead of an anonymous email support system. Non-managerial employees found that HR support was bureaucratic, did not provide equality for people and required improvements in induction and onboarding. The literature supports this finding as the NPM implementation is a transformation of the nature of work in public sector organisations resulting in new approaches to the delivery of goods and services with greater efficiency (Morphet, 2008). This has influenced changes in human resources (HR) role impacting on the function's ability to act as an 'employee champion' due to reduced employee contact and more fragmented HR roles (Harris, 2007; Kessler and Coyle-Shapiro, 2000).

In conclusion, the qualitative aspect of this study contributes to the gap in the employee-focused HRM literature as it relates to employees' reactions to HRM practices, the quality of working life and well-being at work. The findings reveal that managerial employees view HRM as a strategic partner. In contrast, non-managerial employees view HRM as unfair and unjust practices that does not act as an employee champion but rather HRM practices bullies and mistreats them. Managerial respondents revealed that HRM practices that are important to them are associated with talent and performance management, work-life balance, training and development, succession planning and communication. Non-managerial employees highlighted that the same polices are important to them but also included that they would like HRM practices that allowed equality, fairness at work, and trust (Grant et al., 2007; Hayworth and Hart, 2007). The respondents had similar and in some cases different responses regarding their views about which HRM practices should be improved to enhance their well-being and performance at the local government organisation. These findings reveal that 21 HRM practices once improved in this public sector organisation, it will likely create a work environment conducive to enhancing the quality of working life and well-being of these public sector employees, which in turn will enhance service delivery and efficiency to end users in the community. Managerial and non-managerial employees highlighted 16 HRM practices that once improved, will enhance their quality of working life and well-being at work. These HRM practices include: flexible and fair recruitment and selection strategies, fair internal recruitment, clarify and simplify discipline and grievance procedures, team working, involvement in decision making, employee voice, harmonisation and status differential, pay and rewards, absence management, career development opportunities, management performance evaluation, HR support, return the 'human focus' back to HRM, recognition and appreciation, succession planning, health and safety office ergonomics, equality in training and development, coaching and mentoring, reduction in bureaucracy, improve flexible working to reduce dispersed teams, and reduction in change processes. The findings support Pfeffer's (2005) and Redman and Wilkinson (2009) claim to the 'bundles' of high commitment HRM practices that signal management dedication towards employee engagement and well-being drawn from Pfeffer (2005) and are now widely recognised and universally accepted, and have been modified by Marchington and Wilkinson (2005) for the UK context. These include (1) employment security and internal labour markets, (2) selective hiring and sophisticated selection, (3) extensive training, learning and development, (4) employee involvement, information sharing and worker voice, (5) self-managed teams/team working, (6) high compensation contingent on performance, and (7) reduction of status differentials and harmonisation (Currie, 2001; Cooper et al., 2001; Redman and Wilkinson, 2009). The findings from

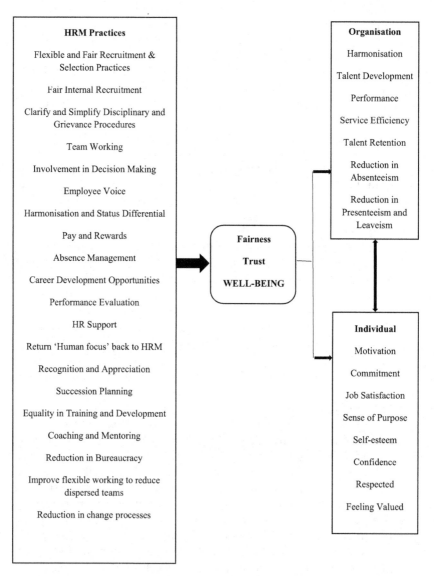

Figure 10.1 Employees' evaluation of HRM practices that influence fairness, trust, well-being at work in the public sector

this study also extends this model to include: clarify and simplify disciplinary and grievance procedures, absent management, career development opportunities, HR support, performance evaluation, return 'human focus' back to HRM, recognition and appreciation, succession planning, coaching and mentoring, reduction in bureaucracy, reduction in change processes and improvement in flexible working to reduce dispersed teams. In the case of the public sector, reform has resulted in budget limitations, cost reduction and the NPM ideology that adopts the management styles and business practices from the private sector (Beaumont et al., 2007). The public sector employees' reactions to HRM practices and well-being shows that within the NPM work environment, fairness at work HRM practices, and the material aspect of the employment relationship has to first be addressed for public sector employees before their well-being at work can be promoted (Whitfield, 2009).

Figure 10.1 shows employees' evaluation of HRM practices that influences fairness, trust and well-being at work in the public sector.

Notes

1 £10,001–£20,000 = six respondents; £20,001–£30,000 = nine respondents; £30,001–£40,000 = five respondents; £40,001–£50,000 = four respondents; £50,001–£60,000 = one respondent.
2 Less than five years (11 respondents); 6–10 years (6 respondents); 11–15 years (3 respondents); 16–20 years (4 respondents) and 21–25 years (3 respondents).
3 Questions related to meanings of HRM are: What do you understand by the term HRM? Which HRM practices are most important to you and why? And how can HRM practices be modified and/or improved to develop your well-being at work?

References

Albrecht, S., and Travaglione, A. (2003) 'Trust in Public-Sector Senior Management', *International Journal of Human Resource Management*, Vol. 24(1): 76–92.

Appelbaum, E., Bailey, R., Berg, P., and Kalleberg, A. (2000) *A Manufacturing Competitive Advantage: The Effects of High Performance Work Systems on Plant Performance and Company Outcomes*, New York, NY: Cornell University Press.

Aryee, S., Budhwar, P.S., and Chen, Z.X. (2002) 'Trust as a Mediator of the Relationship between Organisational Justice and Work Outcomes: Test of a Social Exchange Model', *Journal of Organisational Behaviour*, Vol. 23(3): 267–285.

Baird, M. (2002) 'Changes, Dangers, Choice and Voice: Understanding What High Commitment Means for Employees and Unions', *The Journal of Industrial Relations*, Vol. 44(3): 359–375.

Bakke, D.W. (2005) *Joy at Work: A Revolutionary Approach to Fun on the Job*, New York: Penguin Group (USA) Inc.

Baptiste, N.R. (2007) 'Line Management Leadership: Implications for Employee Well-Being', Developing Leadership Research, Chapters from the Northern Leadership Academy Fellow 2007 Conference, Edited by G.P. Clarkson, Leeds

University Business School, Leeds University Press Financial Services, Leeds, pp. 229–238.

Baptiste, N.R. (2008) 'Tightening the Link between Employee Well-Being and Performance: A New Dimension for HRM', *Management Decisions*, Vol. 46(2): 284–309.

Baptiste, N.R. (2009) 'Fun and Wellbeing: Insights from Senior Managers in a Local Authority', *Employee Relations*, Vol. 31(6): 600–612.

Beaumont, P., Pate, J., and Fischbacher, M. (2007) 'Public Sector Employment: Issues of Size and Composition in the UK', in P. Dibben, P. James, I. Roper, and G. Wood (Eds.) *Modernising Work in Public Services: Redefining Roles and Relationships in Britain's Changing Workplace*, Basingstoke: Palgrave Macmillan.

Becker, B., and Gerhard, B. (1996) 'The Impact of Human Resource Management on Organisational Performance: Progress and Prospects', *Academy of Management Journal*, Vol. 39(4): 779–801.

Black, C. (2008) 'Dame Carol Black Review of the Health of Britain's Working Age Population: Working for a Healthier Tomorrow', Presented to the Secretary of State for Health and the Secretary of State for Work and Pensions, 17th March, London: TSO.

Blau, P.M. (1964) *Exchange and Power in Social Life*, New York: Wiley Publishers.

Blau, P.M. (2006) *Exchange and Power in Social Life: New Introduction by the Author*, 10th Edition, London: Transaction Publisher.

Bolton, S. (2006) 'The UK's Best Could Do So Much Better', *Personnel Today Magazine*, 7th March.

Boxall, P., Purcell, J., and Wright, P. (Eds.) (2007) *The Oxford Handbook of Human Resource Management*, Oxford: Oxford University Press.

Browning, V., and Edgar, F. (2004) 'Reactions to HRM: An Employee Perspective from South Africa and New Zealand', *Journal of the Australian and New Zealand Academy of Management*, Vol. 10(1): 1–13.

Bryson, A., Charlwood, A., and Forth, J. (2006) 'Worker Voice, Managerial Response and Labour Productivity: An Empirical Investigation', *Industrial Relations Journal*, Vol. 37(5): 438–455.

Clarke, J., Gewirtz, S., and McLaughlin, E. (Eds.) (2000) *New Managerialism, New Welfare?*, London: Sage Publications.

Cohen, A. (2003) *Multiple Commitments in the Workplace: An Integrative Approach*, London: Lawrence Erlbaum Associates Publishers.

Cook, J., and Wall, T. (1980) 'New Work Attitude: Measure of Trust, Organisational Commitment and Personal Need Non-fulfillment', *Journal of Occupational Psychology*, Vol. 53: 39–52.

Cooper, C.L., Dewe, P.J., and O'Driscoll, M.P. (2001) *Organisational Stress: A Review and Critique of Theory, Research and Application*, Newbury Park, CA: Sage Publications.

Cox, T., and Jackson, C.A., (2006) 'Health and Well-Being of Working Age People: Mapping the Public Policy Landscape', *ESRC Seminar Series*, London: Economic and Social Research Council.

Coyle-Shapiro, J.A.-M., and Conway, N. (2005) 'Exchange Relationships: An Examination of Psychological Contracts and Perceived Organisational Support', *Journal of Applied Psychology*, Vol. 90: 774–781.

Cropanzano, R. (Ed.) (1993) *Justice in the Workplace: Approaching Fairness in Human Resource Management*, New York: Lawrence Erlbaum.

Cropanzano, R., and Folger, R. (1991) 'Procedural Justice and Worker Motivation', in R.M. Steers and L.W. Porter (Eds.) *Motivation and Worker Behaviour*, pp. 131–43, 5th Edition, New York: McGraw Hill.

Crouch, C. (2004) *Post Democracy*, Cambridge: Polity.

Currie, D. (2001) *Managing Employee Well-Being*, London: Chandos Publishing.

Department for Work and Pensions (2006) *A New Deal for Welfare: Empowering People at Work, CM 6730, Stationery Office*, London, w.dwp.gov.uk/welfarereform/docs/A_new_deal_for_welfare-Empowering_people_to_work-Full_Document.pdf (accessed 19th July, 2007).

Dibben, P. (2007) 'Employment Security and Job Insecurity in Public Services: Tow Sides of the Same Coin?', in P. Dibben, P. James, I. Roper, and G. Wood (Eds.) *Modernising Work in Public Services: Redefining Roles and Relationships in Britain's Changing Workplace*, Basingstoke: Palgrave Macmillan.

Dibbens, P., James, P., Roper, I., and Wood, G. (2007) *Modernising Work in Public Services: Redefining Roles and Relationships in Britain's Changing Workplace*. Basingstoke: Palgrave Macmillan.

Diener, E., Oishi, S., and Lucas, R.E. (2003) 'Personality, Culture, and Subjective Wellbeing: Emotional and Cognitive Evaluations of Life', *Annual Review Psychology*, Vol. 54: 403–425.

Eisenberger, R., Huntington, R., Hutchison, S., and Sowa, D. (1986) 'Perceived Organisational Support', *Journal of Applied Psychology*, Vol. 71(3): 500–507.

Fiorito, J. (2002) 'Human Resource Management Practices and Worker Desires for Union Representation', in J. Bennett and B. Kaufman (Eds.) *The Future of Private Sector Unionisation in the United States*, Armonk, NY: M.E. Sharpe.

Gallie, D., Felstead, A., and Green, F. (2001) 'Employer Policies and Organisational Commitment in Britain 1992–1997', *Journal of Management Studies*, Vol. 38(8): 1081–1101.

George, C. (2009) *The Psychological Contract: Managing and Developing Professional Groups*, Work and Organisational Psychology, Berkshire: Open University Press.

Gibb, S. (2001) 'The State of Human Resource Management: Evidence from Employees' Views of HRM Systems and Staff', *Employee Relations*, Vol. 23(4/5): 318–336.

Gouldner, A.W. (1960) 'The Norm of Reciprocity: A Preliminary Statement', *American Sociological Review*, Vol. 25: 161–128.

Gould-Williams, J. (2003) 'The Importance of HR Practices and Workplace Trust in Achieving Superior Performance: A Study of Public-Sector Organisations', *International Journal of Human Resource Management*, Vol. 14(1): 28–54.

Gould-Williams, J. (2004) 'The Effects of High Commitment HRM Practices on Employee Attitude: The Views of Public Sector Workers', *Public Administration*, Vol. 82(1): 63–81.

Gould-Williams, J. (2007) 'HR Practices, Organisational Climate and Employee Outcomes: Evaluating Social Exchange in Local Government', *International Journal of Human Resource Management*, Vol. 18(9): 1627–1647.

Graen, G.B., Novak, M.A., and Sommerkamp, P. (1982) 'The Effects of Leader-Member Exchange and Job Design on Productivity and Satisfaction: Testing a Dual Attachment Model', *Organisational Behaviour and Human Performance*, Vol. 30: 109–131.

Grant, A., Christianson, M., and Price, R. (2007) 'Happiness, Health or Relationships? Managerial Practices and Employee Well-Being Tradeoffs', *The Academy of Management*, Vol. 21(3): 51–63.

Grant, D., and Shields, J. (2002) 'In Search of the Subject: Researching Employee Reactions to Human Resource Management', *The Journal of Industrial Relations*, Vol. 44(3): 313–334.

Green, F. (2006) *Demanding Work, the Paradox of Job Quality in the Affluent Economy*, Woodstock: Princeton University Press.

Guest, D. (1998) 'Is the Psychological Contract Worth Taking Seriously?', *Journal of Organisational Behaviour*, Vol. 19: 649–664.

Guest, D. (1999) 'Human Resource Management: The Workers' Verdict', *Human Resource Management Journal*, Vol. 9(3): 5–25.

Guest, D. (2001) 'Human Resource Management and Performance: A Review and Research Agenda', *International Journal of Human Resource Management*, Vol. 8(3): 263–276.

Guest, D. (2002) 'Human Resource Management, Corporate Performance and Employee Well-Being: Building the Worker into HRM', *The Journal of Industrial Relations*, Vol. 44(3): 335–358.

Guest, D., and Conway, N. (2004) *Employee Well-Being and the Psychological Contract*, London: The Chartered Institute of Personnel Development.

Guest, D.E. (2006) 'Human Resource Management: The Workers Verdict', *Human Resource Management Journal*, Vol. 9(3): 5–26.

Harrington, S., and Rayner, C. (2010) 'Look before You Leap or Drive Right in? The Use of Moral Courage in Response to Workplace Bullying', in P.A. Linley, S. Harrington, and N. Garcea (Eds.) *Oxford Handbook of Positive Psychology and Work*, pp. 265–276, Oxford: Oxford University Press.

Harris, L. (2007) 'The Changing Nature of the HR Function in UK Local Government and Its Role as 'Employee Champion', *Employee Relations*, Vol. 30(1): 34–47.

Haworth, J., and Hart, G. (2007) *Wellbeing: Individual, Community and Social Perspectives*, Basingstoke: Palgrave MacMillan.

Health and Safety Executive (2004) 'Managing Sickness Absence and Return to Work: An Employers' and Managers' Guide', *Health and Safety Executive*: 1–60.

Homans, G.C. (1961) *Social Behaviour: Its Elementary Forms*, New York: Harcourt, Brace and World.

Huselid, M., Jackson, S., and Schuler, R. (1997) 'Technical and Strategic Human Resource Management Effectiveness as Determinants of Firm Performance', *Academy of Management Journal*, Vol. 40(1): 171–188.

Keenoy, T. (1990) 'Human Resource Management: Rhetoric and Reality and Contradiction', *International Journal of Human Resource Management*, Vol. 1(3): 363–384.

Kersley, B., Alpin, C., Forth, J., Bryson, A., Bewley, H., Dix, G., and Oxenbridge, S. (2006) *Inside the Workplace: Findings from the 2004 Workplace Employment Relations Survey*, London: Routledge and Taylor & Francis Group.

Kessler, I., and Coyle-Shapiro, J. (2000) 'New Forms of Employment Relations in the Public Services', *Industrial Relations Journal*, Vol. 31(1): 17–34.

Legge, K. (1995) 'HRM: Rhetoric, Reality and Hidden Agendas', in J. Storey (Ed.) *Human Resource Management: A Critical Text*, pp. 33–61, London: Routledge Publishers.

Lewis, D., and Rayner, C. (2003) 'Bullying and Human Resource Management: A Wolf in Sheep's Clothing?', in S. Einarsen, H. Hoel, D. Zapf, and C.L. Cooper (Eds.) *Bullying and Emotional Abuse in the Workplace: International Perspectives in Research and Practice*, pp. 370–382, London: Taylor and Francis.

MacDonald, L.A.C. (2005) *Wellness at Work: Protecting and Promoting Employee Well-Being*, London: Chartered Institute of Personnel and Development.

Marchington, M., and Grugulis, I. (2000) 'Best-Practice' Human Resource Management: Perfect Opportunity or Dangerous Illusion?', *International Journal of Human Resource Management*, Vol. 11(6): 1104–1124.

Marchington, M., and Wilkinson, A. (2005) *Human Resource Management at Work: People Management and Development*, London: The Chartered Institute of Personnel and Development.

McLaughlin, K., Osborne, S.P., and Ferlie, E. (2008) *New Public Management: Current Trends and Future Prospects*, London: Taylor and Francis Group.

Meyer, J.P., and Allen, N.J. (1997) *Commitment in the Workplace: Theory, Research, and Application*, London: Sage Publications.

Morphet, J. (2008) *Modern Local Government*, London: Sage Publications.

Noblet, A.J., and Rodwell, J.J. (2009) 'Integrating Job Stress and Social Exchange Theories to Predict Employee Strain in Reformed Public Sector Contexts', *Journal of Public Administration Research and Theory and Advance Access*, Vol. 19(1): 555–524.

O'Donnell, M., and Shields, J. (2002) 'Performance Management and the Psychological Contract in the Australian Federal Public Sector', *Journal of Industrial Relations*, Vol. 44: 435–457.

Pfeffer, J. (2005) 'Producing Sustainable Competitive Advantage through Effective Management of People', *Academy of Management Executive*, Vol. 19(4): 95–108.

Punch, K.F. (2005) *Introduction to Social Research: Quantitative and Qualitative Approaches*, London: Sage Publications.

Purcell, J. (1999) 'Best Practice and Best Fit: Chimera or cul-de-sac?', *Human Resource Management Journal*, Vol. 9(3): 26–41.

Purcell, J., and Hutchinson, S. (2003) *Bringing Policies to Life: The Vital Role of Front Line Managers in People Management*, London: CIPD.

Redman, T., and Wilkinson, A. (2009) *Contemporary Human Resource Management: Text and Cases*, London: Prentice Hall and Financial Times.

Renwick, D. (2003) 'HR Managers, Guardians of Employee Wellbeing', *Personnel Review*, Vol. 32(3): 341–359.

Renwick, D. (2009) 'Line Managers', in T. Redman and A. Wilkinson (Eds.) *Contemporary Human Resource Management: Text and Cases*, pp. 227–242, 3rd Edition, London: Pearson Education.

Rousseau, D.M. (1995) *Psychological Contracts in Organisations: Understanding Written and Unwritten Agreements*, Thousand Oaks, CA: Sage Publications.

Saunders, M., Lewis, P., and Thornhill, A. (2009) *Research Methods for Business Students*, 5th Edition, London: Pearson Education, Financial Times, and Prentice Hall.

Sheehan, K., and Hoy, M. (2004) 'On-Line Surveys', in C. Seale (Ed.) *Social Research Methods: A Reader*, pp. 105–110, London: Routledge Taylor and Francis Group.

Silcox, S. (2007) 'Health Work and Well-Being: Rising to the Public Sector Attendance Management Challenge', *ACAS Policy Discussion Chapter*, No. 6, May.

Silverman, D. (1993) *Interpreting Qualitative Data: Methods for Analysing Talk, Text and Interaction*, London: Sage Publications.

Smith, J.A., and Osborn, M. (2003) 'Interpretative Phenomenological Analysis', in J.A. Smith (Ed.), *Qualitative Psychology: A Practical Guide to Research Methods*, Sage Publications: London.

Storey, J. (2007) *Human Resource Management: A Critical Text*, 3rd Edition, London: Thomson Learning.

Tehrani, N., Humpage, S., Willmott, B., and Haslam, I. (2007) 'What's Happening with Well-Being at Work?', in *Change Agenda*, London: Chartered Institute of Personnel Development.

Torres, L., and Pina, V. (2002) 'Changes in Public Service Delivery in EU Countries', *Public Money and Management*, Vol. 22(4): 41–48.

Van Mannen, M. (1990) *Researching Lived Experience: Human Science for an Action Sensitive Pedagogy*, New York: State University of New York Press.

Ulrich, D. (1997) *Human Resource Champions: The Next Agenda for Adding Value and Delivering Results*, Boston, MA: Harvard Business School Press.

White, M., Hill, S., McGovern, P., Mills, C., and Smeaton, D. (2003) 'High-Performance' Management Practices, Working Hours and Work-Life Balance', *British Journal of Industrial Relations*, Vol. 41(2): 175–195.

Whitfield, K. (Ed.) (2009) 'Employee Well-being and Working Life: Towards an Evidence-Based Policy Agenda', An ESRC/HSE Public Policy Project, Report on a Public Policy Seminar held at HSE, London, February.

Wilkinson, A., Dundon, T., Marchington, M., and Ackers, P. (2004) 'Changing Patterns of Employee Voice: Case Studies from the UK and Republic of Ireland', *The Journal of Industrial Relations*, Vol. 46(3): 298–322.

Williams, M. (2002) 'Generalization in Interpretative Research', in T. May (Ed.) *Qualitative Research in Action*, London: Sage Publications.

Willmott, H. (1993) 'Strength Is Ignorance: Slavery Is Freedom: Managing Culture in Modern Organisations', *Journal of Management Studies*, Vol. 30(4): 515–552.

Wood, S. (1999) 'Human Resource Management and Performance', *International Journal of Management Reviews*, Vol. 1(4): 367–413.

11 The workers' voice

Concepts and improvements in well-being for individual, group and organisational effectiveness

Employee well-being at work

Well-being has become one of the most important issues of the twenty-first-century world of work – a challenge not just for individuals, in terms of their mental and physical health, but for employers and governments who have started to assess its social and financial implications (Baptiste, 2009). The definition and meaning of work-related well-being is emergent with a number of competing meanings, making a precise definition of it open and can take many forms (Renwick, 2003). Proponents of employee well-being indicate that it is a complex concept with multiple dimensions (Baptiste, 2009; Diener et al., 2003; Grant et al., 2007; Ryan and Deci, 2001; Ryff, 1995). Peccei (2004) suggests that well-being at work concerns an overall sense of happiness, physical and mental health of the workforce (Currie, 2001; Haworth and Hart, 2007). Grant et al. (2007) distinguish between three dimensions: the psychological dimension (satisfaction, attitudes and emotions in relation to work); the physical dimension (relating to employees' health and safety at work); and the social dimension (relating to interpersonal relationships, team work and management style). However, Baptiste (2010) proposes a broader and more holistic explanation for well-being at work which includes the individual, group and organisation that are addressed through 16 domains which include *individual dimension* (i.e. psychological, physical, mental health, intellectual, reward/material, career, spiritual, financial and work/family well-being); *social dimension* (i.e. social, compassionate leadership and stakeholders well-being); and *organisational dimension* (i.e. humanistic and fair practices, organisational financial, wellness management and work/organisation well-being). Baptiste (2010) further argues that this explanation invokes not just specific practices of 'wellness' programmes and initiatives, such as health screening, healthy eating, subscriptions to the gym, employee assistance programs or indeed fun programmes, but a broader and more material aspects of the employment relationship, individual satisfaction, mental health and emotions related to work and life, interpersonal relationships and management styles, fairness at work and other social and financial factors associated with wider experience of fulfilment and functioning and work.

The concept of employee well-being at work promotes advantages to organisations of having a healthy workforce and is pivotal to understanding of the different domains that affect the quality of life at work (Baptiste, 2008, 2009). Personal well-being does not exist in isolation but within a social context (Tehrani et al., 2007) and individual lives are affected by social relations with organisational agents, lifestyle and employment changes (Kersley et al., 2006). Contemporary organisations that foster well-being are perceived as employers of 'best practice' and are recognised by current and prospective employees as offering a desirable place to work (Grant et al., 2007). Yet whilst well-being at work is being promoted as a potential avenue for providing meaning and fulfilment at work, the factors that foster well-being at work have attracted limited empirical research. Organisations that embrace employee wellbeing appear then to prioritise the protection and promotion of employee satisfaction (Baptiste, 2008; Tehrani et al., 2007); embraces a praise and rewards culture (Baptiste, 2009); trust (Albrecht and Travaglione, 2003), fulfilment and health (Bakke, 2005; Ryff, 1995).

Public sector working environment and employee well-being

The realities of the public sector work environment show the challenges that employee well-being at work approach can face. Managers' daily realities are inundated with social and moral problems in corporate life (Jackall, 1988), often further challenging espoused rationality and efficiency. Research by Baptiste (2009) shows that as with any other group of employees, for senior managers material aspects of the employment relationship (i.e. working time arrangements, stress management, communication, rewards, training and development, team working, relationships and reduction in change initiatives) are key to their well-being. Furthermore, non-managerial employees' daily realities are likely to be affected by challenges of increasing workloads, job insecurity, work stress, lack of autonomy, control initiatives, redundancies etc. Based on these findings from research done in the public sector, managerial and non-managerial employees may find it difficult to embrace and instigate 'well-being at work' initiatives and it is an essential question to explore the degree to which these employees' individual experiences of work can be characterised as happiness or well-being. This chapter conceptualises a relevant model to better understand and normalise employees' perspective as it relates to employees' concepts of well-being at work in the public sector, as well as employees' voice regarding line management leadership and its implications on employee well-being. There has been little research done in these areas and this chapter begins to address these gaps and proposed recommendations for policy makers, leaders, managers, employees and researchers.

Methodology

This research is part of a larger study investigating employees' experiences of HRM practices, working life and how such experiences have contributed to their well-being at work in the local government context. A local authority was chosen in the North West of England. This authority professed to have adopted well-being policies and practices to establish a positive attendance culture, promote fun at work and enhance staff welfare. This present study focuses on particular groups within the local authority: senior managers, managers, professionals, associate professional and clerical/secretarial staff regarding their views concerning concepts of Employee Well-being at work in the public sector[1] and line management leadership and employee well-being.[2] 'The prominent points cited by respondents as those most frequently mentioned are highlighted in the findings. Local government was considered an appropriate context to examine employee's concepts and definition of their well-being at work in the public sector as well as respondents' voice that relates to line management leadership and well-being at work. This is in keeping with best value regimes placing a statutory duty on local government organisations (i.e. Councils) to review the processes used in delivering services in an attempt to enhance the effectiveness and efficiency of service provision and performance with limited government funding. Can well-being at work philosophy be promoted in the NPM work environment given the government mandate of budget reduction and efficiency savings? This study seeks to address this question as well as the other research questions.

In-depth, face-to-face interviews were conducted with senior managers, managers, professionals, associate professionals, and clerical/secretarial staff with the aim of understanding their perspective of employee well-being at work as well as employees' line management leadership and well-being at work. For simplicity senior managers, managers and professionals will be referred to as 'managerial employees', and associate professionals and clerical/secretarial will be referred to as 'non-managerial employees'. Purposive sampling was used to ensure that all departments within the Council were reflected, and 15 managers (Male = 8, Female = 7) and 12 non-managers (Male = 3, Female = 9) participated in the study. All 27 were Caucasian; (23 respondents) aged from 40 to 59 years, and (4 respondents) aged from 20–39 years; had educational attainment and professional qualifications to master's degree for managers and AGVNQ to HNC/D for non-managers; 25 worked full-time and 2 part-time, reported a range of incomes of (£1,000 to £10,000) for part-time staff,

(£10,000 to £30,000) for full-time employees, and (£30,000 to £60,000) for the managerial group; and held a variety of tenures with the organisation: less than 5 years (11 respondents), 6–10 years (6 respondents), 11–15 years (3 respondents), 16–20 years (4 respondents) and 21–25 years (3 respondents).

Interviews lasted for 60–90 minutes, and were tape-recorded, transcribed verbatim and analysed using Hermeneutic Phenomenological Analysis (HPA) (Van Maanen, 1994). The study commenced with an initial question: 'Can you tell me what you understand by employee well-being?' The interview schedule covered five broad topics: the meaning and definition of well-being; importance of well-being; how employee well-being can be improved; responsiveness of line manager to promote employee well-being; line manager's approach that can promote well-being. The findings from this research is concerned with the employment experiences of local government employees, a moderate generalisation can be made for managerial and non-managerial employees more broadly (Williams, 2002: 211).

Both managerial and non-managerial employees were asked to respond in relation to their own experiences and priorities as employees, rather than from an espoused practice point of view. Initial transcripts were reviewed through immersion in the data to establish an orienting gestalt that drove later coding. Interviews were coded line by line necessary for thematic analysis. Concepts, themes and sub-themes were identified. Half of the transcripts were separately coded by an independent researcher to identify emerging themes, and the resulting coding match of 85% provides evidence of reliability in the coding process (Silverman, 2005). Final themes were also verified by informants to ensure they appropriately captured the meaning that the informant sought to convey. The representation of themes is based on salient points raised (Lyons, 2007) and has been structured on the assumption that a theme cited by a larger number of interviewees have officiate more importance to the respondents as a whole (Miles and Huberman, 1994). The resulting patterns provide an enriched understanding of the factors pertinent to employees' perspectives of the concepts of well-being at work in a NPM environment as well as their perspectives about their line manager's leadership and the implication of the leadership styles on their well-being at work in local government.

Employees' concepts of well-being at work

The setting of the experience and resources

The research findings reveal from observations made that the practices and philosophies of a New Public Management (NPM) environment are central to this local authority. These include a managerialist approach, cost-containment, efficiency savings, changing structures, controlled delegation, and the production of more efficient, effective and responsive services. Harrow (2002) corroborates this view and highlights that the nature of NPM as a collection of government-led activities displaying recognisable characteristics including controlled delegation, increased emphasis on user orientation and the measurement of performance, most commonly by 'business' style measures. The review of company documents reveal that the Council experienced external economic, political and demographic challenges. These include the changing expectations and demands of citizens for speedier responses to inquiries and service provision; attracting and retaining talent; and responding appropriately to the needs of a more diverse society. The modernisation agenda also challenged the council to improve its efficiency, demonstrate value for money, improve service delivery, to make a reduction in expenditure, and to improve the well-being of the local community. The Council's response to this mandate resulted in reductions in budgets and service cuts; workforce transformation by merging departments for greater efficiency; capital asset reduction; the introduction of flexible working options like 'the new ways of working'; and partnership working.

These changes have implications for work demands from workforce reductions, dispersed teams as a result of flexible working, challenges with relationship building due to centralisation, silo working and the use of excessive emails, increased workloads, work pressures and work-related stress. These factors affected managerial and non-managerial employees differently.

Respondents were asked via the semi-structured interviews to delve into their work experiences in the NPM environment and share their perspective, meaning and understanding of well-being at work. Open ended questions associated with the meaning of well-being, definition of well-being, importance of well-being, the effects of change on well-being, and what things you would like to see improved at the Council to promote your well-being at work.

The meaning and understanding of well-being

Managerial and non-managerial employees discussed their understanding and definition of employee well-being at work and shared their perspectives that revealed eight key themes which include work-life-satisfaction, wellness management, stress management, flexible working, safety at work, respect, fairness at work and equality.

Work and life satisfaction

Respondents were asked about their understanding and definition of well-being. Managerial employees' responses reveal a wide range of themes that include feeling valued and supported, listened to, autonomy to do job, job enrichment and variety, can manage the balance between work and life, adequate remuneration and holidays. One manager shares her perspective. She says:

> My understanding of employee well-being is where somebody is feeling valued and supported, listened to, can do their job, are sufficiently stretched but isn't bored, sufficient variety, that they can manage the balance between work and life, that there's some leeway there. That there's adequate remuneration and holidays.
>
> (Manager, Female, Age 50–59 years, Tenure 11–16 years)

Another manager echoes the point of work and life satisfaction as essential to his understanding and definition of well-being and performance at work. Salient points raised are work and life satisfaction, heavy workloads, interesting work, more holidays and leave allowances, and pay and rewards. He claims:

> I think work and life satisfaction does make me more productive at work. I'm lucky, I am a positive thinking person and while there are things that irritate me, I've got a bit too much to do but what I have to do is interesting. That counts for a lot doesn't it. I would like a little bit more in the way of holidays leave allowance. I think we are poor on that.
>
> (Manager, Male, Age 30–39 years, Tenure 20–25 years)

Wellness management programmes

The findings reveal that both managerial and non-managerial employees understanding and definition of well-being relate to the salient point of wellness management programmes. The wellness initiatives highlighted include healthy food in the canteen, cycling and walking to work, walking up the stairs instead of using the elevators, staff counselling and messages.

One managerial employee's account for their understanding and definition of employee well-being was the introduction of a Wellness Programme by the Council called The Health Wise Challenge that addressed a diverse range of wellness management initiatives that were implemented to reduce employee absence levels and promote employees' health, well-being and performance. She said,

> The Health Wise challenge is being promoted because it will reduce our absence levels by 10.6 days per year downwards and was introduced to try and improve employees' health in terms of healthy foods in the canteen, cycling to work, walking more and not using our

cars as much, staff counselling service, messages . . . all linked to the business plans of central government view that we are going to work longer because we are going to live longer.

(Manager, Female, Age 40–49 years, Tenure 6–10 years)

Managers discussed their awareness of the wellness management programmes that were implemented by the Council. Initiatives such as walking up the stairs, losing weight, discounts for gym memberships, yoga sessions, and healthy eating options at the staff canteen. One manager shares:

The Council offers wellness opportunities like nice little note at the bottom of the stairs telling you how much weight you will lose if you went up the stairs instead of using the lift, and that you can get discount for gym memberships. Then you have yoga sessions and various things like that . . . there is some unhealthy food in the canteen but there are also very healthy options. There's always salads and baked potatoes and all that sort of thing. There are always good portions of vegetables . . . these are some of the ways to do it.

(Manager, Male, Age 40–49 years, Tenure 6–11 years)

Stress management

Another manager's understanding and definition of employee well-being at work was associated with stress management, good morale, stress and pressure reduction, improve health and performance. He explains,

Managing stress equates to good morale by not being under too much stress and pressure which can affect health and performance so it is important to manage stress . . . not being too anxious or uptight . . . stress can make you feel unwell and not perform.

(Manager, Male, Age 40–49 years, Tenure less than 5 years)

Another manager's perspectives on understanding and meaning of well-being echoes the notion of stress management associated with long hours working. She also highlighted the removal of evening meetings, decision making is best when staff are not beleaguered, team morale, stretched team and rewarding staff. She reveals a personal experience that gives meaning to the theme of long working hours and stress management. She explains,

Somehow we have to persuade the members that we can't have evening meetings, they must meet during the daytime . . . persuade them that the best place to make decisions is when officers are not tired having worked for maybe 12 hours before the meeting starts. . . .

I don't think that is the best place to make decisions . . . or helpful to my team to be there at 10:00pm or 11:00pm at night . . . it's not the best decision making for the Council either and if that can be removed this will improve my well-being at work . . . possibly rewarding staff as well.

(Manager, Female, Age 40–49 years, Tenure 6–10 years)

Another manager highlights the meaning and definition of her well-being by likened it to the reduction of time constraints, heavy workload, feeling pressured, stress management, managing and enjoying life. She said:

Just having enough time to have lunch would be good, but maybe I should control that myself. Feeling you've got enough time to work hard but to achieve. I think one of the problems is that you work so hard but there's always more to do. That's my sense of things. I feel quite pressured at times . . . so it's about managing my stress, managing and enjoying my life.

(Manager, Female, Age 50–59 years, Tenure 11–16 years)

Flexible working

Respondents also discussed that flexible working and work-life balance was their understanding and definition of employee well-being at work. One manager shares;

Flexible working is really the key one for me. . . . I just think it adds so much to the quality of your life . . . and the business case of work-life balance assisting in the retention of staff is certainly true and the feedback we have had from staff has been good.

(Manager, Female, Age 50–59 years, Tenure 20–25 years)

Safety at work

Non-managerial employees' understanding and definition of well-being at work relates to safety at work. Contentment and satisfaction with the job was also raised; negative emotions, team working, approachable line manager, supported, and absence of worry at work. One employee stated,

I hope that the Council would not put me in any danger and attempt to maintain my well-being. . . . I would say that I am reasonably happy and content . . . not causing us to feel any negative emotions. . . . I work in a nice team . . . my manager is approachable so there is that support, I don't worry about coming into work as I did when I first started.

(Employee, Female, Age 20–29 years, Tenure less than 5 years)

Respect and fairness at work

Another employee associated well-being at work to being respected, rewarded, team working, and flexibility. She asserts that;

> to be treated with respect as part of a team, to be given clear instructions, that my development needs are addressed, to be communicated to about things that are going on, to have access to flexible working or being allowed time off to do things, paid fairly . . . just that whole great big package.
>
> (Employee, Female, Age 40–49 years, Tenure, 16–20 years)

Fair treatment and equality

Another manager relates fair treatment to his definition of well-being. He said:

> I would say that recognition, ensuring that my pay is up to the level, keeping on with my development, giving me support that I need so that I'm happy and confident in work and not changing things for the sake of it.
>
> (Manager, Male, Age 30–39 years, Tenure less than 5 years)

Table 11.1 illustrates managerial and non-managerial employees' perspective, understanding and definition of employee well-being at work in the UK local government organisation in North West of England.

Importance of well-being at work

Sense of purpose, appreciation, and achievement

The analysis of company documents reveals a central theme of the council espousal of recognising and valuing its employees as important assets to the organisation. However, respondents' perspectives were mixed in terms of feeling valued and supported. Rhoades and Eisenberger (2002) argue that employers value employees' dedication and loyalty, whereas employees who are emotionally committed to the organisation show heightened performance, reduced absenteeism and a lessened likelihood of quitting their job (Mathieu and Zajac, 1990; Meyer and Allen, 1997). Employees who perceive that they are valued by the organisation can yield benefits of approval, respect, pay and promotion (Rhoades and Eisenberger, 2002) and are likely to reciprocate in positive attitudes and behaviour. The findings highlight themes of autonomy, more people focused, sense of worth, job design, support and motivation, feeling valued, trusting people to do the job, a sense of achievement, praise and recognition and being respected.

Table 11.1 Managerial and non-managerial employees' perspectives, understanding and definition of employee well-being at work

Dimension	Well-Being Domains	Managerial Employees	Non-Managerial Employees
Individual	Psychological	Feeling Valued Performance Good Morale Reduced Pressure Time constraints	Safety at Work Satisfaction Healthy Emotions
	Physical	Heavy Workloads Improved Employee Health Healthy Food Cycling and Walking to Work Walking up Stairs	–
	Intellectual	Autonomy Interesting Work Job Design Practices	-
	Mental Health	Stress Management Stress Reduction Anxiety Depression Long Working Hours Enjoy Life	Anxiety Opposite of Worry or Fear
	Rewards/ Material	Adequately Rewarded Holidays Leave Allowance	Pay
	Career	Job Enrichment Job Variety Enough time to perform at work	Career Development
	Spiritual	-	-
	Financial	-	Paid Fairly
	Work/Family	Work-Life Balance Work-Life-Satisfaction Stop Evening Meetings Enjoy Life Flexible Working Quality of Life	Access to Flexible Working Allowed Time off
Group	Social	Supported	Team Working Supported Communication
	Compassionate Leadership	Listened To	Approachable Manager Clear Instructions Listened To Regular Feedback Respect
	Stakeholders	-	-

Dimension	Well-Being Domains	Managerial Employees	Non-Managerial Employees
Organisation	Humanistic and Fair Practices	Stop Evening Meetings Decision making with beleaguered staff	Fairness at Work Respect
	Organisational Financial	-	-
	Wellness Management	Health benefits notes to staff about weight loss Healthy Eating at Staff Canteen Encouraged to Walk Stairs instead of using Elevator Staff Counselling Messages Yoga Sessions Discount for Gym Membership	–
	Work/ Organisation	Reduced Absence Levels Staff Retention	–

One manager shared his perspective regarding the importance of well-being and the key themes highlighted relates to a sense of purpose, making a difference, appreciation, adequately rewarded, team working, and career advancement. He said,

> It is important to know that what you do counts, that what you do is making a difference, that there is a purpose to your life . . . and in order to do that you have to be valued, you need to be rewarded and be a part of a team . . . at the end of your career you need to be able to look back and say 'I did this, I did that'.
>
> (Manager, Male, Age 40–49 years, Tenure 6–10 years)

Another manager echoes the this view and claims that well-being is important as people need to feel valued, exposed to humanistic practices, respect employees' contribution, workplace civility, removal of bureaucratic tick-box management approach, appreciation, anti-career stagnation, autonomy, employee commitment, and employee retention. He comments,

> People need to feel valued even if my manager got that performance agenda, she can still, within that, be human and value what you're doing and bring out from you what she needs, if she's skilled enough. . . . I understand where she's coming from I'm not politically naive and I know she has to tick these boxes and I'll help her tick

these boxes, but if she does not value me or doesn't clip my wings, maybe I'll start to think I want to be somewhere else and stuff her boxes.

(Manager, Male, Age 40–49 years, Tenure less than 5 years)

In contrast, non-managerial employees also pointed out that it is important to feel valued and appreciated by their employer. They also echo similar themes of the managerial employees regarding the importance of well-being. There comments touched on some additional themes which include; equal opportunities, embracing workplace diversity, anti-discrimination practices, fair treatment, support, training and development, and mentoring and coaching. These themes are captured by an employee's comments regarding the importance of well-being. She states:

> It's important that people feel valued in terms of what they can offer to the organisation as an individual . . . respecting people's differences in terms of childcare, religious, cultural backgrounds or disability . . . that your needs are respected and the organisation does what they can to try and support you to be the best employee you possibly can . . . whether that's in your specific post or you wanting to carve out a career within the organisation.
>
> (Employee, Female, Age 30–39 years,
> Tenure less than 5 years)

Another employee relates the importance of well-being to valued and supported by the organisation. He also highlighted themes of involvement and participation, anti-discrimination, workplace civility and dignity at work. He states:

> Looking after employees so they feel part of the organisation . . . we feel like individuals and don't feel as though they're discriminated against . . . that you are supported in line with other employees.
>
> (Employee, Male, Age 50–59 years,
> Tenure less than 5 years)

These respondents' views about the importance of well-being are clustered into key salient points that relates to fairness at work, workplace civility, appreciation, a sense of purpose, supported, training and development, career advancement opportunities, and involvement and participation in decision making. These salient points are associated with individual, group and organisational well-being dimensions. Table 11.2 outlines managerial and non-managerial employees' perspective as it relates to the importance of well-being at work.

Table 11.2 Managerial and non-managerial employees' perspectives on the importance of well-being at work

Dimensions	Well-Being Domains	Managerial Employees	Non-Managerial Employees
Individual	Psychological	Sense of Worth Feeling Valued Making a Difference Appreciation Motivation Employee Commitment Retention	Feeling Valued
	Intellectual	Autonomy Sense of Achievement	-
	Rewards/ Material	Rewarded	Training and Development
	Career	Career Advancement	Career Advancement Mentoring and Coaching
Group	Social	Support Team Work	Support Involvement Participation
	Compassionate and Respectful Leadership	Respect Approval Trust Motivation Humanistic approach to people management Dignity at Work Civility at Work	Respect Looking after employees Engagement
Organisational	Humanistic and Fair Practices	People-Focused Humanistic Practices Workplace Civility	Respecting People's Differences Equal Opportunities Embracing Workplace Diversity Anti-discrimination practices Fairness at Work Dignity at Work
	Healthy/Work Organisation	Job Design Anti-Bureaucratic Tick-Box/ Target approach to work	-

Organisational improvements to promote employee
well-being at work

Budget restrictions

Most managers held the view that they face challenges with the budgets and all face problems with government mandates for efficiency savings with finite resources. The budget challenge is associated with political and government pressures, increased workloads, work-related stress, a new public management environment, being stretched, and having to deliver more with less. One manager comments:

> Everything we do relates to the budgets, like organisational development, but yet again you have to think in the context of the budget. That is the difficult thing about working in a local authority, the political necks are assuring, the resources are very finite, sometimes too finite. I know that budgets have to be finite but sometimes it just feels too hard. We have had quite a crisis in the budget. I would like to see more discussions and arguments about budget pressures at national and local levels. It's not just the Council, it's government across the board. I think about the demographic pressures we encounter, it's phenomenal.
> (Manager, Male, Age 50–59 years, Tenure 20–25 years)

Another manager shared her views about budget restrictions having a negative impact on well-being, worry and anxiety, heavy workloads, budget challenges being an unpleasant part of managerial employees working life realities. One manager shares,

> Budget restrictions makes me feel worried, worried. We work hard with what we have but it's a perpetual thing, particularly in social services. It *(budgets)* has a negative effect on everyone's well-being and that's worrying. It's part of life, you get used to it but it's awful.
> (Manager, Female, Age 40–49 years, Tenure 6–11 years)

Work-life balance

Some mangers highlighted work-life balance as important to them to improve and promote their well-being at work. Other salient points mentioned are flexibility, less pressure, supporting staff, more holidays and pay. The manager says:

> I am very committed to the Council but I will like less pressure. In terms of work-life balance, I would like it to balance a little more . . .

slightly more in favour of home, but not much as I am at the stage of life where I have not got young kids. I try to manage people as flexibly as I can and you always get the rewards back. If someone needs some time, they get it because I know I'll get it back in performance – it's very important. I have been there so I know what it is like to be having to rush off and the pressure of being part-time as well. . . . I would also like some more holidays and pay and they all go together.

(Manager, Female, Age 50–59 years, Tenure 11 to 20 years)

Sickness management

Managerial respondents highlighted the importance of sickness management and the support from HRM to assist them to manage sickness absence in their respective department. Additional key themes mentioned include: employee health, team morale, employee disciplinary, termination and HR support to evaluate genuine cases and evaluate HR systems for effectiveness. He stated

Sickness management is important to me as it assists me to cope with absence and sickness in the department . . . this affects team morale, the individual, their health, the fact that you may end up sacking someone rightly or wrongly so that has been key in terms of what I wanted out of HR. . . . The policy restricts effectiveness and needs evaluation to help support genuine cases as there are loopholes in the present system.

(Manager, Male, Age 40–49 years, Tenure less than 5 years)

Derelict working environment

Non-managerial employees highlighted that they were exposed to derelict working environment and working conditions and claim that once the Council improves what they perceive as basic factors, this will improve their well-being at work. Themes highlighted include; depression, poor working conditions, inadequate office lighting, inadequate workplace ergonomics, dilapidated physical work environment, safety at work, and feeling anxious at work. These factors were captured by one employee's view of factors that should be improved by the Council to promote her well-being at work. She states;

The offices are absolutely the pits – the physical environment was really disgusting very depressing, poor daylight, really basic stuff they just weren't meeting quality standards. . . . I used to be very edgy and I actually felt unsafe . . . it took me a long time to relax.

(Employee, Female, Age 40–49 years, Tenure 6–10 years)

Feeling valued and making a contribution

Employees perspectives reveal the importance of feeling valued and being able to make a contribution to the Council and communities. Additional themes mentioned include, receiving more feedback, communication about employee contribution, feeling appreciated, respected, more flexibility, fairness at work and dignity at work. One employee shares:

> I would like the Council to make sure that employees feel more valued and that they are contributing. It's important to make sure that employees get more feedback about the way that they are contributing to the organisation because this is difficult in the public sector. If you work in the private sector, you can clearly see contribution by profits or targets or sales outputs as these are all very measurable, whereas in the public sector it is not. In the public sector, people get in trouble for overspends rather than anything else and its always negative. I think it would be much better for everybody's well-being if they felt much more appreciated. Having the 'WOW' awards event is okay, but it's once a year so what about the rest of the days in the year when people are feeling a bit grumpy . . . so making people feel more valued and giving them more flexibility, and treating people like individuals are all important to promote employee well-being.
>
> (Employee, Female, Age 40–49 years, Tenure 15–20 years)

Both managerial and non-managerial respondents accounts on the factors that they would like to see the Council improve to promote their well-being at work were clustered into five super-ordinate themes which include; budget restrictions, work-life balance, sickness management, derelict working conditions, and feeling valued and feedback about making a contribution. These themes are in alignment with the individual, group, and organisational dimensions and the multidimensional domains of well-being at work. Table 11.3 explores these findings.

Discussion

Definition of Well-Being. The findings that relates to understanding and meaning of well-being, the importance of well-being, and factors that the Council can improve to promote employee well-being at work reveal similarities and differences between managerial and non-managerial employees. Baptiste (2009) and George (2009) argue that significant differences can exist between organisations in the degree to which their organisational cultures tolerate, facilitate, embrace, or embedded well-being. Currie (2001) and Warr (2002) point out that individuals are likely to differ in their attitudes regarding the importance, appropriateness, and perceived consequences of having well-being at work. These differences

Dimension	Well-Being Domains	Managerial Employees	Non-Managerial Employees
Individual	Psychological	Budget Pressures Commitment Motivation Negative Well-Being Committed	Feeling Valued Appreciated
	Physical	Sickness Absence Employee Health	Safety at Work
	Intellectual	-	-
	Mental Health	Worry Anxiety Heavy Workloads Less Pressure	Depression Anxiety
	Rewards/ Material	Holiday Leave Allowance Pay	-
	Career	-	-
	Spiritual	-	-
	Financial	-	-
	Work/Family	Work-Life Balance More Balance in terms of home working Managing people flexibly	More Flexibility
Group	Social	Team Morale Disciplinary Termination HR Support	Respected
	Compassionate Leadership	-	Respected
	Stakeholders	Pressure to deliver services to communities	More feedback about work making a contribution to communities
Organisation	Humanistic and Fair Practices	Evaluate HR Systems for effectiveness	Fairness at work Dignity at Work
	Organisational Financial	Budget Restrictions Budget Pressures Limited Resources	
	Wellness Management	-	-
	Work/ Organisation	Political Environment Organisational Development Performance Management Sickness Absence Management	Poor Working Conditions Inadequate Office Light Inadequate Workplace Ergonomics Dilapidated physical environment

can be aligned to different groups of workers' having different psychological contracts (George, 2009; Rousseau, 1995).

The meaning and definition of employee well-being at work according to respondents touched on the individual, group and organisational dimensions. Both managerial and non-managerial employees defined well-being as a psychological well-being domain as they claimed that well-being is promoted when an individual feels valued and supported by their employer. They both also highlighted that promoting an individual's mental health, can also define well-being at work. Being adequately rewarded, given the opportunity for career development and work-life balance can contribute towards employee well-being at work. They further define employee well-being as being supported, respected and listened to by their line managers in the employment relationship, and from an organisational perspective, to have humanistic and fair practices that will provide equal opportunities for all employees. In contrast, managerial employees' definition of well-being at work were extended to include the physical, intellectual, wellness management and work/organisation well-being domains. Managerial employees also define their well-being to include the absence of heavy workloads and pressure at work, promoting employee health practices and diverse wellness management initiatives. Intellectually, managerial employees define their well-being through having autonomy over their jobs, stimulating job design practices, and having interesting work and the opportunity to work on exciting projects. Managerial employees also define their employee well-being through the reduction of absence levels and staff retention. These findings suggest that managers are concerned about their 'human resources' that they need to be able to respond to their heavy workloads, increased targets within limited budgets.

In contrast, non-managerial employees also define their well-being differently through financial well-being domain. These respondents define their well-being as being paid fairly as being compensated equitably contributes to their overall well-being at work and quality of life. Grant et al. (2007) argue that perceptions of well-being at work may be dependent on employee's personal outlook, socialisation processes, gender, work experiences and personality characteristics – each accounting for varying attitudes and perceptions regarding the importance of workplace well-being. The findings of this research extends the perceptions of well-being at work and suggest that it is also dependent on employees' working within certain work environments as there is no one-size-fits-all as it relates to work environments. For example, employees working in a NPM environment of the public sector is likely to define their well-being differently compared to private sector employees that embrace the well-being ideology through the provision of wellness management initiatives. The findings clearly reveal that these public sector employees' definition of well-being touched on the financial stability of the organisation, limited government funding and budgets, adequate resources, talent retention, heavy workloads, fairness at work, and the material aspects of the employment relationship have to be addressed first before these public sector employees' well-being at work can be promoted. Van Wanrooy et al. (2011) assert that the British economy has been facing economic challenges due to the recession which resulted in a financial crisis with the public sector employment falling with a pattern of unstable growth and uncertainty compared with the private sector (CIPD, 2019). Van Wanrooy et al., further points out that public sector organisations are stretched further to withstand the challenging financial crisis which places a tighter and perhaps unforgiving squeeze on their already limited resources within the New Public Management (NPM) environment.

The Importance of Well-Being. Managerial and non-managerial employees were asked their perspectives regarding why well-being at work is important to them. The findings reveal that there are similarities and differences that exists between managerial and non-managerial respondents. Both groups held the view that the importance of well-being relates to individual, group and organisational dimensions. From an individual perspective, the importance of well-being to respondents relates to psychological, rewards/material, and career well-being domains. These respondents view that once they are appreciated, rewarded, given an opportunity for career advancement, access to training and development, as well as coaching and mentoring, these practices are important for the promotion of their well-being at work. In contrast, managerial employees also highlighted intellectual well-being domain in terms of working with autonomy and being able to accomplish successes with work projects are the importance they place on well-being at work. From a group perspective, both groups state that employee well-being is important because it provides support for employees, builds trust, respect, dignity at work, workplace civility, and facilitate team work, involvement and participation, motivation, employee engagement, and will promote a more humanistic approach to people management by line managers and organisational leaders. Mullins (1993) argues that employee well-being at work promotes the advantage to organisations of having a healthy workforce, and the quality of life at work (Green and Whitfield, 2009). Individual lives are affected by social relations with organisational agents, lifestyle and employment changes (Tehrani et al., 2007) and employees expect their employers to value, support and respect their efforts towards attainment of organisational goals and objectives (Guest, 2002).

From an organisational perspective, both employee groups claim that employee well-being is important because it fosters an organisational culture of dignity, fairness, civility, anti-discriminatory practices, embraces diversity in the workplace and respecting people's differences, advocates equal opportunities, and a more 'people-focused' and employee-centred approach to human resources management, organisational practices, line management leadership, and the psychological contract within the employment relationship. Wilson (2010) argues that a substantial portion of our lives are spent at work that provides individuals status, economic reward and growth potential. For others, working provides a sense of worth, dignity, and that people and employment structure our lives and shape the inequalities that we face (Terkel, 1977). Bolton and Houlihan (2007) claim that maintaining dignity at work is something that workers from all walks of life struggle to achieve and can be attained through taking pride in productive accomplishments, and assistance against abusive bosses or bad management. In contrast, managerial employees also felt that well-being is important for job design practices, and as a tradeoff for a bureaucratic tick-box target approach to work adopted in the New Public Management environment. Weick (1992) argues that managerial practices can have implications on employee well-being and can lead to well-being tradeoffs or exchange, which is a common feature of organisational life.

Organisational Improvements to Promote Employee Well-Being. The findings reveal similarities and differences between both employee groups. Respondents perspective on what they perceive the Council should do to promote their well-being entails individual, group, and organisational dimensions. From an individual perspective, respondents' suggestions for improvements in the Council to promote their well-being involves psychological, physical, mental health, rewards/material, and work/family well-being domains. The budget restrictions that formed the working life realities of workers resulted in heavy workloads and a highly stressed and pressurised working environment that had a negative impact on employees well-being. These pressures affected employees physical and mental health resulting in high sickness absence, anxiety and depression amongst employees. Both employee groups would like to see improvements in these areas, which they perceive will improve their well-being at work, commitment, motivation and performance. Simonet (2013) asserts that the New Public Management ideology influences how decisions are made in the public sector environment and have implications for human resource management, working life and well-being at work for public sector employees working with diminishing confidence in government, declining budgets, increasing demands for service and productivity and human resource activities (Livesey et al., 2006). Respondents also mentioned improvements in work-life balance with more flexibility with the new ways of working in terms of working more from home and access to work-life balance opportunities for employees. MacDonald (2005) posits that the challenges of the changing world of work have a wide-ranging effect on work and family interaction which has major concerns for both employees and employers. In support, Cooper and Robertson (2001) point out that workers are experiencing life changes and aspirations and family time is coming under pressures, intensifying work-family conflict, resulting in psychological strains and ill-health. The strive for more of a balance between work and life mainly affects professionals and managerial workers who are increasingly pressured to work faster and longer hours (Baptiste, 2009; George, 2009).

In contrast, managerial employees would like to experience less pressure in their jobs and respective departments. They would also like to have more remuneration in terms of holiday, leave allowance, pay, and more flexibility in managing people to balance work and their lives. Non-managerial employees would like to feel valued and appreciated by the Council and would like the Council to address employees Safety at work. From a group perspective, both employee groups wanted to be respected by their employer for their contribution to the Council and the communities they serve. In contrast, managerial employees claim that they would like improvements in team morale, and HR support when it comes to disciplinary and terminations. Managers are pressured to deliver more services to stakeholders with less resources and would like the Council to alleviate or improve the pressure that managers are faced with daily which fundamentally are as a result of budget restrictions so managers are having to jump through many hoops to meet target expectations and service outcomes. In contrast, from a group perspective, non-managerial employees would like more feedback and communication from their line managers regarding their work contributing to communities. Meechan (2018) argues that given that employee well-being is now high on senior leaders' and management agenda it is now time to better understand the importance of developing the social and interpersonal skills of empathy and compassion a to enhance their own and others well-being for the good of the organisation.

From an organisational perspective, both groups perspective reveal improvements in humanistic and fair practices, and work/organisation practices. The findings reveal differences in perspectives between managerial and non-managerial employees. From fair practices perspective, managers would like to see improvements in the evaluation of HR systems for greater effectiveness. They would also appreciate the reduction in budget restrictions and less pressure, which in turn will have implication on sickness absence management. They would like to see improvements in organisational development, performance management and a less political environment, which all have implications for a NPM ideology and employee well-being at work. The importance of fair treatment and a 'people-focused' approach to social interactions within organisations will improve experiences of a series of injustices, hurt feelings, frustrations and feelings of inferiority preoccupying the minds and thinking of employees (Robertson et al., 2008). Dehumanised and unfair practice is that of bullying and other mistreatment in the workplace that has negative implications for mental ill-health, workplace absence, stress levels and well-being at work.

In contrast, non-managerial employees would like to see improvements in fairness and dignity at work. The working conditions of the offices were regarded as poor, with inadequate office lighting, poor workplace ergonomics and dilapidated physical work environment. These employees pointed out that improvements in these areas will improve their well-being at work in the local government organisation (i.e. the Council).

In conclusion, the fulfilment of employee well-being can be challenging for this case local government organisation and other public sector organisations alike given the complexity, politicised, and efficiency savings 'doing more with less' oriented work environment that these employees function in. Small steps taken in the process can reap great rewards in terms of enhancement of employees' experiences of working life and well-being at work that can positively influence performance and service delivery. It will take a further step, given the complexities and daily challenges faced by local government employees before the well-being ideology can be successfully promoted and implemented. The mantra of 'working hard', is evident for local government managers and employees, as for so many contemporary professionals, however the Utopian state of 'well-being at work' is likely to remain a subjective phenomenon in the pursuit of happiness for the foreseeable future.

Notes

1 Questions related to meanings of well-being are: What do you understand by the term employee well-being at work? If you have to use words to define your individual well-being at work what would they be? Why is well-being at work as defined by yourself important to you? And what things would you like to see improved in the council to promote your well-being?
2 Questions related to meanings for line manager's leadership and well-being are: How responsive is your line manager to the promotion of your well-being at work? And what can your line manager do differently to promote your well-being at work?

Reference

Albrecht, S., and Travaglione, A. (2003) 'Trust in Public-Sector Senior Management', *International Journal of Human Resource Management*, Vol. 14(1): 76–92.

Bakke, D.W. (2005) *Joy at Work: A Revolutionary Approach to Fun on the Job*, Seattle: Penguin Group.

Baptiste, N.R. (2008) 'Tightening the Link between Employee Wellbeing at Work and Performance: A New Dimension for HRM', *Management Decisions*, Vol. 46(2): 284–309.

Baptiste, N.R. (2009) 'Fun and Wellbeing: Insights from Senior Managers in a Local Authority', *Employee Relations*, Vol. 31 (6): 600–612.

Baptiste, N.R. (2010) 'Beneath the Melting Ice: The Relationship between Employee Well-Being, HRM Practices and Social Exchange in Local Government', *Doctoral Thesis at Roehampton University*, London.

Bolton, S., and Houlihan, M. (2007) 'Beginning the Search for the H in HRM', in S. Bolton and M. Houlihan (Ed.) *Searching for the H in Human Resource Management: Theory, Practice and Workplace Context*, Basingstoke: Palgrave Macmillan.

CIPD (2019) *Health and Well-Being at Work*, Survey Report, April 2019, in Partnership with Simplyhealth, London: Chartered Institute of Personnel and Development.

Cooper, C., and Robertson, I. (2001) *Well-Being in Organisations: A Reader for Students and Practitioners*, Chichester: John Wiley and Sons Limited.

Currie, D. (2001) *Managing Employee Well-Being*, Oxford: Chandos Publishing Oxford Limited.

Diener, E., Oishi, S., and Lucas, R.E. (2003) 'Personality, Culture, and Subjective Wellbeing: Emotional and Cognitive Evaluations of Life', *Annual Review Psychology*, Vol. 54: 403–425.

George, C. (2009) *The Psychological Contract: Managing and Developing Professional Groups*, Work and Organisational Psychology, Berkshire: Open University Press.

Grant, A., Christianson, M., and Price, R. (2007) 'Happiness, Health or Relationships? Managerial Practices and Employee Well-Being Tradeoffs', *The Academy of Management*, Vol. 21(3): 51–63.

Green, F., and Whitfield, K. (2009) 'Employees Experiences at Work', in W. Brown, A. Bryson, J. Forth and K. Whitfield (Eds.) *The Evolution of the Modern Workplace*, Cambridge: Cambridge University Press.

Guest, D. (2002) 'Human Resource Management, Corporate Performance and Employee Wellbeing: Building the Worker into HRM', *Journal of Industrial Relations*, Vol. 44(3): 335–358.

Harrow, J. (2002) 'New Public Management and Social Justice: Just Efficiency or Equity as Well?', in K. McLaughlin, S.P. Osborne, and E. Ferlie (Eds.) *New Public Management: Current Trends and Future Prospects*, pp. 141–159, London: Routledge, Taylor and Francis Group.

Haworth, J., and Hart, G. (2007) *Wellbeing: Individual, Community and Social Perspectives*, Basingstoke: Palgrave MacMillan.

Jackall, R. (1988) *Moral Mazes: The World of Corporate Managers*, New York: Oxford University Press.

Kersley, B., Alphin, C., Forth, J., Bryson, A., Bewley, H., Dix, G., and Oxenbridge, S. (2006) *Inside the Workplace: Findings from the 2004 Workplace Employment Relations Survey*, London: Routledge.

Livesey, D., Machin, A., Millard, B., and Walling, A. (2006) 'Public Sector Employment 2006: Seasonally Adjusted Series and Recent Trends', Office for National Statistics, Labour Market Trends, December.

Lyons, M. (2007) *Lyons Inquiry into Local Government, Place-Shaping: A Shared Ambition for the Future of Local Government*, London: The Stationery Office.

MacDonald, L.A.C. (2005) *Wellness at Work: Protecting and Promoting Employee Well-Being*, London: Chartered Institute of Personnel and Development.

Mathieu, J.E., and Zajac, D.M. (1990) 'A Review and Meta-Analysis of the Antecedents, Correlates and Consequences of Organisational Commitment', *Psychological Bulletin*, Vol. 108, pp. 171–194.

Meechan, F. (2018) *Compassion at Work Toolkit*, https://researchgate.net/publication/322404395 (accessed May 30th, 2019).

Meyer, J., and Allen, N. (1997) *Commitment in the Workplace*, London: Sage.

Miles, M.B., and Huberman, A.M. (1994) *Qualitative Data Analysis: An Expanded Source Book*, London: Sage Publications.

Mullins, L.J. (1993) *Management and Organisational Behaviour*, London: Pitman Publishers.

Peccei, R. (2004) *Human Resources Management and the Search for the Happy Workplace*, Erasmus Research Institute of Management, Rotterdam School of Management. Erasmus University, Rotterdam.

Renwick, D. (2003) 'HR Managers, Guardians of Employee Wellbeing?', *Personnel Review*, Vol. 32(3): 341–359.

Rhoades, L., and Eisenberger, R. (2002) 'Perceived Organisational Support: A Review of the Literature', *Journal of Applied Psychology*, Vol. 87(4): 698–714.

Robertson, I.T., Tinline, G., and Robertson, S. (2008) 'Enhancing Staff Well-Being for Organisational Effectiveness', in R.J. Burke and C.L. Cooper (Eds.) *Building More Effective Organisations: HR Management and Performance Practice*, Cambridge: Cambridge University Press.

Rousseau, D.M. (1995) *Psychological Contracts in Organisations: Understanding Written and Unwritten Agreements*, Thousand Oaks and London: Sage Publications.

Ryan, R.M., and Deci, E.L. (2001) 'On Happiness and Human Potentials: A Review of Research on Hedonic and Eudaimonic Wellbeing', *Annual Review of Psychology*, Vol. 51: 141–166.

Ryff, C. D. (1995). 'Psychological Well-Being in Adult Life', *Current Directions in Psychological Science*, Vol. 4: 99–104.

Silverman, D. (2005) *Doing Qualitative Research: A Practical Handbook*, 2nd Edition, London: Sage Publications.

Simonet, D. (2013) 'The New Public Management Theory in the British Health Care System: A Critical Review', *Administration & Society*, Vol. 47(7): 1–25.

Tehrani, N., Humpage, S., Willmott, B., and Haslam, I. (2007) *What's Happening with Well-Being at Work?*, Change Agenda, London: Chartered Institute of Personnel Development.

Terkel, S. (1977) *Working*, Harmondsworth: Penguin Publishers.

Van Maanen, M. (1994) *Researching Lived Experience: Human Science for an Action Sensitive Pedagogy*, Michigan: Althouse.

Van Wanrooy, B., Bewley, H., Bryson, A., Forth, J., Freeth, S., Stokes, L., and Wood, S. (2011) *The 2011 Workplace Employment Relations Study: First Findings*, The Workplace Employment Relations Study (2011 WERS).

Warr, P. (2002) *Psychology At Work*, Suffolk: Penguin Group Books.

Weick, K.E. (1992) 'Agenda Setting in Organisational Behaviour', *Journal of Management Inquiry*, Vol. 1(3): 171–182.

Williams, M. (2002) 'Generalisation in Interpretative Research', in T. May (Ed.) *Qualitative Research in Action*, London: Sage Publications.

Wilson, F. (2010) *Organisational Behaviour and Work: A Critical Introduction*, Oxford: Oxford University Press.

12 Employees' perspectives on the working life realities, line management leadership and well-being in the public sector

Introduction

The book was introduced as an attempt to understand the meaning of what lies 'beneath the melting ice' of employees' reaction to HRM practices, working life realities, line management leadership and well-being at work in local government in the North West of England. This chapter discusses the findings as they relate to the aims of the main research discussed throughout this book. This chapter discusses the intricacies of the salient themes in this chapter, which includes respondents' evaluation of their working life realities as public sector employees in a local government organisation in North West of England. The chapter also explores the meanings public sector employees give to their jobs and its implication for employees' identity-work-life integration; the lack of trust is shown as an integral thread that runs through the fabric of the New Public Management (NPM) work environment and social interactions between line managers and employees. The exploration of employees' reactions and voice as it relates to their line manager responsiveness to promote well-being at work, as well as employees' perspectives regarding improvements in line management leadership to promote their well-being in the NPM work environment. The chapter concludes with an integrated model of the relationship between HRM practices, the quality working life, leadership and well-being in the public sector as perceived by employees. The chapter concludes with a summary and conclusion of the key issues discussed.

Working life realities and well-being

The first aim of the main study in this book is to explore whether employee well-being ideology can be successfully promoted and maintained in a NPM environment given continuous proposals for reformation and expenditure reduction. This aim is associated with the first two research objectives (see Chapter 1). This research critically examined organisational policies and practices that relate to high commitment HRM practices, working life and well-being at work in a NPM context.

Furthermore, an exploration of how a NPM context impacts on employees' experiences of HRM practices, working life, line management leaders, and well-being at work was completed. Methodologically, the main research adopted the hermeneutic phenomenological analysis approach, which facilitated employees' consciousness, meanings and how they understood and made sense of their working world, the processes, conditions, interactions, structures and experiences. This approach helped to uncover key principles that formed part of employees working life realities, and through this, reveals the implications for employee well-being at work. This was reflected in managerial and non-managerial employees' mixed responses relating to experiences of HRM practices, working life realties, line management leadership, and consequently well-being at the Council. Salient points emerged from the research and include; restricted resources, workplace stress, job insecurity, bureaucracy and control, constant change and instability, bullying and psychological violence, a lack of trust, excessive emails adding to the pressurised work environment, job dissatisfaction and poor public sector ethos, dilapidated office environment, and work-life balance. These factors framed the working life realities of both managerial and non-managerial employees work-life. These factors clearly outline that both employee groups were not having fun at work and their well-being at work was far from being met as they had to face multiple challenges working within a NPM environment as well as jump through many bureaucratic hoops to meet service delivery targets with already limited and stretched resources (Morphet, 2008).

Although wellness management initiatives were adopted and implemented in the local government organisation like the private sector, these public sector employees were so pressurised with heavy workloads, long working hours, meeting targets, faced with constant changes (Clarke et al., 2000), the respondents lacked the crucial elements of 'time' and 'motivation' to appreciate and participate in the wellness management programmes provided. Furthermore, for these two groups of employees, for their working life realities to improve and their well-being at work to be promoted required focusing of the government funding mandates and policies, organisational structure and culture, the strategic approach to change management, the psychological contract that frames the relationship between line managers and their staff within the employment relationship, a focus on improving the aesthetics and safety of the work environment, and be open to introduce a broad range of flexible working arrangements to cater for both employee groups' work-life balance. Clarke (2001) argues that both men and women have significant responsibilities both at work and with the families, now with the growing number of single parents, working women, dual-career couples, and fathers heavily involved in parenting (Fullerton, 1995). For these individuals and for other interested in both work and family, balance between these two spheres has become a major life issue (Clarke, 2001; Kemske,

1988). In response for this need to balance work and life employers have implemented a number of pragmatic changes to working. For the local government case organisation (i.e. the Council), mentioned in the main research, this organisation implemented what they referred to as the 'New Ways of Working' that involved flexible working arrangements of working from home, working from different physical locations, flexi-time, job-sharing, hot-desking for managerial employees, and other types of flexible arrangements to support employees and assist them to manage work-related stress. Flexible working arrangements also assisted the organisation with the budget limitations by offsetting the financial burden of having to find office space to accommodate all employees. By introducing the need to balance work and life, through flexible working arrangements, the Council showed their corporate social responsibility as a supportive employer. Freeney and Stritch (2017) point out that modern public sector workplace, informal family-friendly culture and formal family-friendly policies are considered important components of creating a healthy work environment. Daniels and French (2006) view that workers are experiencing life changes and aspirations and family time are coming under pressure intensifying work-family conflict resulting in psychological strains and ill-health (Cartwright and Cooper, 2009).

In contrast, with such a broad range of flexible working arrangements, line managers show resilience in response to now being faced with another challenge of having to supervise and manage dispersed teams to ensure that service delivery and targets are met in keeping with set objectives, limited resources and radical (UK) public sector reform, which Hesketh et al. (2014) state has implications for and results in changes with the employees' relationship with their organisation. Furthermore, with the adoption of the flexible working arrangements, line managers will also have to work beyond their fear of making mistakes to ensure that they effectively manage the relationships with their employees so that they perform and trust the process, are mentally healthy, are enthusiastic, motivated, committed, and experience positive well-being to prevent sickness absence, presenteeism or leaveism of employees. Cooper et al. (2005) argue that the cost of employee absence and employees being anything than fully productive can have an enormous impact on operational effectiveness as there is a proven link between well-being and increased performance. Hesketh et al. (2014) posit that 'Leaveism' emphasises that sickness amongst employees can be a hidden phenomenon, and that effective workplace well-being strategies can contribute to successful work-life integration that reduce these practices. Hesketh et al. (2014) further argue that the practice of Leaveism may cease or reduce as employees reach their personal resilience limits and may impact significantly on sickness absence levels. Looking at employee absence from the workplace and workload overload, Hesketh and Cooper (2014) introduced the concept of 'Leaveism', which is the practice of employees utilising allocated time off such as annual leave entitlements, flexi hours banked, re-rostered rest days, etc., to take time off when they are in fact unwell. Leaveism also entails employees 'taking work home' that cannot be completed in normal working hours; and employees working whilst on leave or holiday to catch up.

The practices and attitudes of leaveism and presenteeism as a result of heavy workloads and sickness absence have negative implications for work-life integration and employee well-being, with particular reference to public sector managers who the research shows work long working hours and do not have the leisure time in respect to ongoing responsibilities to decide the balance between work and life as it is perceived that there work is ongoing, so they expend their effort trying to separate, aspiring for balance. Robertson and Cooper (2011) state that the notion of having a sense of purpose and meaning is important to leading a successful working life and work ought to be interesting, challenging and suite to an individual's personality (Diener and Biswas-Diener, 2008). Moreover, Hesketh et al. (2014) argue that the challenge is to know where to draw the line, and on whose terms? It is important to question, whether these beleaguered public sector managers and employees can 'draw the line' or distinguish between the pressure of the workplace (i.e. attending diverse daily meetings, answering emails at night, increasing demands on service delivery, reading reports outside of the workplace etc.) and finding that much needed balance to facilitate their work-life integration. Once can question whether the UK North West local government organisation expect managerial and non-managerial employees to be 'present for work', at work and at home? Hesketh et al. (2014) states that organisations need to pay attention to the weakening personal resilience of employees who may abandon the practice of 'Leaveism', with potentially far reaching consequences, with reference to sickness absenteeism that would rise sharply, work would radically be slowed or stopped as a consequence of changes in employee behaviour and a break in the psychological contract (Rousseau, 2003). The quantitative part of the main research outlined in this book is the leanest part of the methodological approach adopted in the study. The findings from the questionnaire reveals that there is a significant difference between managerial and non-managerial employees' working life experiences, HRM practices, the psychological contract and social exchange constructs and their views about their well-being at work.

Identity-work-life integration

Managerial and non-managerial employees' perspectives that relate to the meaning they give to their job highlighted eight key salient points, which includes that the job is; professionally stimulating and engaging, conveys financial stability, community contribution, a sense of purpose that promotes confidence and self-esteem, fulfilment and gratitude, career advancement, relationships, and the job is in close proximity to the home. Both employee groups responses were associated with the individual, and group perspectives. From an individual perspective, the meaning of the job touched on the psychological, physical, intellectual, career, spiritual and financial well-being domains. From the group perspective, the meaning of the job focused on relationships with their line manager as well as their job making a contribution towards the community. For these public sector employees, their job provided a sense of purpose and identity that allowed them to feel valued and appreciated and provided satisfaction that their contribution and efforts mattered for the greater good of the communities they served. Wilson (2010) states that work is perceived and can have different meaning for individuals and the prime reasons that individuals give for working is to earn money, to use their skills, to feel a sense of worth and for a sense of dignity (Bolton and Houlihan, 2007; Terkel, 1977).

Both groups also identified that their job provided the opportunity for career advancement and achievement. Furthermore, managers attributed the meaning of their job to job design practices as they appreciated that they were professionally stimulated and engaged in their jobs. Both groups agreed that their job provided them with financial well-being and life satisfaction as the job provided an avenue where they can pay their mortgage, rent and enjoy life satisfaction. Percy (2018) points out that in 2017, research by the UK's Money and Mental Health Policy Institute found that over two-thirds of employees are struggling financially, which is one sign of poor mental health that could affect their ability to function at work. These signs include loss of sleep, poor concentration and reduced motivation. Therefore, financial well-being is clearly an issue that leaders and managers need to take seriously.

In contrast, non-managerial employees highlighted spiritual and social well-being domains to describe the meaning of their job and attributed it to relationships with line manager, and gratitude and fulfilment. Non-managerial employees meaning is associated with their perception of the psychological contract, justice and fairness perception and their experiences with leader-member exchange relations with their line manager. Therefore, having good relationships at work is integral to non-managerial employees' views of their job. The CIPD (2014) research reveal that line managers sit at the heart of the relationship between the employer and the employee and if this relationship is challenged it can lead to serious problems within the employment relationship. The CIPD further states that managing the employment relationship rests heavily on the shoulders of line managers, but their competence in this area is, in general, seriously neglected. As such, organisations need to focus on building line management capability, which is a common factor within organisations.

Trust makes lives better

The findings from the review of company HRM policy documents from the main research throughout this book that explored employees' reactions to HRM practices, quality and working life and well-being at work, were different to that which was espoused. The findings reveal that the local government organisation advocated working in partnership to facilitate efficient inter-departmental working, collaboration with the delivery of services, and cost minimisation were not in alignment with the employees' reactions to company policy and practices, their working life realities and well-being at work. Although these practices were professed to be adopted, employees' reactions to these practices were different to that which was alleged. For example, the local government organisation (i.e. the Council) professed that team working was promoted throughout the Council. In reality, according to both employee groups, there exists tensions between teams and different departments, creating an atmosphere of mistrust with managers in particular fighting to protect their already stretched resources in keeping with their political and work agendas. The lack of team working also fostered a 'Them and Us' and 'Blame' culture, silos working, ineffective partnerships across the Council, which all had implications for employee well-being as well as service delivery and stakeholders' satisfaction and well-being.

Both employee groups also highlighted the existence of status differentials and a lack of harmonisation between line managers and employees as well as senior leaders and line managers. The presence of status differentials nurtured a lack of trust and anti-harmonisation environment throughout the Council between social actors that in turn negatively affected relationship building, partnership working, service delivery and employee well-being. The notion of an anti-trust environment was captured from the findings from the questionnaire and interviews. The findings from the questionnaire disclosed that managerial and non-managerial as well as male and female employees disagreed that they trusted management to look after their best interests. Males were less trusting than females as their responses were statistically significantly different from their female counterparts. The interviews reveal that both employee groups held the view that trust was not promoted in the Council. Managerial employees pointed out that the 'lack of trust' also extended to outside the organisation with Council officers have to frequently 'fight off attacks' from external stakeholders like Councillors, Members of Parliament (MPs) and Customers. From an internal perspective, the 'lack of trust' was as a result of senior leaders' reluctance to take risks and trust individuals in decision making that could affect change. Managerial employees also held the view that there was a 'lack of trust' from senior leaders to line managers and employees as senior leaders were fearful of losing control of particular budgets, organisational structures and processes, and the formal and informal culture (*i.e. the way things are done here*). In contrast, non-managerial employees held the view that they lacked confidence and trust in their line manager as they were not given autonomy, independence, and shown confidence and trust from their line manager that they had the ability to do their jobs. These non-managerial employees felt controlled and inadequate which had implications for negative well-being and performance. They perceived that this lack of trust from their line manager about their ability to perform effectively contributes to the existence of a 'controlled' working environment – which the researcher observed as a prominent point in this working environment.

Respondents also related the lack of trust to bureaucracy. Managerial and non-managerial employees described the work environment as being saturated with bureaucracy and 'red-tape'. They regarded that this resulted in individuals having to 'jump through many hoops' before decisions were made – this was also observed and experienced by the researcher. They also perceived that bureaucracy contributed to employees not being able to use their initiative or work independently, which stifles creativity and innovation throughout the organisation. Morphet (2008) and Cooper and Robertson (2001) state that to promote employee performance it is important to create a sense of trust, which forms the basis of all professional and personal relationships and interactions. Organisation, particularly the public sector that are able to create and promote trust in the workplace is better able to weather the storms of budget restrictions and cost minimisation to promote harmonisation, improved morale, team working, build relationships, increased productivity, and a clear vision throughout the organisation (Baptiste, 2007).

The lack of trust was also implied by the high neutral responses from the questionnaire. Non-managerial employees had higher neutral responses than managerial employees. Managerial employees' neutral responses were in relation to the existence of employee voice, management responding to suggestions from employees and dealing with problems in the workplace. Non-managerial employees' neutral responses related to the existence of internal recruitment, involvement in decision making, the existence of team working, trust, motivation, work-life balance, autonomy and work demands. Trust is central to team working, support and fairness perceptions found in the psychological contract. This is a key principle of the psychological contract, perceived organisational support and organisational justice. Trust relates to respondents' cognitive expectations of the psychological contract and underpins relational and transactional obligations. It also forms employees' perceptions of support and fairness at work. Sharkie's (2009) research found that there was strong evidence that the vulnerability of employees in the employment relationship had increased the importance of trust in encouraging employee extra-role behaviour outside their contractual obligations.

Grant et al. (2007) and Guest (2007) posit that trust is built through actions and words of social agents within the employment relationship. Managers need to demonstrate that they trust employees or team not merely by saying the word 'trust' but by supportive and justice actions through empowering staff to be accountable and responsible for their daily work (Grant and Shields, 2002). Manager should also involve staff in decision making that affects them and will benefit the organisation, avoid nepotism, show appreciation and acknowledgement for a good job done, show respect, equality and workplace dignity to all employees.

Line management leadership and well-being

This section reveals both employees group voices and perspectives about their line manger as it relates to the responsiveness of their line manager to promote their well-being at work, and improvement that the line manager can implement to promote their well-being at work. This section presents empirical research from 27 semi-structured interviews that formed part of the major research outlined in this book. The respondent's perspective as it relates to the responsiveness of their line manager to promote their well-being clustered into three prominent points and include, supportive with work responsibilities, trust employees' capabilities, and knowledge transfer are the key themes that respondents highlighted that their line manager displays that they claim promotes their well-being at work and subsequently mental health and performance.

Responsiveness of line manager to promote well-being at work

Supportive with work responsibilities

Non-managerial employees held the view that their line manager was supportive of them and trusted their capability to do a good job. Other themes highlighted include, receipt of positive feedback, appreciation, respectful, attentive and considerate. One employee shares her experience. She said,

> My manager is exceptionally supportive and knows my capabilities . . . he challenges me, and trusts me and knows that I can go ahead and do things, he promotes my confidence by providing me with feedback . . . . he always asks me 'how has your day been?' 'have a good evening, have a good weekend?'
>
> (Employee, Female, Age 20–29 years, Tenure less than 5 years)

Similarly, managerial employees held the view that their line managers were supportive to them and the team in terms of assistance with reprioritisation and heavy workloads. One manager comments:

My manager is very supportive. I have no complaints at all. I've have just changed managers and my existing manager is in the room as well with my former manager and both of them are very good. They realise when I am a bit snowed under . . . it's the same way I support my teams, I will say 'well let's have a look a things'. I think sometimes it's just having somebody else help you take that step back and reprioritise perhaps.

(Manager, Male, Age 40–49 years, Tenure 6–11 years)

Employees echoes the view that their managers are supportive to them by giving direction to the work. One employee shares:

My manager directs the work that we're going to this is how he supports me in terms of he very much decides the work programme which we're going to follow, so that's probably how he supports me.

(Employee, Female, Age 20–25 years, Tenure less than 5 years)

Trust employee capabilities

Managerial employees highlighted that their line manager is responsive in promoting their well-being by trusting their capabilities to do a good job. Providing feedback, praise and recognition, and admiration were also mentioned. One manager comments echo this theme. He said:

I get interesting projects to do. He is pleased usually with what I do. I get fairly immediate feedback. He provides me with praise and give recognition for work done. I've worked with him for a while and trust and admire him.

(Manager, Male, Age 40–49 years, Tenure 6–11 years)

Knowledge transfer

Some managers reveal that sharing knowledge with their line manager in an exchange of information, learning from each other, brainstorm exercises, or to resolve workplace challenges promotes their well-being and empowers them to learn and develop in skill areas that that requires development. One manager shares her perspective regarding this theme. She states:

He is very different, he is more low key, very driven and very task oriented. There is that want of support. He comes to me sometimes on some of the people management stuff. . . . He is very strategic, very bright, but sometimes the relationship stuff he comes to me for help on this. So there is a recognition there that I have a lot to learn from him, I'm quite looking forward to working with him more because he is so

much of a strategist and a political animal, and those are less skills of mine. He says to me 'well, there's quite a lot I can gain back from you'.
(Manager, Female, Age 40–49 years, Tenure 6–11 years)

The preceding findings reveal similarities and differences in employees' perspective regarding their view about how responsive their line manager is to the promotion of their well-being at work. Both employee group agreed that their line manager promotes their well-being by being supportive with respect to work responsibilities. In contrast, managerial employees touched on their line manager trusting their capabilities and ability to do a good job as well as knowledge sharing with their line manager. Managerial respondents all agreed that these two themes demonstrate to them that their line manager cares about them and this leader-member-exchange fosters the promotion of their well-being at work.

Line management improvement to promote employee well-being

Empowerment and autonomy

Some employees' perspectives reveal that they would like their line manager to provide them with autonomy regarding their job to foster creativity and performance. Yet other employees highlighted the need to be empowered towards professional development and advancement, which these employees claim will enhance their well-being at work. One employee's comments echo these points. She shares;

> I would like my manager to be more responsive to me. He knows my personality as he has worked with me for eighteen months and I had two performance reviews where I made it perfectly clear that I would like more responsibility, I want to develop, I'd like to be left alone to get on with some more work, be more˙creative about things . . . so he knows all of this but he still doesn't take it on-board and that's extremely frustrating and I don't know what more I can do to spell it out about what I would like from him. I just don't think he's interested, I don't think he cares.
> (Employee, Female, Age 30–39 years, Tenure less than 5 years)

Another employee's perspective about the lack autonomy touched on being able to use own initiative and trusted to do a good job are echoed by the comments of this employee. She explained,

> Employees are not allowed to think and use their own initiatives and there is no autonomy . . . employees should feel motivated at work and be able to use their own initiatives and trusted to do a good job.
> (Employee, Female, Age 20–25 years, less than 5 years)

Other employees' comments reveal the lack of autonomy and poor relationship as central to the employment relationship, the psychological contract and their well-being at work. One employees share her experience:

> I much prefer if my line manager allows me to be able to determine some of the work within the work programme . . . because of this my relationship with him is dreadful. . . . It's absolutely dreadful at the moment although I don't know whether he realises it's as dreadful. I try to be professional about how annoying I find him. I am sure he does realise that he's not my favourite person in the entire world but we are not to the stage where we're rude to each other and ignoring each other because that will be deeply unpleasant when you are sharing a room.
>
> (Employee, Female, Age 40–49 years, Tenure 6–10 years)

People-focused approach to leadership

Managers held the view that their line manager required to have a more people-focused approach to their leadership style to promote their well-being at work. Additional themes mentioned includes team management, trusting staff competencies, support to do your job and more delegation. One manager comments highlighted these points. He said;

> More people oriented and he can develop more specific skills around team management, facilitation of teams, and team building, those sort of things. Complimentary skills like believing in you, and believing in your skills and supporting you to do your job. He does not scrutinise, there's not that requirement, there is a nice balance . . . he sometimes need to delegate a bit better.
>
> (Manager, Male, Age 40–49 years, Tenure 6–10 years)

Empathetic and compassionate

Some employees highlighted that their line manager was indifferent and apathetic, lacking interests in their satisfaction, motivation and well-being. Employees held the view that they would like their line manager to have more empathetic and compassionate skills which are in alignment to a more people-focused approach to people management. These respondents perceive that if their line managers possess these people-focused skills, it will promote their well-being at work, mental health and performance. One employee highlights these themes. She said:

> My manager has to be replaced or I get another role within the organisation. I think I am just going to have to look at moving jobs as nothing seems to be working in terms of getting her to change. I

have been giving her some indicators in her 360 feedback and with some gentle conversations with her but it does not matter . . . so I think, I will have to look for another job.

(Employee, Female, Age 20–25 years, Tenure less than 5 years)

Dignity and civility at work

Managerial respondents shared their experiences of there being a 'blame culture' that exists within the organisation that leaves managerial employees fearful of experiencing the growing pattern of psychological violence behaviours such as threats, being shouted at, intimidation and other incivility and mistreatment. Managerial employees reveal that improvements in dignity and civility in the workplace through their line managers will improve their mental health, well-being and performance. One manager shares his experience that highlight these themes. He said:

I almost feel that there are managers out there that are ready looking for something to pounce on, on some individuals when something has gone wrong . . . there is this fear of getting blamed when things go wrong when you are dragged in and practically shouted at . . . you can feel quite threatened and almost bothered and intimidated and it gets to a point, that you almost become immune to it.

(Manager, Male, Age 40–49 years, Tenure 6–10 years)

Another account of incivility at work, a lack of dignity at work, and psychological violence was revealed by a manager's account of her experiences with her line manager who used power, victimisation, and threats to control her. The manager likened her experiences to feelings of powerlessness, bullying and unfairness. She said:

After my manager was told by HR that he was wrong he apologised afterwards but I did not think it was a sincere apology . . . you read the dignity at work act and you think this is not acceptable to the council standards. . . . It doesn't feed through and if I put in a grievance against my boss, I still have to work with him on the daily basis, he can make my life hell and he let me know he would make my life hell if I took it further . . . it made me feel powerless and I thought that I have to get out of this job.

(Manager, Female, Age 40–49 years, Tenure 21–25 years)

Another manager relates her experiences of a lack of dignity at work to her experiences of the 'back to work' interview with her line manager which she describes as unsupportive, confrontational and also noted the lack of following things through and mistrust of her line manager. This manager shares her experience. She states,

> I was off sick for three and a half weeks as I dislocated my shoulder . . . I have never been off sick before and when I came back to work I was given one of these back to work interviews which made me feel that I made up being ill. . . . I didn't feel supported, it felt like I was being quizzed, it certainly did not feel like 'how can we make things comfortable for you or what could be done for you?' . . . there was a tiny bit of that and there was some reference to physiotherapy but after that meeting I never heard another word, my manager told me that I was referred for physiotherapy and just like everything else it was never done, never ever done . . . and it made me feel cynical.
>
> (Manager, Female, Age 50–59 years, Tenure less than 5 years)

Another manager's experience of incivility at work and psychological violence was associated with his knowledge of the existence of poor relationships with his line manager and his manager. Managerial respondents held the view that respecting people at work, anti-bullying and violence, and fostering dignity and civility will promote their well-being at work. One manager explains;

> My boss who had this awful relationship with his line manager and it affected him all day every day, he was taking it home with him and I'm sure it must have been awful.
>
> (Manager, Male, Age 40–49 years, Tenure less than 5 years)

Impartiality and fairness at work

Some managerial respondents held the view that there was a lack of gender equality as it relates to the access to flexible working arrangements as it relates to home working. Some male managers felt that they experience unfair treatment when they applied to work from home based on their gender. This practice was perceived as bullying and unfair. Managers reveal that line managers being impartial and fair as it relates to work-life balance practices will improve their stress, mental health, well-being, and performance. One employee shares his experience. He commented,

> My manager had the biggest resistance to a lot of these changes . . . he did not feel they were appropriate for everybody and it was seen as a perception that people weren't working. . . . There was this fear that people working at home wouldn't be working . . . they're other mangers in the section which were totally against the principles. . . . My manager eventually embraced it but it wasn't an altruistic act as he wanted to do home working as his circumstances changed where

he became a career and he could see the benefits for himself. . . . I had a big gripe about the sexist thing and I think that sexism should apply both ways . . . I have had comments from management saying 'well, looking after kids, can't your wife do that?' . . . 'this is not fair on us as an employer because your wife should be staying at home and looking after kids' . . . I went to HR and made an issue and things were resolved eventually.

(Manager, Male, Age 40–49 years, Tenure less than 5 years)

Another manager's account of unfair treatment was highlighted as she described her experience after taking out a grievance against her line manager. She likened the experience of not receiving an apology from her line manager and the strained relationship that now exists between herself and her line manager. This manager reveals that better relationship and fairness at work from her line manager would promote her well-being. She said,

I took out a grievance against my manager as I thought that I was unfairly treated because I brought various issues up at a supervision meeting and I think I was then treated unfairly and I put in a formal complaint about it . . . my managers manager addressed the complaint and the judgement came that I won the grievance and was sent a formal letter giving the verdict stating that 'she has now apologised' except that she never apologised to me, she apologised to her manager but it was I who was aggrieved . . . I never received an apology . . . she was asked to develop an action plan to address some issues and it must be 6 months since the verdict and nothing has been done . . . . I think I made my point but it has brought up all wariness in the relationship.

(Manager, Female, Age 40–49 years, Tenure 6–10 years)

Another manager related unfair treatment to being denied access to training courses and career development opportunities by his line manager. Managerial respondents reveal that fair treatment and access to opportunities by their line manager would enhance and promote their well-being at work. One manager shares:

To be unfairly denied courses that would have been perfectly suitable, despite the fact that all this talk about what sort of training and career development needs and so on they all get documented, but nothing happens about them anyway. . . . I was asking to do this course and I was blocked and I do feel there is a blocking and I feel there is a way in which, there is a lot of fear about staff and junior managers becoming more competent than the senior managers.

(Manager, Male, Age 40–49 years, Tenure less than 5 years)

In contrast, non-managerial employees related unfair treatment to rewards and pay scales compared to their counterparts in other Councils. Employees would like their line managers to improve their well-being at work through pay and reward increases. One employee stated:

> The pay scales are lower in the Council as compared to other authorities it is as if there is a glass ceiling on pay scales. . . . I am not happy about my pay.
>
> (Employee, Female, Age 40–49 years, Tenure less than 5 years)

Other employees related unfair treatment to the lack of equal opportunities and access to flexible working arrangements for all employees regardless of their work/family circumstances. Employees would like their line manager to be impartial, compassionate, and people-focused in decisions that relates to flexible working arrangements. One employee commented:

> Flexible working is definitely skewed to people with families and those that are single or divorced like myself you don't feel like the opportunities are quite the same.
>
> (Employee, Male, Age 50–59 years, Tenure less than 5 years)

The preceding discussion regarding impartiality and fairness at work were revealed by both managerial and non-managerial employees as a key factor that they declared that they would like their line manager to improve, which would consequently enhance their mental health, workplace stress, well-being and performance. The findings reveal that these two groups of employees have experiences of disrespectful social interactions with their line managers that hindered their dignity at work and perception of fair treatment. Fairness is underpinned in organisational justice literature that relates to the quality of social interaction at work and focuses on perceptions of fairness in organisations that can affect individuals' psychological, physical and social welfare (Cropanzano, 1993; Greenberg, 1987). This section explains the views and feelings of respondents about their own treatment and that of others within the local government environment reviewing the extent to which respondents were treated fairly. The review of company documents discloses that the Council views employees as valuable assets and professed that policies have been implemented (i.e. dignity at work) to ensure the promotion of a fair and conducive environment to promote employees' mental and physical health. In contrast, the working life realities of both employee groups were the opposite to what was espoused by the Council leadership and written in policy documents. The research shows that these public sector employees were exposed to a pattern of incivility at work; psychological violence such as threats, blaming, and intimidation; deliberating withholding access to training and career development; the lack of equal opportunities; unfair pay and rewards practices; poor relationships between employees and their line manager; victimisation; and bullying and harassment. Fineman (2007) argues that psychological violence begets violent emotions such as rage, anger, revenge and betrayal and inevitably trades on fear, and is intimately connected with the subjective meaning of the event to the victim. Fineman (2007) further points out that organisational violence is embedded in the values of the organisation and is translated into practices that systematically cause danger, risk or exploitation to employees.

From a government perspective, 'Fairness at Work' legislation was promoted by the New Labour government's 1998 White Paper that focused on unfair dismissal, the rights of the trade union, grievance and disciplinary, and extending family friendly policies. Proposals for employment legislation was intended to form employment relations settlement (CIPD, 1998; Lourie, 1998). The White Paper points out that employment security, guarding against the exploitation of vulnerable individuals by introducing safeguards through employment tribunals, is geared towards assisting with the building of effective partnership relationships between employers and employees in the progress towards better healthier workplace relations. These 'best practice' 'Fairness at Work' ideology was embraced by the local government organisation (i.e. the Council) through the implementation of policy documents (i.e. job security, recruitment and selection, internal recruitment, learning and development, team working, work-life balance, rewards, dignity at work to name a few). Furthermore, 'Fairness at Work' ideology was also declared by senior leadership of the Council, who claimed that fairness assisted with partnership working, and the Council's leadership expressed their commitment to adhere to these best practice principles. The findings demonstration disparities in the Council's espousal of high commitment HRM 'best practices' and 'fairness at work' ideology compared to the working life realities of both managerial and non-managerial employees. In particular, the results show that managerial employees were experiencing more incivility at work and psychological violence compared to the non-managerial employees.

However, the findings reveal that there was a prevalence of mistreatment, incivility, disrespect, psychological violence, and bullying and harassment occurring between the social interactions between line managers and the employees that reports to them. In support, the WERS's 2004 survey revealed self-reported claims of employee experiencing bullying at work, poor relationships with line managers, unfair treatment, pay conditions and annual leave in the public sector compared to their private sector counterparts (Kersley et al., 2006). The WERS 2004 research went on to disclose that these 'uncivil, unfair and mistreatment' practices were all higher in the North West of England compared to the National Standard (Forth and Stokes, 2006; Kersley et al., 2006). For bullying and harassment, the CIPD (2008, 2009) reports highlights that the proportion of people experiencing bullying and harassment in the workplace is higher for the public sector compared with the private sector or voluntary sector counterparts. Public sector staff are also more likely to experience violence or to have been threatened with violence, and women are marginally more likely than men to say they are experiencing bullying (CIPD, 2007, 2009). The effects of bullying behaviour have significant impact at the individual, team and organisational levels (Cooper and Marshall, 1976; Hoel et al., 2001). CIPD (2004) estimates that bullying costs UK employers £80 million lost working days annually and up to £2 billion in lost revenue via sickness absence, turnover, reduced productivity, formal and legal investigations, damage to employer branding, disturbance to working relationships, lower morale and commitment (CIPD, 2009). For individuals, the cost can be even higher, with lasting psychological, mental health and physical damage (CIPD, 2007).

The preceding managerial and non-managerial accounts of psychological violence can negatively affect the psychological contract of respondents as well as the perception of being supported, justice perceptions and well-being at work. The perception of psychological contract breach can negatively affect the psychological, physical, mental health, intellectual, career, work/life, and social well-being of employees which in turn has implications for commitment, absenteeism, presenteeism, leaveism, turnover and citizenship behaviour.

Effective communication and involvement

One manager equates her experiences of downward communication and dissemination of information ineffective. Claims of status differentials, and a lack of appreciation were highlighted. One manager shares her experience. She states,

> There needs to be better communication with staff from above that needs to be filtered down better . . . when they have these corporate meetings, these thinking outside the box and samples of staff attend these meetings, and it's the division that causes problems . . . but when staff know that they are appreciated you will get the best from them . . . they need to communicate better with staff and improve things.
>
> (Manager, Female, Age 50–59 years, Tenure less than 5 years)

Another manager echoes this view and suggests that improvements are required with upward communication, employee voice, participation and involvement in decision making. He also related these practices are important to his well-being at work and that of others throughout the organisation. He comments,

> I will like to see improvements in upward communication because it's linked to creating an environment that staff will be able to say what they want to say . . . to come up with even wacky ideas without

thinking 'I would not be disciplined for wacky ideas' . . . this can create job satisfaction and therefore will improve people well-being.
(Manager, Male, Age 40–49 years, Tenure less than 5 years)

Another manager discussed her experiences with her line manager with respect to ineffective communication and the lack of involvement, team working, and coaching and mentoring to facilitate professional development. She said

My manager doesn't harness all the energy or initiatives of her team . . . she could communicate more effectively and try to encourage a bit more team working or involving us more so we can improve.
(Manager, Female, Age 40–49 years, Tenure 21–25 years)

Non-managerial employees also shared the view the communication, involvement, and employee voice are integral to their feeling of appreciation and well-being at work. One employee commented,

It is important to communication with staff and involve people, front line staff in decision making much earlier in the process, just asking for your views, if you bring in this policy – how this and this affects you.
(Employee, Female, Age 40–49 years, Tenure 16–20 years)

Other employees claim that communicating and listening to people will motivate the staff teams and facilitate engagement and well-being amongst employees. One employee shares her perspective regarding the importance of communication towards the promotion of her well-being at work. She states;

I think communicating with people and listening to people is very important . . . finding ways which can benefit the staff team by asking the staff team what they want will go a long way towards staff morale.
(Employee, Male, Age 40–49 years, Tenure 11–15 years)

Another employee highlighted the importance of receiving clear instructions through effective communication, which will create a positive respectful atmosphere, empower individuals, facilitate knowledge transfer and career opportunities. One employee shares her views about improvement in communication to enhance her well-being at work. She shares:

Working as part of a team is also important and receiving clear instructions with development needs being addressed . . . similarly effective communication, encouragement, creating a nice atmosphere to work, to be respected and feeling like an individual is empowering . . . knowledge transfer and career development are also quite important as well.

(Employee, Female, Age 40–49 years, Tenure less than 5 years)

In the local government case organisation (i.e. the Council) leadership claim that they endeavour to become a 'best-practice' employer and introduced a 'communication strategy' which the Council espoused was established to maintain clear efficient and regular two-way channels of communication with internal and external audiences, to encourage an environment of trust and loyalty in which work is supported. The findings reveal disparities existing with respect to what the Council espoused and the working life realities and experiences of respondents. The findings expose that both employee groups experience challenges with effective downward and upward communication with their line managers and the organisation as a whole. This pattern of ineffective communication and the lack of involvement, employees viewed these practices as bullying and unfairness at work. They also claimed that these practices promoted status differentials, the lack of appreciation, stifles employee voice, does not facilitate their line manager listening to their views, hinders clear instructions, does not create a positive atmosphere of trust and respect, does not allow for effective team working, coaching and mentoring or knowledge transfer that will facilitate professional development. Dietz et al. (2009) state that employee involvement/participation and employee voice is a group process, involving groups of employees and their bosses, a process by which the individual employee is given greater freedom to make decisions on his/her own.

In support, Marchington and Wilkinson (2005) suggest that participation can be differentiated into direct communication, upward problem solving, or representative participation. Moorman (1991) states that effective leadership is integral to organisational effectiveness, creating positive organisational cultures, strengthen motivation, clarifying mission and organisational objectives, and steering organisations to more productive and high performing outcomes. At the heart of this Atkinson (2007) and Reichers et al. (1997) indicate that a great place to work requires effective communication, trust and mutual respect between senior executives and their employees and value driven leadership performance with purpose.

Transparency and trustworthiness

Some managers pointed out that there is a lack of trust and openness with their line manager that hinders transparency, confidence and openness which they believe are integral towards the promotion of their well-being at work. One manager's comments echo these points. He shares:

I don't think you can be totally open with management because they're not open with you back. . . . They may try to put a bit of spin on things and almost pretend to be open but, you know, deep down they're doing deals . . . and there's things going on behind the scenes. If we can come to a place of honesty and openness, this will go a long way.
(Manager, Male, Age 40–49 years, Tenure 16–20 years)

Decisiveness – take action

Another manager associated communication and leadership to his line manager's ability to solve problems at work relating it to 'talking to a family member' and does not result in a resolution. He commented,

It's very difficult sometimes to get a slot and be able to pin him down but he does try and make an effort and understand but I never feel that it gets any resolution. . . . It's like talking to a family member about a problem instead of talking to your line manager and asking him for help and assistance . . . it's just talk, you don't feel as though it's going to resolve anything.
(Manager, Male, Age 40–49 years, Tenure 6–10 years)

Attentive, considerate and responsive

Non-managerial respondents claim that their line manager is aware of what they require to improve their working life realities but chooses to ignore feedback received from staff so that changes can be made to improve employees work-life experiences and well-being at work. Employees view this practice as disrespectful and unfair to individuals and the work team. Employees reveal that if their line manager is attentive, considerate, responsive to their needs, and demonstrate fair treatment to everyone this will reduce employees stress levels, and improve their mental health at work, commitment, motivation and well-being at work. One employee shares her experience that highlights these themes:

Yes, my manager is aware of the things that would be really helpful to change and the things that would make my experience of the job so much better. . . . He knows all that so I don't think that he treats me fairly. Because he can't claim that he is not aware of those facts and still he chooses not to do anything about it. We are a very small team for him to manage, so I find that very annoying. I think to myself that if you have a team of thirty, fair enough, it's quite difficult to respond to the needs of your team, but when you have a team of three, it can't be that difficult.
(Employee, Female, Aged 30–39 years, Tenure 6–11 years)

Support with opportunities for career advancement

Some employees held the view that their line managers deliberately with-held training and career advancement opportunities relevant to their job from them. Employees also claim that their line managers were not trans-parent with the sharing of information that can support and empower them in their jobs. Employees view these practices and social interaction as bullying, uncivil, mistreatment, and unfairness, which results in the development of a lack of trust between employees and their line manag-ers. Employees claim that being supported with opportunities for career advancement and transparency and sharing of information will improve their well-being at work. One employee says:

> I don't trust my manager as she does not do anything for me at all. She doesn't even identify training courses that she thinks might be interesting to me or conferences. She held legal framework's changes in key areas of my portfolio and all that stuff to do with human rights. Now, she knows that's important, and it's important for me to know about it as well as her. But she puts herself on a conference some time ago and never bothered to tell me anything about it and when I finally said 'have you heard anything about any training around here in this area?' she sent me something that she clearly responded to back in October last year . . . and this is recently and you just think 'you sat on information that would be useful and empowering to me and is that because you're forgetful or is that because you did it on purpose?' I am undecided as to whether it is because she is forgetful or she does it on purpose. I'd like to think it's because she is forgetful.
> (Employee, Female, Age 30–39 years, Tenure 6–11 years)

Building relationships and narrowing priorities

Employees' perspective about their line manager's interaction in the workplace highlighted themes such as the reluctance to build relation-ships, or use of conflict management skills to deescalate and resolve issues, engaging people, respecting the views of others, embracing diver-sity and equality, people-focused approach, team working and change management. One employee shares:

> My manager scrolls himself away, he's not very assertive but he can be when he is fighting his corner about his stuff. I think he's always felt very beleaguered, him against the world. I think he cre-ated quite a lot of problems for himself by being very much stuck on 'this is legislation, you will be sued, these are the facts, rah, rah, rah'. This approach really antagonised a lot of people so I don't

know if he's then been very good in terms of how you work around those problems, and change management as well in the public sector is a difficult skill I think. So he tends to back away from issues where he's had confrontation which I think is interesting. He does not get along with the marketing department for e.g. but that's so important in terms of diversity and equality, in terms of engaging people in the organisation, and he is reluctant to build these relationships with them. He doesn't have much to do with the rest of the team . . . he is just a private bloke and very much a family guy and comes into work, does his job, overworks at home and is on emails at 9 o'clock at night . . . he is just into his job and into his family.

(Employee, Female, Age 40–49 years, Tenure 15–20 years)

Some managers held the view that the relationships with stakeholders requires improvement as these social interactions with stakeholders have negatively affected managers and the entire organisation and contributed to their heightened stress levels and negative well-being. Clarity about what is important and narrowing priorities are also integral towards the promotion of managers well-being at work. One manager shares his experience. He explains,

Improve the relationship with some of our stakeholders because some of our stakeholders the very few of them are having a disproportionate impact on me and the rest of the organisation . . . we need a bit more clarity about our priorities and need to narrow down our priorities rather than wanting to do everything.

(Manager, Male, Age 40–49 years, Tenure less than 5 years)

The findings in this section outline managerial and non-managerial employees' perspectives regarding how responsive their line managers are to promote their well-being at work, as well as respondents' claims regarding what their line managers can do to improve their well-being at work. The findings contribute to the body of knowledge as it relates to the 'employee-focused HRM' literature as well as well-being at work literature that focuses on public sector employees voice, evaluation of HRM, quality of working life and well-being at work. These areas are afforded little space in literature and the results of this study and the main research outlined in this book have contributed to the gap in these areas. Table 12.1 outlines the workers voice regarding their line managers' responsiveness to promote their well-being at work, as well as their perspectives regarding improvements that their line managers can make to promote their well-being.

Table 12.1 Workers voice: line managers' responsiveness and improvements to promote well-being at work

Workers Voice: Line Manager Responsiveness to Promote Employee Well-Being	Workers Voice: Improvement in Line Manager Leadership to Promote Employee Well-Being
Supportive with Work Responsibilities	**People-Focused Approach**
Trust employees' competencies	Leadership Styles
Positive feedback	Team Management
Appreciation	Trust Employees Competencies
Respect	Delegation
Attentive and Considerate	
Assistance and support with heavy workload	**Dignity and Civility at Work**
Directs work projects	Anti-blame culture
	Anti-Fear and Control
Knowledge Transfer	Anti-Psychological Violence
Exchange and Sharing of Information	Anti-Bullying and Harassment
Learning from each other	Respect
Brainstorming	Employee Engagement
Professional Development	Supported
	Fairness at Work
Trust Employees Capabilities	**Impartiality and Fairness at Work**
Trust employees' abilities and proficiencies	Gender Equality
Provide feedback	Fair Treatment
Praise and Recognition	Anti-Bullying and Harassment
	Grievance and Disciplinary Management
	Respectful Relationships
	Equal Opportunities
	Career Advancement Opportunities
	Fair treatment for Pay and Rewards
	People-Focused
	Compassionate
	Empowerment and Autonomy
	Fostering Creativity and Innovation
	Professional Development
	Use own Initiative
	Trust Employees' competencies
	Build Relationships
	Effective Communication and Involvement
	Upward and Downward Communication
	Removal of Status Differentials
	Harmonisation
	Appreciation
	Employee Voice
	Involvement and Participation
	Listening to Employees
	Team Working
	Coaching and Mentoring
	Giving Clear Instructions
	Knowledge Transfer
	Career Opportunities

(Continued)

Table 12.1 Continued

Workers Voice: Line Manager Responsiveness to Promote Employee Well-Being	Workers Voice: Improvement in Line Manager Leadership to Promote Employee Well-Being
	Empathetic and Compassionate People-Focused Satisfaction Motivation Care about People
	Transparency and Trustworthiness Trust and Openness
	Decisiveness – Take Action Problem Solving
	Attentive, Considerate and Responsive Listen to feedback received Respect Appreciation
	Proving Support Opportunities for Career Advancement Open access to Training and Development Transparency Information Sharing Trust
	Building Relationships and Narrowing Priorities Building Positive Relationships Conflict Management Skills Employee Engagement Respecting the views of others Embracing Diversity and Equality People-Focused Approach Team Working Effective Change Management Clear Instructions Narrowing Priorities

Discussion

Table 12.1 reveals employees voice as it relates to the psychological contract, social interactions, and justice perceptions within the employment relationship. Employees claim that if these factors are implemented, it will change the organisational culture and working life experiences in this local government organisation and other employees in similar related organisations alike. Employees further argue that once these factors are operationalised and positive behaviours and practices are realised it will come into alignment with the government White Paper for Fairness at Work, and the legislative and adopted 'best practice' HRM Policy documents. At present, there is a huge disparity between what the local government organisation declares and the quality of working life of employees. The findings reveal that key themes such as people-focused approach to leadership, fairness at work, civility at work, effective communication and involvement, trust, building relationships to mention a few are integral enhancing the quality of working life, stress reduction, mental health and well-being of public sector workers.

Against this backdrop, the findings revealed that despite the espousal of the adoption of 'best-practice' high commitment HRM practices and wellness management aimed at promoting a committed, healthy and happy workforce, the majority of the sampled respondents that took part in the main research were not happy. Rather, they indicated challenges and tensions experienced by managerial and non-managerial employees operating in an environment with budget limitations, job insecurity, continuous organisational changes, heavy workloads and work pressures, the existence of mistrust and a lack of team working, and challenges with their line manager's leadership practices. These all have implications for increasing levels of work-related stress, which in turn, are likely to affect employee mental health, sickness absence, presenteeism, leaveism, job satisfaction, morale and well-being.

The working life experiences of respondents just quoted can be viewed as oppressive as a result of organisational practices. These can cause employees to feel unfairly treated and oppressed and are associated with a bullying environment. It is important to note here, that the apparent challenges and complexities that exist within this work context can stem from the history and ethos of the public sector that has developed over a long time, resulting in behaviours associated with institutionalised bullying. The complexities and challenges of producing more with less are likely to affect the actions of senior management whose responsibility would be to ensure the successes of the modernisation agenda in keeping with proposals commissioned by central government. This in turn is likely to affect senior management actions and decision making in the process of organisational functioning; resulting in practices that can cause employees to feel victimised while in pursuit of organisational objectives. This view is echoed by Bozeman (1993) who states that public sector organisations are viewed as bureaucratic with red tape, and is as a result of the emphasis on accountability to government, often have more red tape than private organisations (CIPD, 2009).

From a medical perspective, it can become dangerous to leave a wound untreated and as such, the organisation can adopt this principle in terms of ensuring that their key resources (i.e. employees) are not exposed to circumstances and situations that may result in psychological and physical harm. Moreover, the survival strategy depicted by employees explanation of their working life realities, the lack of trust, bullying and unfair treatment, and line manager social interactions affecting their well-being at work are all clustered into the multidimensional well-being model which goes beyond 'satisfaction, contentment, fulfilment and anxiety' ideologies but instead include a holistic approach to an individual's life at work and includes factors that affect the individual, groups, and the organisation that are all geared towards the positive psychological contract within the employment relationship that enhances work experiences and organisational functioning.

To this end, more than four decades have passed from Terkel's (1977) depiction of work, but work appears to hold the same challenging experiences for individuals. The findings from managerial and non-managerial perspectives introduce an alternative conceptualisation of how the quality of working life and well-being should be as perceived by employees. This is illustrated by an integrated model (Figure 12.1) that can be used by policy makers, management and practitioners to minimise or eliminate destabilising experiences like bullying, incivility, psychological violence and unfair treatment at work. Thus, the notion of 'well-being at work' can allow individuals and organisations to unlock the mysteries of individuals, groups and organisational health and potential in the pursuit of happiness of local government public sector employees in the North West of England.

Employees reactions were used to develop an integrated model illustrating the nature of relationship that exists between HRM practices, social exchange, the quality of working life, and well-being as perceived by employees in the NPM environment in the North West of England. In the last twenty years the message of being happy has become a complex collection of theories around the quest to help people find enduring joy (Campbell, 2001; Ulrich, 2010). Thus, the quest for personal happiness, fulfilment, peace and a sense of purpose is ever more important in an increasingly hectic world that places increasing emotional demands on people. More particularly, the emotional demands of employees in the public sector are likely to be numerous given the complexities and challenges faced by those employees who spend a large percentage of their time at work. Ulrich (2010) further argues that too many organisations have failed to help people find happiness in work settings because leaders have not appreciated that employee well-being relates to organisation success and have not fully understood the ways that they can shape organisation setting for individual well-being (Burke and Cooper, 2008; Campbell, 2001).

Even further, leaders in the public sector may not view employee well-being as an integral 'vehicle' that can be used for enhancing service delivery and efficiency savings but may view employee well-being from a narrow perspective of predominantly physical health instead of the holistic approach to employee well-being within the organisation that covers the individual, groups and the organisation as a whole. Wellness management programmes were claimed to be adopted by the local government organisation to promote the well-being of employees as well as an accolade that can be used for employer branding and corporate social responsibility initiatives. Thus, it is likely that the ideology of well-being at work can be re-prioritised for what may be perceived as more important, for example, expenditure reduction. To this end, the findings from this study seek to contribute towards the debate in this area by introducing an integrated model that explains employees' perspectives on HRM practices, working life realities, and well-being at work should be in the employment relationship. Employees perceive that these factors can act as enablers and/or barriers to their happiness, fulfilment, well-being, and productivity at work. The integrated model is shown in Figure 12.1.

The search for happiness and well-being in local government is depicted by respondents in the model which reveals 'what lies beneath the melting ice' of employees' perspectives and reactions to HRM practices, the quality of working life and well-being at work in the public sector. This is highlighted by working life realities, the meaning of well-being, line management leadership, enablers and barriers. Social exchanges and fairness at work are key principles of the psychological contract that are necessary for a positive employment relationship and consequently employee well-being at work. All factors are antecedents to the multidimensionality of well-being at work. Therefore, once well-being at work is promoted, it is likely to have implications for individual and organisational outcomes.

Working life realities. The findings reveal factors that are part of the daily working life realities of respondents in this local government organisation. This brings out the uniqueness and complexity of the working environment. Central themes of changing structures, limited resources, redundancy, heavy workloads and pressures, wellness management, team working, 'Them and Us' and 'Blame' culture, tensions between teams, honesty and openness, trust, controlled environment and bureaucracy that forms part of day-to-day life functioning (Campbell Clark, 2001). These can all have implications for the psychological contract, justice perceptions and well-being at work.

The meaning of well-being. reviews respondents' perspective and meanings associated with the multidimensional well-being at work that forms part of the employment relationship. These include anti-bullying environment, equal opportunities, happiness and contentment, praise and recognition, employee voice, mental and physical health, job design, coaching and mentoring, creativity and innovation, reward strategies, career advancement, a sense of purpose and fulfilment, communication, involvement and participation, relationships with stakeholders, clarifying and narrowing priorities and better work accommodation. These perspectives relate to what employees expectations are of the psychological

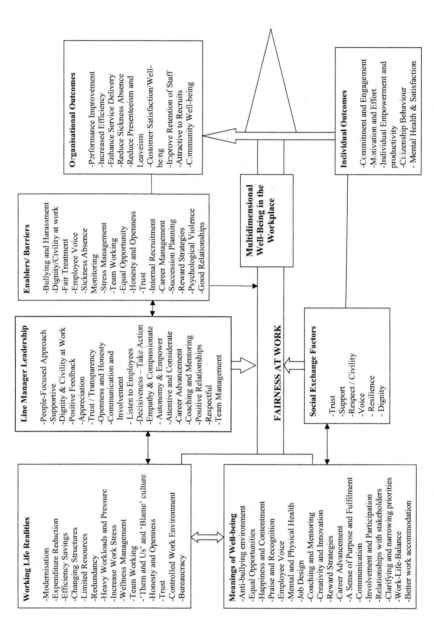

Figure 12.1 Integrated model of HRM, social exchange, leadership, and well-being at work in local government: employees' perspectives

contract between themselves and their employer. If employees perceive that these expectations are not met this can result in the psychological contract breach or violation that can have negative implications for individual, group and organisational well-being. Contract breach can also influence individual and organisational outcomes.

Line management leadership shows the social interactions that should exists between employees and their line managers to promote employee well-being at work in the local government organisation in North West England. The research findings that relates to line management leadership and well-being reveal that employees quality of work life was plagued with psychological violence, the existence of a blaming and controlled culture, a lack of trust between managers and employees, a lack of transparency, ineffective communication and change management processes, bullying and harassment, incivility and unfairness at work, poor relationships, a lack of appreciation and other uncivil and undignified behaviours framed the quality of working experiences of employees; who evidently were like the 'walking wounded' as proclaimed by Terkel's (1977) depiction of work, which in reality still exists for these public sector employees. These experiences of being subjected to constant pressure, heavy workloads, increased stress and lack of control over decisions and outcomes rendered these employees powerless to the functioning of the local government organisation that is working towards efficiency savings based on the UK Public Sector Modernisation agenda that focused on cost minimisation and enhanced service delivery. The promotion of the 'best-practice' HRM philosophy and well-being ideology adopted by the private sector in the public sector makes for a challenging transition and implementation given governmental, political, and limited funding agendas.

Enablers and barriers. The findings reveal 14 categories that are enablers and /or barriers to fairness at work, people-focused approaches, and civility at work, which are antecedents to well-being at work. Each factor if explored from negative and positive experiences at work can have implications for the psychological contract, justice perceptions, leader-member exchange, perceived support and well-being at work.

Social Exchange. The mediating factor that drives the employment relationship. Employees who perceive that their employer supports and trusts them to do the job, shows respect, and treats them fairly are more likely to reciprocate with positive attitudes and behaviours in terms of commitment, engagement, motivation, effort, satisfaction, and citizenship behaviour. This in turn affects organisational outcomes in the form of employee engagement, enhanced performance, increased efficiency, enhanced service delivery, reduction in sickness absence, retention, customer satisfaction and community well-being (MacLeod and Clarke, 2009).

Whilst these findings concern the employment experiences of local government managerial and non-managerial employees, a moderate generalisation can be made for managers and employees more broadly (Williams, 2002: 211). The findings also point to the need for a balance between ideals of 'well-being at work' and human needs (Fineman, 2006). In conclusion, it can be argued that these managers and employees and perhaps more generally, managers and employees in similar contexts have some way to go before they self-actualise and are fulfilled in their well-being at work. It will take a further step towards the strategic focus of a more 'people-focus' ideology and leadership approach to eliminate incivility in the workplace, bullying and harassment, anti-trust, unfairness, and blame and controlled culture that exists in this local authority to usher in a climate of 'respect', 'trust', 'civility', 'resilience' and 'fairness'. These are viewed by the respondents as essential themes that management can embrace to enhance the quality of their working life and well-being at work at this local government organisation in the North West of England. The complexities and daily challenges faced by managers and employees in this local authority may be comparable to those of contemporary professionals at work. An understanding of the organisational practices that are required to promote employee 'happiness and well-being' in local government can be the 'dawning of a new day' in terms of meaning that can contribute to bringing an end to the 'bullying unfair and disrespectful environment' by navigating to the beginning of the way forward. However, the Utopian state of 'Employee Well-being at Work' is likely to remain a subjective phenomenon in the pursuit of happiness for the foreseeable future.

Summary and conclusion

This chapter evaluated the empirical findings from the main research outlined in this book as it relates to the quality of working life experiences of managerial and non-managerial employees of a local government organisation in North West England. Key themes emerged from this research that reveal the challenges faced by these two employee groups were in keeping with the UK's government modernisation agenda of cost minimisation and enhance service delivery. The meaning of the job as declared by both employee groups related that identity-work-life integration, which denotes that employees saw their job as part of their being which flows into other parts of their life. Managerial and non-managerial employees highlighted factors, behaviours, and social interactions with their line manager that promoted and hindered their well-being at work. Employees pointed out areas that can be improved by their line managers to enhance their quality of working life, well-being, mental health and performance at work.

The findings revealed key principles that relate to 'what lies beneath the melting ice' of employees' reactions to HRM practices, the quality of working life, line management leadership, and consequently well-being at work. The research contributes to the employee-focus literature as it relates to employees' reactions to HRM practices, quality of working life, line management leadership, and well-being at work. This research also contributes to the well-being literature by producing a multidimensional well-being model that is practical for the expansion of the well-being theory from an HRM perspective. The study also contributes to the bullying at work literature by highlighting managerial and employees' perspective on their experiences of bullying at work, and its implications for their well-being. The study also contributes to the social exchange literature by highlighting managerial and non-managerial employees' view of the psychological contract, fairness perceptions and well-being at work. The study contributes to the NPM literature as it relates to employee well-being. It also extends the employment relations literature as it relates to employee relations and well-being in North West of England. Finally, the study demonstrates that the use of an alternative methodological conceptualisation allowed the researcher to delve beneath and uncovers an in-depth understanding of the meanings of employees' perspectives of work, the quality of their working life, line management leadership, and well-being in local government in North West of England.

References

Atkinson, C. (2007) 'Trust and the Psychological Contract', *Employee Relations*, Vol. 29(3): 227–246.

Baptiste, N.R. (2007) 'Line Management Leadership: Implications for Employee Well-Being', in G.P. Clarkson (Eds.) *Developing Leadership Research, Papers from the Northern Leadership Academy Fellow 2007 Conference*, pp. 229–238, Leeds: Leeds University Business School, Leeds University Press Financial Services.

Bolton, S., and Houlihan, M. (Eds.) (2007) *Searching for the Human in Human Resource Management: Theory, Practice and Workplace Contexts*, Basingstoke: Palgrave Macmillan

Bozeman, B. (1993) 'A Theory of Government "Red Tape"', *Journal of Public Administration Research and Policy*, Vol. 3: 273–303.

Burke, R.J., and Cooper, C.L. (2008) *Building More Effective Organisations: HR Management and Performance in Practice*, Cambridge: Cambridge University Press.

Campbell Clark, S. (2001) 'Work Cultures and Work/Family Balance', *Journal of Vocational Behaviour*, Vol. 58: 348–365.

Cartwright, S., and Cooper, C.L. (2009) *The Oxford Handbook of Organisational Wellbeing*, Oxford: Oxford University Press

Clarke, J., Gewirtz, S., and McLaughlin, E. (Eds.) (2000) *New Managerialism, New Welfare?*, London: Sage Publications.

Clarke, S.C. (2001) 'Work Cultures and Work/Family Balance', *Journal of Vocational Behavior*, Vol. 58(3): 348–365.

CIPD (1998) *IPD Welcomes Thrust of 'Fairness at Work' White Paper, but Warns That Statutory Union Recognition Could Backfire*, London: Chartered Institute of Personnel Development.

CIPD (2004) *Bullying at Work–Employers Get the Policy Right, but Run the Risk of Leaving the Root Causes Unchallenged*, London: Chartered Institute of Personnel and Development.

CIPD (2007) *Tackling Bullying at Work: A Good-Practice Framework*, London: Chartered Institute of Personnel Development.

CIPD (2008) *Bully at Work and the 2007 Code of Practice*, London: Chartered Institute of Personnel Development.

CIPD (2009) *Harassment and Bullying at Work*, London: Chartered Institute of Personnel and Development.

CIPD (2014) *Developing Managers to Manage Sustainable Employee Engagement, Health and Well-Being*, Research Insight, November 2014, London: Chartered Institute of Personnel and Development. In association with Affinity Health at Work and IOSH.

Cooper, C.L., Cartwright, S., and Robertson, S. (2005) 'Work, Environments, Stress and Productivity: An Examination Using Asset', *International Journal of Stress Management*, Vol. 12(4): 409–423.

Cooper, C.L., and Marshall, J. (1976) 'Occupational Sources of Stress: A Review of the Literature Relating to Coronary Heart Disease and Mental Ill-Health', *Journal of Occupational Psychology*, Vol. 49: 11–28.

Cooper, C.L., and Robertson, I. (2001) *Well-Being in Organisations: A Reader for Students and Practitioners*, Chichester: John Wiley and Sons Limited.

Cropanzano, R. (Ed.) (1993) *Justice in the Workplace: Approaching Fairness in Human Resource Management*, New York: Lawrence Erlbaum.

Daniels, G., and French, S. (2006) *Regulating Work-Life Balance*, Centre for Industrial Relations, Keele University, Keele.

Diener, E., and Biswas-Diener, R. (2008). *Happiness: Unlocking the Mysteries of Psychological Wealth*, Oxford: Wiley-Blackwell.

Dietz, G., Wilkinson, A., and Redman, T. (2009) 'Involvement and Participation', in A. Wilkinson, N. Bacon, T. Redman, and S. Snell (Eds.) *The Sage Handbook of Human Resource Management*, London: Sage Publishers.

Fineman, S. (2006) 'On Being Positive: Concerns and Counterpoints', *Academy of Management Review*, Vol. 31(2): 270–291.

Fineman, S. (2007) *Understanding Emotions at Work*, London: Sage Publishers.

Forth, J., and Stokes, L. (2006) 'A Regional Perspective on Employment Relations: Tabulations from the 2004 Workplace Employment Relations Survey', Report to the Advisory, Conciliation and Arbitration Services (ACAS), Final Report 8th September.

Freeney, M.K., and Stritch, J. (2017) 'Family-Friendly Policies and Work Life Balance in the Public Sector, *Review of Public Personnel Administration*, 27th September. https://doi.org/10.1177/0734371X17733789

Fullerton, H.N. (1995) 'The 2005 Labour Force: Older and Larger', *Monthly Labor Review*, Vol. 118(11): 29–44.

Grant, A., Christianson, M., and Price, R. (2007), 'Happiness, Health or Relationships? Managerial Practices and Employee Well-Being Tradeoffs', *The Academy of Management*, Vol. 21(3): 51–63.

Grant, D., and Shields, J. (2002), 'In Search of the Subject: Researching Employee Reactions to Human Resource Management', *Journal of Industrial Relations*, Vol. 44(3): 313–334.

Greenberg, J. (1987), 'A Taxonomy of Organisational Justice Theories', *Academy of Management Review*, Vol. 12: 9–22.

Guest, D. (2007) 'HRM and the Worker: Towards a New Psychological Contract? In P. Boxall, J. Purcell, and P. Wright (Eds.) *The Oxford Handbook of Human Resource Management*, pp. 128–146, Oxford: Oxford University Press.

Hesketh, I., and Cooper, C.L. (2014) 'Leaveism at Work', *Occupational Medicine*, Vol. 64(3): 146–147.

Hesketh, I., Cooper, C.L., and Ivy, J. (2014) 'Leaveism and Work-Life Integration: The Thinning Blue Line?', *Policing Advance*, Vol. 9(2): 1–12, http://policing.oxfordjournals.org/ (accessed 14th September, 2014).

Hoel, H., Rayner, C., and Cooper, C. (2001) 'Workplace Bullying', In. C.L. Cooper and I.T. Robertson (Eds.) *Wellbeing in Organisations: A Reader for Students and Practitioners*, pp. 55–90, Chichester: John Wiley and Sons Limited.

Kemske, F. (1988) 'HR (2008): A Forecast Based on Our Exclusive Study', *Workforce*, Vol. 77, January: 46–60.

Kersley, B., Alphin, C., Forth, J., Bryson, A., Bewley, H., Dix, G., and Oxenbridge, S. (2006) *Inside the Workplace: Findings from the 2004 Workplace Employment Relations Survey*, London: Routledge.

Lourie, J. (1998) 'Fairness at Work', Business and Transport Section, House of Commons Library, Research Paper 98/99, House of Commons cm 3968.

Macleod, D., and Clarke, N. (2009) Engaging for Success: Enhancing Performance Through Employee Engagement, A Report to Government, Department for Business, Innovation and Skills.

Marchington, M., and Wilkinson, A. (2005) *Human Resource Management at Work: People Management and Development*, London: CIPD.

Moorman, R.H. (1991) 'Relationship between Organisational Justice and Organisational Citizenship Behaviours: Do Fairness Perceptions Influence Employee Citizenship?', *Journal of Applied Psychology*, Vol. 76(6): 845–855.

Morphet, J. (2008) *Modern Local Government*, London: Sage Publications.

Percy, S. (2018). 'Why Leaders Need to Look after Their Employees Financial Well-Being', www.forbes.com/sites/sallypercy/2018/11/20/why-leaders-need-to-look-after-their-employees-financial-wellbeing/#311bc63b67d0 (accessed 20th February, 2019).

Reichers, A.E., Wanous, J.P., and Austin, J.T. (1997) 'Understanding and Managing Cynicism about Organisational Change', *Academy of Management Executive*, Vol. 11(1): 48–59.

Robertson, I., and Cooper, C. (2011) *Well-Being*, New York: Palgrave Macmillan.

Rousseau, D.M. (2003) 'Extending the Psychology of the Psychological Contract: A Reply to Putting Psychology Back into Psychological Contracts', *Journal of Management Inquiry*, Vol. 12(3): 229–238.

Sharkie, R. (2009) 'Trust in Leadership Is Vital for Employee Performance', *Management Research News*, Vol. 32(5): 491–498.

Terkel, S. (1977) *Working*, Harmondsworth: Penguin Publishers.

Williams, M. (2002) 'Generalisation in Interpretative Research', in T. May (Ed.) *Qualitative Research in Action*, London: Sage Publications.

Wilson, F. (2010) *Organisational Behaviour and Work: A Critical Introduction*, Oxford: Oxford University Press.

Ulrich, D. (2010) 'The Abundant Organisation', in P. Linley, S. Harrington, and N. Garcea (Eds.) *Oxford Handbook of Positive Psychology at Work*, pp. xvii–xxi, Oxford: Oxford University Press.

Author biography

Dr. Nicole Cvenkel (nee Baptiste) obtained her PhD in Human Resource Management and Organisational Behaviour at Roehampton University Business School. Her research focused on employees' perspectives and reactions to HRM practices, the quality of working life, line management leadership and well-being at work. Nicole also graduated with an MBA from London Metropolitan University, a Master of Science in Research and Business Management from Manchester Metropolitan University and a Bachelor's Degree in Business Administration from the University of Lincoln. She worked as an Associate Professor in the field of Human Resources Management and Organisational Behaviour at diverse universities in the UK, Canada and in other countries. She has published many journal articles on HRM, line management leadership and well-being at work and has published a book on promoting healthy workplaces. Nicole also held academic administrative positions as an Associate Regional Director for the College of New Caledonia in British Columbia Canada as well as the Dean of Business at the University College of the North in Manitoba, Canada. Nicole is a leadership associate of the Association of Canadian Community Colleges (ACCC) of Canada. She also holds membership for the Senior Women Academics Administrators of Canada (SWAAC); an Associate Professional member of the Chartered Institute of Personnel and Development (CIPD); a fellow of the Higher Education Academy of the United Kingdom; a research fellow of the Northern Leadership Academy of the United Kingdom; and a member of the Chartered Management Institute; and Certified Coach, Teacher and Speaker with the John Maxwell Team; and is an Affiliate of the Workplace Bullying Institute (WBI) and an expert in the complex phenomenon that is based on empirical research, principles of neuroscience and social sciences, and organisational best practices as introduced in the prestigious Workplace Bullying University. She works along with her clients to enable the achievement of their organisational strategic goals and objectives. And make many presentations on these topics.

Abbreviations and acronyms

ACAS	The Advisory, Conciliation and Arbitration Services
BIS	Department for Business, Innovation and Skills
BREXIT	British Exit
CCMD	Canadian Centre for Management Development
CCOSH	Canadian Centre for Occupational Health and Safety
CIPD	Chartered Institute of Personnel and Development
CSR	Corporate Social Responsibility
DOH	Department of Health
DWP	Department of Works and Pensions
EAP	Employee Assistance Programme
EIP	Employee Involvement and Participation
ESRC	Economic and Social Research Council
EU	European Union
GM	Greater Manchester
HRM	Human Resource Management
HSA	Health and Safety Authority
HSE	Health and Safety Executive
HWWE	Health Work and Well-Being Executive
IIP	Investors In People
ILO	International Labour Standard
LMX	Leader-Member Exchange
NIERS	The National Institute of Economic and Social Research
NPM	New Public Management
NW	North West
OCB	Organisational Citizenship Behaviour
OJ	Organisational Justice
PC	Psychological Contract
POS	Perceived Organisational Support
TUC	Trade Union Congress
UK	United Kingdom
UKCES	The UK Commission for Employment and Skills
WERS	Workplace Employment Relations Survey
WHO	World Health Organisation
WSIA	Workplace Safety and Insurance Act
WVMS	Workplace Violence Management Standards

Index

Printed in the United States
by Baker & Taylor Publisher Services